Becoming a Better Sports Coach

Research on coaching education and development highlights, repeatedly, the difficulties of traditional coaching education to impact coaching practice. Practice seems to be disconnected from scientific theory with few coaches accessing the scientific literature as it too often is presented in dry, academic tones. This volume sets out to provide an integration of theory and everyday practice that to date has not yet been published in the field of coaching science in a text easily used by sports coaches.

In order to bridge this theory to practice gap, *Becoming a Better Sports Coach: Development through Theory Application* presents theory and science connected to practice in a way that makes it possible for coaches to test, evaluate and improve upon their existing coaching practice.

This hands-on approach sets out to improve coaches' cognition and raising self-awareness as well as improve coaches' learning using specific tools for behavioural feedback and reflection. Improving on self-reflective skills and eliciting feedback on the coach's own behaviour is how coaching practice is improved. What coaching practice includes and what is laid out for coaches in this new text is motivational climate, coaching behaviours, pedagogy, feedback, coach–athlete relationship, each in one chapter. Reflection and behavioural feedback are applied to each of these areas.

Andreas Carlsson has over 10 years of experience in coaching basketball, including four seasons in Swedish National Team organization and currently conducts workshops, lectures and constructs education material for NGB's, private organizations, schools and club organizations as well as being part of the Swedish sporting federation's network of advisors for sport psychology.

Becoming a Better Sports Coach

Development through Theory Application

Andreas Carlsson

NEW YORK AND LONDON

First published 2021
by Routledge
52 Vanderbilt Avenue, New York, NY 10017

and by Routledge
2 Park Square, Milton Park, Abingdon, Oxon, OX14 4RN

Routledge is an imprint of the Taylor & Francis Group, an informa business

© 2021 Taylor & Francis

The right of Andreas Carlsson to be identified as authors of this work has been asserted by him in accordance with sections 77 and 78 of the Copyright, Designs and Patents Act 1988.

All rights reserved. No part of this book may be reprinted or reproduced or utilised in any form or by any electronic, mechanical, or other means, now known or hereafter invented, including photocopying and recording, or in any information storage or retrieval system, without permission in writing from the publishers.

Trademark notice: Product or corporate names may be trademarks or registered trademarks, and are used only for identification and explanation without intent to infringe.

Library of Congress Cataloging-in-Publication Data
A catalog record for this title has been requested

ISBN: 978-0-367-86069-1 (hbk)
ISBN: 978-0-367-86276-3 (pbk)
ISBN: 978-1-003-19515-3 (ebk)

Typeset in Bembo
by KnowledgeWorks Global Ltd.

To all, including my family, that have deliberately or unintentionally fed my desire for learning and piqued my curiosity.

CONTENTS

List of Figures   viii
List of Tables   ix

1   Background   1

2   Coaches' Learning and Reflection   20

3   Motivation and Motivational Climate   63

4   Coaching Behaviours   95

5   Pedagogy   133

6   Feedback   176

7   Coach-Athlete Relationship   209

8   Long-Term Development   245

Appendix A   260
Appendix B   278
Index   281

FIGURES

1.1	Interactive model of leadership.	4
2.1	Importance of different learning situations as coaching competence develops.	23
2.2	Different levels of learning.	25
2.3	Paths for coach's learning.	28
2.4	Development of coaching practice through reflection.	36
2.5	The relationship between different reflections and knowledge development.	43
2.6	Knowledge development through shared reflection.	47
3.1	The self-determination continuum.	66
3.2	Interaction of goal orientation and motivational climate that create the goal state involvement in the individual.	77
3.3	Goal-orientations dispositions.	78
3.4	Consequences of different motivational climates.	80
4.1	Different leadership styles related to effectiveness and activity of a leader.	103
4.2	Four possible responses from coaches to athletes' behaviours.	110
4.3	Four different combinations of focus.	117
5.1	Illustration of the stimulus-behaviour (response)-consequence chain.	136
5.2	Types of consequences and their effects.	136
5.3	Phases of the self-regulation cycle.	141
5.4	The four pieces of a jigsaw puzzle.	155
6.1	Four functions of feedback.	178
6.2	Time periods between first and second performance in relation to feedback.	183
7.1	Relationships between direct and metaperspective.	215
7.2	Empathy model.	218
7.3	Factors influencing coach's judgement of athletes.	220
7.4	The communication process.	233

TABLES

2.1	Puzzle analogy to describe levels of learning.	26
2.2	General comparison of surface and deep learning.	27
2.3	Characteristics of different reflection depths.	51
2.4	Phases of development of reflective skill in relation to the book's content.	54
3.1	Reasons for acting.	68
3.2	Supportive coaching behaviours and their respective targeted need.	71
3.3	Controlling coaching behaviours.	73
3.4	Characteristics of motivational climates.	79
3.5	Different athletes created by different motivational climates.	82
3.6	TARGET dimensions and strategies.	83
4.1	Categorization of 'sport-specific' coaching behaviours in relation to athletes' behaviours.	98
5.1	Central characteristics of pedagogical methods.	151
5.2	Stages of practice according to 1-2-3 template.	156
6.1	Sensitive words, possible implications and alternatives.	194
7.1	Suggestions on how to improve the 3 C's of a coach-athlete relationship.	215
7.2	Framework for constructing an I-statement.	232
8.1	Phases of behavioural change.	249
8.2	Potential barriers for goal completion and remedies.	251
8.3	States of expertise.	254

1
BACKGROUND

Aim of the chapter: Provide a background to research on coaching development and introduce the content and structure of the present book.
Learning goals of the chapter:
Grow an understanding of…

1. an interactive model of leadership.
2. challenges in coaching development.
3. coaches' preferences for learning and development.

Introduction

Working as a sports coach for many years, my main focus was to develop athletes. To accomplish this goal, coaching knowledge and skill is paramount. In my quest for improved knowledge and skill, I turned to more experienced coaches as well as attended clinics and workshops. However, the discussions with coaches were often based upon our own quite arbitrary experiences. Sometimes, one coach's account contradicted another's. A glaring need for outside input became apparent, as the coaches I met seemed to mostly resort to their tried and proven procedures. Some explicitly referenced their coaching decades ago as a rationale for specific decisions, even though the sport had evolved considerably since then. Initially, I tried to replicate behaviours from better coaches, thinking that was the fastest way to success. Sometimes it worked out fine. Other times it had none, or almost the opposite effect to my dismay. Thus, I turned to other sources. Starting to read up on the sports coaching literature, I found numerous books presenting what could be effective in areas such as motivating and development of athletes' technical skills. Trying out specific recommended tips, however, did not always fit together with other parts of my coaching. From these experiences, it became obvious that to develop my coaching, a deeper approach creating a greater understanding of concepts and their interrelation was needed. Coaching was certainly much more complex than copy-paste.

A curiosity for more knowledge led me to the academic world, which by many coaches was not held in very high regard, as research was viewed as too theoretic, difficult to understand or inapplicable to the world outside of universities. Once, I was even advocated not to enter into a tertiary education in sports, as this pathway 'was not how coaches traditionally were developed'. At the same time, scholars often regretfully told stories of how sporting organizations and coaches were resistant to their advice. This 'conflict' between practitioners and researchers intrigued me. To me, there should be a way to merge the two sides for the benefit of both. Incorporating scientific information into my sports coaching should give me a competitive edge. At least, that was my thinking. After an extensive literature review, it was clear that scientific articles have as much variation when it comes to quality and content as there are among coaches and their practices. If not already difficult to pick out the most relevant information, many times scientific studies do not target the exact issue one is looking for. Even when they do, one single study is seldom enough to come to a sound conclusion. Clearly, there was some validity to the coaches' suspiciousness towards research.

After a few years, I got into coaching education as an educator in the Swedish Basketball Federation. Originally, the coaching courses I ran through this national governing body (NGB) were mostly centred around a prescriptive content which, in a sometimes incoherent manner with various topics stacked on top of each other, described what coaches should do. Little, if any, energy was spent on how the coaches actually develop these skills or make judgments during everyday practices. After a typical course, participants were filled with inspiration and energy to go back to their groups of athletes and use the 'new stuff'. Nevertheless, and not without cause, I had my own doubts about the probability of this ever materializing into major improvements in their everyday coaching. Gradually, my interest shifted from developing athletes to developing coaches. What was lacking though, was a structured way of turning theoretically based advice into coaching craft on the practice venue without being artificial or disingenuous. To solve this issue, I began investigating *how* to develop at craft, like sports coaching and not just *what* a coach should do. Surprisingly, I found a lot of useful ideas in, for sports coaches, lesser-known domains of research such as medicine and teaching. Drawing from this information, I started to develop coaching education courses for various organizations and governing bodies. This allowed me to get applied experiences in coaching development by testing out these ideas, sometimes at a rainy practice ground. Over the years, the content of this book evolved to help coaches avoid my own coaching mistakes.

By then, the challenge became spreading this knowledge to other coaches. Eventually, it was tried out in annual season-long interventions in one of the largest top-level football clubs in Sweden. An opportunity among many that I am very grateful of. In short, this has been my odyssey. Along the way, I had countless of interesting discussions and made quite a few life-long friends, without whom this journey had not been possible (nor as fun). Nowadays, many sports are moving towards having greater access to more advanced statistics and performance data than previously imagined. In a world with more information, a coach needs to be able to digest, adjust and incorporate this information into everyday coaching practice in an efficient manner. In this book, an approach for learning on the job is sketched out. This approach can be used for improving selected coaching areas within this book and others such as sport-specific content. The rest of this chapter will be devoted to presentation of an interactive model of leadership, what is known about coaching education, coaches' learning and the setup of this book for you, the reader, to have a sound background knowledge of coaching development before digging into the subsequent chapters. With this apprehension, it is easier to appreciate the structure of the book and how it will fill a void in the world of coaching development.

For all ambitious coaches striving to get better at the coaching of everyday practices, regardless of being in the early stages of the coaching journey or being a well-travelled senior coach looking for that extra edge, this book offers something for everyone.

Interactive Model of Leadership

Leadership, or coaching, can be regarded from various perspectives. Traditionally, leadership has a long history of being viewed from the *Great Man Theory*. This perspective argues that great leadership is something that is innate in the leader. The person either is or is not a qualified leader. By finding the great leader, any situation or followers can be added with an equally positive outcome. An often-cited example is that of Winston Churchill, who successfully led the allied nations to victory in World War II by rallying the exhausted British people with his charismatic and effective leadership. However, what is less known is that during the First World War he was First Lord of Admiralty, but was removed after the defeat at Gallipoli. Arguably, not even Churchill was a universally successful leader. Needless to say, the Great Man perspective makes it difficult to argue for leadership development as leader identification would be more important. Fortunately, for people involved in coaching development, and not least the coaches themselves, there is ample evidence from science that leadership is something that can be developed (Avolio, Reichard, Hannah, Walumbwa, & Chan, 2009), as can be seen from such diverse domains as finance and military, not to mention sports (Wright & Côté, 2003). The person-situation interaction explains a larger part of one's actions than personal traits alone (Mischel & Shoda, 1995). Hence, it is more effective to view leadership as a dynamic process where components of leadership interact, rather than coexist in a static disposition. This view is also supported from research investigating implicit theories (Hoyt, Burnette, & Innella, 2012),

4 Background

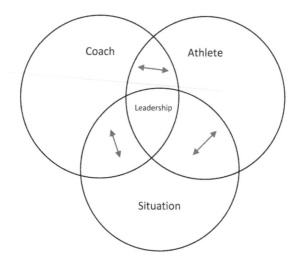

FIGURE 1.1 Interactive model of leadership.

as it is essential for coaching development to view leadership as dynamic. The leadership will emerge at the point of interaction of the three components: leader (i.e., coaches), followers (i.e., athletes) and situation (see Figure 1.1).

A big advantage of viewing leadership as not synonymous with the leader him-/herself is that the blame will not entirely fall on the leader when things go less than perfect, as is often the case when media, parents or other stakeholders are looking for short-term solutions to a struggling sports organization. With this tenet, it will be easier for the coach to observe the coaching as an object and not only from the perspective of a subject. Conversely, it is never entirely the athletes' fault when a practice does not go as smooth as planned. Rather, the interaction between coach, athlete and situation is what counts. This implies that the same coach's characteristics influence the leadership in different ways depending on the athletes and situation. Côté, Salmela, Trudel, Baria, and Russell (1995) proposed that coach characteristics consist of factors such as the coach's philosophy, perception and private situation. Athlete's characteristics include personality, skill level and previous knowledge. Situational characteristics include unstable factors neither directly related to coach nor athlete, such as working conditions, competition system or objectives from club management.

To illustrate the complex and somewhat messy environment a sports coach is working in, a short example of a fictional coach is presented here:

> Instructor Ingram is coaching a group of young track athletes currently working on shot put at the infield of the stadium just inside the running track. Ingram is trying to give everyone feedback on their technique to generate maximum force. While demonstrating how deep one athlete's knee bend was, the rest has to wait so that Ingram can observe their respective performances. One athlete waiting for his turn, getting a little bored,

suddenly throws away a shot toward the running track. Ingram sees this in the corner of his eye and has to make a quick decision on how to act.

What Ingram decides to do in this situation is influenced by a number of aspects from coach, athlete and situational components. To what extent can the athletes be expected to know behavioural rules? Are there any specific cognitive or emotional issues to consider with this particular athlete? What relationship and history do Ingram have with this athlete? How will the rest of the athletes be impacted by Ingram's decision? How are situational factors such availability of shot puts to keep the activity going or other groups of athletes who are interfered by the rolling shot put? Are there any club guidelines on how behaviours like this will be treated, and if so, how will Ingram take them into consideration in this situation? What kind of knowledge on subjects such as motivation, behavioural regulation and coach–athlete relationship does Ingram possess that can be useful in this decision? Clearly, Ingram's decision is influenced by aspects from all three components of coaching. Coaches' decision-making like Ingram's will be informed by experience, knowledge and skills. Therefore, it is worthwhile to investigate how coaching knowledge and skill are best developed.

Challenges in Coaching Development

Traditional coaching education, often given from NGB's, has repeatedly been shown to have trouble impacting coaches' everyday practice. It is far too tempting and easy for a coach to go on with one's business as usual, instead of implementing some of the ideas from the education. Coaches' actions are often influenced more by experiences as an athlete, traditional procedure in the sport or cultural expectations of how a coach should act, rather than scientifically grounded information (Partington & Cushion, 2013). Reasons for ignoring new information vary from not believing in its substance to, out of pure convenience, reverting to the 'proven and known stuff'.

Some of the challenges in coaching development presented by various researchers such as Cushion and colleagues (e.g., Cushion, Armour, & Jones, 2003; Cushion, Armour, & Jones, 2006; Nelson, Cushion, & Potrac, 2013; Stodter & Cushion, 2016) and Abraham and Collins (1998) are summarized in the following seven points:

- Everyday coaching is much harder to capture, and unstructured, than what many coaching models and advice suggest. This can hamper the possibilities to apply information or ideas in practice.
- Scientific information presented is often too technocratic and coach education is often very sport-specific in nature, sometimes entirely ignoring other parts of coaching, or in other cases covering them only briefly.
- Information presented tend to be decontextualized, which can be seen as somewhat artificial and enhance the gap between theory and practice.

- A widely recognized conceptual framework underpinning coaching is lacking. Consequently, the coach as a person and the coaching are easily viewed as synonymous and as a single entity. Thus, critical examination of coaching is hampered as critique risks being interpreted as a threat to the coach's own person.
- Reflective skills are severely underdeveloped and often misunderstood, leading to even further difficulties in developing these elusive and valuable skills.
- Coach educators are often previously successful coaches when it comes to coaching athletes, rather than experts at developing other coaches in their endeavours, and while having practical first-hand experience is useful, it is certainly not sufficient.
- A coach's attitude, values and biographical account can be more powerful than new information, making coaches resist change and development.

Finally, coaches need practice to develop just like the athletes, and mostly coaches' opportunities for practice consist of real-life practices and competitions. During those events, focus often is on improving the athletes' skills or perhaps winning. Obviously, sport practices should be formed around the athletes and their interests, although arguably a coach who develops will over time be able to improve the sporting experience for the athletes as well. To overcome some of the issues raised above, coaching development has to take place to a large extent during real-life practices as this venue carries the most fidelity and poses authentic problems and situations for coaches (Woodburn, 2020). An incorporation of structured and deliberate coaching development during everyday practice should thus benefit both coaches and athletes in the long-run.

However, for optimal development to happen, experience and anecdotal evidence needs to be complemented by external input. Otherwise, the same traditional manners risks being repeated with little progress. This problem is illustrated by pseudoscientific myths being widespread among coaches (Bailey, Madigan, Cope, & Nicholls, 2018). As previously mentioned, coach educators tend to be drawn from the pool of existing coaches, and if false lay-beliefs are prevalent within this group, there is a high risk of the same beliefs being transferred to the next generation of coaches if no external input is received. Beliefs are in themselves not enough to be considered as knowledge since they also need to be true (for more than one person) and be backed up by some form of good ground or evidence (Wikforss, 2020). Alas, coaches' philosophies are often grounded in self-referenced anecdotal arguments (Cushion & Partington, 2016). In contrast to empirical evidence, anecdotal evidence lacks larger and systematic context and is based on isolated personal experiences, highly susceptible to everyday randomness. Philosophies therefore risk ending up in a circular argument, were 'anything goes'. Why did you do so? 'Because that is my philosophy as a coach'. Why is it your philosophy? 'Because I do these things, and they work well for me.' Experiences alone, are not given to produce development or learning, as 50 years of experience in reality might consist of one year almost being repeated over and over again in a non-developmental manner, rather than experiences being built upon through critical reflection and conscious processing (Jarvis, 2006). Altogether, coaches benefit from having their experiences structured and critically scrutinized as well as accompanied by external information. Of course, coaches do not have the means, nor should they, to conduct research for peer-review publication, but a nuanced view on their experiences, comparing them to external information or placing experiences within a larger context is beneficial for coaching development.

In absence of additional input, those experiences are in danger of being used unconsciously for cherry-picking in order to support the 'already-decided-upon' philosophy. In general, people show a clear tendency to choose information in line with their existing views, rather than uncongenial, but more accurate, information (Hart et al., 2009). This is a considerable risk for coaches acting in high-stakes situations under the scrutiny of other stakeholders such as parents, other coaches and club board members. Without critical thinking, a coaching philosophy can be used as a means to justify poor coaching practice rather than develop the coaching. Therefore, any quality coaching development needs to incorporate an easy and systematic manner of evaluating and critically examine one's own beliefs and actions in connection to everyday practices.

Perhaps even more important than having a grasp of sound scientific information is having a scientific mindset to ward coaching. A scientific approach means being constantly curious of new information, thinking critically about experiences, putting experiences into a wider perspective by referring to previous experiences as well as outside input (e.g., an opinion from a peer or a text on a similar subject) and testing out hypothesis in real-life and evaluating tests' results. This path lays an excellent foundation for continuous coaching improvement. On one hand, there is the potential for erring on relying too much on personal experience and, on the other hand, having a too theoretically laden information inapplicable to practice. Accordingly, even if there are generalizable research findings pointing in one direction, for a single coach, there is no guarantee that the cause-and-effect relationship will be identical. This book will walk the thin line in this tough balancing act by offering science-based information while presenting hands-on methods for practical application of this information. Through these means the coach gets to become a little more scientifically orientated in his/her approach, acting like a critical researcher. If so, experiences will no doubt become a more fruitful ground for development and better practice. With these challenges in coaching development, it is time to take a look at coaches' own reported preferences for learning.

Coaches' Preferences for Learning and Development

Conceivably, continuous learning is equally important for a coach as it is for an athlete to keep improving (Armour, 2010). Studies investigating expert coaches have found that a salient characteristic of the best coaches is their constant curiosity and hunger for new learning (Vallée & Bloom, 2005; Wiman, Salmoni, & Hall, 2010). By necessity, coaches need to develop since every sport will evolve over time as technical executions and strategies develop. Coaches will also be provided with new challenges as they meet new athletes and new groups. Currently, the world of information is constantly changing at an ever more rapid pace, placing a greater need than ever to keep learning. Thus, the need for improvement is on-going for coaches. If traditional coaching educations arguably are a dubious ground for effective coaching development, how do coaches themselves prefer to learn? Research has investigated this question both relating to content of and approach to coaching development and the following section will review the literature examining coaches' preference.

Content

Level of experience seems to moderate preferences as more novel coaches prefer sport-specific information, while more experienced coaches value other areas to a larger extent, such as communication skills (Abraham, Collins, & Martindale, 2006). Coaches are often driven by short-term needs and these naturally revolve around sporting issues, like how to find a new drill or improve fitness. With that said, sport-specific information may be prioritized at the expense of interpersonal skills, even though the significance of the latter is supported by its importance for athletes' development over time (Gulbin, Oldenziel, Weissensteiner, & Gagné, 2010). A reason for this might be traced to possibilities of selection bias of coaches being more likely to be chosen from athletic positions incorporating more social skills (Leonard, Ostrosky, & Huchendorf, 1990), thus taking social competence for granted. Furthermore, research has highlighted the risk of coaches being unaware of their advantageous developmental needs, as short-sighted goals and procedural, copy-paste actions are preferred over more conceptual understanding (Stoszkowski & Collins, 2015).

Approach

As coaching expertise grows, coaches tend to increasingly emphasize individualization, and problematize the content for a deeper understanding, but this type of approach is simultaneously more likely to lead to furthering of high competence as well in a circular relationship. Additionally, informal conversations and active involvement during coaching courses are usually preferred by the coaches, probably because coaches generally like to be in charge, and they prefer to direct their own learning (Lemyre, Trudel & Durand-Bush, 2007). Coaches have reported to use plenty of trial-and-error approach to their development, although they simultaneously remark that a more structured path would be extra effective. Again, more senior coaches have an affection for using own coaching practice as fruitful ground for development (Mallett, Rynne & Billett, 2016). Accordingly, mentorship has repeatedly been proposed by coaches both as an effective way of development (Jones, Harris, & Miles, 2009; Nash & Sproule, 2009), and as a desirable way of developing (Erickson, Bruner, MacDonald, & Côté, 2008), as this can serve as a foundation of both the reflective conversation, has access to external, and high quality, information as well as receiving behavioural feedback on one's coaching practice. A trusting relationship will also be helpful in overcoming the challenges of receiving feedback without this being seen as a threat to a coach's personal sphere.

Clearly, coaches prefer coaching education to be more of the interactive variety rather than one-way communication. This factor seems to be more important than the scientific credibility of received information. Lave and Wenger (1991) showed that learning is situated in real-life practice, which certainly mirrors coaches' preference. It is also quite possible that a person being attracted to the coach occupation is a person who likes to voice his/her opinion and is most comfortable in a role of influence. If so, that means that coaches in general prefer educational interventions where they have a more active, rather than a passive role, which is usually found in networking, workshops and mentorship compared to listening to a lecture or reading an article. As much as a coach is sort of a director of athletes' development in practice, coaches prefer to be in the driving seat when it comes their own development.

Summarizing coaches' preferences for content of, and approach to developmental interventions, the most interesting topic is highly relevant information that is readily applied in their own practice. However, by looking at the studies that have examined this area, it is quite likely that coaches are interested in information emanating from non-sport-specific areas such as psychology concerning both their interpersonal skills as well as their intrapersonal knowledge if they are fully aware of the short-term benefits with improvements in these areas. The main issues seem to be that the information should be applied in coaching practice with the coaches' themselves being in charge of how this application is carried out, rather than being presented with a strict, prescriptive, one-size fits all manner. Coaches clearly show a preference for self-directed modes of learning, even though this might be an artefact of lack of viable developmental options. Persistent in coaching is a potentially inhibiting treadmill where existing culture is replicated while dramatic change and large influence from science is resisted (Partington & Cushion, 2013). This is explained by situated learning (Lave and Wenger, 1991), which suggests that a novice coach works his or her way to legitimate participation within the coaching community by adhering to the advice of more experienced coaches. This transition is only accomplished by accepting the pre-existing culture, discourse and tradition. Thus, further increasing the difficulties to break out of old habits. Coaches' preferences might not always be guided by what is best for long-term coaching development. Moreover, by using 'declaratively based critical approaches, formal coaching education would move beyond the simple transference of specific knowledge and skills and, instead, help coaches to move towards a more critical understanding of their thinking, reasoning and behaviour' (Stoszkowski & Collins, 2015, p. 801). In order to enhance coaching, additional contribution is needed in a way that draws from scientific literature and blends into the existing culture in a smooth and non-threatening manner. Efficient and continuous learning requires a structured approach to learning. Coincidentally, time is more crucial than ever, which increases the demands on learning. One cannot use the same coaching knowledge of yesteryear. A possible solution to both the quest for quality continuous learning and time-efficiency is learning from, and during, one's own practice.

Two Metaphors for Coaching Development

In relation to the aforementioned approaches to coaching education, Sfard (1998) has detailed how learning can be viewed from two different perspectives (metaphors). This distinction is highly relevant and cast further light on how to best develop coaches.

Acquisition Metaphor

For a long time, learning has been seen as acquiring something where an accumulation of concepts, which first needs to be understood at a basic level, leads to richer cognitive structures within the learner. This perspective has the learner as a container to be filled with knowledge. When the knowledge has been acquired, it can then be applied to novel situations. This knowledge primarily resides within, and is possessed by the learner. The role for the educator in this perspective is to deliver sound information and facilitate knowledge development in the learner.

Participation Metaphor

Recently, learning has been viewed as a process of the individual becoming a more central member within a community of practice. Here, language, norms and cultural interactions are essential. Learning is not a property of the learner, but entrenched within the community itself. The learning process is ongoing and not separate from the context. Learning is viewed as more active and instead of a state of knowledge, the activity of knowing is emphasized. The role for the teacher, educator or coach in this perspective is as an expert participant and maintainer of the discourse.

Sfard argues that both views of learning are needed and they are not meant to be mutually exclusive. The two metaphors are neither to be seen as individualistic (acquisition) nor social (participation) learning theories, rather the distinction is made regarding the very nature of learning. The acquisition metaphor asserts that learning is acquiring the thing called knowledge, while the participation metaphor argues for learning by becoming a legitimate participant in a group or community. Although, the social aspect is necessary within the participation metaphor, it could feature just as prominently when acquiring knowledge.

Traditionally, acquisition has had a strong grip on coaching education, while participation has been the norm for learning during every day coaching. For coaching development to really take off, a merger between the two perspectives needs to be negotiated.

Setup and Structure of the Book

The present book is more than just an academic text that is read from cover to cover. Rather, it is more of a workbook where the reader is asked to stop and think about the theory just read, in addition to try out some theory during real-life practice. The book sets out to merge the challenges in coaching development with coaches' preferences for learning in an accessible format. The critiques reviewed above might even cause dejection among practitioners or be seen as 'nothing is ever good enough'. However, there are potentially fruitful avenues in attacking these issues. First, a common ground has to be established when it comes to coaching. This can be seen in the interactive model of sports coaching presented above. Second, scientific information has to be presented in an easily accessible manner that coaches both can understand as well as handily try out at the practice field themselves. Chapters 3–7 cover this. Third, this information must not be conveyed in 'my way or highway style', rather it has to be adaptable to the current coach's situation, skills and preferences. In order to accomplish this, the most beneficial vehicle as a means to test in real-life, evaluate and try to draw conclusions in a systematic manner is suggested to be guided reflection, which will be thoroughly explored in Chapter 2 and applied in the subsequent chapters.

In order to bridge the aforementioned gap between theory and practice in sports coaching, and in line with Sfard's (1998) contention that both acquisition and participation is needed for learning, the present book tries to integrate two different and important aspects of development. These aspects are called *What* and *How*. *What* is the content of the learning material, whereas *How* define the process of learning this content. Both are informed by a rich scientific literature considering *What* has been found important in sports coaching, and *How* this is best introduced, problematized and applied to everyday practice. While the former to a large extent is not by any means new information, the latter is something that has been absent in many educational texts and educational interventions alike. Plenty of texts exists where sound research-based information is presented. However, often this presentation leaves out guidelines on how to modify, test and evaluate this information in everyday, real-life practice. With a little imagination, the ambitious and creative coach can solve this by him-/herself, but just as likely is the scenario of having read a great content and still having somewhat unsatisfying effect on coaching practice. Consequently, an ambitious coach tries to read something else similar hoping for the next text to be the magic potion that accelerates practical development. This can be repeated over and over again, with the unsatisfactory effect on coaching being a driver for continued search. Likely, the lack of an effective *How* is one major reason why scientific information has struggled to reach the practice field in sports coaching. In short, *What* is the main topics described within Chapters 3–7, while *How* is the backbone of the present book, outlined in Chapter 2 and then used as a recurring theme within the subsequent chapters where their respective *What* are applied and tested both through short questions, exercises and real-life applications. In the present book, the aim is for the scientific information to be presented in a more problematized manner and highlighting the multicausality (i.e., plenty of factors interact and have effects on many other factors) existing in real-life coaching. For example, running a specific quickness drill might improve an athlete's reaction speed, but at the same time could prove detrimental to the same athlete's motivation. It is skilled negotiation of trade-offs like this that constitutes the core of the coaching craft. In order to make excellent informed decisions, a coach needs to have both awareness of the experience itself as well as understanding of some quality external information. This knowledge will not in itself guarantee a perfect or best solution, but rather a decision to take pros and cons of different alternatives into account. The current book will prevent an element of haphazardness in coaching development and present a road map to structured improvement through its integration of coaches' previous experience and (new) theory in selected areas pertaining to coaching. Up until now, such a take – which truly takes theory into coaches' own everyday practice and back again to the drawing table – has been lacking in the coaching literature. Trial-and-error will still be present, but more so in a systematic fashion and with a greater understanding of the cognitive coaching process. As a vehicle for development, templates and hands-on tools for reflection and behavioural feedback (both through questionnaires and through observation) are provided. Gathering data from various sources with different methods increases the chance of getting a more thorough picture and less risk of blind spots (Wright & Irwin, 2018). Throughout the book's design, the drawback of science seldom having clear cut and comprehensive answers to a single question will be somewhat mitigated as the theory is not stand-alone, rather easily tested in the coach's own reality. There, personal adaptations and lessons learnt will make the theory more useful than if it is, as is common within academic coaching literature, presented free-standing and, at best complemented with a later section of applications or some open-ended questions.

As the present book is made for practitioners who strive to develop themselves, there are hazards to beware of, as self-development is never guaranteed from just reading a text. Orvis and Ratwani (2010) propose a model consisting of several features of instructional design for successful self-development of leaders. They are *content relevancy, learner engagement, practice and progress evaluation information, challenge, structure* and *experiential variety*. All are included within this book. Content relevancy and engagement are provided as the book addresses knowledge/skills in need of improvement and not just learning theoretically about a subject. These skills are honed during real-life sports practices along with behavioural feedback provided by questionnaires and observation schedule other can use to provide feedback. Additionally, the application exercises and reflective activities provide opportunities to problematize sports coaching challenging any coach regardless of level of expertise. These exercises and activities are structured around the framework of reflection and learning detailed in Chapter 2. Through integration of the book's content onto the practice venue with all its changing circumstances, experiences will certainly be varied and authentic. All this provides opportunities for coaches to integrate theory with their coaching practice and not just reading about theories and leaving the application somewhat hanging. Orvis and Ratwani advise against just reading or watching and recommend that action must be taken for self-development to occur.

In the subsequent chapters four types of exercises will surface signified by different icons.

This icon signifies *application exercises* where the reader is asked to think, write opinions or draw upon previous practical experience. These exercises connect the previously described theory to the reader's everyday coaching practice and own reality. These exercises vary in degree of stimulation of reflection depth. They also present opportunities to problematize and tailor the theory to own preferences and personally relevant situations.

This icon signifies *case exercises* where the reader is asked to think about a description of an event and apply the previously presented theory or prior knowledge. It can be perceived to be both easier and less intrusive to ponder a fictive example, especially so when starting to reflect. After having de-dramatized scrutinization of another 'person', often it is less threatening to do the same on oneself.

This icon signifies *reflective activities* where the reader is asked to reflect in connection to practice. One type of activity consists of *reflection cards* that should be used at the practice venue. Make sure that reflection cards are of convenient size if using paper, as they are not supposed to be used for writing extensively. Another option is using a cell phone to make the in-practice recordings. The other type of activity is *reflective sheet* to be used after practices as explained in Chapter 2.

This icon signifies *quantitative measurement* with a questionnaire. The questionnaires will be gathered in an appendix to allow for easy reading of the chapters and convenient opportunities to make copies of the questionnaires for easy distribution to the athletes. The final section of this chapter provides information on quantitative measurements.

The book is divided into eight chapters, starting with outlining learning goals for the chapter and concluding with a quiz containing one question for each learning goal. Chapters 2–7 also includes vignettes presenting two coaches and their mentor's discussions of that chapter's content, providing a fictional description of real-life dilemmas and application, which will be returned to at the end of each chapter. Throughout the chapters additional examples are provided, which are not to be seen as neither the only possible nor best application of theory, but to stimulate creativity, give a more hands-on description of the theory and perhaps even provide a new idea for coaches.

Chapter two (*Coaches' learning and reflection*) covers four main areas. First, coaches' learning is discussed, both from the various situations in which a coach can learn, for example, a mediated learning situation which consists of typical traditional classroom type of lectures where the learning material presented is prepared with a clear learning outcome in mind. Second, reflection skill is measured using a self-report questionnaire in order to elicit a sound baseline measure, before the reader has gained increased knowledge of reflection skill. Then, reflection skill is unpacked and described. Third, different methods for reflection are explained. Mainly, they are *reflection card* (focusing primarily on reflection engagement) and *reflection sheet* (focusing primarily on reflection insight) and will be used in subsequent chapters with their respective contents. Fourth, research has consistently found it difficult to develop reflective practice in coaches, and even when it has been used, reflection more often than not is quite shallow, limiting its effectiveness. Therefore, an important part of this chapter is to facilitate the readers' understanding of different reflection depths and how to apply this knowledge to coach's own reflections.

Chapter three (*Motivation and motivational climate*) covers three main areas. First, Self-Determination Theory (SDT) is briefly described using the SDT-continuum. Second, Achievement Goal Theory (AGT) is presented as this framework is also useful. The theories of SDT and AGT are complementary rather than mutually exclusive, and a coach can benefit by considering each theory's respective key contributions. Third, coaches' own motivation, something severely lacking attention in traditional coaching education and coaching literature, is addressed.

Chapter four (*Coaching behaviours*) covers three main areas. First, some important effects of coaching behaviours on the athletes are reviewed. Second, coaching behaviours in general are divided into 'sport specific', which are behaviours directly related to improving sporting skills and fitness, and 'social competence', which are behaviours more related to leadership in general. Third, factors impacting coaching behaviours will be elaborated using the interactive model presented in Chapter 1 as a framework.

Chapter five (*Pedagogy*) covers five main areas. First, three theories of learning are detailed serving as a foundation for the chapter. Second, five different pedagogical methods are described. Each pedagogical method has their own advantages and drawbacks, entailing various aspects of athlete and coach implications. Third, the '1-2-3 template' is presented. This model consists of three stages within practice and is based on four areas of athletic improvement (technical, tactical, mental and physical). Fourth, three types of practice activities are described. They are *formal exercises*, *playful games* and *game situations*. Fifth, questions are thoroughly described in detail. Compared to many areas in sports coaching, questions are researched quite sparingly.

Chapter six (*Feedback*) covers two main areas. First, and most important part of this chapter, the four potential functions of feedback are elaborated. Second, modality through which channel feedback is provided is scrutinized.

Chapter seven (*Coach–athlete relationship*) covers four main areas. First, the coach–athlete relationship is described using Jowett's (2007) 3 + 1 C's as a starting point. Second, it is imperative for a coach to be able to read and interpret the athlete's feelings and thoughts and this will be addressed. Third, strategies for improving the coach–athlete relationship are explained. Fourth, different techniques for conversating skillfully with the athletes are presented.

Chapter eight (*Long-term coaching development*) covers three main areas in order to facilitate coaches' long-term self-improvement. First, principles of behavioural modification are outlined. Second, features of expertise are detailed. Third, generalizable characteristics of the reflective activities used in previous chapters are outlined, which presents coaches with a *How* for other topics of development.

I have sought to provide a text that can be read by anyone regardless of prior knowledge. A first-time student will have great benefit from each chapter serving as a short introductory text into a range of important subjects, while the more knowledgeable researcher might get some ideas for applied interventions in different areas covered by Chapters 3–7. For the coach, the text is useful in providing a little theory, but first and foremost, also by its linkage to real-life practice with each chapter's suggested applications to coaching that can be tested.

Quantitative Measurements

As a means to elicit behavioural feedback or as a starting point for reflection for the coach, many of the constructs presented within the present book are complemented by questionnaires. These inventories are either self-report where the coach answers questions about him-/herself or for the athletes to report their perception. The measurement can serve as a starting point for either an action plan to improve in a specific area or as a basis for reflection on the coaching. Self-reports are probably more useful as a reflective tool when summing the answers, while athletes' responses provide behavioural feedback. All questionnaires are validated in research and aligned with the theories presented within respective chapters. By getting highly detailed feedback in this manner, a coach can uncover previously hidden areas, in a better way than asking unstructured open-ended questions to the athletes. If the coach is not even aware that a specific area exists or of its importance, it is difficult, if not impossible to reflect on this area or improve upon it. This is where questionnaires come in handy.

However, there are some potential pitfalls when using quantitative measurements (as with all methods extracting information). Consequently, the most pressing issues will be addressed below. The usage of questionnaires has two distinct phases, data collection and data analysis.

Data Collection

When providing answers to a questionnaire it is of outmost importance that the athletes are responding anonymously, voluntarily and understand that there are no right or wrong answers. If not, there is a high risk of social desirability, which means that people answer in a way they think others (e.g., the coach) approve of, rather than honestly (Podsakoff, MacKenzie, Jeong-Yeon, & Podsakoff, 2003), which distorts the feedback. Securing anonymity will be effectively accomplished by having someone else than the coach him-/herself handing out and collecting the questionnaires from the athletes. If the coach him-/herself is the one administering the data collection, one idea is to let the athletes put their filled-out questionnaires in a common envelope for the whole group. Also, the coach should walk out of the room after having provided the instruction leaving the athletes fill out the questionnaire with maximum privacy. The questionnaires should be voluntary to fill out as it is important that the athletes do not feel pressured. However, by explaining that the data collection is important for getting high quality feedback as a coach in order to improve coaching and group environment, instead of evaluating the athletes themselves, a greater proportion of athletes will respond sincerely. In line with this, it is important to stress one more time that the answers are completely anonymous and no team selection or rewards/punishments will be contingent of the answers (Krumpal, 2013).

The questionnaires in the present book should be copied so that every athlete gets a copy. The estimated time for filling out each questionnaire is described in connection to respective questionnaire. In addition to paper copies, each athlete should be provided with a pen or pencil. The verbal instruction for filling out a questionnaire should be the following:

> The coach/I is/am very interested in receiving your opinion on the coaching and group environment. Here is a questionnaire where you can provide your opinion on a number of statements. There are no right or wrong answers – it is your personal opinion that is sought. Answer each statement by making an 'X' in the appropriate box. Do not overthink any statement too long. Go with your initial gut feeling. If you do want to change an 'X' you should make another 'X' and circle the correct one. The coach/I will not know who answered in what way and the coach/I have no interest in individual answers. The important thing is to find out the opinion of the group as a whole. This information will be very helpful for the coach/me in order to improve the coaching and the group environment.

The person administering a questionnaire should take some time to familiarize him-/herself with the content of each item in order to be able to provide a little bit of an explanation if an athlete has a question. However, the statements should be quite self-explanatory as the questionnaires have been validated in previous research. Therefore, it might be better to leave a blank answer rather than the data collector (e.g., coach) trying to change the wording too much by giving a too elaborate explanation to a specific word or an entire statement. Each statement is supposed to fit in a specific category, thus must not drift too far away from its origin.

Data Analysis

Included with every questionnaire is a scoring key. This key will show what statements belong together in what kind of category. Every category is summarized in order to get a point total for that category. Some statements might be scored reversed (i.e., an 'X' in the box to the far right – highest number will get the lowest score and vice versa) when the questionnaire is summarized. When every category is summarized, a profile emerges. The advice is to enter the results into a spreadsheet using a computer programme such as Microsoft Excel, using lines for different responders and columns for the statements. By using the functions in the programme, it is easy to summarize scores on each statement. The statements belonging to the same category should then be averaged, calculating a measure that is comparable to every other category within the questionnaire regardless of the number of statements within the category. The higher the score, the more prominent this category is. In each questionnaire's profile it is possible to see strengths and weaknesses in specific areas, aiding in selection of focus for improvements. A difference between two categories of only .1 or .2 might not mean a real difference as quantitative data always have a little bit of uncertainty about its exactness. However, should one find a substantial difference where one category is clearly rated lower than others, this could serve as a guide for where to try to improve. Another way of analyzing the data is to view the data as a starting ground for reflection. It also opens up avenues for discussion within the group of athletes and coaches. A caveat though, a coach has to interpret this kind of feedback as a help towards improvement rather than a threat to the own person. This is important when talking to the athletes before, and after, the results from the questionnaires are known. Otherwise, the coach could create a group climate where the athletes do not want to provide honest opinions and feelings of distrust and betrayal emerge. Finally, it is important not to dwell too much on the result on a single statement or hamper on a smaller difference between two categories. Rather, it is better to view the broad picture. 'What does this result say about the coaching and how is this information best used to improve the coaching?'

Quiz

1. What statement is most correct about the interactive model of leadership?
    a. Coaching is not synonymous with the coach.
    b. Athletes influence coaching far less than coaches.
    c. Situational factors are independent of coaching.

2. What is a common challenge in coaching development?
    a. Athletes are not interested in helping the coach develop.
    b. Scientific information is overused.
    c. Coaches are prone to repeat traditions uncritically.

3. What approach to development are often preferred by coaches?
   a. Trial-and-error.
   b. Clear one-way communication of hard evidence.
   c. Connected to real-life practice.

References

Abraham, A., & Collins, D. (1998). Examining and extending research in coach development. *Quest, 50,* 59–79.

Abraham, A., Collins, D., & Martindale, R. (2006). The coaching schematic: validation through expert coach consensus. *Journal of Sports Sciences, 24,* 549–564.

Armour, K. (2010). The learning coach… the learning approach: Professional development for sports coach professionals. In J. Lyle, & C. Cushion (Eds.), *Sports coaching: Professionalisation and practice* (pp. 153–164). Oxford, UK: Elsevier.

Avolio, B. J., Reichard, R. J., Hannah, S. T., Walumbwa, F. O., & Chan, A. (2009). A meta-analytical review of leadership impact research: Experimental and quasi-experimental studies. *The Leadership Quarterly, 20,* 764–784.

Bailey, R. P., Madigan, D. J., Cope, E., & Nicholls, A. R. (2018). The prevalence of pseudoscientific ideas and neuromyths among sports coaches. *Frontiers in Psychology, 9,* 641.

Côté, J., Salmela, J., Trudel, P., Baria, A., & Russell, S. (1995). The coaching model: A grounded assessment of expert gymnastic coaches' knowledge. *Journal of Sport & Exercise Psychology, 17,* 1–17.

Cushion, C. J., Armour, K. M., & Jones, R. L. (2003). Coach education and continuing professional development: Experience and learning to coach. *Quest, 55,* 215–230.

Cushion, C. J., Armour, K. M., & Jones, R. L. (2006). Locating the coaching process in practice: Models 'for' and 'of' coaching. *Physical Education and Sport Pedagogy, 11,* 83–99.

Cushion, C., & Partington, M. (2016). A critical analysis of the conceptualization of 'coaching philosophy'. *Sport, Education and Society, 21,* 851–867.

Erickson, K., Bruner, M. W., MacDonald, D. J., & Côté, J. (2008). Gaining insight into actual and preferred sources of coaching knowledge. *International Journal of Sports Science & Coaching, 3,* 527–538.

Gulbin, J. P., Oldenziel, K. E., Weissensteiner, J. R., & Gagné, F. (2010). A look through the rear view mirror: Developmental experiences and insights of high performance athletes. *Talent Development & Excellence, 2,* 149–164.

Hart, W. et al. (2009). Feeling validated versus being correct: A meta-analysis of selective exposure to information. *Psychological Bulletin, 135,* 555–588.

Hoyt, C. L., Burnette, J. L., & Innella, A. N. (2012). I can do that: The impact of implicit theories on leadership role model effectiveness. *Personality and Social Psychology Bulletin, 38,* 257–268.

Jarvis, P. (2006). *Towards a comprehensive theory of human learning.* Abingdon, UK: Routledge.

Jones, R. L., Harris, R., & Miles, A. (2009). Mentoring in sports coaching: A review of the literature. *Physical Education and Sport Pedagogy, 14,* 267–284.

Jowett, S. (2007). Interdependence analysis and the 3+1Cs in the coach-athlete relationship. In S. Jowett, & D. Lavallee (Eds.), *Social psychology in sport* (pp. 15–27). Champaign, IL: Human Kinetics.

Krumpal, I. (2013). Determinants of social desirability bias in sensitive surveys: A literature review. *Quality & Quantity, 47,* 2025–2047.

Lave, J., & Wenger, E. (1991). *Situated learning: Legitimate peripheral participation.* Cambridge: Cambridge University Press

Lemyre, F., Trudel, P., & Durand-Bush, N. (2007). How youth sport coaches learn to coach. *The Sport Psychologist, 21*, 191–209.

Leonard, W. M., Ostrosky, T., & Huchendorf, S. (1990). Centrality of position and managerial recruitment: The case of major league baseball. *Sociology of Sport Journal, 7*, 294–301.

Mallett, C. J., Rynne, S. B., & Billett, S. (2016). Valued learning experiences of early career and experienced high-performance coaches. *Physical Education and Sport Pedagogy, 21*, 89–104.

Mischel, W., & Shoda, Y. (1995). A cognitive-affective system theory of personality: Reconceptualizing situations, dispositions, dynamics, and invariance in personality structure. *Psychological Review, 102*, 246–268.

Nash, C. S., & Sproule, J. (2009). Career development of expert coaches. *International Journal of Sports Science & Coaching, 4*, 121–138.

Nelson, L., Cushion, C., & Potrac, P. (2013). Enhancing the provision of coach education: The recommendations of UK coaching practitioners. *Physical Education and Sport Pedagogy, 18*, 204–218.

Orvis, K. A., & Ratwani, K. L. (2010). Leader self-development: A contemporary context for leader development evaluation. *The Leadership Quarterly, 21*, 657–674.

Partington, M., & Cushion, C. (2013). An investigation of the practice activities and coaching behaviors of professional top-level youth soccer coaches. *Scandinavian Journal of Medicine & Science in Sport, 23*, 1–9.

Podsakoff, P. M., MacKenzie, S. B., Jeong-Yeon, L., & Podsakoff, N. P. (2003). Common method biases in behavioral research: A critical review of the literature and recommended remedies. *Journal of Applied Psychology, 88*, 879–903.

Sfard, A. (1998). On two metaphors for learning and the dangers of choosing just one. *Educational Researcher, 27*, 4–13.

Stodter, A., & Cushion, C. J. (2016). Effective coach learning and the processes of coaches' knowledge development: What works? In P. A. Davis (Ed.), *The psychology of effective coaching and management* (pp. 35–52). New York: Nova Science Publishers.

Stoszkowski, J., & Collins, D. (2015). Sources, topics and use of knowledge by coaches. *Journal of Sports Sciences, 34*, 794–802.

Woodburn, A. (2020). Experiential learning for undergraduate student-coaches. In B. Callary, & B. Gearity (Eds.), *Coach education and development in sport: Instructional strategies* (pp. 20–32). Abingdon, UK: Routledge.

Vallée, C. N., & Bloom, G. A. (2005). Building a successful university program: Key and common elements of expert coaches. *Journal of Applied Sport Psychology, 17*, 179–196.

Wikforss, Å. (2020). Alternativa fakta: Om kunskapen och dess fiender [*Alternative Facts: On Knowledge and its Enemies*] Stockholm, SE: Fri Tanke.

Wiman., M., Salmoni, A. W., & Hall, C. R. (2010). An examination of the definition and development of expert coaching. *International Journal of Coaching Science, 4*, 37–60.

Wright, A., & Côté, J. (2003). A retrospective of leadership development through sport. *The Sport Psychologist, 17*, 268–291.

Wright, P. M., & Irwin, C. (2018). Using systematic observation to assess teacher effectiveness promoting personally and socially responsible behavior in physical education. *Measurement in Physical Education and Exercise Science, 22*, 250–262.

2
COACHES' LEARNING AND REFLECTION

Aim of the chapter: Provide a foundation for using reflection to enhance everyday coaching practice.

Theoretical learning goals of the chapter:
Grow an understanding of...

1. what kind of learning situations exists for coaches.
2. different levels of learning.
3. some key barriers to learning.
4. what characterizes reflection.
5. some important pros and cons of reflection.
6. some methods for structured reflection.
7. some differences between different reflection depths.

Practical learning goals of the chapter:

1. Get accustomed to reflecting-in-action by using a reflection card.
2. Get accustomed to reflecting-on-action by using a reflection sheet.

Vignette

Coach Collin and Leah Leader meet regularly with Ellen Expert, their mentor coach, to discuss coaching issues. This time, they are meeting immediately after they both have finished their respective practices, while still being at the practice venue.

"Everything went smoothly today", Collin started off.

"In what way did the practice go smoothly?" Ellen followed up instantly.

"I don't really know how to explain it", Collin answered. "I just remember the practice starting and then all of a sudden it was over. It must have been a great practice. Otherwise, I would remember that I had plenty of hiccups during the practice", he continued.

"Can it be that you haven't thought much during the practice?" Ellen asked.

"Nah, pretty much like every time", he answered.

"Leah, describe your experience during your practice", Ellen said, as she turned to Leah.

"It was a regular practice, pretty much", Leah replied.

"No issues at all, that you need help with in your coaching?" Ellen probed.

"The main thing I can think of is that I get caught up in my own emotions. I don't really understand why I get so emotional at times", Leah said looking a little bit worried.

"In what kind of situations does this happen?" Ellen queried.

"Hard to tell…", Leah began, before stopping briefly mid-sentence. "I can't tell when and why. It just happens", she continued.

"Would you be interested in learning more about your feelings during practice?" Ellen asked.

"Of course, I just don't know how that could be done. When I think of the practice it is already over, and my memory is not always the best", Leah answered and looked puzzled.

"It sounds like you need some help paying attention during the action itself", Ellen kept going.

"Do you have any ideas?" Leah asked back.

"One thing you could try is to write down thoughts and feelings that you experience during practice. This may develop your understanding of your coaching", Ellen said calmly.

"Do you mean like she could use the practice to learn and practice her coaching?" Collin added.

"A practice could be an important learning opportunity for the coach as well as the athletes. What is the most important thing you have learnt as coaches?" Ellen asked them.

"I would guess that is knowledge about the techniques in my sport. That, and some great new drills I learnt from our level 2 coaching licensing course", Collin quickly replied.

"To me the most important learning has probably been when watching other coaches", Leah added.

"If you want to, you can watch some of my practices to learn some great drills", Collin said confidently.

They closed the discussion having decided upon a date for the next meeting.

> What do you think of the way Collin and Leah reflect upon their coaching practice?
> How do Collin and Leah, respectively, view coaches' learning?

The Learning of Coaches
Different Learning Situations

Plenty of differing circumstances exist for coaches to learn from. In order to structure these learning situations into a perspicuous framework, Werthner and Trudel (2006) categorized the learning situations into three types: *mediated*, *unmediated*, and *internal* learning situations. Mediated learning situations are directed or organized by someone else who has sketched out an agenda, topic, or curriculum for the coach. Mediated learning situations consist of both formal and non-formal learning. The former is often mandatory such as NGB coaching certification courses, whereas the latter is coach-initiated, but still planned and structured in its content by someone else, such as a lecture or a regional coaching clinic. Meanwhile, unmediated learning situations are unstructured and the coach is both the initiator of the learning situation as well as responsible to a larger extent for the content. This is somewhat incidental and covers both peer-learning and individual activities, such as watching YouTube clips and reading a book like this one. Of course, in all learning situations, the learner is chiefly responsible for the learning outcomes regardless of who structures the content. Sometimes, unmediated learning situations are called informal learning, which is a lifelong process where the coach develops knowledge, skills, and attitudes from everyday experiences. This type of learning situations has a connotation of being haphazard and idiosyncratic (Walker, Thomas, & Driska, 2018), but this does not necessarily need to be the case as the opportunities presented within this text will be highly structured and viable for deliberate improvement. In internal learning situations, there is no external learning material or new outside experience. Rather, the learning situation consists of reconsidering and contemplating previous stimuli. Moon (2004) has compared this to a sort of 'cognitive housekeeping'. By effectively reorganizing items in the house cellar, one can find hidden or long-lost items, discover that items previously considered unrelated have commonalities between when they are seen side by side, and get more storing space without throwing away a single thing. Many of these analogies translate well into cognitive outcomes of internal learning situations. For example, the coach can become aware of learning material and lessons learnt that have been forgotten, connect the nature of different episodes and benefit more from previous experiences as they are elaborated on.

All learning situations are potentially valuable for coaches (Erickson, Bruner, MacDonald, & Côté, 2008), but there is reason to believe that internal learning situations are of particular importance as they are frequently triggered by highly relevant coaching issues (Gilbert & Trudel, 2005; Werthner & Trudel, 2006). Arguably, the more experienced a coach is, the more emphasis is placed on internal learning situations, as seen in Figure 2.1. Using internal learning situations is also advantageous as coaches think back and reconsider previous experiences without taxing an already hectic time schedule by squeezing in a new workshop or coaching course.

Schempp (2003) presents another way of categorizing learning sources for coaches into experiences as an athlete, coach experiences, and educations. Experiences as an athlete may provide a source for learning, even if these experiences are long gone as they may still have played a role in forming values, beliefs, or to reflect upon. At least some athletic background is common, if not necessary, among sport coaches (Cushion et al., 2010). However, there is ample support to suggest that not entirely identical memory structures support athletic and coaching performance. In order to execute motor skills, a person uses procedural memories that describe *how* to do something, such as how to ride a bicycle. Procedural memories are difficult to articulate, and might even suffer from being verbalized, as is predicted by the reinvestment hypothesis where motor skills learnt with explicit rules, more easily breaks down under stressful conditions (Poolton & Zachry, 2007). In contrast to procedural memories, declarative memories describe facts and *what* to do and are possible to articulate. The latter are consciously recalled and translated into

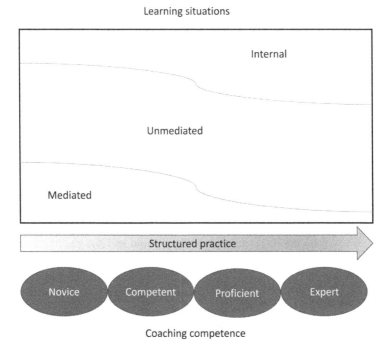

FIGURE 2.1 Importance of different learning situations as coaching competence develops (Trudel & Gilbert, 2013).

words more easily than the former. In conclusion, as an athlete, motor skills stored in procedural memories are essential for performance, whereas declarative memories underpin skilled coaching as coaches need to be able to convey verbal messages to athletes. Of course, experiences as an athlete may help a coach understand the problems and feelings of an athlete in a similar situation. Regardless of how previous experiences interact in a coach's present knowledge, this is something hard to modify, unless the coach is still an active athlete.

Different Areas of Knowledge

Coaches' knowledge consists of various areas, such as *sport-specific*, *social competence*, and *self-awareness* (Côté & Gilbert, 2009). Of course, there is somewhat of an overlap between the areas. This breakdown is more to structure and make coaches' knowledge visible rather than provide absolute distinct categories. Examples of content that fall into the area of sport-specific are technical cues, drill bank for upper body strength, and skills problem identification. Contents that fall into the area of social competence are, for example, non-verbal communication, relationship maintenance, or empathic understanding. The area of self-awareness includes contents like attention to one's own thought-processes, managing one's own emotions, or cognizance of how to learn best.

According to Cushion, Armour, and Jones (2003), sport-specific knowledge is most prevalent in mediated learning situations. Those learning situations often focus on sport-specific details, resulting in coaches being left to other means to round out their total coaching competency. Research on youth sports suggests that other aspects than sport-specific knowledge are more important for athletes' development and well-being (Gulbin, Oldenziel, Weissensteiner, & Gagné, 2010). To some people, social competence is something that you either have or have not, but research in fields such as leadership (Barling, Weber & Kelloway, 1996) and social psychology (Blanch-Hartigan, Andrzejewski & Hill, 2012) has shown this malleable to training. Social competence is usually something picked up in unmediated learning situations. Self-awareness can be developed by reflecting upon experiences. A coach who improves self-awareness increases the probability of also improving his/her sport-specific knowledge and social competence as well. Self-awareness is viewed by Grant (2001) as a driving force for continuous learning. Understanding the self, how one learns and pays attention during real-life practice will no doubt promote development and increase the likelihood for the coach to adapt new learning material into his/her everyday practice.

Different Levels of Learning

Different levels of learning are displayed in Figure 2.2. Some learning consists of pure assimilation where the new information is incorporated in a coach's mind without any major changes to the pre-existing structures such as memories, habits, or perception of previous experiences. At the other end of the spectrum there

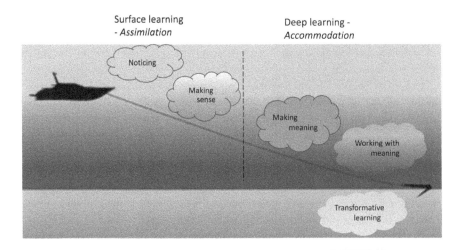

FIGURE 2.2 Different levels of learning.

is accommodation, which means that the coach's already operating structures are modified as the new information is taken into account (Moon, 2004).

Noticing implies that a coach looks at the information and tries to memorize it. *Tina Trainer sees a passing drill run by Instructor Ingram and hopes to remember it for next week's practice, where she could implement it in the same manner with her own team.*

Making sense implies that a coach tries to put together different ideas or pieces of information from quite shallow similarities. *Tina Trainer sees a new passing technique watching Instructor Ingram's use a drill she likes during his practice, and she decides to try to instruct the players in using this technique in a similar drill tomorrow.*

Making meaning implies that a coach really seeks understanding and considers whether new information corresponds to the coach's previous knowledge which might need some modification in order to fit in. At this level, the coach is not just interested in learning, but also understanding. *Tina Trainer sees a way to create numerical advantages for offence in a drill during Instructor Ingram's practice, and she decides to change some of her drills to incorporate this during next practice.*

Working with meaning implies that the new information is adapted along with parts of the coach's previous knowledge, compared to using the information exactly as it was presented. *Tina Trainer sees how the players at Instructor Ingram's practice created numerical advantages, and takes the main concept from this, modifying the players' starting positions to create an entirely new drill for her and the team.*

Transformative learning implies that the coach views his/her own coaching as an object, and not just as a subject. Doing this requires critical scrutiny of experiences including questioning how thoughts and interpretations of past experiences have shaped the individual's learning. The coach is examining personal experiences and relates these to earlier events. *Tina Trainer contemplates how she has impacted the players by introducing this new concept of overlapping from various playing-field positions, and how she can use her experience of successfully implementing this idea to the athletes, when adding new concepts in the future.*

The first two levels of learning, noticing, and making sense are quite shallow forms of learning, while the latter three consist of deeper learning (Trudel, Culver, & Werthner, 2013). In general, deeper learning leads to greater development. Gradually, as the learner gets deeper, the more reconstruction of the coach's previous knowledge structures occurs. As these levels of learning and their differences are quite abstract and hard to really understand, a somewhat more light-hearted analogy to jigsaw puzzles is provided in Table 2.1.

Table 2.2 shows some general differences between surface and deep learning in six different aspects/dimensions. Another important difference is mentioned by Ileris (2007) who argues that deep learning involves emotions, which are not necessary for surface learning. However, emotions potentially also pose barriers for learning as it may be overly upsetting to change one's view of previous knowledge.

> Provide some examples from the first column (*Surface learning*) in Table 2.2 that you recognize from your own experience.
> Provide some examples from the second column (*Deep learning*) in Table 2.2 that you recognize from your own experience.
> What can you do to reach deep learning as a coach more often?

Barriers to Learning

Learning is not always an easy and straight-forward process. Instead, several barriers potentially hamper efficient learning (Ileris, 2007). These barriers may

TABLE 2.1 Puzzle analogy to describe levels of learning.

Level of learning	Approach to jigsaw puzzles
Noticing	Memorizing a single piece.
Making sense	Assembling the puzzle one piece at a time using the nearest piece on the table.
Making meaning	Assembling the puzzle by first looking at the cover picture and then searching for specific pieces.
Working with meaning	Being interested in the cover picture and then building an own jigsaw puzzle that resembles the cover picture that matches one's current desires.
Transformative learning	Pondering which puzzles previously have been seen, assembled and built, and how these experiences can be used with future puzzles.

TABLE 2.2 General comparison of surface and deep learning.

Surface learning	Deep learning
Approach	
Learning something without considering neither purpose nor strategy for learning	Setting a goal and having a possible action plan for integration of learning material in existing knowledge
Connection	
Treating one learning material as entirely separate from another	Relating new ideas to previous knowledge and experiences in order to find new ways forward
Learning strategy	
Rote memorizing facts	Searching for underlying patterns and principles
Usefulness/Usage	
Finding difficulties in creating meaning in new ideas being presented	Exploring what kind of evidence exist for the learning material and drawing conclusions based on own previous experiences and knowledge
Coping	
Feeling unnecessary pressure and worry over the work	Focusing on development as a process and realizing that mistakes are opportunities for learning along the way
Commitment	
Viewing learning material as something to be checked	Getting actively interested in the content

appear anytime, for example, during an unmediated learning situation such as a conversation with a coaching colleague or during a workshop.

Preconception means that the coach deems him-/herself to have prior knowledge of something and because of this does not notice a new learning opportunity. In other words, a chance for learning and development is missed. *Emotional barrier* signifies that although the learning opportunity is registered, there is no further consideration of it. That may be caused by stress or fear for the implications of new lessons learnt. *Rejection* implies that the coach in a more deliberate manner has decided not to learn anything in a new situation. Hence, the coach actively chooses not to take full advantage of the learning opportunity. Argyris (1991) showed that even people skilled in their professions are not immune to these barriers. Rather, emotional barriers or rejections could be powerful in preventing deeper learning. The barriers are illustrated by the filter that consists of the dotted rectangle in Figure 2.3. A coach wanting to improve, regardless of skill level, needs to be vigilant of signs of barriers to learning.

New learning material is filtered through prior knowledge, values, beliefs, and earlier experiences before being more thoroughly examined. Some learning material is rejected immediately because it does not pass the filter, while other may be immediately accepted if deemed useable right away. Both of these processes (*Mismatch* and *Match*, respectively, in Figure 2.3) are examples of surface

28 Coaches' learning and reflection

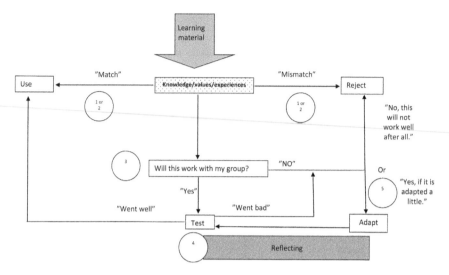

FIGURE 2.3 Paths for coach's learning. The numbers within the circles show which learning level the coach has reached at the respective question formulation or decision process. Adapted from Stodter and Cushion (2016).

learning (*noticing/make sense*). In order to reach a deeper level of learning, it is paramount to investigate further, by asking oneself if the present learning material will work with the current group of athletes. By contemplating this (*Will this work with my group?*), it is possible to reach *making meaning*. To get even deeper learning (*working with meaning* and *transformational learning*), it is necessary to *Test* or *Adapt* the original learning material. The adaptions are made after the coach considered what is appropriate for the current group of athletes or coach's interests. When testing and adapting the original learning material, the coach is engaged in deep learning involving reflection over his/her actions and experiences. This does not necessarily mean that the coach always has to end up in the box *Use*. It could very well be that after testing and trying to adapt the learning material, the coach finds that the most appropriate solution is to *Reject*. However, the learning material has been given a real chance, critically examined and, in all likelihood, the coach has learnt something along the way.

Strean (1995) calls attention to the importance of a coach being aware of, and being able to adjust, firm beliefs regarding coaching in order to prevent these beliefs from impeding deep learning and development. Belief systems and values are often confused with rational knowledge as they share some similarities, but are difficult to distinguish from one another. Values and beliefs might be more complex to reveal compared to behaviours, cognitions, and feelings as they exist at a deeper, less visible, level within the individual. Nonetheless, they have a tremendous impact on coaching (Peel et al., 2013). Thus, for a coach, it is important to uncover some personal values as they otherwise could hinder development. Values are developed in social or cultural interaction and are often traced back to anecdotes in a person's history, such as communications with a coach during the athletic career or interactions with the parents during adolescence. Even though they might not be representative of events in general or logically sound, they are still powerful as they are seldom scrutinized critically, but rather taken for granted. Typical examples of coaches' values concern what is important in sports, how people function, views on competition, or how the power should be shared between coach and athletes. Examples of values that may hamper learning and development as a coach are 'that every practice needs to go flawless', which could lead to anxiety when testing new things during practice. Another example is the assumption 'that a coach needs to know better than the athletes at all times', which could lead to the coach being reluctant to questioning own practice.

> Remember a leader you have met in your life (e.g., a coach, boss, teacher, or someone else in any kind of leadership role) that you think had difficulties in learning. Which of the aforementioned barriers do you think this person struggled with? Provide examples of how the barriers inhibited the person's learning.
> What barriers can inhibit your own learning as a coach and in what way? Give some examples from the following categories:
>
> Your history
> Your feelings
> Your values
> Preconception ('misses')
> Rejection ('active choice')

Reflective Skill

Measuring Reflective Skill

Before delving further into emotions, cognitions, and reflection, it is beneficial to complete the questionnaire *Self-Reflection and Insight Scale* (SRIS: Grant, Franklin, & Langford, 2002) found in the appendix to get a baseline measure of reflective skills. As described in the guidelines for using quantitative measurements in Chapter 1, there are no right or wrong answers and one should not think too long about any statement, but instead go with intuition when placing an 'X'.

As will be elaborated later in this chapter, reflection is somewhat hard to define. Some researchers argue that reflection lends itself to more qualitative approaches such as narrative (Hall & Gray, 2016) or action research (Gibbs, 1988), rather than quantitative. However, the SRIS has been found to validly measure reflective skill and has been used in coaching interventions (Grant, 2003, 2008). The constructs measured by SRIS should be viewed as skills malleable rather than a trait-measure, and serve primarily as a food for thought. It also serves the purpose of making the elusive reflection slightly more tangible. SRIS investigates how well a person is aware of, and understands, emotions and cognitions. Before unpacking components of reflection, it will be necessary to provide a brief overview of emotions and cognitions.

Emotions

Coaches' emotions have received scant interest in research. The relatively few times coaches' emotions have been investigated, studies have almost exclusively been interested in emotional intelligence, how emotions are expressed from the coaches, or emotions pertaining to burnout (cf. Magrum & McCullick, 2019). Thus, coaches' active coping with emotion in specific moments that arise during everyday practice are largely unknown. Still coaches' emotions will be present and impact coaching practice on a daily basis.

Emotions have their origin in both biological and social processes. An individual's disposition constitutes a biological potential for emotions. Throughout our long history, the human species has benefitted from the ability to experience emotions to increase chances of survival and reproduction. Simultaneously, the environmental context constitutes a social potential for emotions. As a member of society, an individual is endowed with social artefacts and symbols encoded during socialization that guide him/her emotionally. Emotions are characterized as episodic and relatively short-term. Three features make up emotions (Averill, 1997), namely *passivity* – there is a sense of the person being out of control (e.g., *falling* in love), *intentionality* – emotions concern something (e.g., being angry *with* someone), and *subjectivity* – emotions are not impartial (i.e., highly dependent on the person experiencing the emotions and not perceived in the same way by everyone).

Various taxonomies exist for arrangement of emotions. It is beyond the scope of this text to provide a detailed account of them, though most have categorized more negative feelings than positive ones. Evolutionary, this makes sense since there have been more practical advantages of being able to recognize the potential danger of a wild animal through feelings of anxiety or fear (among others), compared to being able to feel the joy of smelling a novel and beautiful flower (Power & Dalgleish, 2008). This is important to recognize for the practising coach as the coaching enterprise no doubt will have its emotional ups and downs. When feeling low or negative emotions, this is not something that the coach necessarily should be ashamed of or try to hide from significant others. The feelings rather exist for a reason and serve a function by conveying valuable information.

Cognitions

Similarly to emotions, Abraham and Collins (1998) note that coaches' cognitions traditionally are severely under-investigated in research as much focus has been on coaching behaviours. While certainly having its merits, studies conducted on behaviours seldom take into account the thought processes underlying why and when specific behaviours are carried out as a coach. Arguably, without thorough understanding of cognitions, focus on behaviour will be no more than just a copy–paste manner independent of context and athletes.

Drawing from cognitive psychology, there is a rich database considering cognitive processes. Kahneman (2011) elaborated on two different modes of thought processes called *system one* and *system two*. System one works in quick, automatic, and emotional fashion. In contrast, system two is activated when system one is insufficient and considers the input in a deliberate manner. Conscious processing through system two is necessary, if not more likely, under specific situational characteristics, such as situations experienced as new or unusual, situations evoking a discrepancy, or situations distinguished by a deliberate initiative (Louis & Sutton, 1991). Using system one saves time and energy for the brain, while simultaneously running the risk of making cognitive errors in its haste. These mistakes are sometimes called bias or cognitive pitfalls. For a coach who wants to develop, it is imperative to be alert of this kind of distorted thinking as it can severely hamper both interpreting feedback, as well as decision-making. Because of its speed, system one makes its voice heard before system two can muster a response, regardless of it being right or wrong. System one draws conclusions on superficial qualities inherent to the situation (cf. the well-known Müller–Lyer illusion), that at second thought prove irrational (Sloman, 1996). System one errors are countered by cognitive forcing techniques, which are strategies that make the coach elaborate more deeply than what the quick-minded system one would like to engage in. Mamede et al. (2010) cautioned that expertise might correlate with increased mistakes due to using the non-analytical processes of system one, as individuals with higher skill levels are prone to overuse quick decisions and react instinctively. Thus, it is important for skilled individuals to go back to deliberate pondering every now and then, even on issues that seem very easy. Also, using faster tacit knowledge renders not only the risk of not tracking potential bias but, as Nash and Collins (2006) argued, will serve as a less effective foundation for decision-making than slower declarative knowledge.

Another important concept is metacognition (Veenman, van Hout-Wolters, & Afflerbach, 2006). This is defined as our understanding and control of our cognition. Metacognition consists of two parts: *knowledge of cognitions* and *regulation of the cognitive processes*. In turn, the former includes knowledge of three different kinds, namely declarative, procedural, and conditional, which all have value for a coach. Declarative knowledge regards knowledge of oneself and performance factors. Procedural knowledge concerns execution of skills. Conditional knowledge covers issues of when and why to apply cognitive actions. Metacognitive knowledge does not need to be articulable to be useful, but will help thinking and self-regulating if consciously accessible. Regulation of cognition includes three skills: planning, monitoring, and evaluation. Planning concerns selecting the appropriate strategies and distribution of resources that influence performance. Monitoring covers a person's online awareness of comprehension and performance. Evaluation refers to assessing processes and products of one's learning (Schraw & Moshman, 1995).

> Think of a recent event as a coach – good or bad, positive or negative. Then try to identify what kind of emotions you experienced during the event?
> What do the emotions tell you about your own reactions?
> Think of a recent event as a coach, positive or negative. Then try to identify what kind of thoughts you experienced during the event?
> What do the thoughts tell you about your own reactions?

Reflective Skill in the Research

Reflection is a word often used in commonplace situations, albeit not necessarily with the same meaning as in a research context. Reflection is a somewhat difficult concept to define, though, regardless of being used in the everyday sense or in the research community. In formal coaching education, reflection is used loosely when participants are asked to 'reflect' upon a previously presented subject or about a sporting event just witnessed. There does not seem to exist a consensus among researchers over what reflection really connotes or what its boundaries are (Cushion, 2016). Perhaps, it would be easier to start by describing what reflection is not. Reflection is not just recapitulating a story by going over it again trying to remember as much as possible, nor is it just contemplating a specific event. When solving simple issues, such as figuring out which train to take in order to reach a destination, reflection is not said to be utilized. An unreflective approach views knowledge as absolute, that is, being the same for every person, where one can find a clear-cut right or wrong answer regardless of individuals involved or situational characteristics. Plenty of people probably consider themselves to use reflection most of the time, perhaps by some subconscious process that cannot be explained. In contrast, Cropley, Miles, and Knowles (2018) argue that reflection requires a *purpose*, a deliberate *consciousness*, and a specific *focus*. Thus, reflection has to have a specific content upon which reflection is applied, and it should strive to accomplish a purpose rather than just aimlessly thinking about 'everything' within the present moment. It should also lead to some kind of qualitative change within the person, which is in line with deep learning previously detailed. This change may concern behaviours, values, confirmation/

dismissal of some theory or practical solution, development of self-awareness, or even enhanced knowledge of the environment (Moon, 2004).

Reflection is used when trying to solve complex problems that lack apparent right or wrong answers. Additionally, reflection is used when weighing competing perspectives for and against each other, rather than finding the one panacea standpoint. Situations demanding reflection are often ill-structured and complex where several aspects simultaneously interact, making it difficult to uncover causality between even a few of the many factors involved (Schön, 1991). Complex events need to be viewed in a larger context and examined from different angles. Sometimes one perspective better than the others cannot be found. Regardless if there is an unequivocal best solution or not, the cognitive process in itself will be valuable. This reflective process creates an awareness of the different perspectives' pros and cons which underpins informed decision-making in tough situations or provide a rationale to others for the decision. When reflecting, suppositions taken-for-granted are examined in a critical, systematic, and deliberate way (Moon, 2004). Experiences are the foundation of reflection, although unreflected experiences in themselves are not sufficient for learning or development. Reflection is the vehicle to make sense of experiences and to elicit as much development as possible from experiences (Cushion et al., 2010).

Perhaps reflection has more similarities to problem formulation compared to problem-solving. Setting and formulating the problem is a perquisite before being able to solve an issue and, in contrast to straight-forward text-book examples, in real life the problem itself is not always obvious. When trying to find solutions to issues such as medical diagnosing, reflection has been found to help in complex cases, but not lead to higher accuracy in simple cases (Mamede, Schmidt, & Penaforte, 2008). This underscores the value of system one processing during easy everyday events, not only for saving energy but also for the quality of decisions. Reflection is crucial for practitioners working with people, as those environments are characterized as ever-changing and feature multi-causal relationships between antecedents and outcomes. Oftentimes reflection is elicited in a situation where something unexpected occurs deviating from the norm that Peel et al. (2013) deem *critical incident*. However, this does not imply solely a focus on problems and negative events. Ghaye (2011) highlights the difference of deficit-based questions and strengths-based questions when reflecting, where the former draws attention to problems and negative aspects while the latter focuses on successful and positive events. There is no right or wrong here, but it deserves to mention that reflecting only on mistakes and negative events runs the risk of being less than optimal, as important lessons from the positive event go unnoticed and lead to a more negative state of mind.

Granted, reflection is connected to metacognition as reflective activity will enhance metacognitive knowledge, and all three parts of regulation of cognition will be incorporated in the reflection methods used later in the chapter.

As previously mentioned, reflection is closely connected to deep learning. In order to reach the levels of working with meaning and transformational learning, it is paramount to problematize the learning material, view it from multiple perspectives, and try to put it into different contexts. By reflecting, the coach takes the role of both a subject, the one doing the reflection, and of an object, the entity that is reflected upon. Thus, reflecting is something else than seeing, reading, or hearing about a new drill or another coach. In reflection, old experiences are, so to speak, recycled and viewed in a different light rather than new external learning material being used (Lyle & Cushion, 2017). Knowles, Gilbourne, Cropley, and Dugdill (2014) define reflection as:

> A purposeful and complex process that facilitates the examination of experience by questioning the whole self and our agency within the context of practice. This examination transforms experience into learning, which helps us to access, make sense of and develop our knowledge-in-action in order to better understand and/or improve practice and the situation in which it occurs. (p. 10)

Reflection Engagement and Reflection Insight

In the SRIS questionnaire, reflection is measured in two dimensions: reflection engagement and reflection insight. Reflection engagement is best described as how *often* one in a deliberate way pays attention to inner states, critically examines suppositions, and highlights various perspectives of the current situation. Thus, reflection engagement is a quantitative aspect of the reflective skill. In short, this is related to the amount of reflection. In contrast, reflection insight is best described as how *well* one understands the impact of thoughts, behaviours, and feelings – both on the situation, followers as well as the coach him-/herself. This is related to cognitive flexibility, ability to manage one's thoughts and feelings, as well as the capacity to consciously control behaviours. Thus, reflection insight is a qualitative aspect of reflection skill. In sum, this pertains to how advanced reflections a person is capable of doing.

These two dimensions are distinct from each other. On one hand, it is possible to spend plenty of time observing oneself without reaching any conclusions or insights to speak of. On the other hand, it is equally plausible to be skilled at understanding thoughts and emotions, but for some reason not investigate this inner world particularly often. Both aspects of reflection are necessary for skilled reflection, and also to develop self-awareness.

Zaccaro, Foti, and Kenny (1991) found that leaders' self-monitoring significantly correlated with other's evaluations of leadership emergence. Examinations of learning skills have showed that metacognitive interventions, including self-monitoring, have a significant impact on development (Hattie, Biggs, & Purdie, 1996). Therefore, a coach who develops better self-awareness has good prospects of further development in other areas of interest than the topics covered within the present book. Self-monitoring could be best described as being in line with one's behaviours, cognitions, and emotions, something that overlap to a large extent with reflection engagement.

Leaders in charge of organizational change have been found to have more success when they possess a better understanding of how their own behaviour and role play a part in the change process (Higgs & Rowland, 2010). In domains outside of the sports coaching, metacognitive skill has been found to correlate with measurements of leadership skills (Marshall-Mies et al., 2000). Furthermore, Avolio and Gardner (2005) summarize vast research that concludes that leaders need an understanding of their own emotions and cognitions. These examples of self-awareness support the construct reflection insight.

A word of caution is warranted regarding a relationship that might not be so intuitive though. Trapnell and Campbell (1999) reported complex correlations between neuroticism (i.e., continuously worrying and being somewhat emotionally unstable) and self-monitoring. Primarily, they made a distinction between reflection and rumination, two constructs that overlap to some extent. By having too large focus on negative feelings and personal problems instead of a constructive approach, helplessness could enter the picture. One potential explanation is that an overly high attention to the self increases awareness of shortcomings. In turn, this might lead to ruminating rather than acting. Therefore, it is paramount to also try to improve the insight of reflections, where cognitive flexibility helps finding new ideas and alternative ways (Grant et al., 2002). Also, testing out new ideas and perspectives in real-life practice is necessary to prevent getting stuck in rumination. Real-life testing of new ideas also enhances visibility of these ideas, making them easier to evaluate and build upon (Croskerry, 2003a) and turning theoretical knowledge into skill. To examine the skill properly and make it tangible, it is necessary to set a behavioural goal. This examination, in turn, is based on a reflective approach instead of a more superficial 'plan, do, review' that Nash (2016) argues against. Finally, as mentioned in Chapter 1, it is also important to view the coaching practice as an unfinished process rather than a trait or an end product. This view of coaching makes it easier to accept shortcomings in the present as they are malleable for the future. In summary, Figure 2.4 displays how reflection engagement and reflection insight are connected to systematic coaching development. Also, the model depicts that goal setting and planning mainly concern: *What* of the present book, while action during practice accompanied by reflective activities make up *How* the plan is implemented, leading to development.

 Now, go back and review your score on SRIS. When you see your results on reflection engagement and reflection insight, what do you think?

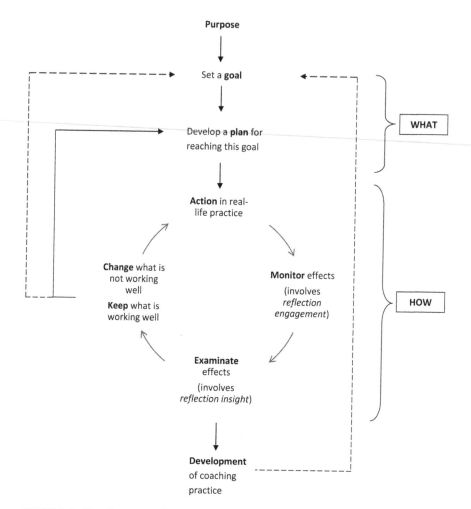

FIGURE 2.4 Development of coaching practice through reflection.

Different Times for Reflection

Reflection is possible to conduct at different times in relation to the event reflected upon such as in the midst of an event, immediately after an event, or long after an event has passed (Gilbert & Trudel, 2001). Additionally, Thompson and Pascal (2012) argued for the merits of reflection carried out before an action, but for the purpose of this book, this will be integrated into the methods for reflection in subsequent chapters, as there will be an element of planning before using reflection activities in practice. The other three time-periods for reflection will be described below.

Reflection-in-action is carried out while the person is in the middle of the event and simultaneously engaged in some kind of action. For a coach, this will most often be during a practice or competition. The purpose of this reflection is often to solve an urgent issue at hand (Gilbert, 2017). While being in the midst of an event, the coach needs to handle some cognitively demanding tasks, detailed by Schön (1991). First, the coach needs to reframe the problematic situation. This is done by considering different perspectives through setting up mental experiments. By doing that, the coach ponders questions like 'what kind of underlying issues are really in effect within the current situation?' and the coach will be less likely to get stuck with the first knee-jerk analysis. Second, the coach needs to draw upon previous experiences to find matter for thought for the mental experiment and find an appropriate intervention for the situation. Similarities between previous and current experiences are examined. In addition to considering previous experiences, it is beneficial to take into account information from other sources as well, such as this book (Abraham & Collins, 2011). This information likely needs some adaptation for use in a real-life situation. Third, the coach needs to make and carry out a decision, materializing the mental experimentation into hands-on experimentation. There are three different hands-on experiments to use. *Exploratory experiment* is when the coach does not know exactly what is going to happen, but it is worthwhile trying something, such as a coach walking around a new practice facility for the first time looking for ideas on how to best use the area during conditioning practice. *Move-testing experiment* is when the coach has a desired outcome in mind, tries some action tentatively, and looks to keep going if the consequences seem satisfactory as a whole even if the action is accompanied by some negatives. An example of this is a basketball coach trying a new defence late in a game when the normal defence has not worked well, even if the new defence has a risk of giving up more easy scores. The result of the experiment leads to new knowledge on how the defence works. *Hypothesis testing* is when the coach has a specific idea of what a certain action will lead to and decides to try it out to see if he/she is right. For example, a coach thinks that a new way of gathering the group before practice will get the practice going quicker and tests this hypothesis out. While move-testing experiment is inductive in nature, creating theory from practice, hypothesis testing is deductive, going from theory to practice.

Evidently, reflection-in-action is closely tied to action. At first sight, deliberate reflection-in-action poses a tough nut to crack, but on the other hand, ignoring problematic issues that arise during practice will no doubt be a less successful path, as will be making decisions without any reason or rationale behind them. By using structured and deliberate practice for reflection-in-action over time, the coach will see the kind of questions and decision-making described here happening more swiftly and effortlessly as the skill is improved. Time is often a crucial factor when solving issues in practice. It is often better to go with one 'good enough' solution relatively quickly, than spending too much time finding the best solution (Mumford, Zaccaro, Harding, Jacobs, & Fleishman, 2000). That further strengthens the case for a coach to be well drilled in thinking on his/her feet. *Tina Trainer contemplates why one of her athletes for the third time in a row chooses to play a short pass to the side instead of a through ball during a small-sided game, in order to figure out what kind of instruction that is appropriate at the moment.*

Reflection-on-action takes place shortly after an event by looking back at the event itself, while there is still an opportunity for a new action in a similar situation. For a coach, this will most often be in between practices or competitions during a season. The purpose is to improve future actions or to develop new knowledge (Gilbert, 2017). One advantage of reflecting after the event is that the time constraints might not be as pressing as they usually are during the event itself. This makes for a great opportunity to go deeper and consider other factors rather than only the most immediate. This will often be carried out as mental experiments resembling 'if I had done this, then that would have happened'. *Tina Trainer ponders why one of the athletes chose to pass to the side during a small-sided game, but not during similar situations during the practice and what triggered the decision to play a through ball to be able to create appropriate situations for practicing this in future practices.*

Retrospective reflection is carried out after an event has passed with some distance to it, while there will not be any obvious possibilities to impact the specific event. For a coach, this could be after the season. The purpose is to evaluate actions and view experiences in a new light to develop new knowledge. Gilbert and Trudel (2001) make the distinction between the previous two times for reflection as they are a means of learning *through* experience, while retrospective reflection is a way of learning *from* experience. This is the time to really dig deeper into a coach's values and biases. Argyris (1991, 2002) advocated reconsidering the underlying factors that influence a coach's actions instead of focusing primarily on an urgent problem's solution. The distance in time to the event reflected upon will enhance the possibilities for the coach to escape the immediacy of the moment and uncover the factors that might be hidden from normal daylight, but still impact coaching. *Tina Trainer dissects her attacking philosophy and tries to introduce drills that value shorter passes more in the upcoming season in the light of the previous season's experience with unexpected creativity from the athletes, because she began to doubt her previous approaches' positive impact on the athletes' development in offence.*

In this book, reflection-in-action will be characterized primarily by testing and experimenting, while reflection-on-action will be characterized essentially by investigating what type of effects these tests had on the coach and the athletes. Retrospective reflection will be used to summarize lessons learnt and think about how experiences will be implemented in future practice as a way of reflecting before action as well.

What types of regularly occurring events during your practices are interesting and perhaps unexpected to you? Provide some examples and describe why these are of particular interest.

> Reflection-in-action
> *An athlete in your group is highly skilled in your sport and has a highly developed physique. During one practice you observe that this athlete is only participating half-heartedly. You talk with the athlete during a break in practice who responds that there is no need for an all-out effort since all drills are easily won and this athlete is already the very best in the group.*
>
> What is important in this situation for the athlete's best interest according to you?
>
> What kind of previous experiences do you have that resemble this event, and what other knowledge do you have that can be useful here?
>
> What do you decide to do in this event?
>
> In what way will your thoughts, feelings, and behaviours in this event impact the athlete's performance (short-term or long-term)?
>
> Reflection-on-action
>
> Considering how you reacted in the aforementioned situation, is there anything that you would like to change when it comes to your thoughts, emotions, or behaviours?
>
> What reasons can you identify for your reactions?
>
> What effects did your reaction in this situation have on this athlete? The other athletes in the group?
>
> What would have happened if you had reacted in another manner?
>
> Retrospective reflection
>
> In your mind, play out a best-case scenario what happened later during the season with your relationship. What could be learnt from this season?
>
> How would you use this lesson learnt in the future?
>
> In your mind, play out a worst-case scenario what happened later during the season with your relationship. What could be learnt from this season?
>
> How would you use this lesson learnt in the future?

Pros and Cons with Reflection

Below, three major potential benefits of reflection found in the literature are described separately, although naturally intertwined.

Increased Self-Awareness

When reflecting upon how you impact a situation and, conversely, how the situation itself influences your cognitions, feelings, and behaviours, a greater understanding of the self is developed. Through increased self-awareness, it is quite possible that the ability to reflect will benefit in a reciprocal manner, as deeper reflections require an examination of the individual's role within the situation. In turn, this examination will enhance the person's understanding of the self. Thompson and Thompson (2008) list some skills that can enhance the ability to both reflect and increase self-awareness, such as analytical skills, critical thinking skills, and communication skills. Analytical skills are used to break down complex and perhaps even messy events into smaller parts that are better structured, in order to get a greater understanding of them. Critical thinking skills are used to uncover underlying factors that impact an event as well as taken-for-granted truths. Communication skills are of outmost importance as reflections that are put into words – either through dialogue with others (Cropley, Miles, & Peel, 2012) or through writing (Moon, 2006) – are more in depth and of better quality. The verbalizing and writing processes help uncover otherwise hidden meanings.

Improved Learning

Moon (2004) argues that for deeper learning to take place, reflection is necessary. Through reflection it is possible to both examine learning material critically from different perspectives, as well as critically evaluate beliefs, previous experiences, and knowledge that make up the coach's existing basis for action. This basis might need to be modified for deep learning to take place.

Enhanced Problem-Solving (i.e., Improved Practice)

No matter the depth or quality of any learning material, such as a book or lecture, there is no way to cover all potential issues or variations of problems that over time will be encountered during coaching. Therefore, it is a must for a coach to be able to resolve urgent matters on the feet, and to accomplish this, viewing existing information and imagined outcomes from different perspectives is necessary. The experimental approach described earlier will enhance problem-solving. Schön (1991) talks about theoretical knowledge being held in higher esteem than practical, despite the latter being key to sound decision-making during practice.

Weaknesses of Reflection

Nevertheless, there are some potential drawbacks of reflection. One problem arises if reflections only repeat own experiences (Abraham & Collins, 2011), perhaps even ruminating them. This is easily experienced as nothing new emanating from the reflections. A potential solution to this problem is to involve some connection to theory. In the subsequent chapters, there will be ample connection between theory and the reflective exercises. Another possible means to counter this problem is to use shared reflections, described in detail below, to elicit another person's input.

Memory failure is another potential obstacle for reflections (Grant, 2016). This can be countered by memory aids in the form of reflection cards that will be presented later in this chapter. Reflection cards help memory in two ways. First, they are a means to focus attention on a specific area during practice when they are prepared before the practice. Second, they capture a moment during the practice, as thoughts and feelings will be noted instantaneously. Then, as will be discussed in the section on two-part reflection, the coach returns to the notes on the reflection cards without having to remember everything by rote.

Another imaginable negative effect of reflections is that they may pose a threat to the self (Nesbit, 2012). Possibly, questioning firm beliefs is experienced as threatening, as people like the world to be predictable and stable. Here it is imperative to have a process focus where a coach's competence is seen as an unfinished product just as is the case with the developing athletes. Also, it will be helpful to have the interactive model of leadership presented in Chapter 1 in mind as it separates the coach as a person from the coaching. If coaching is viewed as dynamic, then if something within the coaching is found to be of unsatisfactory quality, it does not necessarily echo back on the coach as a person. This approach will help create the necessary distance between the coach as a person and the coaching, while simultaneously viewing the coaching as an object and not as a subject. Elaborating on negative feelings, Daley (1999) highlighted that cognizant practice required for new skills' development could be experienced as uncomfortable in the short-term.

From another standpoint, Kovacs and Corrie (2017) draw attention to the potential risk that reflection, with its somewhat single-minded focus on the present and a specific aim, could be viewed awkwardly in today's world of constant multitasking and split attention. There is even the conceivable conflict between a deceptive feeling of good productivity by superficially engaging in multiple tasks simultaneously and what is perceived as more arduous, but actually leading to quality outcomes, such as focused attention over a period of time (Diwas Singh, 2014; Paivio, 1991). By highlighting risks of inner disharmony, coaches are hopefully aware of, and able to bear a little short-term discomfort for long-term gains.

Moreover, time is a scarce commodity for most coaches (Lynn & Lyle, 2010), and reflection could be interpreted as being time-consuming. The solution is to make the reflections convenient. By reflecting during or in immediate connection to the practice, extra time added to the coach's hectic schedule will be minimized. Contrary, it is argued that – if time is scarce – it is even more necessary to make the most out of that time. Thus, high-quality structured reflection offers a great value in such situations.

Finally, by explicitly reflecting during practice and focusing on a coach's own cognitive processes, there is an elevated risk that actions run less smoothly and decisions are executed slower than normally. Though, this is not as, Ericsson (2006) argues, necessarily solely negative. Even though some short-term effects might be less positive, in the long run conscious processing will help prevent arrested development, which occurs when some behaviours or cognitions are automatized before reaching their highest level. By postponing the automatization of coaching actions and reactions, the coach will reach a more advanced level. It is easier to change routines before they are set in stone and performed habitually. Reflection works as a cognitive forcing strategy helping prevent quick system one errors. Much like weight lifting stresses the body in the short term, only to lead to long-term gains, reflecting deliberately will have similar developmental track. To become an expert coach, it is essential not to settle down too early and use the autopilot before becoming a well-developed captain.

Troubleshooting Reflection

Burt and Morgan (2014) investigated potential barriers to coaches' reflection and divided them into two main categories: *internal* and *external*. Among the most common internal barriers, lack of motivation or time was found. Among the most common external barriers were lack of written practice plan and lack of support from others. Moon (1999) highlighted further potential barriers for reflection such as fear of being socially rejected when expressing personal views. Among potential assets that facilitate reflection are supportive environment, technical gadgets for reminders, strengths of coaching group to enable stepping back a little bit from the most immediate concerns of the athletes, or individual disposition to curiosity for learning.

After this basic review of reflection, it is time to think about potential impediments of its use in practice. To be prepared for some potential troublesome issues, it is useful to consider a few crucial areas. In summary, technical aids, social factors, coaching characteristics, and characteristics of athletes are among the factors that constitute assets or barriers for reflection.

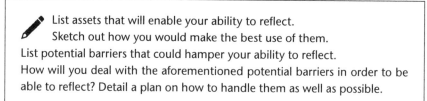
List assets that will enable your ability to reflect.
Sketch out how you would make the best use of them.
List potential barriers that could hamper your ability to reflect.
How will you deal with the aforementioned potential barriers in order to be able to reflect? Detail a plan on how to handle them as well as possible.

Methods for Reflection

Reading and thinking about reflection is not enough to develop reflective skill. Thus, it is now time to turn to hands-on methods and tools for reflection that bring the essential element of structure to reflection. The methods presented aim to provide a systematic way of reflection. General templates for each method are provided, as there is clear evidence for the notion that developing reflective skills requires guidance and education (Cropley et al., 2012). At this point, these

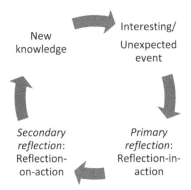

FIGURE 2.5 The relationship between different reflections and knowledge development.

templates serve to illustrate how reflection can be supported in practice and, at the same time, the templates should be tested to get going in structured reflection. In line with earlier presented arguments, the language is paramount for reflections to take place and also to reach quality depth. By putting thoughts into words, the reflection will become clearer, more effective, and deeper compared to a reflection that only stays within the mind. Writing about thoughts and emotions leads to a change processes, compared to only thinking about the event, and results in new perspectives (Pennebaker & Graybeal, 2001). There is also ample evidence for writing both facilitating and enhancing reflections (Black & Plowright, 2010). Furthermore, written reflections are possible to save and keep in the future in a way that emotions and cognitions are not. Thus, written reflections can be returned to and deepened at a later moment. However, this does not imply that a coach has to write an essay during practice. Naturally, the extent of the writing has to be convenient. To definitely make the reflections manageable, two-part reflections will be utilized. Two-part reflection implies dividing the reflection into a primary and a secondary reflection. The former is carried out during practice with the purpose of capturing the immediacy of the moment, such as thoughts and feelings experienced during a specific event (see Figure 2.5). The latter is then carried out at a later time when the person has gotten a little distance from the event and the experiences (e.g., in the locker room when changing or at the bus stop waiting to go home), with the purpose of going above and beyond the original thoughts and feelings by reviewing them in another light (Black & Plowright, 2010). This method can be time-saving, lessen the effort, and improve quality of the reflections.

To cover both reflections at the three time-periods (during, after, long after the event) and make for a reasonable amount of writing, various methods are presented. The methods will benefit from being used together. Reflection cards will primarily be focusing on the development of reflection engagement (and monitoring during practice), while the reflection sheets will primarily be focusing on reflection insight (and evaluating after practice). In subsequent chapters, both reflection cards and reflection sheets will be designed to fit respective chapters' content (*What*). However, to provide a better understanding of the methods and their usage, a generic template for each will be presented in this chapter as well. The templates presented in the present chapter can beneficially be used to practice the methods (*How*) in order to be able to more skilfully apply the content of subsequent chapters. Thus, in the present chapter, the methods are a means to an end.

Reflection Card (Reflection-In-Action)

This method will be carried out in two-part fashion, where the first part focuses primarily on reflection engagement and the second part on reflection insight. The primary reflection is written on the reflection card, which should be printed on paper or any digital device that the coach uses for note-taking. The reflective activities should start by formulating a goal and then converting this into a simple action plan. The goal is chosen from the chapter's content and the action plan describes how this is implemented into real-life practice. However, in this chapter, which is the first with reflective activities, the goal is to become accustomed to the reflective activities themselves. Therefore, the action plan is simply to use the reflective activities during practice and evaluate their usage.

Practice content			Date:_____
Planned activity	Arisen situation	Intervention	Coach's thoughts/emotions

In the first column (*Planned activity*), sketch out a specific practice activity that has been planned, either through text or picture. It might, for example, be a playful game, drill, or game situation that is going to be used. This is done before the practice. In the second column (*Arisen situation*), briefly note something that occurs during this specific practice activity as it is happens. It can be anything from how the activity in general is working out or a specific reaction from a certain athlete. At this stage, the coach needs to frame the current situation appropriately. This could also include finding similarities to prior experiences or knowledge). In the third column (*Intervention*), make a short note describing the actions that were chosen as a response to the arisen situation. A lot of actions are of course possible, but to just name a few possibilities, changing the space in a playful game, having an individual chat with an athlete at the next water break, or nothing at all (which many times is an appropriate 'intervention' as long as there is a rationale for it). In the fourth column (*Coach's thoughts/emotions*), make a short note containing some of the thoughts or emotions either stemming from the situation, the intervention or its effect on the athlete that appear during this very moment.

The first column aims to prepare the coach's focus at a specific moment in practice. As previously mentioned, a quality reflection has to be about something specific. By preparing this prior to the practice, attention is primed to be alert to this part of the practice (Roberts & Bruce, 1989), and the prospect of being successful at making an explicit reflection and remembering to use the reflection card is amplified. Grant (2016) argues that a prompt increases the likelihood of a deliberate action like reflection-in-action is. This preparation enhances the probability that the coach will be vigilant at this moment instead of just randomly trying to reflect on something as an afterthought. An additional reminder could be to put an asterisk on the regular practice plan next to the practice activity of choice that will be in plain sight as the plan is reviewed during practice. The reflection card is purposely designed to be small enough to fit inside pockets of coaching pants along with a pen.

Of course, the final goal is to be able to make this kind of reflection-in-action on the fly with anything that might arise during practice. Perhaps, it seems a little forced to make this preparation in advance, as there is no certain way to know beforehand if the planned situation will lead to something interesting to happen. One suggestion is to follow Davies' (2008) contention that deviations from expectations are a fruitful ground for new learning and reflection, thus choosing a particular practice activity where there are ample opportunities for unexpected events to occur. This might be a drill that is new to the group, a playful game that has certain inherent elements of chaos, or a small-sided game that provides openings for creative initiatives from the athletes. Naturally, to become comfortable with reflection it takes a lot of practice and everyone has to start somewhere. Further, in my own applied work, and in line with recommendations from others regarding the essentiality of structure when developing reflective skill (Cropley et al., 2012), the benefits clearly outweigh the drawbacks. Also, the filling out of reflection cards during practice will probably help in viewing the coaching as an object as distance between the coaching and the coach as a person tends to increase while writing. The purpose of completing the second to fourth columns during practice is not to make an exhaustive and perfectly accurate account of an event, but rather as Grant (2016) puts it, have the notes serve as an 'external working memory support'. In addition, Croskerry (2003b) points to the value of decreasing reliance on memory to avoid cognitive mistakes. The snapshot of an event captured on the reflection card will then be returned to later in the follow-up (see below).

Reflection Card Follow-Up (Secondary Reflection)

This part focuses primarily on developing reflection insight.

> How much time did the filling out of the reflection card take?
> How well did you manage to think deliberately during the practice?
> Look back on what you have written in the section on troubleshooting. Were you able to use the assets as initially thought?
> Which of the potential barriers you noted in the section on troubleshooting were actual difficulties in reality?
> Did you manage to handle the difficulties as you hoped to do?
> Did any unexpected difficulties appear that you did not note in the section on troubleshooting?
> Which of the following words best describe you as you were reflecting-in-action: nervous, doubtful, happy, tense, expectant, calm, confused, strange, hesitant, alleviated, and distracted?
> In what way did your emotions at that moment impact your choice of intervention?
> In what way is the chosen intervention related to your coaching philosophy/idea of what you wanted to accomplish at the practice?
> Would you do anything differently as you look back at this specific event? If so, elaborate on this.

Shared Reflection (Secondary Reflection)

Another method to reflect, and especially to enhance or deepen the primary reflection from the reflection card, is shared reflection (Cropley et al., 2012), which aims at developing reflection insight. When explaining thoughts and feelings around an event to someone else, something 'private' is released into the public light. This will lead to several positive outcomes. The person explaining the event likely scrutinizes the experiences somewhat differently. Sometimes verbalizing thoughts and feelings in itself can lead to an aha-moment, which is well-known within therapeutic literature (Miller & Rollnick, 2013). The positive effects of putting experiences into written word resembles the advantages of conversating with someone else who is able to respond, which have many favourable outcomes (Kuhn, Milek, Meuwly, Bradbury, & Bodenmann, 2017). Simultaneously, the other person can provide new perspectives unknown to the coach. Furthermore, shared reflection has the potential to unlock undiscovered dimensions of critical thinking for novice reflective practitioners. It takes place as secondary reflection (see Figure 2.6). Regardless of primary incentive for using shared reflection, the person whom the reflection is shared with should be chosen with care. Ideally, this person is someone the coach trusts and who is not inclined to condemn. It is possible to have different persons with varying experiences and/or competences to share with. To start off, one is perfectly fine, though. Some coaches will prefer to reflect on their own, and yet others will prefer to reflect through conversation. Before deciding what is best for you, it is beneficial to at least try shared reflection, as reflective discussions must be given time developing to be fruitful (Thompson & Thompson, 2008). Accordingly, Cropley et al (2018) suggest three different types of individuals that

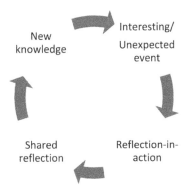

FIGURE 2.6 Knowledge development through shared reflection.

facilitate shared reflections in quite different manners. *Sharing upwards* is when the coach shares reflection with another person who is considered more knowledgeable in coaching or the specific sport, such as a mentor or an expert coach. One advantage of this may be that the more knowledgeable person can provide quality information from own experience or knowledge that might have been unknown to the coach. *Sharing sideways* is when the coach shares reflection with another person who is considered a peer, such as a colleague in the coaching staff or a close friend from an NGB coaching education. An advantage of this may be that peers can engage in an equal and dynamic discussion going back and forth. *Sharing downwards* is when a coach shares reflection with another person who is considered less knowledgeable, such as a person who is not involved in the specific sport at all. Perhaps surprising at first, this way of sharing will often lead to the coach getting questioned about 'obvious' things that have been taken for granted, which is one of the goals of engaging in reflection in the first place – challenging long-held beliefs and traditions associated with the sport.

When sharing a reflection with another person, Davies (2008) distinguishes between 'a fellow participant' and 'an informed non-participant'. Both types of persons have their merits when it comes to helping elaborate a reflection. A fellow participant could be another coach in the same coaching staff who was present at the same practice where the event of reflection happened. This person probably has some similar, but also some different, appraisals of the same event. The differences could emanate from logistics such as being at another physical place and therefore observing the event differently, but also from individual factors such as differing previous knowledge, experience, or dispositional emotional reactions. All in all, this could be a very fertile ground for digging into the reflection from various perspectives. An informed non-participant is a person who was not present at the time of the event for reflection. Similar to the fellow participant, this person has differing individual characteristics and experiences from the coach, but this person also requires a deeper explanation of features within the event compared to what might be necessary when talking to a person who has been present. This deeper explanation in itself requires a more elaborate use of language from the coach, and, as mentioned previously, language is a powerful motor in generating reflection quality. Conceivably, shared reflections have the greatest value early on in the development of reflective skill (Cropley et al., 2012).

> **Shared Reflection**
>
> Follow the six steps below:
>
> 1. Describe the event that is recorded on a reflection card.
> 2. Describe what you thought and felt during the specific event.
> 3. Describe your intervention.
> 4. Explain the most important lessons you have learnt through this event.
> 5. Ask the other to elaborate on his/her thoughts after listening to step 1–4 by providing room for a free mind for the other's comments. After a while, you could ask more specific questions concerning how the other would have thought/felt/acted in the specific event, had he/she been the coach.
> 6. Discuss together what kind of consequences alternative reactions within the event from the coach would have had. Ponder together how athletes and situation impact the coach's decision of action in the event.

Reflection Sheet (Reflection-On-Action)

This method focuses primarily on developing reflection insight. Complete first column before practice and second to fifth columns after practice.

Practice content					Date: _____
Name of and purpose of practice activity	What proportion of the athletes managed to handle the activity well in my estimation?	What adjustments can be made in the practice activity to get a larger portion of athletes to handle the activity well, or to increase the challenge for them?	What kind of pros and cons can I envision with the various adjustments suggested?	What were your own thoughts and emotions during this part of the practice?

Concluding/Other comments:

Reflective Summary (Retrospective Reflection)

This method will focus primarily on trying to learn from experiences and improve self-awareness.

 Choose a specific and important event in your coaching that has occurred over the last three months and describe it briefly.

Then answer the following 12 questions.

What does this event tell you about your thought processes?	Would you like to change something in your thought processes to be more like the coach you would like to be?	How will this change be implemented?
What does this event tell you about your emotional reactions?	Would you like to change something in your emotional reactions to be more like the coach you would like to be?	How will this change be implemented?
What does this event tell you about your values and personal beliefs?	Do you need to update anything within your values or belief systems to be more like the coach you would like to be?	How will this change be implemented?
What is the most important thing you learnt from this event?	How would you take advantage of this lesson learnt in future coaching?	How will you evaluate the consequences of this implementation?

Finally, by deliberately elaborating on reflective exercises during and after practices, the coach will over time improve reflection-in-action and intuition, as important issues have been explored repeatedly. Experiences from structured reflection can lead to improved judgement and decision-making, even if the improved cognitive process is difficult to articulate. The 'hard' work on explicit and structured reflection will pay off through a greater, and better, 'database' to draw intuitive decisions from during subsequent practices, in what Ericsson, Prietula, and Cokley (2007) call 'informed intuition'.

Improving Reflections

Different Depths of Reflection

Reflections can have varying depths. Many times, coaches', just like other labour categories such as nurses' or teachers', reflections tend to be quite shallow (Knowles, Gilbourne, Borrie, & Nevill, 2001). By reflecting with depth, the possibilities to develop self-awareness, and to solve complex issues, are increased. Consequently, both awareness of the existence of different reflection depths and characteristics of different depths are beneficial. Below, four different levels adapted from Hatton and Smith (1995) are laid out. The depths are in some way accumulative and build upon each other where they become more and more advanced.

Telling

Telling does not involve any actual reflection. The person is only describing an event and makes no effort to warrant actions or provide any explanation of what happens. There is no attempt of trying to view larger contexts or possible underlying processes. Telling implies that the coach is only engaged within the moment and does not contemplate particularly much, neither relating to the past nor to the future.

Descriptive Reflection

This depth includes not only a description but also attempts at rationalizing events or actions, though in a fairly shallow manner. The reflection is based only on one perspective and emanates purely from sporting issues. The reflection tries to investigate the best possible way for the specific type of sport. An analysis is carried out from the perspective of the coach alone, as well as known outside information (e.g., information presented at a coaching clinic or in a book).

Dialogic Reflection

This depth incorporates an investigation of different perspectives. Pros and cons with different perspectives are contrasted and subsequently different possible solutions are examined. The person can be said to hear an inner voice while various potential actions are explored. At this depth, an analysis of the coach's self occurs and its role in the event. An analysis is carried out from the perspective of the coach, but known outside information is problematized instead of universally taken for granted. This information is put into context when its appropriateness for the present event is evaluated.

Critical Reflection

This depth takes into account the present event's social and cultural context. The event is problematized from various perspectives, and historical links are taken into account, not just from the first-person perspective, but also in a broader context including the athletes' previous experiences and the sporting organization's history. The reflection is more advanced as the person takes a step back and tries to view not only the event but also his/her own thoughts, feelings, and behaviour from the outside. The coach is an object

TABLE 2.3 Characteristics of different reflection depths.

	Number of perspectives	Starting points	
	'From how many perspectives can I view the event and its consequences?'	'What basis do I have for acting in the way I decide to do?'	*Effects of the actions* 'What consequences can my actions have?'
1. Telling	1	The event itself	–
2. Descriptive reflection	1	The coach, rigid facts	Sports
3. Dialogic reflection	2	The coach, problematized facts	The whole athlete/person
4. Critical reflection	2	Social, cultural, historical, political aspects	Society

for the reflection. An analysis examines the values of the self, others, and the community.

Table 2.3 illustrates some simplified characteristics for the four reflection depths. Note that there are not totally distinct demarcations between two levels (Hatton & Smith, 1995). For example, it is possible to illuminate an event from two different perspectives, but only use rigid facts, as a basis for reflections. When there are characteristics from different depths, it is of course more difficult to categorize the reflections at the correct depth. However, the most important is not to find the perfect categorization, but rather to increase awareness of degrees of differences in different reflections and consequently strive to deepen the coach's own reflections.

In summary, the most important distinction between reflection qualities is between depth two and three. This is where the coach moves on from inquiring from a subjective point of view to taking a wider scope and investigating the impact of, and on, the self as an object entering into the area where reflection becomes a true vehicle for improvement.

Four Worked Examples for Practicing Reflection Depth

Read the fictive examples below and try to find the most appropriate reflection depth for respective example. In Appendix B, an answer key is found with some comments in order to increase understanding for characteristics of the different reflection depths.

The fictive situation is the following: *An athlete in the practice group is highly skilled and has a highly developed physique. Throughout a practice the coach observes that this athlete is only participating half-heartedly. During a break, the coach talks with the athlete, who responds that there is no need for an all-out effort since all drills are easily won and this athlete already is the very best in the group.*

Below are the reflections of four different coaches in this situation. It is important not to value their respective decisions or actions, but focus entirely on the depth of reflection.

Leah Leader

The athlete did not do her maximum to improve in the drills. I decided pretty quickly to talk to her. Because of this I took her aside during water break and asked if there was something wrong. 'You don't look like you are giving your all. I know you can do better', I told her. She looked at me and said that she thought it was too easy and that the competition was too lacklustre in the drill. Subsequently, I asked her if she thought that was the best way to improve, which she at first said she did. After a little discussion I managed to get her to understand the importance of maximum effort. Without maximum effort, little progress will be made. The discussion ended up with me as a coach setting a few tougher goals that focused on her performance in relation to her own capacity, as opposed to the other athletes in the group. I think we came up with a very good solution.

Coach Collin

As the player went at it half-heartedly, I decided to have a chat with her during the next water break. I told her that the team captain cannot do it like that. At first, she did not understand what I was talking about, so I clarified my expectations that the team captain has to be the one working the hardest during practice. As a coach, I have to make sure that my expectations are clear to the athletes in order to get the full potential from them. Usually, individual meetings are an effective way to convey my expectations on the athletes. At the coaching education I went to recently, they emphasised the importance of being clear to avoid misinterpretations of coaches' communication. Perhaps I need to be able to adjust the level of difficulty in drills in order to stimulate the athletes even more. Usually, I like to choose drills where the athletes get involved in one-on-one situations as it is important to get them to compete in order to push them to the max.

Tina Trainer

I chose not to do anything other than a quick question if the athlete was 100% fit. After that I observed her during a number of sequences in the next drill. Normally, I would have gathered the athletes pretty hastily and given a stern talk about the importance of giving maximum effort. This time, though, I chose to observe a little longer before intervening. Either I could take her out of the drill for a longer talk, or I could switch drill for the entire group. If I take her out, she might feel exposed and become upset like last week during the game when she was substituted at half-time. It is important as a coach in situations like this to act immediately, but at the same time it could hurt our relationship if I am too blunt with her. In that case, I need to articulate that I am not upset, but rather have a calm emotional tone. Usually, I can have some troubles with this as I become very engaged in the practice. On the other hand, if she is still in the drill going through the motions, it could affect the others and start creating bad habits in the group.

Instructor Ingram

Immediately when I saw that the athlete did not give an all-out effort, I considered to cut off the drill, but because I talked to the group quite a while before we started the drill, I chose to give them more time. I know that the athletes need to be active during practice since they are not especially active outside of practice time and need to practice for their well-being. Furthermore, I know that their previous coach, whom they weren't fond of, used to talk very much. It would be unwise of me, as a new coach, to keep going in the same track, without having established my own coaching style first. If I can get them to like me first, it will be easier to be a little harsh later, as I will have some confidence 'to spare'. These athletes, with all things they have gone through, need to feel that their coach cares for them so that they won't be engaged in juvenile delinquency in the spare time. A little later during the practice I decided to talk one-on-one with this specific athlete during a natural break in between drills. Normally, I am better prepared to take this kind of talks at a water break than during an ongoing drill.

Initially, reflections using methods described above might not have reached a very advanced depth. This is perfectly fine at this stage. To begin with, focus should be at getting accustomed to the methods and incorporating them into the daily coaching routine. A coach that routinely reaches dialogic reflection has come very far! Also, there are times when, perhaps out of time constraints, it is alright to reflect at a shallower level. Certainly, at the introduction of deliberate structured reflection, it is enough to try out the methods, remember to use them, etc. As Table 2.4 illustrates, there are four phases in the development of reflective skill. Initially, there is a phase of understanding basic concepts, followed by trying out hands-on methods. After getting comfortable with the reflective methods, the methods are refined and eventually used for knowledge and skill development.

> Look back at some of your reflection sheets. At what reflection depth would categorize your reflections? Use Table 2.3 and the worked examples to help you categorize your own reflection.

TABLE 2.4 Phases of development of reflective skill in relation to the book's content.

Chapter	Purpose	Important themes
1–2	Educating	Definition
		Purposes
		Processes
2	Applying	Methods
		Getting comfortable
3–7	Refining	Developing the methods
3–8	Optimizing	Using reflection to develop other skills and knowledges

Deepening Your Reflections

Below are some exercises to deepen your reflections. Using these exercises will increase the ability to reflect at a deeper level during practice as you will get more accustomed to the inherent qualities of deep reflections. To reach a more advanced reflection depth, one can consider three areas: *Pros and cons*, *effects*, and *justifications for actions*. Look at one of the used reflection sheets when answering these questions.

Pros and Cons/Perspectives

Have you included BOTH pros and cons with the suggested adjustments? If not, try to come up with at least one pro and one con.

Have you included different perspectives (e.g., offence vs. defence, individual vs. group, long-term vs. short-term) on the consequences of the adjustment? If not, try to come up with at least two different perspectives.

Effects

What kind of effects do you think your chosen intervention(s) can have in various areas?

Athletically:
Athlete as a person:
Society:

Justifications/Basis/Knowledge for Interventions

What is the basis for your interventions?
The event itself:
Yourself/rigid information:
Yourself/problematized information:
Social/cultural/historic:

> In what way was the chosen intervention related to your coaching philosophy/idea of what you wanted to accomplish at the practice?

Evaluate Your Reflections

'Interrupting' practice to reflect can pose a challenge for a coach. Possibly, coaching actions will be slower and more mechanical when deliberately reflecting. However, just as athletes sometimes need to slow down to develop further, this is likely a phase that the coach will come out of with enhanced reflective skill. To improve reflective skill, it is now important to evaluate the reflections that have been done so far. The questions below aim to pinpoint what have been successful and what needs further improvement so far. This exercise also serves as a metacognitive activity where the coach has to think about his/her own cognitive processes, which in itself enhances both self-awareness and reflective skill.

> What difficulties have you encountered when using the methods for structured reflection so far? How will these difficulties be better handled in the future?
> What benefits have you experienced so far with structured reflection?
> How well have you managed to use the *reflection card* at a specific time planned in advance?
> Do you need to improve something to be able to remember to use the *reflection card* during practice?
> How well have you managed to describe the *Arisen situation* in the reflection card?
> How well have you managed to write down *Coach's thoughts/emotions* in the reflection card?
> How well have you managed to deepen your reflection?
> In what way have your thoughts and actions differed between the original event and what you have considered in retrospect when completing the reflection sheet?
> How well has shared reflections worked out so far?
> What pros and cons have you experienced with *shared reflection* compared to reflecting by yourself?
> Do you think you will have the most benefit from reflecting by yourself or by sharing the reflection?

Challenging Reflection Assumptions

A month later, the three met up again.

Tell me a little about what have happened since we talked about your inner experiences as coaches during practices, Ellen initiated the discussion.

> "Well, first of all, I have to say that the reflection cards you gave me have been wonderful. Completing them has really increased my awareness of both what kind of emotions I go through during a practice, when they occur and how to interpret them", Leah said joyfully.
>
> "I can see that you are delighted. How can this help in your future coaching?" Ellen asked.
>
> "I don't think I am quite there yet, but I do know that I have managed to identify critical situations that arouse me the most", Leah answered.
>
> "And what kind of situations are these?" Ellen kept on.
>
> "Pretty much every time an athlete fails to execute a technique during practice that I consider really simple", Leah replied slowly.
>
> "How do you react then?" Ellen probed.
>
> "First, I get upset or annoyed. But now I have realized that my negative reaction was mostly due to feeling bad for my coaching. If they can't execute, then I haven't done my job and I feel like I'm inadequate as a coach. During the past few weeks, I have really reconsidered that their shortcomings are not solely a reflection of my coaching. Other factors weigh in also. Ellen, I really appreciate our text conversations during this past month. It is so nice to have someone to share my experiences with, and not just write them down", Leah explained.

Ellen smiled affectionately.

> "Also, sometimes the writing process itself makes me grasp something obvious. I feel a little stupid sometimes for not realizing the most apparent connections prior to that", Leah said, having somewhat of a frown on her face.

Up till now, Collin had been quiet. The others were not sure if he was zoning out or not.

> "I see what you're talking about. I have underappreciated practices as a learning opportunity for me as a coach", Collin interjected, to the others surprise.
>
> "In what way can you use practices to learn more about your coaching?" Ellen asked him, happy that he contributed to the discussion.

"To me, I feel that I have previously been using the autopilot too much during practices. It's good when everything goes smoothly, but it also causes me to miss a lot of things that happen", he elaborated.

"How would you describe what you have learnt with this approach?" Ellen enquired.

"I think that I have become much more aware of what's going on. And I have begun to deliberately think back to other situations looking for similarities before deciding what to do", Collin grinned with a sense of satisfaction.

"In your mind, are there any drawbacks to actively reflecting during practice?" Ellen asked.

"Sure, it is hard work. It is much easier to just go about one's own business as usual", Collin said with an afterthought.

"I think I have been slow to process what's going on, sometimes even to the point that I have missed giving feedback to some athletes during practice. However, in the long run, I'm confident these learning experiences will benefit my athletes", Leah said.

"Good to hear that you value deliberate learning during your own practices as coaches. That will give you plenty of developmental opportunities to take advantage of", Ellen wrapped up the meeting.

Quiz

1. What learning situation is likely a spontaneous dinner with a coaching colleague discussing coaching philosophies?
    a. Internal learning situation.
    b. Unmediated learning situation.
    c. Mediated learning situation.

2. Which statement regarding levels of learning is correct?
    a. In deep learning one knows much more.
    b. Deep learning means that cognitive patterns are changed.
    c. Surface learning means to change the new learning material.

3. Which statement is most accurate about barriers for learning?
    a. A person who considers him-/herself knowledgeable may miss a learning opportunity.
    b. Without emotions it is impossible to learn something.
    c. By rejecting uninteresting material, one learns better.

4. What does it mean to reflect?
    a. Critically questioning something in order to find alternative possibilities.
    b. Trying to find a correct answer to a difficult problem.
    c. Writing down what happens.

5. What advantages are important with reflection?
    a. Integration of theory and practice, and complex issues that do not have one apparent solution can be solved.
    b. The coach invests more time.
    c. The coach thinks as much as possible.
6. Which statement is most correct about structured methods for reflection?
    a. When reflecting, one should always talk to a friend.
    b. By writing down reflections become both clearer and easier to remember.
    c. Secondary reflection is less important than primary reflection.
7. Why is dialogic reflection deeper than descriptive reflection?
    a. The best information is used.
    b. There is a clear focus on sports.
    c. Information is problematized and viewed from more than one perspective.

References

Abraham, A., & Collins, D. (1998). Examining and extending research in coach development. *Quest, 50,* 59–79.

Abraham, A., & Collins, D. (2011). Effective skill development: How should athletes' skills be developed? In D. Collins, A. Button, & H. Richards (Eds.), *Performance psychology: A practitioners guide* (pp. 207–229). London: Elsevier.

Argyris, C. (1991). Teaching smart people how to learn. *Harvard Business Review, 4,* 4–15.

Argyris, C. (2002). Double-loop learning, teaching, and research. *Academy of Management Learning & Education, 1,* 206–219.

Averill, J. R. (1997). The emotions: An integrative approach. In R. Hogan, J. A. Johnson, & S. R. Briggs (Eds.), *Handbook of personality psychology* (pp. 513–541). San Diego, CA: Academic Press.

Avolio, B. J., & Gardner, W. L. (2005). Authentic leadership development: Getting to the root of positive forms of leadership. *The Leadership Quarterly, 16,* 315–338.

Black, P. E., & Plowright, D. (2010). A multidimensional model of reflective learning for professional development. *Reflective Practice, 11,* 245–258.

Blanch-Hartigan, D., Andrzejewski, S. A., & Hill, K. M. (2012). The effectiveness of training to improve person perception accuracy: A meta-analysis. *Basic and Applied Social Psychology, 34,* 483–498.

Burt, E., & Morgan, P. (2014). Barriers to systematic reflective practice as perceived by UKCC level 1 and level 2 qualified rugby union coaches. *Reflective Practice, 15,* 468–480.

Côté, J., & Gilbert, W. D. (2009). An integrative definition of coaching effectiveness and expertise. *International Journal of Sports Science & Coaching, 4,* 307–323.

Croskerry, P. (2003a). Cognitive forcing strategies in clinical decision making. *Annals of Emergency Medicine, 41,* 110–120.

Croskerry, P. (2003b). The importance of cognitive errors in diagnosis and strategies to minimize them. *Academic Medicine, 78,* 775–780.

Cropley, B., Miles, A., & Peel, J. (2012). *Reflective practice: Value of, issues, and developments within sports coaching.* Sports Coach UK Research Project. Cardiff: Cardiff Metropolitan University.

Cropley, B., Miles, A., & Knowles, Z. (2018). Making reflective practice beneficial. In R. Thelwell, & M. Dicks (Eds.), *Professional advances in sports coaching: Research and practice* (pp. 377–396). Abingdon: Routledge.

Cushion, C. J. (2016). Reflection and reflective practice discourses in coaching: A critical analysis. *Sport, Education and Society, 23*, 82–94.

Cushion, C. J., Armour, K. M., & Jones, R. L. (2003). Coach education and continuing professional development: Experience and learning to coach. *Quest, 55*, 215–230.

Cushion, C., Nelson, L., Armour, K., Lyle, J., Jones, R., Sandford, R., & O'Callaghan, C. (2010). *Coach learning and development: A review of literature*. Leeds: Sports Coach UK.

Daley, B. J. (1999). Novice to expert: An exploration of how professionals learn. *Adult Education Quarterly, 49*, 133–147.

Davies, L. (2008). *Informal learning: A new model for making sense of experience*. Aldershot: Gower.

Diwas Singh, K. C. (2014). Does multitasking improve performance? Evidence from the emergency department. *Manufacturing & Service Operations Management, 16*, 168–183.

Ericsson, K. A. (2006). The influence of experience and deliberate practice on the development of superior expert performance. In K. A. Ericsson, N. Charness, P. J. Feltovich, & R. R. Hoffman (Eds.), *The Cambridge handbook of expertise and expert performance* (pp. 683–703). Cambridge: Cambridge University Press.

Erickson, K., Bruner, M. W., MacDonald, D. J., & Côté, J. (2008). Gaining insight into actual and preferred sources of coaching knowledge. *International Journal of Sports Science & Coaching, 3*, 527–538.

Ericsson, K. A., Prietula, M. J., & Cokley, E. T. (2007). The making of an expert. *Harvard Business Review, 85*, 114–121.

Ghaye, T. (2011). *Teaching and learning through reflective practice: A practical guide for positive action* (2nd ed.). Abingdon: Routledge.

Gibbs, G. (1988). *Learning by doing. A guide to teaching and learning methods*. Oxford: Further Education Unit, Oxford Polytechnic.

Gilbert, W. (2017). *Coaching better every season. A year-round system for athlete development and program success*. Champaign, IL: Human Kinetics.

Gilbert, W., & Trudel, P. (2001). Learning to coach through experience: Reflection in model youth sport coaches. *Journal of Teaching in Physical Education, 21*, 16–34.

Gilbert, W., & Trudel, P. (2005). Learning to coach through experience: Conditions that influence reflection. *The Physical Educator, 62*, 32–43.

Grant, A. M. (2001). Rethinking psychological mindedness: Metacognition, self-reflection, and insight. *Behaviour Change, 18*, 8–17.

Grant, A. M. (2003). The impact of life coaching on goal attainment, metacognition and mental health. *Social Behavior and Personality, 31*, 253–264.

Grant, A. M. (2008). Personal life coaching for coaches-in-training enhances goal attainment, insight and learning. *Coaching: An International Journal of Theory, Research and Practice, 1*, 54–70.

Grant, A. M. (2016). Reflection, note-taking and coaching: If it ain't written, it ain't coaching! *The Coaching Psychologist, 12*, 49–58.

Grant, A. M., Franklin, J., & Langford, P. (2002). The self-reflection and insight scale: A new measure of private self-consciousness. *Social Behavior and Personality, 30*, 821–836.

Gulbin, J. P., Oldenziel, K. E., Weissensteiner, J. R., & Gagné, F. (2010). A look through the rear view mirror: Developmental experiences and insights of high performance athletes. *Talent development & Excellence, 2*, 149–164.

Hall, E.T., & Gray, S. (2016). Reflecting on reflective practice: A coach's action research narratives. *Qualitative Research in Sport, Exercise and Health, 8,* 365–379.

Hatton, N., & Smith, D. (1995). Reflection in teacher education: Towards definition and implementation. *Teaching & Teacher Education, 11,* 33–49.

Higgs, M., & Rowland, D. (2010). Emperors with clothes on: The role of self-awareness in developing effective change leadership. *Journal of Change Management, 10,* 369–385.

Ileris, K. (2007). *Lärande [Learning].* Lund: Studentlitteratur.

Kahneman, D. (2011). *Thinking, fast and slow.* New York: Farrar, Straus and Giroux.

Knowles, Z., Gilbourne, D., Borrie, A., & Nevill, A. (2001). Developing the reflective sports coach: A study exploring the processes of reflective practice within a higher education coaching programme. *Reflective Practice, 2,* 185–207.

Knowles, Z., Gilbourne, D., Cropley, B., & Dugdill, L. (2014). Reflecting on reflection and journeys. In Z. Knowles, D. Gilbourne, B. Cropley, & L. Dugdill (Eds.), *Reflective practice in the sport and exercise sciences* (pp. 3–15). London: Routledge.

Kovacs, L., & Corrie, S. (2017). Building reflective capacity to enhance coaching practice. *The Coaching Psychologist, 13,* 4–12.

Kuhn, R., Milek, A., Meuwly, N., Bradbury, T. N., & Bodenmann, G. (2017). Zooming in: A microanalysis of couples' dyadic coping conversations after experimentally induced stress. *Journal of Family Psychology, 31,* 1063–1073.

Louis, M. R., & Sutton, R. I. (1991). Switching cognitive gears: From habit to mind to active thinking. *Human Relations, 44,* 55–76.

Lyle, J., & Cushion, C. (2017). *Sports coaching concepts: A framework for coaching practice* (2nd ed.). Abingdon: Routledge.

Lynn, A., & Lyle, J. (2010). Coaching workforce development. In J. Lyle, & C. Cushion (Eds.), *Sports coaching: Professionalisation and practice* (pp. 193–208). London: Elsevier.

Mamede, S., Schmidt, H. G., & Penaforte, J. C. (2008). Effects of reflective practice on the accuracy of medical diagnosis. *Medical Education, 42,* 468–475.

Mamede, S., van Gog, T., van den Berge, K., Rikers, R. M. J. P., van Saase, J. L. C. M., van Guldener, C., & Schmidt, H. G. (2010). Effects of availability bias and reflective reasoning on diagnostic accuracy among internal medicine residents. *Journal of American Medical Association, 304,* 1198–1203.

Magrum, E. D., & McCullick, B. A. (2019). The role of emotion in sport coaching: A review of the literature. *The Sport Journal, 20,* 1–17.

Marshall-Mies, J. C., Fleishman, E. A., Martin, J. A., Zaccaro, S. J., Baughman, W. A., & McGee, M. L. (2000). Development and evaluation of cognitive and metacognitive measures for predicting leadership potential. *Leadership Quarterly, 11,* 135–153.

Miller, W. R., & Rollnick, S. (2013). *Motivational interviewing: Helping people change* (3rd ed.). New York: Guilford Press.

Moon, J. (1999). *Reflection in learning and professional development: Theory & practice.* Abingdon, UK: Routledge.

Moon, J. (2004). *A handbook of reflective and experiential learning.* London: Routledge.

Moon, J. (2006). *Learning journals: A handbook for reflective practice and professional development.* London: Routledge.

Mumford, M. D., Zaccaro, S. J., Harding, F. D., Jacobs, T. O., & Fleishman, E. A. (2000). Leadership skills for a changing world: Solving complex social problems. *Leadership Quarterly, 11,* 11–35.

Nash, C. (2016). Donald Schön: Learning, reflection, and coaching practice. In L. Nelson, R. Groom, & P. Potrac (Eds.), *Learning in sports coaching: Theory and application* (pp. 49–60). London: Routledge.

Nash, C., & Collins, D. (2006). Tacit knowledge in expert coaching: Science or art? *Quest, 58*, 465–477.

Nesbit, P. L. (2012). The role of self-reflection, emotional management of feedback, and self-regulation processes in self-directed leadership development. *Human Resource Development Review, 11*, 203–226.

Paivio, A. (1991). Dual coding theory: Retrospect and current status. *Canadian Journal of Psychology, 45*, 255–287.

Peel, J., Cropley, B., Hanton, S., & Fleming, S. (2013). Learning through reflection: Values, conflicts, and role interactions of a youth sport coach. *Reflective Practice, 14*, 729–742.

Pennebaker, J. W., & Graybeal, A. (2001). Patterns of natural language use: Disclosure, personality, and social integration. *Current Directions in Psychological Science, 10*, 90–93.

Poolton, J. M., & Zachry, T. L. (2007). So you want to learn implicitly? Coaching and learning through implicit motor learning techniques. *International Journal of Sports Science & Coaching, 2*, 67–78.

Power, M., & Dalgleish, T. (2008). *Cognition and emotion: From order to disorder* (2nd ed.). Hove: Psychology Press.

Roberts, T., & Bruce, V. (1989). Repetition priming of face recognition in a serial choice reaction-time task. *British Journal of Psychology, 80*, 201–211.

Schempp, P. G. (2003). *Teaching sport and physical activity: Insights on the road to excellence*. Champaign, IL: Human Kinetics.

Schraw, G., & Moshman, D. (1995). Metacognitive theories. *Educational Psychology Review, 7*, 351–371.

Schön, D. A. (1991). *The reflective practitioner: How professionals think in action*. Aldershot: Avebury.

Sloman, S. A. (1996). The empirical case for two systems of reasoning. *Psychological Bulletin, 119*, 3–22.

Stodter, A., & Cushion, C. J. (2016). Effective coach learning and the processes of coaches' knowledge development: What works? In P. A. Davis (Ed.), *The psychology of effective coaching and management* (pp. 35–52). New York: Nova Science.

Strean, W. B. (1995). Youth sport contexts: Coaches perceptions and implications for intervention. *Journal of Applied Sport Psychology, 7*, 23–37.

Thompson, N., & Pascal, J. (2012). Developing critically reflective practice. *Reflective Practice, 13*, 311–325.

Thompson, S., & Thompson, N. (2008). *The critically reflective practitioner*. New York: Palgrave Macmillan.

Trapnell, P. D., & Campbell, J. D. (1999). Private self-consciousness and the five-factor model of personality: Distinguishing rumination from reflection. *Journal of Personality and Social Psychology, 76*, 284–304.

Trudel, P., Culver, D., & Werthner, P. (2013). Looking at coach development from the coach-learner's perspective: Consideration for coach development administrators. In P. Potrac, W. Gilbert, & J. Denison (Eds.), *Routledge handbook of sports coaching* (pp. 375–387). London: Routledge.

Trudel, P., & Gilbert, W. (2013). The role of deliberate practice in becoming an expert coach: Part 3 – Creating optimal settings. *Olympic Coach Magazine, 24*, 15–28.

Veenman, M. V. J., van Hout-Wolters, B. H. A. M., & Afflerbach, P. (2006). Metacognition and learning: Conceptual and methodological considerations. *Metacognition and Learning, 1*, 3–14.

Walker, L. F., Thomas, R., & Driska, A. P. (2018). Informal and nonformal learning fort sport coaches: A systematic review. *International Journal of Sports Science & Coaching, 13*, 694–707.

Werthner, P., & Trudel, P. (2006). A new theoretical perspective for understanding how coaches learn to coach. *The Sport Psychologist, 20,* 198–212.

Zaccaro, S. J., Foti, R. J., & Kenny, D. A. (1991). Self-monitoring and trait-based variance in leadership: An investigation of leader flexibility across multiple group situations. *Journal of Applied Psychology, 76,* 308–315.

3
MOTIVATION AND MOTIVATIONAL CLIMATE

Aim of the chapter: Develop an understanding of what motivation is and how to improve athletes' motivation during practices.
Theoretical learning goals of the chapter:
Grow an understanding of...

1. that motivation varies in both *quality* and *quantity* (low-high).
2. the three basic needs according to Self-Determination Theory.
3. some important consequences of different types of motivation.
4. some autonomy-supportive and controlling coaching behaviours.
5. different motivational climates and their characteristics.
6. what 'kind of athletes' different motivational climates can create.
7. what the coach can do to improve the motivational climate.
8. aspects that influence a coach's own motivation.

Practical learning goals of the chapter:

1. Become more accustomed to use supportive coaching behaviours by using reflection card.
2. Become able to use a TARGET-strategy during practice by using reflection sheet.

Vignette

Collin and Leah entered the meeting right after their respective practices had finished. Ellen, asked them how their practices went. Collin was still fired up and almost out of breath. For him practice was all-out war. Only the strong survive. Now he was pleased with the group's intensity.

"We started slow, so I stopped the guys about 15 minutes in. I took them back to the locker room and talked about the importance of valuing practice time."

"And you needed to take them back to the locker room to do that?" Ellen intervened.

"We have a competition this upcoming weekend. There is no room for error. I really needed to send a strong message to the guys", Collin explained.

"Did you consider any other alternatives to giving them a speech?" Ellen asked.

"If I am the leader, I have to show them my passion and that this is important to me", Collin replied. "No one has ever accomplished anything without a great heart. Especially the starters were disappointing to me, and I let them know that during the talk."

"What kind of effects did you experience afterwards?" Ellen continued.

"The guys were much more focused and hardly made any mistakes during the rest of the practice. That was very good", Collin kept on.

"I don't have much problem with work ethic in my group. I have established a rewards system. Whenever an athlete shows up early to work on some areas, I give them five points. They can get points for a lot of different things. When anyone has reached a total of 100 points, I let them decide if they want to skip a practice the next week", Leah, who had been quite during the conversation so far, said.

"Perhaps I could use rewards more frequently; I only hand out rewards for winning our end-of-practice game", Collin added. Ellen managed to slip in few words before Collin went on talking about the competitive game that he called the gauntlet which according to him 'would weed out the fainthearted'.

"Are there any other ways that your rewards system has impacted the athletes?", Ellen asked.

"The group was very interested and disciplined initially, but the rewards are important to keep them going throughout the season", Leah responded.

"What if someone is late from school and can't come before practice, but still want the points?" Ellen wondered.

"That's alright", Leah replied. "They can get points for staying after practice as well. As long as they show interest, they are going to get rewarded." Collin had apparently not paid much attention to the others' conversation the last minute as he had begun sketching out next practice on a napkin.

"After the practice I told the guys that this is what I want to see from them during the rest of the season. Every minute of every practice. This is the level they need to be at if we are going to beat our opponents", he finished.

> What do you think of the way the athletes in Collin's and Leader's groups are motivated?
> How do Collin and Leah, respectively, view motivation?

Introduction

Motivation is often described in movies and popular culture as one of three approaches:

- A personality trait, that you either have or have not.
- A coach has to provide motivation to the athletes, preferably through some kind of emotional locker room pitch right before the competition.
- A use of carrots and sticks is necessary to motivate the athletes.

Those descriptions may work well in Hollywood, but reality is often far from it. Of course, there are always exceptions, but contemporary research investigating motivation is quite straight-forward and consistent. Over the years, plenty of theories have set out to explain human drive motives. Recently, an abundance of studies has accumulated evidence for two of them in various domains. First *Self-Determination Theory* (SDT: Deci & Ryan, 1985) will be reviewed, and then *Achievement Goal Theory* (AGT: Nicholls, 1984) will be examined. The two theories overlap somewhat, albeit with a little different terminology. However, they approach motivation from slightly different perspectives as SDT is primarily concerned with the individual level of inquiry, while AGT lends itself to the group level. This distinction makes them complementary rather than competing. Also, by having a fundamental grasp of both, anyone who wants to proceed more in depth has a sound starting position regardless of which motivational theory the next book or coaching education will be built around. According to Roberts (2001) an agreed upon consensus of the construct of motivation is lacking, but most often it is defined as *something that energizes, directs, and regulates behaviour*.

Self-Determination Theory

SDT has received support in many contexts, such as education, nursing, family life and sports, among others. SDT actually consists of six sub-theories, all of which are beyond the scope of this presentation and therefore only the most significant parts for sport coaches are discussed.

SDT Continuum

SDT argues that there are three overarching motivation types – amotivation (i.e., lack of motivation), extrinsic motivation (which in turn is divided into

66 Motivation and motivational climate

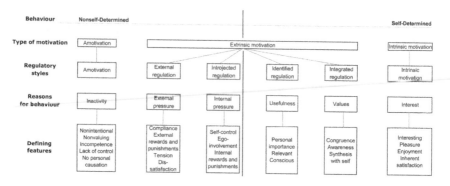

FIGURE 3.1 The self-determination continuum.

several other sub-types of regulations) and intrinsic motivation. These types of motivation are located on a continuum, as seen in Figure 3.1. The thick vertical line separates the self-determined forms of motivation (to the right) from the non-self-determined forms of motivations (to the left). The most important thing with this continuum is not to remember every type of regulation or their respective underlying processes, but rather to realize that there are various degrees of self-determined motivation and not just the well-known classification of inner and outer motivation.

The difference between the overarching types of motivation primarily lies within the individual's intention to act (Ryan & Deci, 2000). An athlete experiencing amotivation is lacking intention to act and action will generally not take place. An athlete experiencing extrinsic motivation acts primarily to get something. The action becomes a means to an end. An athlete experiencing intrinsic motivation acts primarily because it is enjoyable or inherently stimulating, not as a means to an end. There is a temporal distinction between extrinsic and intrinsic motivation. The former is expected to lead to something after the action, while the latter provides immediate satisfaction in the present. Extrinsic motivation consists of four different types of regulations giving the SDT continuum a total of six different regulations. *Amotivation* is characterized by a lack of intent and engagement. The athlete does not feel competent and does not expect the activity to yield any outcome at all. *External regulation* is the least self-determined extrinsic motivation, which means that the athlete performs the activity to get external rewards from others or to comply with threats of punishments. This resembles the classic vision of external motivation, with carrots and sticks controlled by others. *Introjected regulation* is another type of extrinsic motivation and an athlete experiencing this type has internalized parts of the external rewards and punishments system from external regulation. Thus, action becomes a means to deserve internal rewards such as feelings of pride, or to avoid negative emotions (e.g., shame or anxiety). *Identified regulation* is the first form of extrinsic motivation where the perceived locus of causality is within the athlete. The athlete performs the behaviour because it is perceived as valuable and important to the self. *Integrated regulation* is the final form of extrinsic motivation, and even though the behaviour is carried out to get something in the future, this motivation is highly internalized and in concordance with the athlete's view of him-/herself. This regulation shares many of the similarities with intrinsic motivation as there is negligible discrepancy between doing the behaviour and what is desired by the athlete. *Intrinsic motivation* is characterized by behaviour being a purpose of its own where the activity is inherently satisfying regardless of what it will lead to in the future for the athlete (Ryan & Deci, 2000).

Vallerand (2007) distinguished between three hierarchical levels of motivation: *global*, *contextual* and *situational*. The global level refers to a general orientation of motivation, that is, how the athlete predominantly interacts with the environment. The contextual level describes the athlete's typical motivation in a specific context, such as sports or school. The situational level reflects what kind of motivation the athlete experiences at a specific moment during a specific activity. Motivation at different levels interact in both a top-down and a bottom-up manner. The top-down effect means motivation at a more general level influences motivation at a lower level (e.g., an athlete who primarily interacts with his/her environment in an intrinsically motivated way is more likely to be more intrinsically motivated in a specific context compared to a person who is generally extrinsically motivated, all other variables equal). The bottom-up effect means motivation at a lower-level influence more general motivation (e.g., an athlete who experiences plenty of situations of self-determined motivation during practices will be inclined to be more self-determined motivated towards this sport in general).

Of course, an athlete can simultaneously experience a combination of different types of regulations to varying degrees in a specific situation. For the sake of simplicity, in the following we assume that a person is driven by only one form of motivation. Some examples: Amotivation makes Hannah Hammer Thrower skip going out for a 5 km run, despite her coach having told her to improve her fitness, something she is not very fond of, *because she does not really think it will make a difference anyway*. External motivation makes Steven Striker come in before practice to work on his leaping ability, *since his dad has promised him an allowance raise if he can score three goals from corners during the first two months of the season*. Introjected motivation makes Paula Pole Vaulter not eat desert, *since she will be ashamed if she does not manage to keep the target weight her coach has set*. Identified motivation makes Gordon Goalie do some additional crunches in the gym, even though this is not particularly fun to him, *but he has noticed that a stronger core helps him grip the ball when stretching out for a diving saving*. Integrated motivation makes Lola Long Jumper do 100 sit-ups every day, *as she considers having a strong core an important part of being the track and field athlete she envisions herself to be*. Intrinsic motivation makes Nelson Netminder stay after practice trying to save his best friends penalties, *since he loves the challenge and feeling of being solely focused on trying to guess their aims*. Another way to illustrate the difference between nonself-determined and self-determined forms of motivation is displayed in Table 3.1.

TABLE 3.1 Reasons for acting.

Regulation	Reason
External	Because I have to…
Introjected	Because I ought to…
Identified	Because I choose to…
Integrated/Intrinsic	Because I want to…

> What types of motivation do you think the athletes in your group most often experience?

Basic Psychological Needs

What determines which type of regulation an athlete experience is how well three different basic psychological needs are satisfied. They are *perceived autonomy, perceived competence* and *perceived relatedness*. Perceived autonomy concerns how well an athlete perceives having influence on life and decisions, having options and not feeling coerced. Perceived competence pertains to how skilful an athlete feels regarding a specific task or believes in reaching set goals. Perceived relatedness concerns the amount and quality of perceived support from others, how satisfying relations one has, and to what extent the athlete feels understood by others. The more these needs are satisfied, the more self-determined motivation is experienced. The needs do not have an intermutual hierarchy, even if some researchers have speculated that perceived relatedness is somewhat subordinate (Ryan & Deci, 2017). Finally, it is important to emphasize that what is significant for the athlete is his/her perception and not what is objectively so. If an athlete perceives high levels of autonomy, this will lead to self-determined motivation, even if in 'reality' the person is not in charge of many life decisions. The athlete's interpretation of the social and interpersonal context as primarily controlling or informational determines to what extent basic needs will be satisfied. Evaluations and deadlines are examples of factors that normally are viewed as controlling, thus thwarting basic needs and reducing self-determined motivation. In contrast, non-pressure and positive competence information are usually correlated to an informational apprehension, and will therefore lead to more self-determined motivation through greater needs satisfaction.

> ✎ Which one of the three basic psychological needs do you think the athletes in your group most often experience as satisfied during practices?

Consequences of Different Types of Motivation

The six different forms of regulation have been found to lead to different consequences for the athlete. These consequences can be affective, cognitive or behavioural. Vallerand (2007) suggests a motivational sequence where social factors (i.e., coaching behaviours) impact psychological mechanisms (i.e., an athlete's experience of perceived autonomy, perceived competence and perceived relatedness), which in turn leads to a type of motivation (i.e., amotivation, extrinsic motivation or intrinsic motivation), something that affects the athlete's emotions, thoughts and behaviours. Thus, in contrast to some popular beliefs, motivation is dynamic.

Amotivation does not lead to any action in particular, or at best going through the motions indifferently Therefore, this will not be elaborated on. In comparison, both non-self-determined and self-determined motivation (to the left and right respectively of the thick vertical line in Figure 3.1) therefore lead to behaviours. Research is quite unequivocal in that the consequences generally are more positive the more self-determined the motivation is (Ryan & Deci, 2017), although there are a few exceptions, such as a study investigating Bulgarian elite athletes which found that better performance was correlated with less self-determined forms of motivation (Chantal, Guay, Dobreva-Martinova, & Vallerand, 1996). Since not every part of the athletic experience is inherently pleasurable in itself, integrated regulation will have an important role and it is encouraging that its consequences are quite similar compared to those derived from intrinsic motivation. When athletes engage in activities that are not inherently intrinsically motivating, it is imperative to identify a sound rationale that is valued by the athlete. Some of the consequences related to self-determined motivation are higher persistence and less frequency of dropout from sport (Pelletier, Fortier, Vallerand, & Brière, 2001; Sarrazin, Vallerand, Guillet, Pelletier, & Cury, 2002), better performance (Gillet, Berjot, & Gobancé, 2009), increased creativity (Hennessey & Zbikowski, 1993), greater enjoyment (Kazén, Kuhl, & Leicht, 2015), better concentration (Stormoen et al., 2016), less fear of failure (Bartholomew et al., 2018), increased effort (Aelterman et al., 2012), and better subjective well-being (Balaguer et al., 2012), just to name some behavioural, cognitive and emotional outcomes that have been researched quite thoroughly. Thus, it is safe to say that self-determined motivation is preferable. What about the classic stick-and-carrot then? Aside from the quality of behaviours, cognitions and emotions, there is also a great risk that motivation ceases altogether when the external reinforcers are removed, something that will inevitably happen to the athlete during competition or when working out by him-/herself. In that case the behaviour may no longer be carried out at all.

> ✏ Look back at a situation where you were obviously driven by non-self-determined motivation. What kind of consequences (e.g., persistence, creativity, fear of failure, enjoyment, performance) did you experience?
>
> Compare the previous situation and its consequences with a situation where you were obviously driven by self-determined motivation. What kind of consequences (e.g., persistence, creativity, fear of failure, enjoyment, performance) did you experience?

Coaches' Impact on Self-Determined Motivation

The coach is one of the many social factors that influence an athlete's motivation. Of course, intraindividual factors also play a role, such as trait anxiety or cognitive patterns (e.g., Oliver, Markland, & Hardy, 2010), and the coach is not in sole possession of all pieces in the social puzzle of an athlete. However, as this is a text about coaching development, by necessity the focus will be on what the coach can do. Coaches' behaviours have been investigated from different perspectives over the years (cf. chapter 4), and in regard to SDT coaching behaviours have been categorized in *(autonomy-)supportive* and *controlling*. The former increases the likelihood of athletes' motivation being self-determined, whereas the latter increases the likelihood of athletes' motivation being nonself-determined.

Supportive Coaching Behaviours

Most researchers have labelled behaviours of teachers, leaders and coaches leading to increase in followers self-determined motivation as autonomy-supportive (Mageau & Vallerand, 2003). Autonomy is the most investigated need, and for good reasons as Baard, Deci, and Ryan (2004) found that autonomy support facilitates the other basic needs, although competence and relatedness may be targeted as well. Table 3.2 provides an overview of supportive behaviours (with hands-on examples for each one using push-ups, as many athletes do not consider this type of activity inherently pleasurable) and primary need targeted by each behaviour. The most important thing is not to know exactly what basic psychological need that is unfulfilled in a particular athlete. Yet, it is advantageous for coaches to be aware of the athletes' needs and to have a wider arsenal of support, than only supporting autonomy. The list is synthesized from primarily Amorose (2007), Conroy and Coatsworth (2007), Deci, Eghrari, Patrick, & Leone, (1994), Mageau and Vallerand (2003).

TABLE 3.2 Supportive coaching behaviours and their respective targeted need.

Supportive behaviour	Example	Need in focus		
		Autonomy	Competence	Relatedness
Acknowledge the athlete's feelings	'I understand that you do not think push-ups are particularly fun.'	✔		✔
Provide choice	'Do you want to do push-ups with your hands in parallel or diagonal position'	✔		
Provide logical and rational explanations to tasks and limits	'Push-ups will strengthen your upper body so that you can take a hit from your opponent easier.'	✔		
Formulate feedback connected to the athlete's own competence and skills	'Now you have managed to do 21 push-ups, which is only two away from your personal best.' Instead of comparing athletes' performances to each other.	✔	✔	
Healthy approach to winning and losing	Even if athlete A did 30 push-ups (with a personal best of 40), athlete B gets the most attention since he/she set a new personal best, was the closest to the personal best, or exerted the most effort, even if far fewer than 30 push-ups.	✔	✔	
Let the athletes participate in goal-setting	'How many push-ups is reasonable that you will be able do in two months' time?'	✔		
Provide the athletes with leadership tasks	'Today, Gordon Goalie gets to choose three strength exercises that we will do together.'	✔		
Make sure that possible rewards, if any are used, are connected to controllable aspects	'Anyone who comes within 90 % of your personal best in push-ups gets to choose a song for our warm-up play list.'	✔		
Provide opportunities for social company	Let the athletes hang around awhile after practice in the locker room.			✔

(Continued)

TABLE 3.2 (Continued)

		Need in focus		
Supportive behaviour	Example	Autonomy	Competence	Relatedness
Show interest for the athletes' opinions, thoughts and activities	Show up ten minutes earlier than usual before start of practice and use this time to ask early arriving athletes how school is going at the moment.			✔
Express the connection between skill execution and effort exerted over time	'Now you have managed five more push-ups compared to the start of the season. It has really paid off that you chose to work a little extra two times a week on your upper body strength.'		✔	
Emphasize that mistakes are okay, for example by making sure there are some trial-and-error during practice, and not having a zero tolerance against mistakes both when designing activities as well as when interacting with the athletes during practice	'Try some different widths with your hands when doing push-ups today. It is okay if you go too narrow and do not manage a single one. Just change to a little wider stance.'		✔	

> What supportive behaviours do you already use during practices?
> What supportive behaviours can you do more of?
> How will that be done?
> Are there any challenges in accomplishing this? If so, how will you handle them?

Controlling Coaching Behaviours

As a coach it is also possible to behave in a manner that the athletes experience as controlling, thwarting their basic psychological needs, leading to less self-determined motivation. Examples are detailed by Ryan and Deci (2017), such as dominance or control (autonomy), coldness or distancing (relatedness), and criticism or derogation (competence). Predominantly, coaches hamper athletes' autonomy when using controlling behaviours. Relatively innocent comments

TABLE 3.3 Controlling coaching behaviours.

Controlling coaching behaviour	Example
Tangible rewards	The coach promises rewards for participating in practice activities.
Controlling feedback	The coach gives praise in a manner so the athletes learn to exclusively engage in behaviours that the coach wishes/demands.
Excessive personal control	The coach asks controlling questions, hands out orders and uses deadlines.
Intimidating behaviour	The coach disgraces the athletes in front of others when they do something the coach does not like, or emphasizes old mistakes.
Promoting ego-involvement	The coach evaluates athlete's individual performance in front of the entire team.
Conditional regard	The coach pays more attention to athletes when they perform well and less when they perform worse.

from the coach can thwart athletes' needs, leading to athletes' actions to please someone else, or to avoid feelings of shame or guilt. Table 3.3 describes a number of controlling coaching behaviours with corresponding examples to provide a better understanding how the behaviours can look in real-life (Bartholomew, Ntoumanis, & Thørgersen-Ntoumani, 2009). Athletes will not perceive coaches' statements and actions uniformly. A comment from the coach may be perceived as controlling by one athlete, while another athlete's basic psychological needs remain unaffected by the same comment. Though, it is crucial to become aware of comments and recognize behaviours (that might be more common than initially thought) that can be perceived as need thwarting, even if they are not intended that way.

> What do you do as a coach that the athletes might experience as controlling?
> What are the advantages of these behaviours?
> What alternative behaviours that are more supportive and effective could you use instead?

Effects of Rewards on Motivation

Ryan and Deci (2017) present five different categories of contingencies for rewards. *Task-noncontingent* is a reward given to a participant simply for being present. *Engagement-contingent* is a reward given to a participant for spending time on a specific task. *Completion-contingent* is a reward given to a participant for completing a task (perhaps within a set time limit). *Performance-contingent* reward is given to a participant for reaching a specific standard, such as outscoring 75% of all participants. *Competitively contingent* reward is given to only the winner of a competition. To date, the largest review of the effects of rewards by Deci, Koestner, and Ryan (1999) showed interesting impacts on intrinsic motivation. Task-noncontingent seemed not to have any decisive impact on intrinsic motivation. All other types of reward were negatively related to intrinsic motivation. Children's motivation was more negatively affected than college-age students.

Again, the impact on motivation is determined by the individual's own perception, as rewards can be viewed as informational or controlling. Whether the athlete perceives the control of the behaviour to reside within (increase in perceived autonomy) or outside (decrease in perceived autonomy) of him-/herself determines if the motivation will be more self-determined or not after a reward (Deci & Ryan, 1985). Nonetheless, in general, the effect of tangible rewards seems to be negative for intrinsic motivation. Rewards can also come in the form of verbal positive feedback, which is positively related to intrinsic motivation, in contrast to the previously mentioned types of rewards. When college-age students were separated from children, the former were significantly affected in a positive way by verbal positive feedback, whereas the latter, surprisingly, were unaffected (Deci et al., 1999).

> How do you use rewards today?
> What type of impact do you think this has on the athletes' self-determined motivation?
> How could you use rewards more effectively (e.g., increase or decrease use, or use differently)?

Effects of Competition on Motivation

Competition can be either *indirect* (comparison against a personal standard, for example trying to beat a previous personal best) or *direct* (comparison against another person). Indirect competition leads either to increase or decrease in self-determined motivation depending on whether it is viewed as an opportunity to improve one's competence or if it is viewed as pressure to reach a certain standard. Direct competition seems to decrease self-determined motivation regardless of win-loss, since it makes competition the focus rather than the activity itself. Hence, the behaviour becomes a means to an end. Competition, however, just as any extrinsic structure, contain both informational and/or controlling aspects, thus leading to either satisfied or thwarted needs. When the competition is seen as something that *must* be won, the controlling aspect is prominent. Whereas, if the competition is viewed as continuous feedback and optimal challenge, the informational aspect is prominent (Deci & Ryan, 1985).

Granted, for many coaches and athletes, participating in competition is not really much of a choice as it is a 'mandatory' part in numerous sports. Therefore, it is useful to make the best out of it, rather than avoid it altogether. Competition is made up of a number of aspects such as *competitive outcome, interpersonal context, perceived challenge* and *competence valuation* (Reeve & Deci, 1996). Pertaining to outcome, winning increases intrinsic motivation compared to losing. Informational or controlling interpersonal cues play a big role for the effects of competition. If the social context is interpreted as pressure to win, intrinsic motivation will be undermined. In line with flow theory (Csikszentmihalyi, 1990), the perception of being optimally challenged is facilitative of intrinsic motivation. Competition tends to increase the value of competence at display, perhaps as a way of making the skills more meaningful if they are used to reach a competitive goal. For a coach, outcomes are not entirely under personal control, but the other aspects are more manageable.

However, in competition, the outcome might not be everything, as was found by McAuley and Tammen (1989). Participants in their study subjectively rated their performance irrespective of the outcome. The motivation was more impacted by ratings of success versus failure than outcomes of winning versus losing. In another study, Tauer and Harackiewicz (2004) compared three conditions, cooperating, competing, and competing as a group. Although some methodological artefacts may have influenced the results, it points to the advantage of competing as a group, as this uses the best of both worlds (i.e., getting to cooperate with teammates and have an added effect of competition in a positive way). For a coach working within an individual sports context, aspects of cooperation will be useful in enhancing self-determined motivation in the athletes. Taken together, these studies hint that motivation can be more self-determined if the coach is able to frame competitive performances in a positive manner that is under the control of the athlete. Additionally, an intragroup focus in the matchup of a greater opponent facilitate self-determined motivation as this can enhance the perceptions of both autonomy and relatedness. Likewise, goal-setting may play a pivotal role, as reaching a performance goal should lessen the blow of a negative competitive outcome (i.e., defeat). This performance goal should be optimally challenging irrespective of the current opponents' skill level. Coaches' feedback can also serve as a buffer for decrease in intrinsic motivation after a loss, as Vansteenkiste and Deci (2003) showed that losers receiving positive feedback displayed greater intrinsic motivation compared to losers getting other rewards. For a coach to be able to provide positive feedback after a poor outcome, it is necessary to focus on controllable aspects related to the performance, regardless of the opponents' qualities, such as running technique, intragroup communication or number of passes attempted. Finally, one caveat is warranted. Competition easily becomes more important than performance itself, which risks leading to ego-involving, a controlling state, where the person's self-perception is dependent on the outcome of the competition (Deci & Ryan, 1985; Vallerand, Gauvin & Halliwell, 1986).

> How do you currently use competition and cooperation during practice?
>
> What type of impact do you think this has on the athletes' self-determined motivation?
>
> How could you use competition and cooperation in future practices to facilitate athletes' self-determined motivation (i.e., increase informational aspects and/or decrease controlling aspects)?
>
> If you are coaching an individual sport, how could you use cooperation during competitions?

Setting Limits in Regard to Motivation

Limits, such as social rules, have to be set, either by the coach or the group of athletes. From time to time, these boundaries need to be reinforced. When setting or reinforcing limits, the coach can be perceived as informational or controlling. Koestner, Ryan, Bernieri, and Holt (1984) designed an interesting experiment where second-grade children were asked to participate in a painting activity. They found that setting limits with a *passive tone, acknowledge ambiguous feelings* and *include a rationale* – helped the children be creative, which was seen as a way of being self-determined. In contrast, limits set in a manner that included a more *direct voice* ('should' or 'must'), as well as *praise of the person* ('being a good boy/girl') instead of behaviour, affected the children in a controlling way. Below are two examples of limit-setting applied to a sports coaching context.

Instructor Ingram (Informational)

'Before getting into practice, I'd like to tell a few things about how practices are conducted here. I know that you would like to be able to take it easy after school for a couple of hours before practice, but we need to use our allotted practice time since others are using this facility as well. We need to be on time in the locker room. Before leaving the locker room, it is important to clean up, which means picking up our clothes from the floor and empty the trash can, so that no one will trip on them. I understand that some kids don't want to be tidy all the time, but here it is important to be neat.'

Tina Trainer (Controlling)

'Before getting into practice, I'd like to tell a few things about how practices are conducted here. These are the rules for locker rooms and practices. You'll only practice if you are on time. You absolutely must stay in the locker room until our time starts. You've to clean up the floor before you leave the locker room. In general, I want you to be good kids and not mess around in the locker room.'

> How do you set limits for practice and competition today?
>
> What type of impact do you think this has on the athletes' self-determined motivation?
>
> How could you improve your limit-setting in the future to facilitate the athletes' self-determined motivation?

Motivation Measurement

 In the appendix, a questionnaire is presented measuring the coach's motivational style using hypothetical cases (Problems in Sports Questionnaire: Carpentier & Mageau, 2013). The results of the measurements can be used to elaborate the coach's own estimation of autonomous and controlling behaviours. This will facilitate the coach's self-awareness.

> When you view the results on your own motivational style, what do you think?

Achievement Goal Theory

Another motivational theory that has strong support from research in both school and sports setting is Achievement Goal Theory (AGT: Nicholls, 1984). AGT proposes that motivation, called *Goal State Involvement*, is partly determined from an individual's goal orientation and partly from the environmentally inclined climate as Figure 3.2 shows.

An athlete's goal orientation hinges on his/her conception of ability, or how he/she defines performance. This conception is either a differentiated or an undifferentiated view of ability. Early in life, effort, luck, task difficulty and ability are undistinguishable from each other (Nicholls, 1978), creating

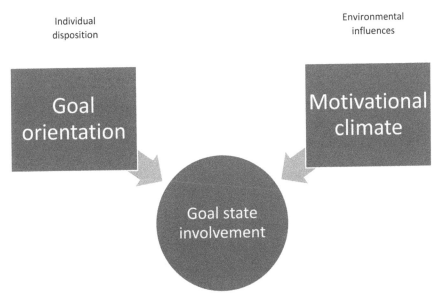

FIGURE 3.2 Interaction of goal orientation and motivational climate that create the goal state involvement in the individual.

		Ego-orientation	
		Low	High
Task-orientation	Low	Low-Low	High-Low
	High	Low-High	High-High

FIGURE 3.3 Goal-orientations dispositions.

an undifferentiated conception of ability. Originally, Nicholls proposed that children are able to differentiate between these aspects of performance around the age of twelve, although this age should probably not be seen as definitive, considering the inconsistencies found between chronological age and maturity (Baxter-Jones, Eisenmann, & Sherar, 2005). An undifferentiated view will lead to high *task-orientation*, where the athlete focuses on the task and self-referenced standards. Meanwhile, a differentiated view will lead to high *ego-orientation*, where the athlete focuses on the self and comparing favourably to others. Further, an athlete also carries a perception of his/her level of competence. This view of one's competence can be high or low. If competence is perceived as high, the athlete will be active, whereas a perception of low competence will lead to avoidance. This distinction is most pronounced when a person holds a differentiated perception of ability. Most researchers have assumed, and found, (cf. Roberts, Treasure, & Kavussanu, 1996) the two orientations to be independent. Thus, it is possible for an athlete to be high in both task- and ego-orientation (and vice versa). This creates four rough possible combinations of goal-orientations (Figure 3.3).

Environmental influences consist of feedback, evaluations, competitions and social relations, to name a few, and make up a motivational climate. Although, Roberts (2001) argues for the malleability of goal-orientation disposition through inclining an individual's early socialization experiences towards task-orientation, motivational climate is more often than not the focus for interventions.

Goal-orientation and motivational climate contribute to create the athlete's goal state involvement. This state is either *ego-involved* or *task-involved* as it is impossible to be focused simultaneously on both ego and task (Roberts, 2001).

When ego-involved, social comparison is salient and the athlete is primarily concerned with either showing competence or hiding incompetence, depending on the athlete's perceived level of competence. An ego-involved athlete with a self-perception of high competence is motivated to succeed, at the expense of less able rivals. Meanwhile, an athlete with the self-perception of low competence is motivated primarily to hide short-comings in order not to reveal low competence in front of others (or for oneself for that matter). Contrastingly, when task-involved, the individual is primarily concerned with learning or improving (Ames, 1992; Schultheiss & Brunstein, 2005). Thus, when task-involved perceived level of competence has less impact as both high and low competent athletes can improve and therefore reach their goals independent of others' skill level.

Motivational Climates

A coach has an important role in creating the motivational climate within the group of athletes. Two types of motivational climates exist: *performance* (ego) climate and *mastery* (task) climate. In a performance climate, success is defined as demonstrating superior competence in comparison to others. Meanwhile, in the mastery climate success is defined as improvement of personal competence, regardless of others' performances. Thus, mastery climate values learning, effort and improvement, while performance climate cherishes favourable normative comparisons and performances outcomes, rather than processes. Mistakes are seen as a logical, and unavoidable part of progress in mastery climate, while performance climate views mistakes as an indication of low competence. The primary reason for engaging in sport within a mastery climate is to learn new skills and improve existing skills, whereas performance climate highlight demonstration of superior competence as the main reason for participation. Finally, the coach focuses on development and learning in mastery climate, while the leader in performance climate concentrates on outcomes and normative rankings (Allen & Hodge, 2006).

The two motivational climates are contrasted by different characteristics along six dimensions displayed in Table 3.4 (Brathwaite, Spray, & Warburton, 2011; Ntoumanis & Biddle, 1999). Of course, the characteristics are somewhat overlapping. In reality, the climates might not be entirely black or white. One aspect from the performance climate may negate some good intentions with one of the aspects from mastery climate, such as varied tasks being negated by public social comparison from the coach (Ames, 1992).

TABLE 3.4 Characteristics of motivational climates.

Mastery climate	*Dimension*	*Performance climate*
Challenging and varied	*Design of practice activities*	Lack of variation and challenge
Athletes are provided choices and leadership opportunities	*Decision-making*	Athletes do not participate in decision-making processes
Individual progress	*Criteria for rewards' distribution*	Social comparison
Mixed ability grouping to encourage learning through cooperation and interaction	*Grouping*	Static groupings based on ability
Based on task mastery and individual development	*Evaluation*	Based on winning and out-performing others
Allotted time for development is adjusted to the individual	*Pace of learning*	Every athlete is expected to learn at the same pace

Consequences of Different Motivational Climates

Even though there are some arguments for positive effects of dispositional ego-orientation (Lochbaum, Kazak Cetinkalp, Graham, Wright, & Zazo, 2016), and state ego-involvement (Roberts, 2001) for elite athletes, the vast majority of research has found quite striking advantages of mastery climates over performance climates. Harwood, Keegan, Smith, and Raine (2015) conducted a meta-analysis covering studies published from 1990-2014 with participants ranging from 10 to 38 years old that investigated correlations of motivational climate within the sporting domain displayed in Figure 3.4. Overwhelmingly, the evidence supports mastery climate.

Adaptive strategies include, among others, increasing effort, persistence, help-seeking, co-operation, and adaptive coping strategies (e.g., solution focused). Maladaptive strategies include among others exercise dependence, avoiding practice, maladaptive coping strategies (e.g., avoidance), and self-handicapping. Also, for international elite level athletes, mastery climate is beneficial (Pensgaard & Roberts, 2002). Interventions trying to foster a mastery motivational climate in physical education have the strongest impact on

Outcome	Mastery climate	Performance climate
Intrinsic motivation	▬▬▬▬▬►	───────
Extrinsic motivation	───────	────►
Amotivation	───────	────►
Adaptive practice and competitive strategies	▬▬▬▬▬►	───────
Maladaptive strategies for practice and competition	───────	────►
Positive affect	▬▬▬▬▬►	───────
Negative affect	───────	────►
Pro-social moral	▬▬▬▬▬►	───────
Antisocial moral	───────	────►
Self-esteem	▬▬▬▬▬►	───────
Performance	▬▬▬▬▬►	───────
Flow	▬▬▬▬▬►	───────
Perfectionism	───────	────►

FIGURE 3.4 Consequences of different motivational climates. Thicker bar indicates increase and thinner bar indicates decrease on various athletes' outcomes.

behavioural outcomes (e.g., health and development). Affective outcomes, such as enjoyment and attitude, are slightly less influenced, although still in a positive way (Brathwaite et al., 2011). As similar results have been found in both the context of physical education and sports, there is a strong argument for mastery climate. In extension, Smoll, Smith, and Cumming (2007) found that athletes who were exposed to a mastery climate over time, changed their goal-orientation to become more task-orientated. Moreover, this positive change for the athletes carried over to their school context. This indicates a bidirectional nature of state and orientation in AGT. Thus, a coach has the potential, through the motivational climate, to influence the orientation in the athletes well beyond the time and context of practices and competitions. Drawing on this, it is possible to 'create' different athletes. Table 3.5 lays out a description of stereotypical athletes and their respective characteristics in some important areas (Ames, 1992; Burton & Raedeke, 2008; Schultheiss & Brunstein, 2005). Certainly, this is a rough estimate of reactions from the athletes, and one individual might not display every characteristic. Still, it is valuable both to identify outcome-orientated athletes risking motivational struggles in the future, and also to get a deeper understanding of consequences of different motivational climates. Mastery climate 'creates' a process-orientated athlete, whereas performance climate 'creates' an outcome-orientated athlete.

Coaches Impact on Motivational Climate

TARGET is an acronym involving the six dimensions (*Task, Authority, Recognition, Grouping, Evaluation, Timing*) that is under coaches' influence, create a task-involving motivational climate. Table 3.6 provides a few hands-on examples of what the coach can do within each dimension (i.e., *strategies*). Brathwaite and colleagues (2011) demonstrated that interventions stretching over longer timeframes had stronger impact. Also, interventions including the entire TARGET model had stronger impact. Thus, coaches working with more than one dimension and persisting in their effort to create a mastery climate will likely be rewarded, and the athletes reap larger benefits.

 How do you use the TARGET dimension today in your coaching?
What strategy could you use more of in your coaching?
How will that be carried out?
Are there any obstacles to overcome with implementing this strategy? If so, how could you possibly handle those obstacles?

Evidently, there is an overlap between the TARGET strategies for a mastery group climate and supportive coaching behaviours according to SDT. However, this should not be seen as redundant, but rather complementing.

TABLE 3.5 Different athletes created by different motivational climates.

Climate	Mastery climate	Performance climate	
Goal-orientation	Task-orientated	Ego-orientated	
'Type' of athlete	Mastery searchers	Success seekers	Failure avoiders
How does the athlete view own competence?	Low or high, as both types can behave in the same manner.	High perceived ability because of favourable social comparison.	Low perceived ability because of poor social comparison.
What kind of goals does the athlete have?	Learning and personal improvement. Both athletes with high and low perceived ability believe they can succeed.	Social comparison and winning. Motivated to succeed.	Social comparison, but fears failure. Motivated to avoid failure.
What kind of tasks does the athlete prefer?	Difficult, challenging. Chooses learning opportunities even at the risk of displaying mistakes.	Challenging, but realistic. Sacrifice learning opportunities if risk of displaying mistakes is high.	Very difficult or very easy. Sacrifice learning opportunities to avoid displaying low ability.
How much effort will the athlete exert?	Consistently strong effort to promote maximum improvement and learning.	Only as high as needed to demonstrate positive social comparison. Excessive effort could signal lower ability.	Low effort on moderately challenging tasks to avoid demonstrating low ability. High effort on easy tasks to avoid failure. May give high effort on very difficult tasks as this can be viewed as being close to success.
What kind of groups does the athlete prefer?	Groups where opportunities for learning are high, and could include athletes of mixed competence.	Groups of lesser competent athletes in order to sustain favourable social comparison.	Groups of more competent athletes if this makes it possible to hide from responsibility in a team sport. In an individual sport, preferred groups will likely be of athletes with lesser competence.
How does the athlete view learning?	Learning is the primary purpose of participation and is intrinsically enjoyable.	Learning is enjoyable as long as it is conducive to displaying competence.	Learning is downplayed and avoided as it often demands plenty of effort, brings the risk of mistakes, or risk revealing initial low competence.
How will the athlete respond to failures and setbacks?	Increased effort and persistence.	Increased effort as long as they believe they can succeed. Probably fears failure more than strives for success.	Gives up and quits trying.

TABLE 3.5 *(Continued)*

Climate	Mastery climate		Performance climate
Goal-orientation	**Task-orientated**		**Ego-orientated**
'Type' of athlete	Mastery searchers	Success seekers	Failure avoiders
How will the athlete explain success and failure?	Success is due to effort and improvement. Failure is temporary and due to something that can be improved, such as effort and skill development.	Success is caused by talent. Failure is generally discounted, and excuses/explanations are often made.	Success is due to luck or an easy task. Failure is caused by a lack of ability.

TABLE 3.6 TARGET dimensions and strategies.

Dimension	Strategies
Task. Skills and competencies athletes are asked to develop and what tasks they are given to complete (e.g., practice activities, structure of practice conditions).	Provide athletes with a variety of moderately demanding tasks that emphasize individual challenge and active involvement. Use activities that facilitate focus on own development and limit comparison with others. Help athletes with goal setting. Create a training environment that is developmentally appropriate by individualizing tasks' demands.
Authority. How decision-making processes are distributed and what they contain (e.g., athlete involvement in decision concerning training, the setting and enforcing of rules).	Encourage athletes' participation in decision-making processes. Provide choice for the athletes regarding when and how to carry out tasks. Develop opportunities for leadership roles. Get athletes to take responsibility for their own development by teaching self-management and self-monitoring skills.
Recognition. Procedures used to motivate and recognize athletes for their progress and achievement (e.g., reasons for recognition, distribution of rewards).	Use individual meetings between coach and athlete focusing on individual progress. Recognize individual progress, effort, and improvement. Ensure equal opportunities for rewards to all.
Grouping. How athletes are grouped or kept apart in training and competition.	Use flexible, heterogenous and mixed ability groupings. Create opportunities for individual work on athletes' own specific needs. Provide multiple grouping arrangement (i.e., individual, small group, and large group activities). Emphasize cooperative solutions to training tasks and activities.

(Continued)

TABLE 3.6 (Continued)

Dimension	Strategies
Evaluation. Standards set for athletes' learning and performance and how performance is monitored in relation to these standards.	Treat competition as an opportunity to test skills and evaluate practice, rather than ranking athletes. Develop evaluation criteria based on effort, improvement, persistence, and progress toward individual goals. Provide assessments of athletes in private. Involve athletes in self-evaluation. Make evaluations meaningful.
Timing. Appropriateness of the time demands placed on learning and performance (e.g., expected pace of learning and development, management of time and training schedule).	Develop training programs that recognize that athletes, even at the elite level, do not train, learn, or develop at the same rate. Provide sufficient time before moving onto the next stage in skill development. Negotiate the time spent on specific skills with the athletes. Spend equal time with all athletes. Assist athletes in establishing training and competition schedules.

Individual athletes will experience enhanced self-determined motivation from supportive behaviours, while the whole group simultaneously will flourish from the mastery climate.

Motivational Climate Measurements

The Perceived Motivational Climate in Sport Questionnaire-2 (Newton, Duda, & Yin, 2000) is provided in the appendix where the athletes rate their perception of the motivational climate within the group.

> When you view the results on the motivational climate in your group, what do you think?

Coaches' Own Motivation

Pressure from Two Sides

Surprisingly, coaches' own motivation has received scant interest, considering the amount of research conducted on athletes' motivation. Within the educational domain, teachers' motivation has been investigated to somewhat larger extent, though not as thoroughly as students' motivation. However, while many similarities exist between coaches and teachers, some deviations exist due to coaching still being comparatively unprofessional work in relation to teaching. A majority of the studies investigating coaches' motivation have examined troubles, stress and factors of negative impact. Coaches report that their level of self-determined motivation is influenced by both the organization and the athletes. Within the organization, coaches can perceive pressure from colleagues comparing their coaching styles or trying to outperform coaching peers. Organizational tasks such as administration, fund raising, or adhering to demands of sports directors (i.e., tasks that might be mandatory, but hardly ever the main reason for entering into coaching) may add pressure. Additionally, practice sessions themselves are conceivably perceived as straining, when planning and decisions have to be made, or when things are not progressing as well as hoped for. Also, interactions with athletes are potentially stressful and demanding for the coach. In particular, coaches' motivation is likely inhibited if athletes are believed to have low self-determined motivation and high extrinsic motivation (Rocchi, Pelletier, & Couture, 2013). At times of struggle, it is easy for coaches to forget the original reasons for starting to coach, as motives over time change or fall into oblivion. Time, or perceived lack thereof, is another potential source of coaches' stress. This is especially pressing when the coaching assignment is voluntary or at least not full time (Roxburgh, 2002). Finally, if motivation becomes really poor, a coach risks entering a state of burnout, which is characterized by emotional/physical exhaustion, reduced sense of accomplishment and devaluation of the sport (cynicism; Radeke & Smith, 2001). Thus, vigilance towards any indicators of burnout is advantageous, so the coach can counteract in time. On a more positive side of motivation, McLean and Mallett (2012) interviewed coaches working on different sports and levels. They reported four distinct areas of fuel for their motivation; namely, *connection with their sport*, *coach and athlete development*, *external influences* (mostly expressed by high performance coaches that mentioned competition), and *internal influences* (e.g., enjoyment, love, and passion for sport and coaching).

Measuring Your Own Motivation

 In the appendix, Coach Motivation Questionnaire (McLean, Mallett, & Newcombe, 2012) is provided to get a baseline measurement of coaches' own motivation.

> When you view the results on your own motivation, what do you think?

Enhancing Coaches' Own Motivation

SDT is a needs-based theory, and therefore basic needs will have to be satisfied to a larger extent for motivation to improve. Then, how does a coach go about fulfilling his/her own needs better? A lot hinges on being able to create a supportive environment benefitting oneself. Additionally, Reeve (2013) examined the possibilities for individuals to engage their own environment. By agentic engagement, a person tries to elicit autonomy-support from significant others. This is accomplished by asking questions, stating own preferences, offering suggestions to improve the situation/relationship or talking to significant others about own interests. For coaches, that social environment is likely made up of coaching peers, perhaps working with the same group of athletes. Else, it is possible to engage in these conversations with family and friends.

In addition, time for recovery, such as spending time away from the coaching environment or undemanding physical activities are oft-cited resources for enhancing vitality (Gerber & Pühse, 2009). Since motivation at different hierarchical levels can influence one another, it is likely that a coach who has self-determined motivation in other contexts of life indirectly positively impact his/her motivation in the context of sports coaching.

Intrapersonal feedback is expressed in either an informational or controlling tone (Ryan, 1982). Accordingly, an internal informational style involves non-pressured monitoring, while a controlling style involves some aspects of verbal rewards/punishments, personal attributes, such as 'I am a good/bad person because…'. Naturally, those two intrapersonal feedback styles have been found to replicate the effects of interpersonal feedback on self-determined motivation described earlier. Similarly, Kazén and colleagues (2015) instructed participants to immerse themselves in a task and think of a way to find something meaningful, personally relevant or interesting with the task at hand. This intervention successfully improved response-time, accuracy and physiological measures such as pulse rate, which were moderated by the task being perceived as more fun. Consequently, self-talk could be a fruitful avenue for enhancing self-motivation.

Adoption of task goals can further enhance a coach's motivation. This is accomplished by focusing on aspects salient in a mastery climate, or using the TARGET structures. Along these lines, setting goals with feelings of intrinsic interest, instead of having goals connected to feelings of introjected guilt or external compulsion is beneficiary (Sheldon & Houser-Marko, 2001). Finally, interested coaches are referred to the compendium created by Knittle and colleagues (2020) for additional ideas on self-motivation.

> What motivates you today as a coach?
> What basic needs could be more satisfied in order to enhance your motivation?
> How can you act agentically and improve your supporting environment?
> Are there any other contexts in your life in which you experience self-determined motivation?

> How can your internal feedback become more informational than controlling?
> What kind of task or intrinsically interesting goals can you adopt as a coach?

Practical Implementation of Motivation and Motivational Climate

Reflection Card

	Motivation		Date: _____
Situation	Need	Intervention	Coach's thoughts/emotions
	☐ Autonomy ☐ Competence ☐ Relatedness		

The goal of this reflective activity is to support athlete's basic needs during practice, perhaps through one of the supportive behaviours listed in Table 3.2. By thinking through how such behaviours are best executed in a coach's real-life practice, an action plan starts to develop. In the first column (*Situation*), briefly describe, either through text or picture, a specific situation where an athlete shows poor motivation. In the second column (*Need*), mark the need, of the athlete in question, deemed most pressing. This is does not have to be 100 percent accurate, but serves to frame the problem. Rather, this exercise serves as a way of trying to improve the coach's analytical skill in relation to theory, in this case SDT. In the third column (*Intervention*), describe the chosen supportive behaviour. In the fourth column (*Effect*), make a short note regarding the effects on the athlete that the supportive behaviour had (e.g., changes in emotional expression, increases or decrease in specific behaviours). First to third columns can all be completed prior to practice, as a coach probably can think of a certain familiar athlete who is likely to be unmotivated during a specific activity, and figure out what need is unsatisfied, and what would be an appropriate remedy. By doing this in advance, the cognitive burden during practice will be eased, since the coach does not need to think as much on the feet. Eventually though, it is desirable to be able to do this analysis on the fly, since that skill will be necessary for a coach to make sure that all athletes' motivation is monitored and if necessary – enhanced. The fourth column is completed during or immediately after practice, before memory fades away.

Secondary Reflection

> *Use the questions below and/or the formula for shared reflection in chapter 2.*
>
> How often did you think about athletes' motivation and searched for indicators of an athlete's motivation during the practice?
>
> Did you miss any opportunities to intervene on an athlete's motivation during the practice? If so, what was the cause that you did not seize the opportunity/made an intervention? What was the main reason for the intervention being made at the time it actually was?
>
> With the used reflection card in hand, what do you think when you look back at that specific situation and the athlete during the practice?
>
> How well could you manage to keep a 'theory' (in the shape of SDT) in the back of your mind as a starting point for your reflection during the practice?
>
> At what point of the practice was it easiest to reflect (at the start/middle/towards the end)? What is the reason for this?
>
> Compare the emotions you experienced during this practice with the emotions during a practice where you 'exclusively' focus on running the practice as normal? What similarities and differences do you find?
>
> In what way does having to think of a theory (e.g., motivational climate) influence your coaching behaviours?
>
> Did your behaviours differ compared to a practice where you only focus on running the practice as 'usual'?

Reflection Sheet

First and second columns should be completed before practice. Third to fifth columns are completed after practice.

Motivational climate Date: _____

Description of and Purpose of practice activity	*Description of TARGET-strategy in focus*	How well could the chosen TARGET-strategy be implemented compared to what you expected?	What pros and cons do you see with the implementation of the specific TARGET-strategy? (Try to think of effects for the athletes as athletes/as individual persons/as a group/for the society.)	What were your own thoughts and emotions during this part of the practice?

Reflective Summary

> When working with supportive behaviours during practice, what has been the most important learning for you?
> How are you going to capitalize on this learning in the future?
> When trying to implement a TARGET strategy during practice, what has been the most important learning for you?
> How are you going to capitalize on this learning in the future?
> From your readings of SDT, your answers to the application exercises, and your reflective activities, how would you best use SDT in your coaching?
> From your readings of AGT, your answers to the application exercises, and your reflective activities, how would you best use AGT in your coaching?

Challenging Motivational Assumptions

A month later, the coaches went into the meeting again with Ellen. Collin was a little distraught as his group had not persisted in its efforts during practice. He had been gone on a business trip for a week and a half, and apparently the athletes had coasted during his hiatus when his assistant was handed the reigns. Reports from the assistant told the story of an unfocused group.

> "I don't understand why the guys don't get it. I've tried to instil some passion in them during every practice", Collin said somewhat dejected.
> "Perhaps you've tried too hard, and they see your micromanaging as the main reason for practicing. When you're not present, they don't have the same incentive for giving their all. Could that be the case?" Ellen asked.
> "Maybe you're right. They might think of me as controlling", Collin said, looking back at Ellen.
> "Are there any other ways you could use to foster a more task-orientated motivation?" Ellen probed.
> "I guess I could try to use the TARGET strategies such as giving the guys some input into decision-making and leadership issues", Collin said.

He immediately began writing up some ways for incorporating this idea into practices. Leah said that her group had kept working and often showed up early and stayed late. However, the technical progress was absent, especially when it came to the new and more difficult skills she had introduced.

> "I get what you mean with the dangers of rewarding an intrinsically motivated behaviour. The athletes used to practice because it was fun. Now, they seem more interested in getting the points and therefore are going through the motions instead of being absorbed by the task. From now on,

I'll show positive appreciation verbally instead of using the point system for reinforcement of extra practice", Leah said regrettably.

"Do you think they'll perceive that as less controlling and more informational?" Ellen replied, in a soothing voice.

"I'll make sure that the extra effort they put in is not because I'm surveillant, but rather that they want to do it themselves", Leah responded.

"How will you do that in practice?" Ellen asked curiously.

"I can leave after practice and ask if anyone wants to stay, they just have to make sure they close the facility after they're done. In that way, they're both provided choice and given responsibility for closing. Simply more practice is not necessarily better. Particularly so, if the emphasis lays on quality execution and not just putting in some repetitions", Leah elaborated.

"Perhaps my own motivation would also be better if I didn't put so much emphasis on the standings and having to beat our opponent every weekend. I'm really upset after a defeat, and it really feels as if I'm less of a person after it happens", Collin, who again was not listening to the conversation, interrupted.

"Do you think a change of mindset when it comes to emphasis of competition will make you happier in the long run?" Ellen questioned.

"Most definitely, now Sunday mornings are real roller-coasters as I'm worrying about the outcome of the afternoon competition", he said while his face seemed to lighting up.

Quiz

1. What statement is most correct regarding SDT?
    a. The most important thing is that motivation is high regardless of the type of motivation.
    b. The type of motivation influences behaviours and thoughts and not just the degree of motivation.
    c. Intrinsic motivation needs to be complemented by extrinsic motivation in order to get the best motivation.

2. Which are the three basic needs that determine an individual's motivation?
    a. Skill, individualization, optimism.
    b. Autonomy, competence, relatedness.
    c. Happiness, fellowship, interest.

3. Which of these consequences are most likely coming from athletes' motivation being more self-determined?
    a. More creative solutions.
    b. More behaviours.
    c. More goals scored.

4. What of the following actions can a coach use to facilitate athletes' self-determined motivation?
   a. Provide performance-contingent rewards.
   b. Be a good role model.
   c. Listen to and acknowledge an athlete's feelings.
5. What statement is most correct about a mastery climate?
   a. Small groups are made up of varying skill levels.
   b. The athletes have many tasks to engage in during practice.
   c. The coach has a clear and well-built practice plan.
6. How does a high-ability athlete, used to practicing in a performance climate, view effort?
   a. High effort on easy tasks displays superiority.
   b. The more effort the better.
   c. Effort is of little value, as a highly competent athlete does not need to exert oneself.
7. What is the TARGET model?
   a. A help for coaches to create a mastery climate.
   b. A model for goal-setting.
   c. A way of reflecting as coach.
8. In what way can coaches' motivation primarily be influenced?
   a. The coach with the most skilled group of athletes will be the best motivated.
   b. Athletes' success in competition is most important to a coach's self-determined motivation.
   c. Pressure from others can be seen as controlling, thus leading to non-self-determined motivation.

References

Aelterman, N., Vansteenkiste, M., Van Keer, H., Van den Berghe, L., De Meyer, J., & Haerens, L. (2012). Students' objectively measured physical activity levels and engagement as a function of between-class and between-student differences in motivation toward physical education. *Journal of Sport and Exercise Psychology, 34,* 457–480.

Allen, J. B., & Hodge, K. (2006). Fostering a learning environment: Coaches and the motivational climate. *International Journal of Sports Science & Coaching, 1,* 261–277.

Ames, C. (1992). Classroom: Goals, structures, and student motivation. *Journal of Educational Psychology, 84,* 261–271.

Amorose, A. J. (2007). Coaching effectiveness: Exploring the relationship between coaching behavior and self-determined motivation. In M. S. Hagger, & N. L. D. Chatzisarantis (Eds.), *Intrinsic motivation and self-determination in exercise and sport* (pp. 209–227). Champaign, IL: Human Kinetics.

Balaguer, I., González, L., Fabra, P., Castillo, I., Mercé, J., & Duda, J. L. (2012). Coaches' interpersonal style, basic psychological needs and the well- and ill-being of young soccer players: A longitudinal analysis. *Journal of Sports Sciences, 30,* 1619–1629.

Baard, P. P., Deci, E. L., & Ryan, R. M. (2004). Intrinsic need satisfaction: A motivational basis of performance and well-being in two work settings. *Journal of Applied Social Psychology, 34,* 2045–2068.

Bartholomew, K. J., Ntoumanis, N., & Thørgersen-Ntoumani, C. (2009). A review of controlling motivational strategies from a self-determination theory perspective: Implications for sports coaches. *International Review of Sport and Exercise Psychology, 2,* 215–233.

Bartholomew, K., Ntoumanis, N., Mouratidis, A., Katartzi, E., Thørgersen-Ntoumani, C., & Vlachopoulos, S. (2018). Beware of your teaching style: A school-year long investigation of controlling teaching and student motivational experiences. *Learning and Instruction, 53,* 50–63.

Baxter-Jones, A. D. G., Eisenmann, J. C., & Sherar, L. B. (2005). Controlling for maturation in pediatric exercise science. *Pediatric Exercise Science, 17,* 18–30.

Brathwaite, R., Spray, C. M., & Warburton, V. E. (2011). Motivational climate interventions in physical education: A meta-analysis. *Psychology of Sport and Exercise, 12,* 628–638.

Burton, D., & Raedeke, T. D. (2008). *Sport psychology for coaches.* Champaign, Il: Human Kinetics.

Carpentier, J., & Mageau, G. A. (2013). When change-oriented feedback enhances motivation, well-being and performance: A look at autonomy-supportive feedback in sport. *Psychology of Sport and Exercise, 14,* 423–435.

Chantal, Y., Guay, F., Dobreva-Martinova, T., & Vallerand, R. J. (1996). Motivation and elite performance: An exploratory investigation with Bulgarian athletes. *International Journal of Sport Psychology, 27,* 173–182.

Conroy, D. E., & Coatsworth, J. D. (2007). Assessing autonomy-supportive coaching strategies in youth sport. *Psychology of Sport and Exercise, 8,* 671–684.

Csikszentmihalyi, M. (1990). *Flow: The psychology of optimal experience.* New York: Harper & Row.

Deci, E. L., Eghrari, H., Patrick, B. C., & Leone, D. R. (1994). Facilitating internalization: The self-determination theory perspective. *Journal of Personality, 62,* 119–142.

Deci, E. L., Koestner, R., & Ryan, R. M. (1999). A meta-analytic review of experiments examining the effects of extrinsic rewards on intrinsic motivation. *Psychological Bulletin, 125,* 627–668.

Deci, E. L., & Ryan, R. M. (1985). *Intrinsic motivation and self-determination in human behavior.* New York: Plenum.

Gerber, M., & Pühse, U. (2009). Do exercise and fitness protect against stress-induced health complaints? A review of the literature. *Scandinavian Journal of Public Health, 37,* 801–819.

Gillet, N., Berjot, S., & Gobancé, L. (2009). A motivational model of performance in the sport domain. *European Journal of Sport Science, 9,* 151–158.

Harwood, C. G., Keegan, R. J., Smith, J. M. J., & Raine, A. S. (2015). A systematic review of the intrapersonal correlates of motivational climate perceptions in sport and physical activity. *Psychology of Sport and Exercise, 18,* 9–25.

Hennessey, B. A., & Zbikowski, S. M. (1993). Immunizing children against the negative effects of reward: A further examination of intrinsic motivation training techniques. *Creativity Research Journal, 6,* 297–307.

Kazén, M., Kuhl, J., & Leicht, E.-M. (2015). When the going gets tough…: Self-motivation is associated with invigoration and fun. *Psychological Research, 79,* 1064–1076.

Knittle, K. et al. (2020). The compendium of self-enactable techniques to change and self-manage motivation and behaviour v.1.0. *Nature Human Behaviour, 4,* 215–223.

Koestner, R., Ryan, R. M., Bernieri, F., & Holt, K. (1984). Setting limits on children's behavior: The differential effects of controlling vs. informational styles on intrinsic motivation and creativity. *Journal of Personality, 52*, 233–248.

Lochbaum, M., Kazak Cetinkalp, Z., Graham, K.-A., Wright, T., & Zazo, R. (2016). Task and ego orientations in competitive sport: A quantitative review of the literature from 1989 to 2016. *Kinesiology, 48*, 3–29.

Mageau, G. A., & Vallerand, R. J. (2003). The coach-athlete relationship: A motivational model. *Journal of Sports Sciences, 21*, 883–904.

McAuley, E., & Tammen, V. V. (1989). The effects of subjective and objective competitive outcomes on intrinsic motivation. *Journal of Sport & Exercise Psychology, 11*, 84–93.

McLean, K. N., & Mallett, C. J. (2012). What motivates the motivators? An examination of sports coaches. *Physical Education and Sport Pedagogy, 17*, 21–35.

McLean, K., Mallett, C., & Newcombe, P. (2012). Assessing coach motivation: The development of the coach motivation questionnaire (CMQ). *Journal of Sport & Exercise Psychology, 34*, 184–207.

Newton, M., Duda, J. L., & Yin, Z. (2000). Examination of the psychometric properties of the perceived motivational climate in sport questionnaire-2 in a sample of female athletes. *Journal of Sports Sciences, 18*, 275–290.

Nicholls, J. G. (1978). The development of the concepts of effort and ability, perception of academic attainment, and the understanding that difficult tasks require more ability. *Child Development, 49*, 800–814.

Nicholls, J. G. (1984). Achievement motivation: Conceptions of ability, subjective experience, task choice, and performance. *Psychological Review, 91*, 328–346.

Ntoumanis, N., & Biddle, S. (1999). A review of motivational climate in physical activity. *Journal of Sports Sciences, 17*, 643–665.

Oliver, E. J., Markland, D., & Hardy, J. (2010). Interpretation of self-talk and post-lecture affective states of higher education students: A self-determination theory perspective. *British Journal of Educational Psychology, 80*, 307–323.

Pelletier, L. G., Fortier, M. S., Vallerand, R. J., & Brière, N. M. (2001). Associations among perceived autonomy support, forms of self-regulation, and persistence: A prospective study. *Motivation and Emotion, 25*, 279–306.

Pensgaard, A. M., & Roberts, G. C. (2002). Elite athletes' experiences of the motivational climate: The coach matters. *Scandinavian Journal of Medicine & Science in Sports, 12*, 54–59.

Radeke, T. D., & Smith, A. L. (2001). Development and preliminary validation of an athlete burnout measure. *Journal of Sport and Exercise Psychology, 23*, 281–306.

Reeve, J. (2013). How students create motivationally supportive learning environments for themselves: The concept of agentic engagement. *Journal of Educational Psychology, 105*, 579–595.

Reeve, J., & Deci, E. L. (1996). Elements of the competitive situation that affect intrinsic motivation. *Personality and Social Psychology Bulletin, 22*, 24–33.

Roberts, G. C. (2001). Understanding the dynamics of motivation in physical activity: The influence of achievement goals on motivational processes. In G. C. Roberts (Ed.), *Advances in motivation in sport and exercise* (pp. 1–50). Champaign, IL: Human Kinetics.

Roberts, G. C., Treasure, D. C., & Kavussanu, M. (1996). Orthogonality of achievement goals and its relationship to beliefs about success and satisfaction in sport. *The Sport Psychologist, 10*, 398–408.

Rocchi, M. A., Pelletier, L. G., & Couture, A. L. (2013). Determinants of coach motivation and autonomy supportive coaching behaviours. *Psychology of Sport and Exercise, 14*, 852–859.

Ryan, R. M. (1982). Control and information in the intrapersonal sphere: An extension of cognitive evaluation theory. *Journal of Personality and Social Psychology, 43*, 450–461.

Ryan, R. M., & Deci, E. L. (2000). Self-determination theory and the facilitation of intrinsic motivation, social development, and well-being. *American Psychologist, 55,* 68–78.

Ryan, R. M., & Deci, E. L. (2017). *Self-determination theory: Basic psychological needs in motivation and wellness.* New York: Guilford Press.

Sarrazin, P., Vallerand, R., Guillet, E., Pelletier, L., & Cury, F. (2002). Motivation and dropout in female handballers: A 21-month prospective study. *European Journal of Social Psychology, 32,* 395–418.

Schultheiss, O. C., & Brunstein, J. C. (2005). An implicit motive perspective on competence. In A. J. Elliot, & C. S. Dweck (Eds.), *Handbook of competence and motivation* (pp. 31–51). New York, NY: Guilford Press.

Sheldon, K. M., & Houser-Marko, L. (2001). Self-concordance, goal attainment, and the pursuit of happiness: Can there be an upward spiral. *Journal of Personality and Social Psychology, 80,* 152–165.

Smoll, F. L., Smith, R. E., & Cumming, S. P. (2007). Effects of a motivational climate intervention for coaches on changes in young athletes' achievement goal orientations. *Journal of Clinical Sport Psychology, 1,* 23–46.

Stormoen, S., Bjørnøy Urke, H., Eikeland Tjomsland, H., Wold, B., & Diseth, Å (2016). High school physical education: What contributes to the experience of flow? *European Physical Education Review, 22,* 355–371.

Tauer, J. M., & Harackiewicz, J. H. (2004). The effects of cooperation and competition on intrinsic motivation and performance. *Journal of Personality and Social Psychology, 86,* 849–861.

Vallerand, R. J. (2007). Intrinsic and extrinsic motivation in sport and physical activity: A review and a look at the future. In G. Tenenbaum, & R. C. Eklund (Eds.), *Handbook of sport psychology* (3rd ed., pp. 59–83). New York: Wiley.

Vallerand, R. J., Gauvin, L. I., & Halliwell, W. R. (1986). Negative effects of competition on children's intrinsic motivation. *The Journal of Social Psychology, 126,* 649–656.

Vansteenkiste, M., & Deci, E. L. (2003). Competitively contingent rewards and intrinsic motivation: Can losers remain motivated? *Motivation and Emotion, 27,* 273–299.

4
COACHING BEHAVIOURS

Aim of the chapter: Develop an understanding of coaching behaviours and its effects on athletes.

Theoretical learning goals of the chapter:
Grow an understanding of...

1. different sorts of coaching behaviours.
2. the four I's of transformational coaching.
3. how athletes' behavioural problems can be handled.
4. how silence is used by the coach.
5. how athlete factors (skill/position, gender, age) influence coaching behaviour.
6. how situational factors (competition, stress) influence coaching behaviour.
7. how coach factors (expectations, self-efficacy) influence coaching behaviour.
8. five main areas that coaches impact athletes in.

Practical learning goals of the chapter:

1. Become able to increase positive reinforcement during practice by using the reflection card.
2. Become able to deliberately use one specific behaviour for social competence during practice by using the reflection sheet.

Vignette

After a long practice, Collin entered the room where Leah and Ellen already had started conversating. "How was practice?" Leah asked Collin.

"I think it went very well", he quickly replied. "The lads ran every drill with laser-like precision".

"What do you mean?" Ellen asked.

"With the current group, I can just stand back and watch. It's been like that for a few months now. Everything is so smooth during our practices. We hardly ever waste any time talking and standing around. All I do is move some cones and call out the name of the drills", Collin said with a smile that did a poor job concealing how proud he was of himself.

"That's a big contrast to my practices", Leah said with a sigh.

"Elaborate", Ellen requested.

"Well, you know I think we should be progressing much quicker. By now, we should be at a totally different level", she answered.

"I've all my practices pre-planned two weeks in advance", Collin interjected.

"Why would you do that?" Leah asked confoundedly.

"I detail the plan for the guys in advance and that keeps them focused", Collin explained.

"Anyway", Ellen interrupted trying to get the focus back to Leah, "what do you normally do during the practice?"

"It feels like I'm instructing all the time. I don't think I could do anything more than that", Leah added.

"Could it be that you overcoach?" Ellen probed.

"Maybe, I don't know. Coaches should be active, shouldn't they?" Leah wondered.

"Well, perhaps, but do you think you have a good balance between observing and intervening during practices?" Ellen questioned.

"When I start to observe, I always find some stuff that could be improved, and then I feel the need to intervene", Leah replied.

"You really need a detailed practice plan. If you have that, the athletes will have a much easier time progressing, and you can stand back a little more, right after you got a drill going after your instructions", Collin spoke up suddenly.

"Do you have any suggestion what you could do to improve?" Ellen asked Leah.

"What do you say about observing one of my practices a few times until our next meeting?" Collin quickly added.

Leah nodded.

"Alright, I'll show you some tricks", Collin said confidently.

 What do you think of the way Collin and Leah talk about their coaching behaviours?

How do you think Collin and Leah, respectively, view a coach's role?

Coaching Behaviours in General

In general, coaches have been found to be quite unaware of their own coaching behaviours. Comparisons between coaches, athletes and third-party observers oftentimes show diverging perceptions. This is especially substantial when it comes to positive behaviours. Coaches tend to overestimate the frequency of their positive behaviours. Negative coaching behaviours are less frequent and likely more salient in the coaches' memory, as it should be easier in retrospect to distinguish between zero and one occurrences compared to discriminating between 15 and 20 occurrences (Millar, Oldham, & Donovan, 2011; Smoll & Smith, 1989). Even though negative behaviours in general occur more seldom than positive, the former seem to make a more profound impact on the athletes compared to the latter. Graziano, Brothen, and Berscheid (1980) claimed that negative behaviours (i.e., criticism) from leaders were more salient to followers than positive. There is an evolutionary advantage of being alert on negative behaviours from others, as they might indicate danger. Possibilities of future interaction with the person providing the negative behaviour makes it advantageous to be aware of what renders criticism, since this would aid in avoiding harm.

Consequently, the balance between positive and negative behaviours is important for the individual athlete. It is similar to a bank account where frequent deposits (i.e., positive behaviours) allows a withdrawal (i.e., negative behaviours) every now and then, while the opposite makes for a negative and unsustainable balance. Thompson (2003) argues in favour of a ratio of at least 5:1 of positive to negative behaviours for a coach. For pedagogical purposes, coaching behaviours are divided below into two sections, *sport-specific* and *social competence*. Naturally, those should not be viewed as mutually exclusive, but rather integrative and complementary.

'Sport Specific' Behaviours

Coaches use plenty of behaviours for athletes' improvement of sport-specific skills. Smith and Smoll (2007) have been very influential in their work focusing on coaches' responses to athlete's performances. Their work is one of the very few evidence-based coaching educations (Langan, Blake, & Lonsdale, 2013). Through extensive observational studies, Smith and Smoll found that coaches use *reactive* and *spontaneous* behaviours. The former is used after a successful or a failed attempt from an athlete. The latter is emitted from the coach with no apparent athlete's action preceding it. Additionally, when a coach shouts some direction towards the whole group or a single athlete in anticipation of an upcoming technique, decision-making, etc., that is considered spontaneous behaviour. In total, 12 different coaching behaviours are displayed in Table 4.1, (two reactive to desirable performance, five reactive to mistakes, one reactive to misbehaviour, three spontaneous sport-related, one

TABLE 4.1 Categorization of 'sport-specific' coaching behaviours in relation to athletes' behaviours.

Type of behaviour	Example
Reactive behaviours	
After a successful performance from an athlete	
Reinforcement	'You had a relaxed stroke during the entire race, very good.'
Non-reinforcement	A coach ignoring a nice tackle in football.
After a failed performance from an athlete	
Encouragement	'Next time you will succeed in executing that technique.'
Instruction	'You need to keep your head up whenever we're on the attack.'
Punishment	'You have such a bad posture during your routine that you will have to do some laps around the gym.'
Punitive instruction	'How many times have I told you moron to extend your wrist when shooting a shot?'
Ignoring mistake	A coach says nothing after a dislodging of the bar in high jumping.
After a misbehaviour from an athlete	
Keeping control	'Hey! You cannot pull him in the hair like that!'
Spontaneous behaviours	
General instruction	'Remember that when we lose possession of the ball, we need to retreat as quick as possible to our defensive positions'.
General encouragement	'Come on girls, give it all you got in the final set!'
Organization	A coach moves cones for an upcoming drill.
Sport-irrelevant	A coach talks to a spectator.

spontaneous sport-irrelevant). Interestingly, the underlying dimensions that the overt behaviours registered by a third-party observer make up are not identical to the dimensions that emerge from questionnaire reports from the athletes. Apparently, the perception is not exactly the 'reality' when it comes to the athletes experiencing their coach's behaviour.

 What kind of performance/skill failure from an athlete is a 'big no-no' for you as a coach?
How do you react when that happens?
In what alternative ways could you react?
How would this alternative reaction impact the athlete?

> How can you enhance the way (amount or quality) of positive reinforcement after an athlete's successful performance?
> How would you go about this?
> What kind of challenges do you perceive that may hinder you from enhancing your positive reinforcement?

Sport-specific coaching behaviours are not constrained to the provision of feedback and reactions to athletes' actions. Other important coaching behaviours are related to planning and execution of various aspects within the sport. For this reason, Côté and colleagues (1999) proposed several areas for coaching behaviours, such as *physical training and conditioning, technical skills, mental preparation, goal setting* and *competition strategies*, which are examined briefly below.

Physical Training & Conditioning

This area has a long history in sports and coaching, which is clearly beyond the scope of this text. Some brief points are warranted, though. Planning is at the centre of attention for physical conditioning, emanating from periodization of work load according to different models (Oliveira et al., 2018). However, as Kiely (2012) pointed out in his critique of mechanistic views of work load responses, generic models are limited in their usefulness. This is especially so for coaches working within amateur or youth contexts. Those athletes seldom have the all-out commitment as sports might not be the top priority competing with family, school and labour activities among others. Hence, it is difficult adhering to a strict work load plan. Still, having a plan that is very flexible might be the way to go, with continuous evaluation considering both the progress and the availability of the athlete.

The physical dimension in sport is divided into five distinct areas: endurance, strength, power/speed, flexibility and gross motor skill. Some physical dimensions (e.g., strength and endurance) seem to inhibit each other's development (Leveritt, Abernethy, Barry, & Logan, 1999). Also, the physical demands of the specific sport impact the importance the coach places on different areas. Finally, if the athletes are very young, they will benefit from more age-appropriate all-round training rather than a narrower sport-specific physical focus. Practice planning is of course important for developing other areas than physical fitness, such as technical skills.

Technical Skills

Much has been written over the years about technical skills in sports and many coaches see technical skill development as their primary task. Two different views on skill acquisition have been very influential for coaches. *Information-processing theories* (Schmidt, 2003) suggest similarities to a computer where a motor programme is drilled repeatedly until it is so well learnt that it is later retrievable. Like the computer having large storage capacity for small bits of information, an athlete may benefit from practicing parts of a movement and then put them together later on. Here, the coach has to know the proper way to sequence and progress drills and techniques for optimal athlete development. In contrast, *dynamical systems theory* proposes that an individual has the capacity to self-organize a complex system that consists of the entire body, including emotions and cognitions (Davids, Button, & Bennett, 2008). From this view point, the constraints within the individual, environment and task itself constitute affordances that allow the skill to 'emerge'. Here, the coach has to manage and adapt these constraints to elicit the optimal movement from the athlete.

An important issue deserving attention is that of movement goal. Gentile (1972) makes a distinction between *open* and *closed* skills. The former consists of constantly varying parameters and factors. Meanwhile, the latter is subject to few (if any) changes from one repetition to another and the conditions are well-known in advance. Open and closed skills are not dichotomous, rather make up opposite end points on a continuum. A one-timer in ice hockey is a very open skill as the pass will have different inherent features every time, such as velocity, height and angle. In addition, the player has to take into account opponents' different positions, including the goaltender, as well as different ice surface conditions and distances to the goal. Comparingly, a skill such as an indoor long jump is more closed, as conditions like length of run-up, take-off foot and pit are identical every time. Of course, the score of the competition and standings will vary from one time to another, thus making hardly any skill exactly identical in its preconditions. Anyhow, where a skill is identified on the continuum between open and closed determines whether it is more fruitful to aim for generalization or automatization of a skill. In open skills, the athletes' benefit from being able to generalize the skill so that it is functional under many different circumstances. The success of the skills is determined by the consequences of the movement (e.g., a weak shot between the goaltender's legs that goes into the net is better than a powerful slap shot striking the goaltender on the pads). Contrastingly, in a sport like artistic gymnastics, it is imperative to automatize a routine, as the movement objective is the movement itself as this is given points by the judges. Gentile warns against goal-confusion, where the objective of the movement is mistaken such as when an athlete is asked to imitate a coach rather than successfully solve the movement problem of an open skill. Another important part of technical skill development highlighted in much literature is feedback (see Chapter 6).

Mental Preparation

A coach can prepare the athletes mentally right before competitions, but it is wise to use deliberate long-term work and not only last-minute actions. Before competition, athletes have been shown to have somewhat deviating opinions from coaches when it comes to pre-game speech content. However, these studies have not examined the impact on actual performance during competition, only preferences (Breakey et al., 2009; Vargas & Short, 2011) and perceived effect on efficacy beliefs (Vargas-Tonsing & Bartholomew, 2006). Athletes' preferences might be influenced by traditional views on sports that fuel expectations of speeches like Al Pacino in the movie *Any Given Sunday*, even if it is not facilitating performance. Further confusing the issue, different sports will likely have different optimal levels of arousal depending on use of fine or gross motor skills. A sport like archery will probably have a much lower optimum than a sport like weight lifting (Landers & Arent, 2006).

Turning to long-term mental skills development, mental toughness is a highly sought-after characteristic. Coaches from both individual and team sports have brought up several ideas on how to build mental toughness. Among them are creating intense and competition-like physical practices, providing learning opportunities either through drills, conversations, or observations, and finally, creating a confident atmosphere with high expectations (Weinberg, Butt & Culp, 2011). Another important area of mental preparation is being able to focus, and particularly under pressure. Singer, Lidor, and Cauraugh (1993) developed an effective five-step approach to self-paced tasks. This approach consists of a) readying; b) imagine the act; c) focus on external cue; d) execute without thought; e) evaluate the act. For execution of dynamic skills, vast research also suggests the advantages of having an external focus compared to focusing on the body (Wulf, 2013). This is accomplished by the coach drawing the athlete's attention to external cues or metaphors during skill execution (see Chapter 5).

Goal-setting

Goals are most effective when they are moderately challenging, spanning both short- and long-term and specific in a way that they are measurable. Publicly stated goals have also been found to have a greater impact than private goals (Kyllo & Landers, 1995). More proximal goals are more effective than more distal as are goals that aim to develop competence rather than demonstrating superiority (Oettingen & Gollwitzer, 2009). The level of goal commitment determines if it is most advantageous by looking forward on future work or back on past accomplishments. Thinking about prior achievements enhances motivation for a goal the individual is poorly committed to, while how much progress is still left until reaching goal enhances motivation for a highly committed goal. Temporally distant goals seem to induce more abstract goal representations and lead the individual to benefit from focusing on how much work is to be done rather than prior achievements (Fishbach, 2009). Goals that are congruent with the person's self are perceived as easier and will lead to more positive experiences compared to goals that aim to avoid something or are chosen to please someone else. Common mistakes when using goals are to set too many, too difficult, too far away into the future, or that multiple goals are in conflict with each other (Koestner et al., 2002). A common issue in group work is social loafing where an athlete does not exert as much effort as possible when more people are involved as it might be difficult to identify a particular athlete's contribution. To remedy this, goals at group level should be complemented by individual goals. Commitment to goals consists of how much an athlete wants to achieve the goal, and also to what extent the athlete believes the goal is achievable and both are beneficial to enhance (Locke & Latham, 2013).

Competition Strategies

This area includes having a pre-planned routine that describes how the competition will be handled. Naturally, there is a huge difference in the competitions faced by an eight year old making a competition debut and an Olympic athlete. However, a sense of security will reduce anxiety for both. For the eight year old, this could be accomplished by having a familiar face (i.e., coach) greet the athlete at the venue, while for the Olympian, having competed at the venue and slept at the hotel a year before might serve the same purpose. At the stage of the competition, the preparations are done and there it is 'only' a matter of feeling good and being in sync to be able to get the most out of one's capacity (Raglin, 2001).

In addition to having a routine for the competition, a coach also needs to be able to react to the changing conditions during a competition, such as an opponent taking the lead, bad weather or an unfair decision made by the referee. To handle setbacks or pressure, athletes have different coping strategies at disposal. Typically, these are defined as problem-focused or emotion-focused (Lazarus & Folkman, 1984). The former are directed at the sources of the distress, while the latter are concerned with managing the emotions caused by the distress. Problem-focused strategies are most useful when the issue is under the person's control (e.g., having the coach design a specific set-play for a tough situation, using the help of teammates when a predetermined problem comes up). Meanwhile, emotion-focused strategies are better when the issue is uncontrollable, for example, using positive self-talk or interpreting arousal signals constructively (Moran 2012). Classical sport psychology has tended to focus on regulation of emotional response, whereas Cognitive Behavioural Therapy and Acceptance and Commitment Therapy are more focused on the problem itself (Beck, 2011). Rather than one size-fits all, both approaches are useful for a coach to have some knowledge in to be able to help the athletes in the best possible way before and during competitions.

In the peer-reviewed literature, little attention is paid to the effectiveness of time-outs that are present in many team sports and some individual sports (e.g., table tennis). In sports where coaches have a large impact on in-competition decisions, such as American football and basketball, timeouts are usually given a significant role by coaches themselves, although empirical evidence does not always back up their assumptions (Kozar et al., 1993). Moreover, athletes' working memory has limited storage space (Cowan, 2001). Athletes' arousal level during competition is commonly higher than optimal for cognitive tasks, and memory capacity shrinks even more. Perhaps, it is wise for a coach to limit instructions during time-outs to one unit of information. A coach taking the 'less is more approach' will have a greater lucidity and inject the athletes some confidence, rather than going over plenty of information that is not being put into successful use. By focusing on a smaller number of things during a timeout the possibilities of crisp execution are elevated and consequently greater perceptions of success.

> From the areas of coaching behaviour described above, which one or two areas are your strongest areas?
> How can you capitalize on these strengths even more?
> Which one or two areas are your weakest?
> What kind of resources would you have to draw upon in order to improve these areas (e.g., mediated, unmediated learning situations)?

'Social Competence' Behaviours

This kind of coaching behaviours revolves around the full range of leadership model (Bass & Riggio, 2006). This framework conceptualizes leadership along two dimensions: effectiveness and level of activity from the leader (see Figure 4.1). Transformational leadership is viewed as the most effective style that is accomplished by an active leader. Less effective and somewhat active is the transactional

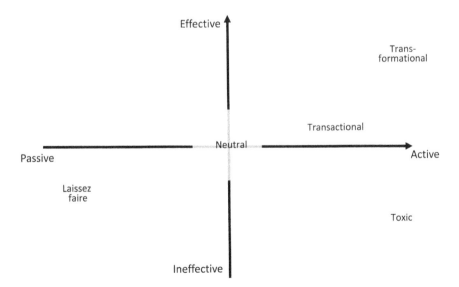

FIGURE 4.1 Different leadership styles related to effectiveness and activity of a leader.

leadership. Neither effective nor active is the neutral leadership style. The least active and very ineffective leadership style is *Laissez faire*. Meanwhile, a leader's behaviour that is very ineffective, but active is characterized as toxic. Over the past two decades, this framework, or variations of it, has been highly popular for studying leadership (Avolio et al., 2009; Turnnidge & Côté, 2016). Additionally, it has recently been used in interventions for sport coaches with promising results (Turnnidge & Côté, 2017; Vella, Oades & Crowe, 2013). Transformational leadership is made up of four components (4 I's). The 4 I's are *idealized influence, individualized consideration, intellectual stimulation* and *inspirational motivation*. Below, each style is described as it pertains to coaching. Of course, it is possible, and even likely, that a coach shifts from one style to another through the full range of leadership.

Toxic

A coach using toxic leadership is highly active, although the energy is not put to best use for the outcome of the athletes. Toxic coaching behaviour occurs when the coach has a negative attitude or negative feelings towards the athletes. This includes behaviours such as expressing anger or hostility, or modelling antisocial behaviours. Yelling at or threatening athletes are other prime examples of this leadership style. The intention of toxic behaviours is often to instil winning attitudes and promote competitiveness. Instead, athletes' development is negatively influenced through hampered motivation and well-being.

Laissez Faire

Laissez faire coaching is manifested in shown disinterest or ambivalence towards the athletes or practice activities. This kind of behaviour is often characterized by a hands-off leadership. It includes paying attention to something else than the athletes or the practice itself, or an avoidance of decision-making. Rather than focusing on practice issues, the coach may be more engaged in his/her cell phone or talk to spectators. Comparing Laissez faire to the toxic style, they are similarly ineffective, while the biggest difference is the coach's activity level.

Neutral

Neutral coaching consists of the coach being occupied with the pure mechanics of the practice without any extra commitment. This is characterized by distance towards the athletes and few emotions or an interest that is best described as neutral. Examples of this type of coaching includes constantly moving cones, only giving the athletes instruction on how to organize during drills (compared to providing feedback on their execution of skills), and provision of brief general descriptive feedback compared to more specific feedback and engaging interactions. In some way, this could be interpreted as an absence of leadership and lack of passion.

Transactional

Transactional coaching behaviours are intended to reinforce hierarchical structures between coach and athlete through an enhanced perception of authority (i.e., the coach has the means that the athlete needs). A coach acting this way reinforces athlete behaviour and expectations, often by mentioning rewards and punishments. The coach is focused on errors and mistakes, and much of the coaching is focused on monitoring performance standards in relation to the athletes' achievements. Tangible rewards are often used such as for the athlete who won a mini-competition during practice or scored the most goals. The rewards are anything from objects to more subtle social reinforcers such as head-nods.

Transformational

Transformational leadership influences the followers through various ways that go deeper than rewards and trading of favours do. Instead, the leader acts as a role model, inspiring, stimulating and caring for each individual. Through the leader's actions, the followers want to emulate the leader and exert extra effort to show their support. If a leader uses a transformational style, followers will evolve into leading themselves (Bass & Riggio, 2006). Thus, of the styles presented, transformational leadership is the most effective. Furthermore, it is possible to develop (Kelloway & Barling, 2000). Recently, Turnnidge and Côté (2019) conducted thorough investigations of transformational leadership behaviours in the sporting domain. They found eleven types of behaviours classified as transformational. Below, a brief description of the 4 I's of transformational leadership is provided.

Idealized Influence

The leader acts as a role model for the followers. By doing this, followers want to emulate the leader, who is admired, respected and trusted. An important aspect is that the leader is willing to take risks for the greater good. The leader displays highly ethical and moral values and conduct. Followers trust the leader to do what is right in a consistent manner. Sometimes, followers attribute special capabilities to the leader and hold him/her in high regard (Bass, 1998). Two coaching behaviours were described by Turnnidge and Côté (2019), which are in italics, with corresponding examples provide after each.

1. *Talking about and modelling prosocial values and behaviours*
    - Do what is right rather than take the easy way out
    - Demonstrate personal values

2. *Showing vulnerability and humility*
    - Apologize for own mistakes
    - Share personal experiences

Inspirational Motivation

The leader provides meaning for tasks to the followers, who are also challenged in a positive manner. By providing an attractive future state that is shared by the followers, the leader increases team spirit. Positive expectations on the followers are important, signalling they can accomplish tremendous achievements. Through clear communication, the leader displays enthusiasm and optimism (Bass, 1998). Four coaching behaviours were identified by Turnnidge and Côté (2019):

1. *Talking about goals*
    - Create a shared understanding of where you are at going and how to get there
2. *Expressing confidence in the athletes' capacity*
    - Encourage the athletes to believe in themselves
    - Clarify when the athletes have reached their goal
3. *Implementing a collective vision for the group*
    - Connect the athletes to the group by using symbols and stories
4. *Providing meaningful and challenging tasks and roles*
    - Present rationales and explanations for tasks, roles and rules
    - Enhance the athletes' understanding for actions and tasks during practice and competition

Intellectual Stimulation

The leader stimulates followers' intellect to be creative and challenge assumptions. By reframing problems into opportunities, followers may see new aspects than. By no means, the leader publicly criticizes faults from followers, as mistakes are viewed as stepping-stones along the journey of improvement. Creative approaches are encouraged and solicited. This is true even when followers' ideas diverge from those of the leader (Bass, 1998). Three coaching behaviours were described by Turnnidge and Côté (2019):

1. *Eliciting athletes' input*
    - Encourage athletes to contribute new and alternative ideas
2. *Sharing decision-making*
    - Provide opportunities for the athletes to lead activities or help others

3. *Emphasizing the learning process*
   - Encourage the athletes to engage in challenging tasks
   - Value effort and learning instead of only focusing on outcome

Individualized Consideration

The leader creates a supportive environment where each individual has the opportunity to improve and grow as a person. An acceptance of individual difference is displayed by the leader, where different needs from different people are taken into account during interactions. This is demonstrated when a leader remembers something personal about a follower during an interaction, regardless if this is a connection to a previous conversation or a question about his/her family members. Tasks are delegated to followers, although the leader still, in a non-intrusive manner, monitors progress standing ready to provide additional support or direction if necessary (Bass, 1998). Two coaching behaviours were described by Turnnidge and Côté (2019):

1. *Showing interest in the athletes' emotions and their personal world*
   - Adjust activities to fit the athletes' individual needs
   - Show genuine regard and care for aspects of athletes' life both within and outside of sport
2. *Paying attention to the contributions of performances and unique contributions from athletes*
   - Provide feedback on both sport-specific and nonsport-specific behaviours
   - Make regular use of the phrase 'thank you'

Which one of the 4 I's do you currently use in your coaching practice?
Which one of the 4 I's could you use more of in your coaching practice?
How would you go about implementing this behaviour?
What type of challenges do you envision when trying to implement this behaviour?

Turnnidge and Côté (2019) suggested that sport-specific and social competence behaviours could be integrated. For example, a coach can respond to an athlete trying to improve athletic stance in a variety of manners including both sport-specific instruction and a social dimension. 'Your base of support gives you too little balance, how could you improve that?' (Intellectual stimulation). 'If you widen your base of support, you can get into the competition this weekend' (transactional). 'What don't you understand, stop standing with your feet so narrowly together!' (toxic). Again, the athlete's perception of the coach's behaviour is what counts (Smoll & Smith, 1989).

When to Use Specific Behaviours

In order for an athlete to have a reasonable chance to execute a skill or behaviour successfully, it is necessary to have realistic expectations. Although expectations should be high, simultaneously the athlete has to be able to reach them. If not, positive reinforcement will be scarce, and many times athletes report a desire for more positive feedback. Furthermore, a coach can use *shaping* (i.e., positive reinforcement even if the preceding behaviour is not perfectly executed), as long as the behaviour is approaching the goal-behaviour and closer then previous attempts. Shaping provides positive reinforcement as an encouragement that the athlete should keep working and information that the athlete is on the right track. As the athlete progresses, the approximation of the desired goal will need to improve successively, in order to elicit further positive feedback from the coach (Smith, 2006). Importantly, effort should be reinforced regardless of successful outcomes. In reaction to an unsuccessful performance, encouragement is advocated. Another important note is to, at all costs, avoid hostile, aggressive or punitive instructions. Still, all too many coaches resort to using physical punishments, such as push-ups or running laps, in response to failed performances. By using a physical activity as a consequence of an unsuccessful performance, the athlete will associate this activity with negative emotions, which will present a problem when the coach wants to use the same activity for training purposes (e.g., doing push-ups to strengthen the upper body). Further possible consequences of using punishments are provided by Albrecht (2009), such as wasted practice time on executing the punishments instead of developmental activities, increased performance anxiety, lowered risk-taking as fear of failure is increased, and severe damage to the relationship between coach and athlete.

Intriguingly, there is a potential problem when evaluating the effects of punishment, though. After an uncharacteristically poor performance an athlete is likely, on a statistical basis, to return to 'normal' level because the poor performance was out of norm. If the coach used punishment (e.g., given the athlete an earful) following the poor performance, that 'improvement' can be interpreted as if punishments are indeed effective. Conversely, if an athlete has a terrific performance and the coach provides positive feedback, subsequently, it is likely to see a drop in the athlete's performance because the previous one was 'a little too good' and not representative of 'real ability'. Perhaps the normal performance fluctuation was a little larger than usual (at least partly) due to external influences, such as optimal weather conditions, strategies used by the opponent or simply pure luck. Anyway, a decrease in performance can lead the coach to the conclusion that positive feedback is bad for performance, maybe through reasoning that the athlete has become complacent or needs to be threatened to be alert. This phenomenon is called *regression fallacy*. It means that eventually, everything will return to the norm, regardless of outer influences, but our judgement might lead us to believe that an exceptional event (either better or worse than normal) might be in line with a new trend, rather than a single deviation from the norm

(Kahneman, 2011). This is an excellent example of how important it is to use more systematic data (as provided by research), than just anecdotal or self-experienced episodes.

Effective coaching is likely to be characterized by deliberate and predictable patterns of behaviours (Erickson et al., 2011). The athletes need to be able to predict a coach's behaviour in order to feel comfortable and have a grasp of what to expect during practice. Too much unpredictability in a coach's behaviour will be ineffective as athletes become insecure about what they should do in order to please the coach. Also, a lot of time needs to be spent silently observing. Research has been equivocal on coaches' usage of silence. Still, it remains one of the most common categories of coaching behaviours. Early on, silence was primarily interpreted as the coach being off-task (Claxton, 1988). Later studies have found coaches to be highly engaged in the practice while silent and have proposed a more deliberate usage of silence where the coach is contemplating, observing and analysing the next step. A common cycle for coaches consists of starting up a practice activity, observing and intervening, followed by new observation. (Cushion & Jones, 2001; Rupert & Buschner, 1989). Silence can also be used to encourage the athletes to use their intrinsic feedback and learn to take responsibility for their own learning (Smith & Cushion, 2006).

> How do you use shaping?
> How do you use silence during practice (e.g., purpose, thoughts, emotions)?

Behavioural Problems from Athletes

Sometimes an athlete misbehaves unacceptably. Behaviours that qualify in this category are unrelated to sport specific performance. Instead, they are socially problematic, such as fighting, being late for practice or teasing another athlete. In such cases, a coach needs to keep control.

Both positive and negative reinforcements increase the probability for the preceding behaviour occurring in the future (see Figure 4.2). However, negative reinforcement has the potential to lead to more negative emotional and cognitive reactions for the athlete compared to positive reinforcement (i.e., it is much better to do something in order to *achieve* or *reach* a positive consequence, rather than to *avoid* a negative consequence). Punishment decreases the likelihood for the behaviour to occur again, but for punishments to be effective, three conditions must to be met: a) immediate, b) highly aversive and c) always present. It will be hard to consistently meet all three. Additionally, punishments will elicit negative emotions within the athlete and the coach will role model aggressive behaviour. In comparison, *response cost* is an advantageous alternative (upper right box in Figure 4.2). Response cost implies taking away something the athlete values.

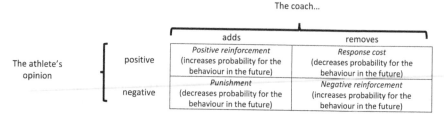

FIGURE 4.2 Four possible responses from coaches to athletes' behaviours.

This decreases the likelihood for the preceding behaviour to be repeated in the future, but without many negative side-effects of punishments. Even if response cost can create strong emotional reactions from the athlete, these are more temporary. Additionally, fear is easier to avoid compared to when using punishment (Smith & Smoll, 2012).

Aside from removing something positive in the eyes of the athlete, two conditions need to be satisfied for the consequence to work as response cost: a) the response cost needs to be logically connected to the misbehaviour and b) the response cost needs to be connected in time to the misbehaviour. Thus, if the coach chooses to withdraw Christmas gifts for an athlete who was late to repeated practices in May, this consequence is neither connected by logic nor time to the misbehaviour. Therefore, this consequence will have more of punishments' negative effects rather than a response cost (Smith, 2006). Perhaps, a more logical response cost is that athletes late for practice have to warm up by themselves on the side-line, while the rest of the group partake in a playful game (that the late athlete really likes), since the late athlete would not be physically ready to join the game before being warmed up, as a rationale provided to the athlete.

Another method to counter behavioural problems is *token economy*. The coach and the athlete agree on a system of token rewards that are to be earned whenever a desirable behaviour is performed (e.g., showing up to practice on time). A predetermined number of tokens can then be exchanged for a reward the athlete is interested in (i.e., the coach adds something positive). This way of postponing the real reinforcer makes it easier for an athlete to adhere to a behaviour that is otherwise nonattractive. By using the token economy, the athlete gets more repetitions of an acceptable behaviour. Token economies have been used successfully with severe behavioural problems. Clear consequences of this kind are more effective in changing problem behaviour, then lecturing or nagging (McGoey & DuPaul, 2000). To enhance the adherence and acceptance from the athletes to team rules, *sanctions by reciprocity* is suggested. This means the athlete will be able to decide when he/she is ready to behave in an acceptable manner and when so – return to the activity (Toner, Moran & Gale, 2016). Moran (2012) also highlights advantages of letting the athletes participate in construction of team rules. In such discussions, the coach can allow the athletes to come up with suggestions for consequences of breaking a rule.

> Describe a common behavioural problem in your sport.
> What kind of response cost or token economy would be appropriate to decrease the likelihood of this behaviour occurring again?

Factors Impacting Coaching Behaviours

Some of the more prominent aspects of each of the three interactive factors of coaching (athlete, situation, coach) will be examined below. In comparison to the findings of outcomes for sport specific and social competence behaviours, the research investigating how different factors influence coaching behaviour is more scattered across many areas. These findings rest mostly on fewer number of studies, and in many cases just a single one. Hence, this section should be viewed as more tentative, serving as food for thought for coaches to put into their own perspective.

Athletes

Position/Skill/Psychological Characteristics

In a study of handball players, goalkeepers reported significantly higher levels of anxiety compared to players at other positions (Meeûs, Serpa & De Cuyper, 2010). The authors speculated this was caused by goalkeepers' isolated playing position. Some coaches noted that they forgot about the goalkeepers, instead opting to focus on the outfield players. Coaches were found by Leonard, Ostrosky, and Huchendorf (1990) being recruited from the most central playing positions on the field as athletes. Thus, coaches likely have a harder time identifying with positions or roles they have not had themselves.

In contrast to athlete's position, skill levels are examined more thoroughly, with athletes usually divided into high vs. low expectancy groups or starter vs. nonstarter. Markland and Martinek (1988) found that starters received more positive and negative feedback than non-starters. They proposed that the coaches preferred to spend more time on the better players as these athletes are key to coaches' competitive success, and therefore need to be kept in shape, satisfied etc.

To the contrary, lesser skilled athlete may be given positive feedback as a 'consolation prize'. Hence, athletes risk interpreting overly large amounts of positive feedback as the coach feeling sorry for them, especially so, if feedback is non-contingent or too general (Horn, 1985). Highly anxious athletes are especially sensitive for punitive feedback and desire higher amount of positive and informational feedback (Horn et al., 2011).

Gender

Gender differences are easy to exaggerate, as many popular opinions through media and folk theories are expressed in this direction. However, there are some differences, albeit often quite small. Some of these differences could very well be artefacts of historically masculine perspectives on sports.

Given that females generally report somewhat lower self-esteem (Kling et al., 1999), the finding that coaches have a larger impact on athletes with lower self-esteem is noteworthy (Coatsworth & Conroy, 2006; Smoll et al., 1993). How low self-esteem influences coach's behaviour is unclear, but it is plausible that an athlete with lower self-esteem will either elicit more empathy from the coach or be met with antipathy, due to the coach thinking that the athlete is not developing/extroverted as one 'should'.

Girls seem to receive less feedback on their performance (Black & Weiss, 1992), although their own perception is a higher frequency of feedback (Smith & Smoll, 2007). One possible explanation is that coaches provide more unspecific feedback to girls (e.g., 'Good job') that is noncontingent of their actual performance. Another potential explanation for these correlations is that girls in general might be more vigilant on the environment, whereas boys are more focused on their own performance, thus missing a lot of feedback from the coach, although Moreno, Cervelló, and Gonzalez-Cutre (2008) found no gender differences in dispositional flow. More research is clearly needed to uncover gender differences in perceived feedback.

Girls prefer coaches who to a larger extent emphasize enjoyment, whereas boys prefer coaches that emphasize fitness, performance and challenge. While both genders prefer democratic coaching, this preference is even more pronounced among girls (Martin et al, 1999; Martin, Dale & Jackson, 2001). In line with this, boys have reported higher ego-orientation, and are more likely to report participating in a performance climate. (Moreno et al., 2008). This is either due to boys eliciting more performance climate behaviours from the coaches perhaps through their disposition, or they perceive coaches' behaviour more in this way.

In general, boys get more encouragement from family members to participate in sports compared to girls. In relation to girls, boys perceive themselves as more competent in sport (Fredricks & Eccles, 2005). This is an important issue for a coach to try to counteract. Instead of assuming that girls always have the same opportunities to participate in logistically difficult practices or competition (time of day, distance, etc), a coach might prove valuable in encouraging even a small sacrifice from a young female athlete (or her parents).

Age

Coatsworth and Conroy (2006) found that younger athletes' self-esteem (below 12 years old) was more influenced by a coach than older athletes. Contradictingly, Black and Weiss (1992) found that athletes aged 12–18 were more influenced than 10–11-year-olds. Evidently, what age of athletes is most impacted by coaching is still unclear.

Athletes aged eight to nine years old, differentiate between better and worse coaches on the provision of punishment and punitive behaviour. Slightly older athletes (ten to twelve years old), categorize primarily on the basis of a coach's positive reinforcement and encouragement. Meanwhile, as athletes become older (13–15-year-olds), they value amount of and quality of instruction more than other coaching behaviours (Smith & Smoll, 2007).

Riemer (2007) reported that with increasing age, athletes' preference for positive feedback decrease, while more social support is preferred, although others have provided somewhat ambiguous results (Høigaard, Jones & Peters, 2008). It is quite possible that older athletes have learnt to rely more on intrinsic feedback rather than the coaches' feedback. Arguably, the rigours and pressure experienced at higher levels will put more emphasize on social support structures compared to youth sport's participation for fun.

Finally, humour has been proposed to be favourable for enhancing learning for younger athletes, whereas older ones, easily perceive jokes from a coach as non-serious and possibly ineffective (Burke, Peterson & Nix, 1995).

> In what way do you think that the athletes' characteristics influence your coaching behaviours (skill/position/psychological characteristics/gender/age)?

Situation

Competition

Walters, Schulter, Oldham, Thomson, and Payne (2012) found comparatively high rates of negative coaching behaviours (over 20% of all behaviours coded) when studying side-line behaviours during competitions. Even higher rates of negative behaviours were used by male coaches and towards male athletes. This is obviously a troublesome finding giving cause for concern. Naturally, a coach who has an ego-orientation (see Chapter 3) will probably be more stressed-out during competitions as this will be viewed as highly threatening. In line with effects of a performance climate, Bolter and Weiss (2013) showed that coaches who prioritized winning to a large extent had athletes who displayed more anti-social behaviours towards both teammates and opponents. This could be an effect of favourable social comparisons being so valuable that athletes are prepared to cheat even a friend.

Smith, Shoda, Cumming, and Smoll (2009) examined how score of competition interacted with coaching behaviour to influence athletes' liking of their coach. When the score was tied, no difference was found between behaviours of most and least liked coaches. Contrastingly, when the athletes were behind, negative coaching behaviours (e.g., scolding, punitive instruction) negatively impacted their impression of the coach, whereas positive behaviours made no difference. Conversely, when the athletes were ahead, positive coaching behaviours (e.g., instruction, support) positively impacted their liking of the coach, while negative behaviours had no influence in this situation. Although, only one study has investigated the interaction of game score and coaching behaviour to date, it is intriguing to think about this relationship in your own coaching.

 In what way do your behaviours change in relation to the score of the competition?

What can you do to decrease your negative coaching behaviours when the competition does not go as well as you would like?

What can you do to increase your positive coaching behaviours when the competition is going very well?

Stress

Coaches' experience of stress has recently been investigated quite thoroughly. Initially, environmental stressors are perceived by the coach, whose appraisal of this perception consequently leads to an emotional response and perhaps eliciting coping resources (Fletcher & Scott, 2010). Under stress, coaches are prone to be more autocratic and involve athletes less in decision-making, provide less instruction and offer less support and empathy to the athletes (Olusoga & Thelwell, 2017).

Stress is viewed by Lazarus and Folkman (1984) as a balancing act between environmental demands and available resources. Thus, it is possible to work in two separate ends. One means is to reframe the view of the stressor, making it less threatening or demanding. Another means is trying to improve the resources to handle the stressor (e.g., coping strategies).

Typical stressors for coaches can be divided into four categories (Chroni, et al., 2013; Thelwell et al., 2008): *athlete performance-related* (e.g., concern for injuries, coachability), *coach performance-related* (e.g., competition issues; such as team selection, communication during competition), *organizational-environment* (e.g., access to facilities, travels) and *organizational-leadership* (e.g., staff/board members, handling large group of athletes).

Coaches have reported using a wide variety of coping strategies (Norris, Didymus & Kaissler, 2017). These can be divided into *problem-focused* (e.g., help-seeking), *emotion-focused* (e.g., self-talk) and *avoidance-focused* (e.g., alcohol consumption). In general, if the situation is controllable, problem-focused strategies are preferable, while in an uncontrollable situation, emotion-focused strategies have added value.

> Think of a stressful situation? What aspects of this situation are most salient to you?
> What did you feel?
> What did you think?
> What did you do?
> How could you reframe the situation to interpret it as less threating/demanding?
> What will you do to cope with the stressors better even if they still appear threatening/demanding?

Coach

Naturally, the coaches themselves can impact the leadership that is in effect within the group. Some studies have investigated the influence of gender of the coach or traits of the leader. However, in the following, focus lays on aspects within the coach that are easier to change.

Expectations

Coaches' behaviour risks being governed by expectations of an athlete, rather than the athlete's actual behaviour. A cycle of self-fulfilling prophecy consisting of four steps explains this. First, a coach makes an assessment of an athlete based on various cues (e.g., personality, performance, psychological characteristics). Second, these assessments influence coaching behaviours. Third, the athlete adapts his/her own behaviour in accordance with the coach's behaviours, and this in turn impacts the performance positively or negatively. Fourth, the expectation from the coach is therefore confirmed, and this leads to the coach being further strengthened in the belief of the accuracy of his/her own assessments (Solomon & Buscombe, 2013).

Being a 'coach's favourite' can have tremendous positive effect on an athlete's development, and conversely, being a 'coach's reject' can severely hamper development. Coaches have been shown to persist in their assessments of athletes and resist updating initial judgements. Interestingly, even a parameter that should be open for the athletes to control regardless of a coach's treatment, such as effort spent seem to be affected by coaches' expectations (Wilson, Cushion & Stephens, 2006). Furthermore, when coaches expect the athletes to be extrinsically motivated, it leads them to behaving in a more controlling way, even if this expectation does not reflect athletes' true motivation (Sarrazin et al., 2006). Coaches' expectancy driven behaviours influence various outcomes for the athletes, such as reported enjoyment, interest in participating in the same relationship and the time spent voluntary on the same activity (Pelletier & Vallerand, 1996). In division 1 college basketball, head coaches have been shown to provide more reinforcement and encouragement to high expectancy athletes (Solomon et al., 1996). Perhaps, highly competitive environments like NCAA division 1 creates additional tension on the coach to win, thus focusing on the best athletes.

Suggestions for minimizing expectancy effects include varying athletes' training partners during the season, deliberately varying coaching patterns within training sessions and regularly updating coach expectations, yet conveying positive and high expectations of all athletes (Solomon & Buscombe, 2013).

> What expectations do you have of the athletes you are coaching?
> In what way do you think your expectations impact the athletes?

Coaching Efficacy

Feltz, Chase, Moritz, and Sullivan (1999) propose four sources of information for coaching efficacy: *extent of experience and preparation*, *prior success*, *perceived skill in athletes* and *support from others*. Information from these sources lead to efficacy beliefs in four dimensions: *competition strategy* (e.g., confidence in the ability to lead the athletes to competitive success), *motivation* (e.g., confidence in the ability to affect athletes' psychological skills and states), *technique* (e.g., confidence in the ability to instruct and knowledge of sport-specific skill) and *character building* (e.g., confidence in the ability to influence athletes' personal development and athletes' attitude towards the sport). Coaches with high coaching efficacy tend to provide more positive reinforcement and encouragement, while spending less time on instruction and organization. Contrastingly, another study, using self-report measures from coaches showed a positive relationship between instructional behaviours and coaching efficacy (Sullivan et al., 2012). Thus, the influence of coaching efficacy on amount of instruction is somewhat unclear. Possibly, coaches high in efficacy overrate their usage of instruction due to some self-serving bias, or perhaps these coaches provide high quality of instruction, resulting in less need for subsequent interventions observable by others. Moreover, Myers, Vargas-Tonsing, and Feltz (2005) found that all four efficacy beliefs were positively related to coaches' usage of efficacy-enhancing behaviours, such as verbally persuading an athlete to believe in his/her abilities. Coaching efficacy is positively impacted by participation in formal coaching education (Malete & Feltz, 2000).

> Which are your primary sources for coaching efficacy?
> How confident do you feel about your coaching in the four areas: competition strategy, motivation, technique and character building?
> What can you do to enhance your coaching efficacy?

Effects of Coaching Behaviours on Athletes

The effect that coaches' behaviours have on the individual athlete is divided into five categories (cf. Côté et al., 2010): *competence, self-concept, connections, character* and *well-being*, which are detailed below. Additionally, one area of impact at the group level, *cohesion*, is included.

Competence

Here, the focus will be on more 'objective' aspects of sport-skills, leaving the 'subjective' perception to the next section (*Self-concept*). An athlete's competence in sport can be categorized into four categories: *technical, physical, mental* (cognitive and emotional) and *tactical*. The first two have received most attention in the existing coaching literature as well as in traditional coaching education. Technical competence means being able to solve movement problems with or without an object, such as getting a pass through to a teammate, having an efficient running stride or keeping a tight tuck position during high diving. Physical competence pertains to being able to execute the movements rapidly, on balance, for long-time, or perhaps withstanding physical contact from an opponent.

Mental skills include being able to keep focus in the presence of distractions. Nideffer and Sagal (2006) distinguish between width and orientation of focus. This creates four different types of focuses as Figure 4.3 displays. *Narrow-internal focus* is used when an athlete mentally rehearses an upcoming action. *Narrow-external focus* is used for aiming at a target, such as a dart board. *Broad-internal focus* is used for analysing bodily reactions that an athlete experiences during practice or competition. *Broad-external focus* is used for scanning the playing field for opponents and teammates movements. Not to be forgotten is the ability to be able to shift between the different types of focuses during dynamic conditions. *Cybill Cyclist scans the field of competitors, decides to zero in on one in particular who looks tough to determine the opponent's fatigue level and then shifts again to feel if her own legs allow her to crack the field open.*

Being able to regulate emotions is another important area for athletes and occurs when there is a discrepancy between current and desired emotions within oneself. It is possible to manage emotions from different directions, either aimed at antecedents or aimed at responses. Examples of the former

		Width	
		Narrow	Broad
Orientation	Internal	Narrow-Internal	Broad-Internal
	External	Narrow-External	Broad-External

FIGURE 4.3 Four different combinations of focus.

are choosing a situation that is advantageous, modifying aspects of the situation, directing attention to influence emotions, such as distracting oneself, and reinterpreting the situation. Examples of actions aimed at the emotional response are listening to calm or upbeat music, progressive muscle relaxation and exercising (Lane et al., 2012).

Tactical skills differ from strategy in that the former consists of decisions made by the athlete close to the action under time pressure. On the other hand, strategy is decisions made far in advance, usually before a competition, and this kind of decision-making is not really a property of an individual athlete, thus it does not necessarily transfer to another situation with another coach (who might have another strategic philosophy). Tactical skills can be described involving three levels; perception of the situation, comprehension and assessment and prediction and execution of motor skill (Mascarenhas & Smith, 2011).

Self-concept

Although self-concept is somewhat of an ambiguous construct, it is encompassing of many 'self-constructs'. All in all, self-concept answers the question 'Who am I?', as it is an appraisal of self, rather than an objective assessment (Oyserman, 2001). *Self-esteem* is a valuing of ourselves. This tells us how satisfied we are with ourselves and how much we can trust ourselves (Johnson, 2003). Self-esteem is made up of a global and quite stable part, but also a momentary part that changes due to situational factors (Heatherton & Polivy, 1991). The athletes with the lowest self-esteem are the ones who are influenced the most by coaches' behaviours. This is likely because low self-esteem individuals are more inclined to search for external cues of their value, such as how the coach is acting towards them. Self-confidence is used quite often in everyday language, though *self-efficacy* probably has a stronger evidence base. Self-efficacy is closely tied to a specific behaviour compared to the more global self-confidence. According to Bandura (1977), self-efficacy pertains to how much an individual believes in his/her own capacity to perform a specific behaviour or to achieve a specific outcome. Having control over one's environment is of outmost importance for the entire self-concept. Being able to connect effort over time to skills and proficiency is significant, while simultaneously having a sense of being alright no matter what performances achieved or skills developed. Motivation may also be considered a part of a wider self-concept.

Connections

Connections cover bidirectional relationships with other people, such as peers (e.g., school mates), subordinates (e.g., employees) or superiors (e.g., teachers). Furthermore, many individuals need to have relations with an organization (e.g., the sport's NGB). Typically, parents are the most influential persons early in life as an individual can develop working models for relationships that are *secure* (i.e., 'it is easy to get close to others'), *avoidant* (i.e., 'it feels uncomfortable to get close to others'), or *anxious* (i.e., 'others are difficult to get as close to as preferred'), as described by Shaver and Mikulincer (2009). During adolescence the influence from teenage peers take over parents' high-influence position (De Goede et al., 2009). These relationships tend to grow more equal, positive and take an increasingly larger place as the individual becomes older. In sport, an athlete's relationship with the coach is important (see Chapter 7), as well as with peers. Peer relations provide positive dimensions such as pleasant play, practical help, intimacy and emotional support, while also having the possibility for more negative aspects such as conflict, betrayal and inaccessibility (Weiss, Smith & Theeboom, 1996). By working together, being part of a group and improving the cooperative aspects inherent in many sports, the athlete will develop interpersonal skills.

Character

Character implicates having respect for social rules, integrity (e.g., having honest and strong moral values), as well as empathy for other people. This is mirrored in how well the individual follows rules both within and outside of sports, how the individual views right and wrong, and handles situations where other people are in trouble. Sports participation is argued to be beneficial for character development when conducted in a sporting environment that is respectful towards participants, coaches, referees, parents as well as the rules of the sport. Also, abiding to unwritten rules such as giving your best effort, fair play and joint efforts as a part of a group are other displays of character (Côté et al., 2010). Prosocial behaviour (e.g., taking responsibility), self-regulation (e.g., being able to postpone rewards for oneself) and handling setbacks (e.g., showing resiliency) are also included in the development of character. Correspondingly, moral values, like taking a stand against aggressive behaviour against opponents, and complimenting a successful teammate are parts of quality character (Bolter & Weiss, 2013).

Well-being

Well-being has been intensively investigated in the psychological domain over the years. In sports though, it has much shorter history, (Lundqvist, 2011). In all likelihood, this is at least partly due to the performance focus that traditionally has had a tight grip on sports. To some extent, a 'win-at-all-costs' attitude might have promoted a masculine culture where focusing on well-being is seen as soft or weak. It has often been said that sports participation facilitates well-being. A more accurate depiction is probably that *healthy* sports participation promotes well-being, rather than participation *per se* (cf. Becker, 2009; Gearity, 2012). Ryff (1989) stresses that well-being hinges on balancing negative and positive emotion that constitute two different dimensions rather than just opposites of the same continuum. Aspects included in well-being are acceptance of the self, positive relations with others, autonomy, sense of environmental mastery, purpose in life and personal growth.

Cohesion

At the group level, cohesion is an important outcome in both team and individual sports (Brawley, Carron, & Widmeyer, 1987). Cohesion is seen as dynamic, associated with positive feelings and reflects the groups' intentions to form and stay together (Carron, Shapcott & Burke, 2007). People hold two types of cognitions about cohesiveness of their group. *Group integration* is a perception of the closeness, similarity and bonding among group members. *Group attraction* is a perception of the personal motivations to retain an individual in the group. Further, the group is involved in both *task* and *social* aspects, creating a 2 x 2 manifestation of cohesion in sport, such as group integration – task, that shows how similar individuals are working on a specific task (Carron, Colman, & Wheeler, 2002). All four manifestations of cohesion can have a positive impact on performance. However, a combination of high social cohesion and low task cohesion (paired with low commitment to group norms) has been found to underlie a perception of teammates not giving their all (Høigaard, Säfvenbom, & Tønnessen, 2006).

Which one of these areas do you think is the most important for the athletes/group to develop?

Which one of these areas do you think the athletes themselves consider most important to develop?

Which one of these areas is currently the strongest suit in your coaching?

Which one of these areas is currently the weakest suit in your coaching?

Measuring Coaching Behaviours

In the appendix, two different questionnaires for measurement of athletes' opinions on coaching behaviours are provided. Coaching Behaviour Scale for Sports (CBS-S; Côté et al., 1999) measures sport-specific coaching behaviours. Transformational Teaching Questionnaire (TTQ; Beauchamp et al., 2010) measures social competence behaviours.

> When you view your results from CBS-S, what do you think?
> When you view your results from TTQ, what do you think?

Practical Implementation of Coaching Behaviours

In addition to the reflective methods in this section, an observational schedule is provided. This observational schedule is used by a person during practice observing the coach while trying to implement of specific social competence behaviours. Getting behavioural feedback using a structured observation is valuable for coaches (Brewer & Jones, 2002). This means has further potential, along with reflective activities, to increase a coach's self-awareness.

Reflection Card

Positive reinforcement			Date:_____
Situation	Reinforcement	Effect	Coach's thoughts/emotions

Certainly, the reflection card can be used for increasing/decreasing any coaching behaviour. But as positive reinforcement has been demonstrated to be harder for coaches to be aware of and athletes wanting more of this behaviour, for most coaches it is an important issue. Thus, an appropriate goal is to increase positive reinforcements. In the first column (*Situation*), briefly describe a specific situation where positive reinforcement after a successful performance from an athlete is desirable to be enhanced. This could be during a specific practice activity, in response to a specific athlete's successful performance, or when a specific skill is executed during practice regardless of by whom or when. In the second column (*Reinforcement*), describe the way positive reinforcement was used. If this is done prior to practice, it constitutes the action plan. Otherwise, it is possible to separately sketch a simple plan for how the goal of increasing positive reinforcements are conducted and then hopefully something along those lines is carried out during practice (which then is noted in the second column). In the third column (*Effect*), describe the observed effect on the athlete following the reinforcement irrespective of the effect being emotional or behavioural. In the fourth column (*Coach's thought/emotions*), note some reactions emanating from either the reinforcement or the observed effect on the athlete. As with the reflection card in Chapter 3, the first columns (in this case, the first two) can be prepared beforehand. The last two should be completed during the practice.

Secondary Reflection

 Use the questions below and/or the formula for shared reflection in chapter 2.

Did you miss any opportunities to reinforce an athlete that you had in mind during the practice? If so, what was the cause that you did not seize the opportunity/made an intervention? What was the main reason for the reinforcement being made at the time it actually was?

With the used reflection card in hand, what do you think when you look back at that specific situation and the athlete during the practice?

How would you interpret your thoughts and emotions from this particular moment?

What do you now think will be the effects for the athlete after your reinforcement?

In what way is the chosen reinforcement related to your coaching philosophy/idea of what you wanted to accomplish at the practice?

Would you do anything differently as you look back at this specific event? If so, elaborate on this.

What is the main lesson learnt that you take away from the experience?

Reflection Sheet

First to third columns are completed before practice. Fourth and fifth columns are completed after practice.

Social competence behaviour

Date: _____

Description of and Purpose of practice activity.	Circle the 'I' of the selected trans-formational leadership.	Description of how the chosen behaviour is going to be implemented.	Briefly answer the following questions: How did it feel to use the chosen behaviour? How did the athletes respond to the chosen behaviour? How could this behaviour have been more effective?	What were your own thoughts and emotions during this part of the practice?
	II IM IC IS			
	II IM IC IS			
	II IM IC IS			

Observation schedule

Description of practice activity.	Circle the 'I' of the selected trans-formational leadership.	Description of implementation of the chosen behaviour.	Other coaching behaviours of note.	Reactions from the athletes.
	II IM IC IS			
	II IM IC IS			
	II IM IC IS			

Overall comments:
How did you perceive the coach's social competence behaviours?
How could the behaviours have been even more effective?

Reflective Summary

> When working with increasing positive reinforcement during practice, what has been the most important learning for you?
> How are you going to capitalize on this lesson learnt in the future?
> When trying to implement a transformational coaching behaviour during practice, what has been the most important learning for you?
> How are you going to capitalize on this lesson learnt in the future?
> From your readings of sport-specific coaching behaviours, your answers to the application exercises, your and reflective activities, how would you best use these behaviours in your coaching?
> From your readings of transformational coaching behaviours, your answers to the application exercises, and your reflective activities, how would you best use transformational coaching?

Challenging Behavioural Assumptions

A month later, Ellen met the two coaches again.

> "Tell me, what did you experience by observing each other's practices?" Ellen began.

Almost immediately the two others began talking over each other before both burst into laughter.

> "You seem pretty upbeat, don't you?" Ellen tried to quiet them down.
> "The observations were really helpful", Collin alleged. "I could never have imagined seeing so many wrinkles through structured observation of another coach. It is too easy to get caught up in your own thinking."
> "I agree", Leah said. "By having someone watching you and giving you valuable behavioural feedback, you can discover blind spots."
> "Sounds good. It is often very good to get a second opinion on your behaviours. What were your main conclusions", Ellen asked?
> "To me, I think I have realized that the kids benefit from me spending some time during practice on other things than reorganizing the drills or playing areas. Perhaps, I should show some vulnerability every now and then", Collin said.
> "What effect do you think that would have on the athletes?" Ellen asked.
> "I think their connection to me would be better. They would not only see me as a sports coach, but a leader they would want to be like", Collin elaborated.

Yes, that was actually my exact thinking too", Leah interrupted. "Remember when you told them that you hadn't succeeded in preparing a drill for your last opponent that upset you last weekend?"

"Yeah", Collin responded looking a little bit down.

"Don't be sad", Leah continued. "You showed that you are a human with good and bad sides. Like all of us."

"Could it be that they will identify more with you as they see that you have similarities to themselves?" Ellen asked.

"I guess so", Collin responded a little more upbeat than a few seconds ago. "It is easy to forget that sport specific skills are just one area where the kids could improve."

"Some of them might not be full-time professionals in the future and may therefore have more gain from learning other skills, don't you think?" Ellen queried.

"Uhum. I also think it was very useful watching a few of Leah's practices", Collin expanded.

"I agree", Leah replied immediately. "I am very grateful for the feedback you gave me. Now I realize that I didn't give as much positive feedback as I thought I did."

"Why is that?" Ellen probed.

"I might have had too large expectations on the athletes. They could never be good enough. Now I try to set the bar a little lower and Collin can verify that the number of positive reinforcements has gone up tremendously from the first practice he visited", Leah said and looked at Collin who responded with a light nod. "Previously, I would have ignored an athlete who performed reasonably well, as I wanted even more."

"Are there any downsides to your new approach?" Ellen asked.

"Not really, at least not as long as I am positive and show that I believe in their abilities to succeed in the long-term even if the current drills are a little easier than an international championship final", Leah said happily.

Quiz

1. What statement is most correct about different coaching behaviours?
   a. Coaches generally use more positive behaviours than the athletes prefer.
   b. Athletes and coaches have usually the same perception of the coach's behaviours.
   c. Negative coaching behaviours have a larger impact than positive behaviours.

2. How can transformational coaching behaviours be used to improve coaching?
   a. These coaching behaviours will get more order within the group.
   b. These coaching behaviours will inspire the athletes.
   c. These coaching behaviours will generate more competitive success.

3. How can response cost be used to counter behavioural problems?
    a. The coach removes something the athlete values.
    b. The coach adds something the athlete dislikes.
    c. The coach emphasizes the rules in front of the group.
4. What is known about coaches' silence?
    a. Coaches who remain silent a lot are usually lower skilled.
    b. Silence can be used off-task and on-task so the purpose is hard to tell for an outsider.
    c. Silence indicates that the coach is off-task.
5. What statement can be said to be most accurate about athletes' factors?
    a. Girls will likely get the same amount and quality of feedback compared to boys.
    b. Regardless of age athletes prefer the same type of coaching behaviours.
    c. More skilled athletes generally get both more positive and negative feedback.
6. How is stress usually impacting coaches' behaviours?
    a. Not at all if the coach is competent.
    b. The coach will make a larger proportion of the decisions instead of eliciting athletes' input.
    c. The coach will spend more time on social support.
7. What statement can be said to be the most accurate regarding coach's expectations?
    a. Expectations are formed solely on the basis of the athlete's behaviour.
    b. Expectations are regularly updated by the coach.
    c. Expectations can be stable over a long period of time.
8. What areas can be said to capture most of a coach's influence on an athlete?
    a. Competence, self-concept, connections, character, well-being.
    b. Quickness, game sense, strength, skills.
    c. Sports, family, school, work.

References

Albrecht, R. (2009). Drop and give us 20, seifried: A practical response to "Defending the use of punishment by coaches". *Quest*, *61*, 470–475.

Avolio, B. J., Reichard, R. J., Hannah, S. T., Walumbwa, F. O., & Chan, A. (2009). A meta-analytical review of leadership impact research: Experimental and quasi-experimental studies. *The Leadership Quarterly*, *20*, 764–784.

Bandura, A. (1977). Self-efficacy: Toward a unifying theory of behavioral change. *Psychological Review*, *84*, 191–215.

Bass, B. M. (1998). *Transformational leadership: Industry, military, and educational impact*. Mahwah, NJ: Lawrence Erlbaum Associates.

Bass, B. M., & Riggio, R. E. (2006). *Transformational leadership* (2nd ed.). Mahwah, NJ: Lawrence Erlbaum Associates.

Beauchamp, M. R., Barling, J., Li, Z., Morton, K. L., Keith, S. K., & Zumbo, B. D. (2010). Development and psychometric properties of the transformational teaching questionnaire. *Journal of Health Psychology, 15*, 1123–1134.

Beck, J. S. (2011). *Cognitive behaviour therapy: Basics and beyond* (2nd ed.). New York: Guilford Press.

Becker, A. (2009). It's not what they do, it's how they do it: Athlete experiences of great coaching. *International Journal of Sports Science & Coaching, 4*, 93–119.

Black, S. J., & Weiss, M. R. (1992). The relationship among perceived coaching behaviors, perceptions of ability, and motivation in competitive age-group swimmers. *Journal of Sport & Exercise Psychology, 14*, 309–325.

Bolter, N. D., & Weiss, M. R. (2013). Coaching behaviors and adolescent athletes' sportspersonship outcomes; Further validation of the sportsmanship coaching behaviors scale (SCBS). *Sport, Exercise, and Performance Psychology, 2*, 32–47.

Brawley, L. R., Carron, A. W., & Widmeyer, W. N. (1987). Assessing the cohesion of teams: Validity of the group environment questionnaire. *Journal of Sport Psychology, 9*, 275–294.

Breakey, C., Jones, M., Cunningham, C-T., & Holt, N. (2009). Female athletes' perceptions of a coach's speeches. *International Journal of Sports Science & Coaching, 4*, 489–504.

Brewer, C. J., & Jones, R. L. (2002). A five-stage process for establishing contextually valid observation instruments: The case of rugby union. *The Sport Psychologist, 16*, 138–159.

Burke, K. L., Peterson, D., & Nix, C. (1995). The effects of the coaches' use of humor on female volleyball players' evaluation of their coaches. *Journal of Sport Behavior, 18*, 83–91.

Carron, A. V., Colman, M. M., & Wheeler, J. (2002). Cohesion and performance in sport: A meta-analysis. *Journal of Sport & Exercise Psychology, 24*, 168–188.

Carron, A. V., Shapcott, K. M., & Burke, S. M. (2007). Group cohesion in sport and exercise: Past, present and future. In M. Beauchamp, & M. A. Eys (Eds.), *Group dynamics in exercise and sport psychology: Contemporary themes* (pp. 117–139). Abingdon: Routledge.

Chroni, S., Diakaki, E., Perkos, S., Hassandra, M., & Schoen, C. (2013). What stresses coaches in competition and training? An exploratory inquiry. *International Journal of Coaching Science, 7*, 25–39.

Claxton, D. B. (1988). A systematic observation of more and less successful high school tennis coaches. *Journal of Teaching in Physical Education, 7*, 302–310.

Coatsworth, J. D., & Conroy, D. E. (2006). Enhancing the self-esteem of youth swimmers through coach training: Gender and age effects. *Psychology of Sport and Exercise, 7*, 173–192.

Côté, J., Bruner, M., Erickson, K., Strachan, L., & Fraser-Thomas, J. (2010). Athlete development and coaching. In J. Lyle, & C. Cushion (Eds.), *Sports coaching: Professionalisation and practice* (pp. 63–83). London: Elsevier.

Côté, J., Yardley, J., Hay, J., Sedgwick, W., & Baker, J. (1999). An exploratory examination of the coaching behavior scale for sport. *Avante, 5*, 82–92.

Cowan, N. (2001). The magical number of 4 in short-term memory: A reconsideration of mental storage capacity. *the. Behavioral and Brain Sciences, 24*, 87–114.

Cushion, C., & Jones, R. (2001). A systematic observation of professional top-level youth soccer coaches. *Journal of Sport Behavior, 24*, 354–376.

Davids, K., Button, C., & Bennett, S. (2008). *Dynamics of skill acquisition: A constraints-led approach*. Champaign, IL: Human Kinetics.

De Goede, I. H. A., Branje, S. J. T., Delsing, M. J. M. H., & Meeus, W. H. J. (2009). Linkages over time between adolescents' relationships with parents and friends. *Journal of Youth and Adolescence, 38*, 1304–1315.

Erickson, K., Côté, J., Hollenstein, T., & Deakin, J. (2011). Examining coach–athlete interactions using state space grids: An observational analysis in competitive youth sport. *Psychology of Sport and Exercise, 12*, 645–654.

Feltz, D. L., Chase, M. A., Moritz, S. E., & Sullivan, P. J. (1999). A conceptual model of coaching efficacy: Preliminary investigation and instrument development. *Journal of Educational Psychology, 91,* 765–776.

Fishbach, A. (2009). The dynamics of self-regulation. In J. P. Forgas, R. F. Baumeister, & D. M. Tice (Eds.), *Psychology of self-regulation: Cognitive, affective, and motivational processes* (pp. 163–181). New York: Psychology Press.

Fletcher, D., & Scott, M. (2010). Psychological stress in sports coaches: A review of concepts, research, and practice. *Journal of Sports Sciences, 28,* 127–137.

Fredricks, J. A., & Eccles, J. S. (2005). Family socialization, gender, and sport motivation and involvement. *Journal of Sport & Exercise Psychology, 27,* 3–31.

Gearity, B. T. (2012). Poor teaching by the coach: A phenomenological description from athletes' experience of poor coaching. *Physical Education and Sport Pedagogy, 17,* 79–96.

Gentile, A. M. (1972). A working model of skill acquisition with application to teaching. *Quest, 17,* 3–23.

Graziano, W. G., Brothen, T., & Berscheid, E. (1980). Attention attraction and individual differences in reaction to criticism. *Journal of Personality and Social Psychology, 38,* 193–202.

Heatherton, T. F., & Polivy, J. (1991). Development and validation of a scale for measuring state self-esteem. *Journal of Personality and Social Psychology, 60,* 895–910.

Høigaard, R., Jones, G. W., & Peters, D. M. (2008). Preferred coach leadership behaviour in elite soccer in relation to success and failure. *International Journal of Sports Science & Coaching, 3,* 241–250.

Høigaard, R., Säfvenbom, R., & Tønnessen, F. E. (2006). The relationship between group cohesion, group norms, and perceived social loafing in soccer teams. *Small Group Research, 37,* 217–232.

Horn, T. S. (1985). Coaches' feedback and changes in children's perceptions of their physical competence. *Journal of Educational Psychology, 77,* 174–186.

Horn, T. S., Bloom, P., Berglund, K. M., & Packard, S. (2011). Relationship between collegiate athletes' psychological characteristics and their preferences for different types of coaching behavior. *The Sport Psychologist, 25,* 190–211.

Johnson, M. (2003). *Självkänsla och anpassning [Self-esteem and adaptation]*. Lund: Studentlitteratur.

Kahneman, D. (2011). *Thinking, fast and slow*. New York: Farrar, Straus and Giroux.

Kelloway, E. K., & Barling, J. (2000). What we have learned about developing transformational leaders. *Leadership & Organization Development Journal, 21,* 355–362.

Kiely, J. (2012). Periodization paradigms in the 21st century: Evidence-led or tradition-driven? *International Journal of Sport Physiology and Performance, 7,* 242–250.

Kling, K. C., Hyde, J. S., Showers, C. J., & Buswell, B. N. (1999). Gender differences in self-esteem: A meta-analysis. *Psychological Bulletin, 125,* 470–500.

Koestner, R., Lekes, N., Powers, T. A., & Chicoine, E. (2002). Attaining personal goals: Self-concordance plus implementation intentions equals. *Journal of Personality and Social Psychology, 83,* 231–244.

Kozar, B., Whitfield, K. E., Lord, R. H., & Mechikoff, R. A. (1993). Timeout before free-throws: Do the statistics support the strategy? *Perceptual and Motor Skills, 76,* 47–50.

Kyllo, L. B., & Landers, D. M. (1995). Goal setting in sport and exercise: A research synthesis to resolve the controversy. *Journal of Sport & Exercise Psychology, 17,* 117–137.

Landers, D. M., & Arent, S. M. (2006). Arousal-performance relationships. In J. Williams (Ed.), *Applied sport psychology: Personal growth to peak performance* (5th ed., pp. 260–284). New York: McGraw-Hill.

Lane, A. M., Beedie, C. J., Jones, M. V., Uphill, M., & Devonport, T. J. (2012). The BASES expert statement on emotion regulation in sport. *Journal of Sports Sciences, 30,* 1189–1195.

Langan, E., Blake, C., & Lonsdale, C. (2013). Systematic review of the effectiveness of interpersonal coach education interventions on athlete outcomes. *Psychology of Sport and Exercise, 14*, 37–49.

Lazarus, R. S., & Folkman, S. (1984). *Stress, appraisal, and coping*. New York: Spring Publishing.

Leonard, W. M., Ostrosky, T., & Huchendorf, S. (1990). Centrality of position and managerial recruitment: The case of major league baseball. *Sociology of Sport Journal, 7*, 294–301.

Leveritt, M., Abernethy, P. J., Barry, B. K., & Logan, P. A. (1999). Concurrent strength and endurance training: A review. *Sports Medicine, 28*, 413–427.

Locke, E. A., & Latham, G. P. (Eds.) (2013). *New developments in goal setting and task performance*. New York: Routledge.

Lundqvist, C. (2011). Well-being in competitive sports – The feel-good factor? A review of conceptual considerations of well-being. *International Review of Sport and Exercise Psychology, 4*, 109–127.

Malete, L., & Feltz, D. L. (2000). The effect of a coaching education program on coaching efficacy. *The Sport Psychologist, 14*, 410–417.

Mascarenhas, D. R. D., & Smith, N. C. (2011). Developing the performance brain: Decision making under pressure. In D. Collins, A. Button, & H. Richards (Eds.), *Performance psychology: A practitioners guide* (pp. 245–267). London: Elsevier.

Markland, R., & Martinek, T. J. (1988). Descriptive analysis of coach augmented feedback given to high school varsity female volleyball players. *Journal of Teaching in Physical Education, 7*, 289–301.

Martin, S. B., Jackson, A. W., Richardson, P. A., & Weiller, K. H. (1999). Coaching preferences of adolescent youths and their parents. *Journal of Applied Sport Psychology, 11*, 247–262.

Martin, S. B., Dale, G. A., & Jackson, A. W. (2001). Youth coaching preferences of adolescent athletes and their parents. *Journal of Sport Behavior, 24*, 197–212.

McGoey, K. E., & DuPaul, G. J. (2000). Token reinforcement and response cost procedures: Reducing the disruptive behavior of preschool children with attention-deficit/hyperactivity disorder. *School Psychology Quarterly, 15*, 330–343.

Millar, S.-K., Oldham, A. R. H., & Donovan, M. (2011). Coaches' self-awareness of timing, nature and intent of verbal instructions to athletes. *International Journal of Sports Science & Coaching, 6*, 503–513.

Moran, A. (2012). *Sport and exercise psychology: A critical introduction* (2nd ed.). New York: Routledge.

Moreno, J. A., Cervelló, E. C., & Gonzalez-Cutre, D. (2008). Relationship among goal-orientations, motivational climate and flow in adolescent athletes: Difference by gender. *The Spanish Journal of Psychology, 11*, 181–191.

Myers, N. D., Vargas-Tonsing, T. M., & Feltz, D. L. (2005). Coaching efficacy in intercollegiate coaches: Sources, coaching behavior, and team variables. *Psychology of Sport & Exercise, 6*, 129–143.

Nideffer, R. M., & Sagal, M.-S. (2006). Concentration and attention control training. In J. Williams (Ed.), *Applied sport psychology: Personal growth to peak performance* (5th ed., pp. 384–403). New York: McGraw-Hill.

Norris, L. A., Didymus, F. F., & Kaissler, M. (2017). Stressors, coping, and well-being among sports coaches: A systematic review. *Psychology of Sport and Exercise Psychology, 33*, 93–112.

Oettingen, G., & Gollwitzer, P. M. (2009). Making goal pursuit effective: Expectancy-dependent goal setting and planned goal striving. In J. P. Forgas, R. F. Baumeister, & D. M. Tice (Eds.), *Psychology of self-regulation: Cognitive, affective, and motivational processes* (pp. 127–146). New York: Psychology Press.

Oliveira, A. L. B., et al. (2018). Comparison of the mateev periodization model and the verkhoshansky periodization model. *Journal of Exercise Physiology Online, 21*, 60–67.

Olusoga, P., & Thelwell, R. (2017). Coach stress and associated impacts. In R. Thelwell, C. Harwood, & I. Greenlees (Eds.), *The psychology of sports coaching: Research and practice* (pp. 128–141). Abingdon, UK: Routledge.

Oyserman, D. (2001). Self-concept and identity. In A. Tesser, & N. Schwarz (Eds.), *The blackwell handbook of social psychology* (pp. 499–517). Malden, MA: Blackwell.

Pelletier, L. G., & Vallerand, R. J. (1996). Supervisors' beliefs and subordinates' intrinsic motivation: A behavioral confirmation analysis. *Journal of Personality and Social Psychology, 71*, 331–340.

Raglin, J. S. (2001). Psychological factors in sport performance: The mental health model revisited. *Sports Medicine, 31*, 875–890.

Riemer, H. A. (2007). Multidimensional model of coach leadership. In S. Jowett, & D. Lavallee (Eds.), *Social psychology in sport* (pp. 57–73). Champaign, IL: Human Kinetics.

Rupert, T., & Buschner, C. (1989). Teaching and coaching: A comparison of instructional behaviors. *Journal of Teaching in Physical Education, 9*, 49–57.

Ryff, C. D. (1989). Happiness is everything, or is it? Explorations on the meaning of psychological well-being. *Journal of Personality and Social Psychology, 57*, 1069–1081.

Sarrazin, P. G., Tessier, D. P., Pelletier, L. G., Trouilloud, D. O., & Chanal, J. P. (2006). The effects of teacher expectations about students' motivation on teachers' autonomy-supportive and controlling behaviors. *International Journal of Sport and Exercise Psychology, 4*, 283–301.

Schmidt, R. A. (2003). Motor schema theory after 27 years: Reflections and implications for a new theory. *Research Quarterly for Exercise and Sport, 74*, 366–375.

Shaver, P. R., & Mikulincer, M. (2009). Attachment theory: I. Motivational, individual differences and structural aspects. In P. J. Corr, & G. Matthews (Eds.), *The Cambridge handbook of personality psychology* (pp. 228–246). New York: Cambridge University Press.

Singer, R. N., Lidor, R., & Cauraugh, J. N. (1993). To be aware or not aware? What to think about while learning and performing a motor skill. *The Sport Psychologist, 7*, 19–30.

Smith, R. E. (2006). Positive reinforcement, performance feedback, and performance enhancement. In J. Williams (Ed.), *Applied sport psychology: Personal growth to peak performance* (5th ed., pp. 40–56). New York: McGraw-Hill.

Smith, M., & Cushion, C. J. (2006). An investigation of the in-game behaviours of professional, top-level youth soccer coaches. *Journal of Sports Sciences, 24*, 355–366.

Smoll, F. L., & Smith, R. E. (1989). Leadership behaviors in sport: A theoretical model and research paradigm. *Journal of Applied Social Psychology, 19*, 1522–1551.

Smith, R. E., & Smoll, F. L. (2007). Social-cognitive approach to coaching behaviors. In S. Jowett, & D. Lavallee (Eds.), *Social psychology in sport* (pp. 75–90). Champaign, IL: Human Kinetics.

Smith, R. E., & Smoll, F. L. (2012). *Sport psychology for youth coaches: Developing champions in sports and life*. Plymouth, UK: Rowan & Littlefield Publishers.

Smith, R. E., Shoda, Y., Cumming, S., & Smoll, F. L. (2009). Behavioral signatures at the ballpark: Intraindividual consistency of adults' situation–behavior patterns and their interpersonal consequences. *Journal of Research in Personality, 43*, 187–195.

Smoll, F. L., Smith, R. E., Barnett, N. P., & Everett, J. J. (1993). Enhancement of children's self-esteem through social support training for youth sport coaches. *Journal of Applied Psychology, 78*, 602–610.

Solomon, G. B., & Buscombe, R. M. (2013). Expectancy effects in sports coaching. In P. Potrac, J. Denison, & W. Gilbert (Eds.), *Handbook of sports coaching* (pp. 247–258). London: Routledge.

Solomon, G. B., Striegel, D. A., Eliot, J. F., Heon, S. N., Maas, J. L., & Wayda, V. K. (1996). The self-fulfilling prophecy in college basketball: Implications for effective coaching. *Journal of Applied Sport Psychology, 8*, 44–59.

Sullivan, P., Paquette, K. J., Holt, N. L., & Bloom, G. A. (2012). The relation of coaching context and coaching education to coaching efficacy and perceived leadership behaviors in youth sport. *The Sport Psychologist, 26*, 122–134.

Thelwell, R. C., Weston, N. J. V., Greenlees, I. A., & Hutchings, N. V. (2008). Stressors in sport: A coach perspective. *Journal of Sport Sciences, 26*, 905–918.

Thompson, J. (2003). *The double-goal coach*. New York: HarperCollins.

Toner, J., Moran, A., & Gale, L. (2016). Jean Piaget: Learning and the stages of athlete development. In L. Nelson, R. Groom, & P. Potrac (Eds.), *Learning in sports coaching: Theory and application* (pp. 89–100). London: Routledge.

Turnnidge, J., & Côté, J. (2016). Applying transformational leadership theories to coaching research in youth sport: A systematic literature review. *International Journal of Sport and Exercise Psychology, 16*, 327–342.

Turnnidge, J., & Côté, J. (2017). Transformational coaching workshop: Applying a person-centred approach to coach development programs. *International Sport Coaching Journal, 4*, 314–325.

Turnnidge, J., & Côté, J. (2019). Observing coaches' leadership behaviours: The development of the coach leadership assessment system (CLAS). *Measurement in Physical Education and Exercise Science, 23*, 214–226.

Vargas, T. M., & Short, S. E. (2011). Athletes' perceptions of the psychological, emotional, and performance effects of coaches' pre-game speeches. *International Journal of Coaching Science, 5*, 27–43.

Vargas-Tonsing, T. M., & Bartholomew, J. B. (2006). An exploratory study of the effects of pregame speeches on team efficacy beliefs. *Journal of Applied Social Psychology, 36*, 918–933.

Vella, S. A., Oades, L. G., & Crowe, T. P. (2013). A pilot test of transformational leadership training for sports coaches: Impact on the developmental experiences of adolescent athletes. *International Journal of Sports Science & Coaching, 8*, 513–530.

Walters, S. R., Schulter, P. J., Oldham, A. R. H., Thomson, R. W., & Payne, D. (2012). The sideline behaviour of coaches at children's team sport games. *Psychology of Sport and Exercise, 13*, 108–215.

Weinberg, R., Butt, J., & Culp, B. (2013). Coaches' view of mental toughness and how it is built. *International Journal of Sport and Exercise Psychology, 9*, 156–172.

Weiss, M. R., Smith, A. L., & Theeboom, M. (1996). "That's what friends are for": Children's and teenagers' perceptions of peer relationships in the sport domain. *Journal of Sport & Exercise Psychology, 18*, 347–379.

Wilson, M. A., Cushion, C. J., & Stephens, D. E. (2006). "Put me in coach…I'm better than you think I am!" Coaches perceptions of their expectations in youth sport. *International Journal of Sports Science & Coaching, 1*, 149–161.

Wulf, G. (2013). Attentional focus and motor learning: A review of 15 years. *International Review of Sport and Exercise Psychology, 6*, 77–104.

5
PEDAGOGY

Aim of the chapter: Develop an understanding of how athletes learn during practice and what coaches can do to facilitate this learning.

Theoretical learning goals of the chapter:

Grow an understanding of…

1. three different theories of learning
2. five different pedagogical methods
3. aspects that influence the effectiveness of how information is presented to athletes
4. types of practice activities and some of their distinctions
5. the 1-2-3 template and how it can be used during practice
6. questions and their potential usage during practice

Practical learning goals of the chapter:

1. Become able to use the 1-2-3 template during practice by using reflection card.
2. Improve the variety of pedagogical methods used comfortably during practice by using reflection sheet.

Vignette

"Leah, you look concerned. Tell us a little about your last practices", Ellen inquired.

"They complain a lot about that they know the drills we're using. That we do things over and over. Then after growing tired of these complaints, I bought a book with 100 new drills. Some were quite complicated, so I figured they would like them", Leah explained.

"Did they?" Ellen looked at her distressed face.

"Of course not! Now they complain that they just stand around listening to my instructions", Leah replied, looking even sadder now.

"Some of my athletes do that too every now and then", Collin interjected. "Last month, though, I read a book about sport psychology. We have implemented those things 15 minutes after every practice. It works great!"

"How about trying to integrate the mental aspect of the game in the regular practice activities you run?" Ellen asked Collin.

"How, should I do that?" Collin asked, with some irony in his voice. "We need to work on our technique, so I have them follow my demonstrations. That way they will get proper execution."

"But, during contests, the athletes have to handle themselves, right?" Ellen queried.

"Yes...", Collin was interrupted.

"Hello?!? I am still in the room", Leah cried. "I don't know what to do. At all. And you guys talk about psychology. It's just an add on to sports."

"Sorry", Ellen apologized. "It seems you're stuck between repeating the same stuff and spending too much time organizing new things. What do you think you could do to spice up your old drills?"

"It isn't that the old drills are bad or anything. I just need to find a way to challenge the athletes more. Maybe spice up the techniques used in the drills"; Leah sounded a little more unscathed.

"Then you could save some time instead of organiz...", Ellen couldn't finish her sentence.

"And that time could be spent of working on these challenges instead", Leah lit up a smile for the first time during this meeting.

"Collin, do you see any issues in competitions with the athletes primarily repeating your movements during practice?" Ellen probed.

"Sometimes the guys have some trouble handling new situations at a faster tempo", he confessed.

"How could you incorporate more individual learning, that have a greater carry-over to competition?" Ellen asked.

"Maybe they should give each other some feedback", Collin replied.

"You're the one providing all the feedback now, aren't you?" Ellen asked almost knowing what Collin's response would be.

"It seems like that. They only hear what I view as correct. Perhaps they could help each other out a little more", he said.

"How would you make sure that they are getting their own optimal execution then?" Ellen questioned, liking the opening up in Collin's attitude to more diverse approaches to practice.

"I guess, if we focus more on the outcome of the movement rather than the motion itself. That would be good", Collin finished, while picking up his stuff and taking off to the next practice.

> What do you think of the way Collin and Leah construct their practices? How do you think Collin and Leah, respectively, view pedagogy?

Introduction

Berliner (1991) notes the lack of research investigating expertise within the field of pedagogy compared to other domains. Reasons for this include a belief that ill-structured domains such as pedagogy lack clear-cut right or wrong answers, and while true to some extent, this assertion simultaneously opens up for an unreflective 'anything goes' perspective, as mentioned in Chapter 1. Of course, pedagogy does not obey the laws of natural sciences, though there are some interesting findings in research that can serve as, at least, a starting point for testing out in real-life practice. Also, pedagogy might be hampered by being viewed as a feminine endeavour, overlapping childcare, opinions that anyone easily can acquire pedagogical knowledge as it is basically common sense, and pedagogical jobs are often engaged in by members of a social class whose status is not necessarily very high (Berliner, 1991). Altogether, pedagogy lives in the shadow of more 'established' sciences such as physics and even psychology. Nonetheless, Jones (2007) claims that coaching will be enhanced by viewing it from a pedagogical lens. This chapter starts off with a review of some theories of learning and from there on moves towards more hands-on practical applications for the coach.

Theories of Learning

Over the years, many different ideas have been promoted on learning. Naturally, an exhaustive review of them is beyond the scope of this chapter. Thus three distinct major theories are briefly reviewed. By having some basic knowledge of these three, it will be easier to grasp the pedagogical methods described later in the chapter. This review does not aim to endorse one or the other theory as superior. They all have their distinct advantages and complement each other. A coach could make great use of each one of them at different times in varying situations.

Behaviourism

According to behaviourism, an individual's behaviour is regulated by its consequences in a backwards manner. A person will undertake a specific action in order to receive or avoid a specific consequence. This is illustrated in Figure 5.1. When a certain stimulus appears, the athlete will respond with a specific behaviour, which is believed to elicit a desired consequence, or prevent an unwanted consequence. This expectation determines which behaviours that are used. An example of this happens when an athlete, in response to the stimulus of a coach scolding another athlete for not having his head under his hands when starting

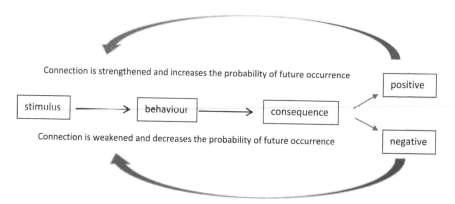

FIGURE 5.1 Illustration of the stimulus-behaviour (response)-consequence chain.

from the blocks in freestyle swimming, makes sure his hands are forming a perfect arrow in order to avoid the negative consequence of being scolded himself.

Four types of possible consequences exist (see Figure 5.2). Positive reinforcements and negative reinforcements both increase the likelihood for the preceding behaviour to happen again. However, in the swim example provided above, short-term it might work out perfectly fine, but in the long run, negative reinforcements are definitely more harmful than positive reinforcements. It is much better to do a behaviour in order to get a positive consequence than to avoid a negative one. The latter has a greater risk of leading to severe negative emotions, such as anxiety or fear, rather than more functional experiences of joy and creativity. Withdrawal of positive consequences is characterized as *extinction*. If a particular stimulus triggers a specific response, and this behaviour is not reinforced through a positive consequence, the link is weakened and eventually disappears altogether. During extinction, it is common to see the person increase the frequency of responses or trying a myriad of alternative responses in order to keep receiving the wanted outcome. This is called *extinction burst*. When trying to use

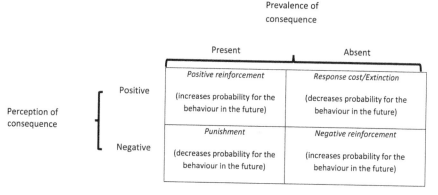

FIGURE 5.2 Types of consequences and their effects.

extinction, a coach needs to be prepared for this surge and refrain from providing the consequence the athlete desires, as that would contradict the extinction process. What determines the response from the individual is the strength of the connection between a specific stimulus, the response and a desired outcome is. In any given situation, plenty of stimuli exist. Therefore, an individual perceptually has to recognize a unique stimulus from background noise. After being exposed to a certain stimulus over time, *habituation* operate to ignore irrelevant stimuli. This occurs when an athlete learns not to respond to a specific stimulus as there are neither positive nor negative consequences from inaction. The outcome of habituation is that the individual does not respond to the stimulus in question, such as when an athlete does not hear the audience cheering when he/she has participated in enough competitions not to be startled by them (Domjan, 1998). Further, *generalization* and *discrimination* are two processes that are important for causation of a response. Generalization occurs when an individual has received a desirable outcome and later tries to use the same response for a slightly different stimulus. The opposite process is called discrimination and occurs when a desirable outcome has been absent. In this case, the individual tries a different response in order to elicit the desired outcome. Discrimination happens when the individual notices distinguishable aspects within two seemingly similar situations, and from these differences respond in different ways (Snowman & McCown, 2015).

Ways of Learning According to Behaviourism

Learning is dictated by reinforcements. Woollard (2010) categorizes reinforcers into groups of *intrinsic, environmental* and *social reinforcers*. Intrinsic reinforcers are more difficult to control and pertain to emotion and motivation, such as feelings of anger, fear, joy, relief, excitement, pleasure or impulses like a sudden smile across the face or a rampage in anger. Environmental reinforcers pertain to systems, such as gamification or milestones achieved (e.g., having participated in a set number of practices during the season). Social reinforcers refers to actions of others around the athlete, such as facial expressions, verbal feedback, pat on the back or showing empathy. The following sub-categories review some tools for a coach to impact an athlete's learning.

Shaping

An athlete trying to learn something complex will probably not get it perfectly right immediately. For this reason, shaping is a powerful tool. Shaping means that the athlete's behaviour is reinforced when it is getting closer to the target behaviour. Actions from the athlete that are further away from the target behaviour are ignored. By reinforcing steps along the way, a potentially long and tedious journey without any success is easier for the athlete to undertake. The reinforcements contain both motivation for future attempts, as well as information on how to execute these attempts (Snowman & McCown, 2015).

Reinforcement Schedule

The frequency of reinforcement provision is called reinforcement schedule. There are four different types of reinforcement schedules differing on two dimensions: fixed vs varied, and interval vs ratio. When reinforcements are provided using a fixed schedule that means that the athlete know when the reinforcements will appear, and when varying schedules are used, the reinforcements appear randomly. When reinforcements are provided on the basis of an interval, the athlete has to use the behaviour for a time period before the reinforcement will appear. When reinforcements are provided on the basis of ratio, the determining factor for when the reinforcement will appear is the number of times the specific behaviour is done. This makes for four variants of reinforcement schedules.

Fixed interval schedule is used when the athlete is reinforced after a set time engaging in the activity. Once the reinforcer has been provided a new interval begins. As the end of an interval nears, the activity is usually increased, while immediately after a new interval has been started the activity is normally reduced.

Variable ratio schedule is used when the athlete is reinforced after varying time periods. On average, the length of the periods evens out, but the length of one specific period is unknown to the athlete. This will make it more likely that the athlete keeps going for a longer period of time, as the reinforcement may appear any minute.

Fixed ratio schedule is used when the athlete is reinforced after a set number of repetitions. This type of schedule will normally produce high amounts of behaviour as the athlete can predict how many repetitions that will be needed, but immediately after the reinforcement a drop in intensity is common.

Variable ratio schedule is used when the athlete is reinforced after a different number of responses each time. This unpredictability tends to eliminate variation after reinforcements have been given, meaning the athlete keeps going even immediately after being reinforced as the next reinforcement may appear after the very next behavioural response. Highly addictive slot machines use this kind of reinforcement schedule with great success (Snowman & McCown, 2015).

Regardless of which reinforcement schedule is adhered to, in the early stages of learning it is recommended to use high frequency of reinforcement and reduce the frequency as the athlete progresses. By diluting the reinforcement, the athlete will have to keep going longer and perhaps also increasing the quality of the behaviour. However, if the reinforcements are too rare initially, the athlete may not cope with practicing difficult tasks, and consequently might quit.

Token Economy, Response Cost, Extinction, Time-Out

Token economy and response cost were described in Chapter 4. Extinction and time-out are variations of similar phenomena. Extinction means that a desirable outcome is withheld. Often, coaches are advocated to ignore troubling behaviour within the group. Although theoretically sound advice, it might not solve the issue completely, as athletes also get reinforcement from peers and not only from the coach. Time-out in behaviourism has a slightly different meaning from time-outs used in many sports during competition. Contrastingly, time-out in this account is used when an individual is removed from the action. Thus, positive reinforcement will temporarily be removed, leading to a weakened link between response and consequence. When using the time-out, it is important to remain calm and not overuse excessive force, otherwise this will likely have the same negative consequences as punishments (Snowman & McCown, 2015).

Premack's Principle

Another means to increase the likelihood of an athlete doing a less desired task is to use Premack's principle. It states that a highly desired behaviour is used as reinforcer for another behaviour of lower attractiveness. A coach can tell the athletes that they will get to play a game of tag (i.e., highly desired behaviour), after they have cleaned the locker room (i.e., minimally desired behaviour). In order for Premack's principle to be effective, the athletes must know in advance that they will be rewarded with a desirable behaviour after engaging in something less desirable (Woollard, 2010).

> Which of your own behaviours could be explained by a desire to reach a specific outcome or to avoid a specific outcome?
> What type of consequences are particularly interesting for the athletes you are coaching?
> What do you already do as a coach that relates to behaviourism?
> What else could you incorporate in your coaching from behaviourism?

Social Cognitive Theory

According to Bandura (1989), an individual's future behaviours are a result of the interaction of three factors. *Behaviour, personal factors* and *environmental influences* operate in a bidirectional way so that they all influence each other. Nevertheless, this does not mean that they are of equal strength or that they are in effect simultaneously. Behaviour (B) includes, among other things, patterns of self-observations and self-evaluations through various means. Personal factors (P) include emotions, metacognition and self-efficacy. Environmental influences (E) include elements like explanations provided by others, nature of task and consequences to responses (Snowman & McCown, 2015).

Two examples are provided on how this reciprocal causation might look in reality:

> *One of Instructor Ingram's athletes has very high self-efficacy for another technique (P). Because of this, the athlete chooses to use this technique as often as possible in competitive drills during practice (B) instead of other techniques. Ingram, who really wants this athlete to use other techniques, provides a concurrent instruction including*

a rationale for this specific technique (E) to the athlete. When hearing this, the athlete starts thinking more about the choices of technique during drills rather than just reacting instinctively (P).

Tina Trainer explains a new drill for her group of athletes (B). When the athletes get going, they show clear signs of boredom (E), which generates anxiety in Tina (P). She starts to question her instructional ability and chooses to stop the drill (B).

Two important concepts in social cognitive theory are *self-regulation* and *self-efficacy*.

Self-regulation

Self-regulation pertains to the individual's ability to be in charge of his/her own behaviours in spite of a lack of external reinforcers. This is important because it signifies an important development to go from being disciplined in a well-known situation to showing the same discipline under new circumstances. This is exhibited in the increased self-regulation of going from squatting by 'yourself' when the coach is in the same gym along with the other athletes, to working out on an off-day when no one else is present in the gym. Additionally, it is displayed when going from practicing with a familiar coach to switching to a more advanced group. With increasing age, more responsibility is assumed when it comes to being able to direct one's own development. Still, it is plausible that external temptations increase accordingly as the individual grows more conscious of the options that exist in the world. Particularly crucial is this in today's world with its accessible technical advancements and rapid flow of information. Zimmerman and Kitsantas (2005) describe a self-regulation cycle of three phases (see Figure 5.3). This view of learning puts much emphasize on deliberate actions.

Forethought consists of task analysis and creation of an action plan. Additionally, the athlete's motivational beliefs will affect how (and if at all) this phase is adhered to. Performance consists of focusing attention appropriately and self-instruction. In this phase, the athlete will also make some sort of recording (e.g., in memory or writing) of one's own behaviours. Self-reflection consists of evaluation of one's own behaviour and attribution of success/failure (e.g., luck, talent, task-difficulty, effort). In this phase, the individual will also undertake an analysis of how everything went. Eventually, conclusions from self-reflection will be brought into next cycle starting with forethought.

Self-efficacy

Bandura (1977) proposes that how much effort and how long an individual persists is determined by the level of self-efficacy, which is how much the individual believes that he/she can either perform the behaviour or reach a desired outcome. Self-efficacy has a number of sources, of which four are presented in descending

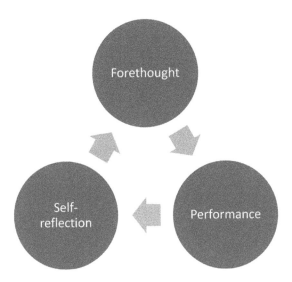

FIGURE 5.3 Phases of the self-regulation cycle.

order of strength. First, *previous performances* are personally experienced successes. To make previous performances salient, coaches can use statistics, video recordings, goal-setting focusing on controllable aspects and outline appropriate training progression. Importantly, 'previous performances' do not necessarily have to be an 'entire performance', but could consist of a part of a performance, or a process that went well. Hence, the wise coach uses some creativity to provide the athlete with opportunities not only to succeed but also as evidence of success in retrospect. Second, *vicarious experience* consists of modelling success by observing someone else (or self-modelling through watching film clip of previous performances before an injury for example). To make modelling effective, the athlete should be able to identify him-/herself with the model. Third, *verbal persuasion* can consist of augmented feedback or inspiring discussions with the coach, but possibly also of purposeful self-talk. Verbal persuasion is often combined with the other sources. Fourth, *appraisal of arousal* means that the individual can interpret bodily reactions both as a sign of weakness or unpreparedness but also as a sign that the body is getting ready to perform (e.g., without any kind of muscle tension or arousal it would be impossible to do much else than sleep). Feeling those butterflies in the stomach before a big competition is a healthy sign of bodily preparation for action. Understanding this relationship will provide more self-efficacy (Feltz, Short, & Sullivan, 2008).

Ways of Learning According to Social Cognitive Theory

Two overarching categories of learning strategies are *memory-directed* and *comprehension-directed*. In an athlete's situation and endeavour, the latter is probably more fruitful. However, two memory-directed are included first in the presentation below, followed by three comprehension-directed.

Rehearsal

Rehearsal includes repeating something until it is recalled by rote memory. Perhaps this is best likened to repetitive practice of a closed skill or routine, as can be seen in shooting or figure skating. Cumulative rehearsal is a somewhat more advanced version that includes rehearsal of several listed tasks. After the most recently introduced task is practiced, it is then rehearsed in conjunction with the previous tasks. Then another task is introduced until all tasks have been practiced. This way all skills are kept up to date.

Mnemonics

Some skills or routines that consist of several smaller parts are possible to label verbally. In this case, two useful mnemonics are *acronyms* and *acrostics*. In the former, the first letter of every word is used to create a new word, such as *HIIT* (High Intensity Interval Training). In the latter, the first letter of each item to be remembered is used to create a word, which in turn make a full sentence to remember the order of the items, such as *Fat Whales' Entertainment Show*, to remember the order in which body parts (Fingers, Wrist, Elbow, Shoulder) are supposed to hit the water during a freestyle stroke.

Self- and Peer Questioning

By posing and trying to answer questions, the athlete's comprehension is improved. Different types of questions are elaborated in a section below. There are two benefits of using questions. Obviously, it helps understanding the subject, but it also provides an opportunity to monitor progress as number of questions asked or answered is an indication of comprehension. Athletes can self-question their execution of a specific skill evaluating the effects of the movement, such as how the wind was countered with aim and point of impact on the golf ball. Questions for the athletes could be provided in a sheet by the coach.

Note Taking

Two main benefits are seen with note taking. First, the process of making the notes themselves enhances both retention and understanding. Second, reviewing the notes will be an additional opportunity for learning. An example of note taking useful for athletes, comes in the form of writing a training diary that records progress and/or experiences.

Observations

Magill (2011) mentioned four processes governing observational learning. First, the observer gets information from the model. Second, when the observer thinks back on the model, symbols derived during the observation are transformed and restructured in memory. Third, this memory is then translated into a behaviour trying to reproduce the model. Fourth, there is a motivational incentive to perform like the modelled action.

> Which of your own behaviours could be explained by the self-regulatory cycle and/or your level of self-efficacy?
> Think of an athlete in your current group that you consider to have low confidence. Which one of the aforementioned sources could you use to enhance this athlete's self-efficacy?
> What do you already do as a coach that relates to social cognitive theory?
> What else could you incorporate in your coaching from social cognitive theory?

Constructivism

Constructivism has evolved into many variations over the years. A shared aspect for them is that learning is viewed in, and dependent of, a larger context and not just the learner. In this context, social relationships such as the one between athlete and coach become important. Thus, learning is more than mere memory functions or probabilistic calculations of consequences. Instead, the athlete becomes a creator of his/her own learning and knowledge. Two persons will not learn the same despite reading the same book. Knowledge is seen more as a process rather than an end-product (Slavin, 2009).

Four common assumptions are typical of constructivist theories. First, learning has to be *meaningful* to the learner. The athlete builds a personal view of the world by drawing from previous experiences, interests, values and knowledge. Prior knowledge can facilitate learning of new issues. Perhaps similarities between new and existing experiences need to be highlighted by a coach (Snowman & McCown, 2015). Second, *social interaction* is emphasized. During social interactions athletes have the opportunity to use the language to learn with, and from, each other. Also, a knowledgeable other makes it possible to 'scaffold' the learning experience. This means that a person with someone else's support manages far more than when working alone. Thus, it is always a negotiation between what 'can be done alone' and 'what can be done with another'. Hence, scaffolding is supposed to be gradually withdrawn for the learner to emerge as capable in his/her own right (Slavin, 2009). Experiencing others' perspectives through social interaction facilitates and broadens learning. To accomplish this, language plays a huge role. Learning can happen in and through a narrative, where the individual expresses a story of a lived experience. This narrative is also expressed through an internal conversation. Thus, language is central to learning (Goodson, Biesta, Tedder, & Adair, 2010). Correspondingly, the social context serves to enhance the experience of meaningfulness of tasks. Third, *self-regulation* is, similarly to social cognitive theory, important in constructivism. The individual is seen as active in creating knowledge and needs to be able to test theories in practice for substantial learning to develop. This cannot be accomplished without activity, and, as Cervone, Mor, Orom, Shadel, and Scott (2011) conclude, judgement of both the person's existing knowledge as well as goals for improving the same knowledge will determine if the person takes action. Fourth, *authentic problems and real-life situations* are used to a large extent. The problems are holistic in nature and not small bits and pieces of information being taught one at a time for the athlete to put into a coherent unit. Because of this, scaffolding from a coach or peer might be needed as the tasks are too difficult to handle alone. Real-life situations also make it possible for the athlete to draw upon previous experiences, in addition to being a fruitful ground for collaborative work in a group (Snowman & McCown, 2015).

Ways of Learning According to Constructivism

Change of Perspectives

Multiple perspectives are emphasized in constructivist learning. Change of perspectives is highly advocated as this both leads to novel approaches being visible, while simultaneously make features of known approaches more salient, thus better understood. The multiple perspectives could be presented by a coach, or could emerge in a discussion with peers. Content of these perspectives could concern any aspects of sports, such as technique, decision-making, mental facets or physical aspects. Pertaining to sports, an athlete that views, or tries, different techniques to accomplish the same movement goal will enhance motor learning and likely deepen cognitive understanding of pros and cons with different technical executions.

Group Discussions

Group discussions are another important means for learning. Discussions may be initiated by elaborating on an issue that already has a conclusion (at least according to some). Another way to initiate a group discussion is presenting a topic that has no single, easy answer. In sports, athletes may have a discussion (with or without a coach's presence) about techniques, tactics, team strategies, previous experiences of training and improvement, just to name a few subjects. During discussions, it is advantageous to emphasize contrasts between different approaches or solutions, stimulate informed guessing (e.g., pose a hypothetical question about 'what would happen if...') and to encourage participation by providing a safe and inclusive climate as everyone's opinion is of interest for the benefit of the others' knowledge development (Snowman & McCown, 2015). The number of people within a group is important to consider to ensure proper space for interaction, as both speaking time and engagement tend to increase with less participants. Of course, the number of people depends on practical logistics and task type, but if possible, no more than five athletes is recommended.

Cognitive Apprenticeship

Constructivism highlights that learning is individualized and a single correct universal solution seldom exists. Therefore, guidance is more important to learning than telling a predetermined answer. Much of the interaction between coach and athlete depends on how the athlete responds. In a way, this happens through negotiation between coach and athlete. That supportive relationship is a *cognitive apprenticeship*. A coach tries to bring only as much support as necessary for the athlete to keep going. If too much support is provided, risks are the athlete loses responsibility of learning and becomes passive. Learning is facilitated by observations, questions, participation and testing out solutions and behaviours. Gradually, the athlete will develop more and more expertise and the relationship will change to a more equal one (Slavin, 2009).

Problem-solving

Problem-solving consists of five steps according to Snowman and McCown (2015). First, a person needs to identify the problem. This might seem easy, but in reality, we often have far less training in problem identification compared to the solving part. In educational settings, the problem is often presented as a given and the participants are asked to work on only solving. The athlete needs to recognize that he/she actually has a problem, which takes an open mind and curiosity. Second, the athlete needs to understand the nature of the problem. One should strive to frame the problem optimally, as there are likely multiple ways to frame the same problem. With the help of the coach's extensive content knowledge, the athlete is assisted in recognizing important features in the current issue and from this, draw upon previous experiences to create an optimal representation. Third, relevant information has to be compiled. There are different ways to accomplish this, such as looking at other successful athletes or getting some advice from the coach. Fourth, a solution has to be tested out. Many different strategies exist for athletes' problem-solving. Among those available are a) trying to solve an analogous problem (e.g., coming up with a similar issue regarding aspects/information that the athlete is more knowledgeable about), b) break the problem into smaller and more convenient parts, c) working backward from the intended solution or d) work on a simpler version of the problem (e.g., take into consideration fewer parameters). Some of these strategies might lend themselves more to a group of athletes' tactical problems, while others might be more appropriate for individual technical problems. Fifth, the solution needs to be evaluated. This evaluation should be based both on the efficacy of the solution and outcomes. However, other aspects worthy of consideration include energy- and time-efficiency of the solution, and lessons learnt from the process as a whole.

Well-structured problems might only need steps 2, 4 and 5 (i.e., understand the problem, work out a solution, evaluate the solution), while ill-structured problems demand all five. Problems during coaching practice tend to be ill-structured, as they are complex (i.e., lots of factors influencing each other simultaneously), cues for solution procedures might be scarce and less definitive criteria for when the problem is solved exists.

> Which of your own behaviours could be explained with the learning taking place in a realistic context or through social interaction?
> What types of athletes' prior experiences could you take advantage of to enhance their learning in the current sport?
> What do you already do as a coach that relates to constructivism?
> What else could you incorporate in your coaching from constructivism?

> Remember a leader that you have met in your life (e.g., a coach, boss, teacher or someone else in any kind of leadership role). Which one of the three theories of learning do you think this person most identified with? Provide examples from the most salient theory from the leader's actions.
> What theory do you find most appealing as a coach right now? Provide some examples.

Pedagogical Methods

Five different pedagogical methods will be presented. Their features are discernible from different theories of learning. Some methods have their roots in more than one theory. Neither of these five methods is to be viewed as always superior to the others. Consequently, coaches who have a grasp of more than one pedagogical method are better at varying practices and are prepared for different circumstances and demands, compared to coaches who exclusively rely on one. As coaches seem to be shaped by their own athletic experiences to a large extent, it is not unlikely that one method is seen as more appropriate. Conversely, one method may initially be deemed impossible to use or inappropriate for a particular sport setting. However, coaches are advocated to keep an open mind throughout this section. It is possible that even without going all-in on a specific method, at least a few aspects could look attractive to test out. Each method has its own advantages as well as drawbacks. In order to make each method more salient, they are contrasted against each other. The five methods are *direct instruction* (the coach leads), *task method* (athletes work independently with activities), *peer teaching* (athletes help each other), *guided discovery* (coach guides the athlete indirectly towards a movement goal) and *problem-solving method* (effects of movements are in focus). They are situated on a continuum where direct instruction means that the coach owns most of the decisions to problem-solving where the athlete owns most of the decisions. The methods are derived from Cassidy, Jones, and Potrac (2009), Metzler (2005), and Mosston and Ashworth (2002), unless other references are provided.

Direct Instruction

The coach leads the practice while the athletes' objective is to execute movements as close as possible to the model/demonstration provided by the coach. The aim of this method is to quickly improve performance, and it is assumed that this method will lead to high precision in the performance, at least on short-term basis. Practice time is used with high efficiency (at least in a way that athletes complete many and accurate repetitions). The coach is the one who explains what to do and how it is to be done. Athletes' actions are directed very clearly by the coach. When the coach directs attention to certain parts of demonstrations or specific cues, important details are effectively conveyed to the athletes. By executing movements correctly, athletes are assumed to develop. Much of the work is carried out in a whole-group setting. The athletes try to automatize a movement, often after a visual demonstration or verbal cue from the coach to start or stop a movement. It is also possible for the coach to pass the torch to another athlete who takes the role the others are supposed to follow.

Implications of the Method

The coach is assumed to have a large sport-specific competence (at least more than the athletes) regarding the area that is practiced. Additionally, the coach needs to be able to demonstrate movements physically, or otherwise use a proficient athlete for this purpose. Plenty of prescriptive feedback should be provided by the coach to correct deviations from the athletes. As the coach has a lot of power in this method, this position should not be abused, but rather complemented with care and empathy. Athletes do not make many decisions, but try to imitate coach's demonstration, and they will have to believe in the coach's competence to 'show and tell'. Athletes are expected to conform to group norms and behave in their respective roles. All athletes are making the same movement and strive for similarity in their executions to a large extent. Individual variations are seen as deviations that should be moulded away. Thus, some frustration can be experienced when executions are not up to standards, either by the athlete or by peers waiting for others to get it right before the whole group will move on. Some athletes like practices where focus is on clear physical execution on behalf of making-decisions, and such athletes will probably like this method.

Task Method

For each task used during practice, the coach has pre-planned instructions and evaluation criteria, which are provided by text, pictures or video. The group as a whole will not need the coach for instruction or continuous feedback during practice itself. Consequently, the coach spends more time during the practice with individualized instruction and interaction with the athletes deemed to be in need of this extra support. Meanwhile, the athletes are responsible for the pacing of the tasks, and as they finish one level of difficulty, they progress to the next on their own. The coach is relieved from managerial duties during the practice and can engage in more individual interactions with certain athletes. Of course, every now and then every athlete needs to get attention from the coach. Using the task method, individual adjustments for specific athletes are quite easily done, perhaps by having variations of the instructions. Individual goals are an excellent addition to this method. Compared to direct instruction, task method use practice time more efficiently as more repetitions can be performed since quick athletes do not have to wait around for the rest of the group to finish or for the coach to present the next activity. Factors under the influence of the athletes are starting, pace, rhythm and intermissions in-between repetitions. Athletes will also develop their capacity to give themselves feedback by comparing their performance to the evaluation criteria. However, the order of exercises and how they are supposed to be executed are determined by the coach. If a large portion of the athletes commits the same mistake, the coach can gather the group for reinstruction.

Implications of the Method

The coach needs to get used to not constantly directing and commanding athletes. Further, the coach has to value individual decision-making and athletes' responsibility over their own practicing. In reality, the coach needs to trust the athletes will do their best, and when athletes are occupied with their activities in an efficient manner, the coach has to be content with observing rather than intervening. As the athletes are given more responsibility for the pace of practice, they will develop accountability for their own development. For the athletes it should be quite easy to recognize the connection between number of repetitions and improvements. Because the athletes primarily work on their own, they learn to take responsibility and evaluate their own progress. This method can also bring a greater experience of independence in the athletes.

Peer Teaching

Peer teaching is described with the phrase 'I teach you, then you teach me'. In this method, athletes work in dyads, or perhaps even trios. In a dyad, one athlete is the *learner* while the other acts as a *tutor*. If using groups of three, the role of *observer* is added. The tutor's task is to observe the learner providing feedback on his/her movement execution. After a stipulated time or number of repetitions, the athletes switch roles. In short, the tutor takes over the primary supervising responsibility from the coach. Many other responsibilities still rest with the coach. If the coach sees something worthy of feedback or attention in a learner's execution, the coach does not intervene directly with this athlete. Instead, the coach interacts with the tutor, leading the tutor's attention to the specific area of concern, in extension providing this information to the learner. Additionally, the tutor has the opportunity to learn through observational learning. When working with younger children, it is beneficiary to have them active for large portions of the practice time. However, due to spatial constraints, sometimes it will be difficult to have all athletes active during a specific activity simultaneously. In this case, peer teaching makes athletes who are not physically involved in the activity still engaged. If the spatial limitations are even more severe, groups of three are appropriate. The observer monitors both the learner and the tutor and provides the tutor with feedback on how this task was performed. During some work, it is beneficiary to incorporate some recovery time (e.g., sprint work aimed at improving maximum speed). In that instance, peer teaching serves dual purposes. Initially, it will be preferable to use pairs of good friends to avoid social conflicts obscuring the method itself. After the athletes have become more comfortable with the method though, it is advocated to change the pairings every now and then.

Implications of the Method

The coach needs to view the socializing process between tutor and learner as a desirable goal for sports participation. An advantage of this method is that athletes get more feedback per person compared to if the coach is the only one responsible for feedback provision. Shea, Wulf, Whitacre, and Wright (2000) showed that this method can be as effective as methods that have twice as many physical repetitions. Furthermore, the coach has to help the athletes to give each other accurate feedback. Hattie (2009) highlighted that peer feedback in classrooms often is inaccurate, furthering the need for a coach to clarify how the feedback should be provided and then monitoring that the tutors actually follow the guidelines.

Guided Discovery

Similarly to the three previous methods, the coach using guided discovery has a clear goal for the movement execution. However, the way to find the movement solution rests to a larger extent with the athlete. Two different athletes might not have the same path to the goal. Instead, they are encouraged to engage in more cognitive activity compared to the previous methods. In guided discovery, questions are used as a primary tool to elicit the desired response. Though, the questions are of convergent character since they aim to lead the athlete to discover a predetermined movement. Four rules direct this method. First, avoid telling the answer explicitly. Second, wait for the athlete's response and evaluate it, before providing another intervention. Third, provide frequent feedback for the athlete to explore instead of replicating demonstrations of instructions. Fourth, have patience with learning progress, and foster a climate of acceptance. The argument for this method is that it takes advantage of the idiosyncrasies of the athlete and lays the foundation for a more robust learning over long time, as the athlete needs to be more engaged in the movements. Also, the potential for developing metacognition is enhanced compared to the previous methods presented.

Implications of the Method

First and foremost, the coach has to have a vision of what the athlete should be able to accomplish. Then the coach has to break down the end-goal into manageable steps that are in sequence, and after this, accompany each step with appropriate clues or questions. Anticipation of potential responses from the athlete will also be necessary in order to construct fitting questions. The coach needs to have questions ready for disposal, and these questions need to be evaluated in the event of plateauing progression. The questions have to be provided in a non-authoritative manner so that the athlete feels ownership of the learning process. The athlete has to be curious and sometimes needs to put off a thirst for short-term solutions. This method requires more thinking from the athlete. Both coaches and athlete (or even parents or other stakeholders) might have to fight traditional expectations on the coach being the one providing the answers. Likely, old-school expectancies are pre-empted by an explicit information about the method's mode of procedure.

Problem-solving Method

From a constructivist point of view, the athlete should own the learning process and this is evident in this method. Using problem-solving method, the only given is the problem itself (e.g., hit opponent with an upper-cut or prevent opponent from scoring). The effect of the movement is the only important. Thus, any means (within the rules of the specific sport) that produce the desired effect are considered appropriate. There is no optimal movement template prescribed for every athlete since they all have their individual differences in everything from physical dispositions to previous experiences. This method takes guided discovery a step further as the coach does not have a prescribed aesthetic opinion of the movement. The assumption is that the athlete can, and will, self-organize when it comes to finding the optimal movement according to what the constraints allow. Some might view this method as Laissez Faire leadership as the coach is not explicitly demonstrating how movement should be executed to the same extent that is more common in the previous methods. However, nothing could be further from the truth, as this method calls for more cognizance in adapting the tasks and environment to fit the current behaviours of the athletes.

Implications of the Method

The coach has to have patience, as this method might see slower short-term gains than other methods. Additionally, it is absolutely vital that the coach uses creativity in manipulating the environment, task or individual constraints in order to elicit an efficient movement-solution. Therefore, it is helpful to make a plan that includes some potential interventions for the most common troubles the athlete will run into. For example, when power cleaning, an athlete might throw the barbell too far out from the body. If so, the coach may place the athlete in front of a wall in the gym which will enhance the probability that the barbell will travel closer to the athlete's body. This is an example of a manipulation of the environmental constraints without explicitly telling the athlete how to do it. After getting more accustomed to this method, these manipulations should be easier to invent on the spot. Compared to other methods, this method could demand somewhat less focus on pre-planning activities and much more energy spent during the actual practice, as the coach needs to adapt to the responses from the athletes, instead of relying mostly on a predetermined practice schedule. More robust long-term learning is assumed with this method.

To sum up, the methods have their respective pros and cons with some central characteristics displayed in Table 5.1. The most effective pedagogical method is hard to discern, as there are many antecedents to consider and perhaps as many outcomes to evaluate. For instance, Kember and Wong (2000) found that passive students preferred more direction from the leader. Contrastingly, active students preferred looser reigns from the leader and more personal input. On the other hand, Simon and Bjork (2001) compared two different practice schedules where participants after practice got to estimate how well they would perform on a retention test the next day. Their findings supported the notion that people in

TABLE 5.1 Central characteristics of pedagogical methods.

Method	Origin learning theory	Essential coaching tasks	Crucial question for the coach to answer
DI	Behaviourism	Demonstrating, instructing	Will one size fit all?
TM	Behaviourism	Planning, creating instructions that can be easily understood by athletes on their own	Will the athletes understand the instructions on their own?
PT	Social cognitive theory	Grouping, monitoring athletes' feedback provision to one another	Will the athletes cherish the role of tutor?
GD	Constructivism	Preparing questions/methods to lead the athlete toward the goal	Will the athletes respond in the anticipated way?
PS	Constructivism	Focusing on effect, manipulating environmental constraints	Will the athletes have the patience?

general are poor at judging their own learning, as participants had greater confidence in their upcoming performance after the less effective practice schedule. In conclusion, a coach clearly needs to juggle a lot of factors for pedagogy to be optimal for the athletes. No predetermined answer seems to exist, and perhaps worse, it is tricky to trust even athletes' own preferences. Best advice seems to be having a dialogue with the athletes about pros and cons of potential pedagogies and to keep reflecting on their impact on various outcomes.

> Which one of the methods do you currently use the most?
> What are the reasons for this preference (e.g., mediated/unmediated/internal learning situations, or own athletic training)?
> Which method could you use more of?
> How would that be carried out?
> What kind of challenges do you see in using this method?
> Which one of the methods do you think would be most difficult for you to use?
> What could you do to overcome these difficulties?
> What would be the consequences for the athletes if you used this method?

Presentation of Information to Athletes

This section briefly covers information presented to the athlete before his/her movement. Presentation of information during and after a movement is reviewed elsewhere (Chapter 6). Two typical measures for presenting information about a skill before an athlete engages in a specific movement are *demonstration* and *instruction*. Cognitive development might be a factor deciding if visual demonstration or verbal instruction is most beneficiary. A study comparing eight- and eleven-year-old dancers found that the younger children reported a greater reliance on visual information, while the older reported greater preference on verbal information (Cadopi, Chatillon, & Baldy, 1995).

Demonstration

Two different aspects can be discerned from watching a demonstration. First, the observer studies the effect or goal of the movement. Second, the observer studies the movement pattern itself. However, it is not a given that demonstrations always enhance athletes' performance. If demonstrations contain redundant information (e.g., a very simple skill), they will not enhance performance. Other aspects to consider are both the skill level of the model and the observer (McCullagh & Weiss, 2001). Usually, demonstrations are thought of as an expert illustrating a movement. Although there is support for the notion that correct movement execution will enhance performance, novice observers also benefit from seeing a learning model, as this can make them explore a greater range of movements. Magill (2011) argued that this kind of problem-solving exploration is especially effective if it is accompanied by feedback. This is similar to the peer teaching pedagogical method.

An athlete observing a difficult movement he/she is trying to learn, spends much of the attentional capacity to grasp the task execution and therefore demonstration highlighting small details risks lead to cognitive overload. Instead, it is advantageous to mix demonstrations with physical repetitions as the athlete can get a hold of a few basic aspects of the movement before returning to a more detailed observation (Ong & Hodges, 2012). Some evidence exists that the primary role of a demonstration is to present strategies that are viable solutions of the task at hand. Therefore, variations in demonstration may help the observer to perceptually discriminate the variables that are crucial to reaching the movement goal (Buchanan & Dean, 2010). Using a model that is similar to the observer is beneficial. Attributes that likely convey similarity are ability, age, body composition and sex. Though, skill level has been found to be more salient and is probably more important than sex for observers to identify with the model (McCullagh & Weiss, 2001).

Instruction

Explicit instruction may enhance or inhibit performance (Wulf & Weigelt, 1997). Too much verbal information easily overloads athletes' attentional capacity. A sound guiding principle is to provide only as much information as necessary to communicate to the athlete what is requested to do. Too much is no better than no instructions at all (Magill, 2011). An important feature of instruction is whether it draws attention to internal or external aspects. Instructions pertaining to effects of movement are more efficient learning tools and lead to better long-term outcomes (Wulf, 2007). Instructing a slalom skier to exert force on the outer *ski* compared to the outer *foot*, or instructing a golfer to move the *club head* compared to move the *hands* have proven to be beneficial for the athletes. It does not sound like much of a difference, but studies have repeatedly shown a significant effect. One way of conveying lots of information in an implicit way is to use a metaphor. Liao and Masters (2001) effectively taught table tennis players to hit a forehand loop through the analogy of a right-angled triangle and to move the racket along the hypotenuse (longest side in a right-angled triangle). Naturally, for a metaphor to provide information in a convenient manner, it has to be relatable for the athlete.

Verbal instructions can also be provided in a shorter version such as a 'cue'. Landin (1994, p. 299) defined verbal cues as 'concise phrases, often just one or two words, that either direct the student's attention to relevant task stimuli or prompt key movement pattern elements of a motor skill'. Cues used in conjunction with demonstration serve to draw the observer's attention to some specific features of the demonstration. In extension of augmented verbal instruction, athletes themselves can provide cues. This has two utilities. First, it increases the active involvement in the activity, and second, similarly to the task method, it frees up the coach for work with other athletes. Telling the athlete prior to movement execution what he/she should focus on increases the likelihood for the athlete to actually have this cue in mind. Timing of the cue seems important as well. A verb before the movement is started will be beneficial, while a verb during the execution might interfere as the athlete's cognitive processes can be overloaded with competing tasks (i.e., processing the verbal information and executing the motor task). An exception to this is when cues are used to trigger a rhythmical pattern, such as coordinating the timing of leg kick in a butterfly swim stroke (Winkelman, 2020).

> How do you use demonstrations during practice?
> How do you provide instruction during practice?
> What could you do to improve presentation of information for the athletes?

The Four Pieces of the Jigsaw Puzzle

When it comes to full-scale competition at the senior and elite level, the performance is made up of *technical*, *tactical*, *mental*, and *physical* aspects (Janelle & Hillman, 2003). Actually, this would be true regardless of the level of competition, albeit adjusting for degree of difficulty. For example, an eight year old experiencing her first basketball game will need to be able to execute a movement (technical: e.g., making a pass), after making a decision (tactical: choosing between passing and dribbling), while simultaneously handling the anxiety of grandmother watching (mental: emotional regulation), at a given time before the moment is gone (physical: speed) while withstanding an opponent's physical contact (physical: core stability). Traditionally, sports practice has followed the pattern of first working on skills (i.e., technique), and when athletes have proven sufficiently proficient technically, they are allowed to move on to some kind of competition-like game. During the 1980s, Games-Based Approaches (GBA) were introduced to complement practices' overly focus on technical execution by early incorporation of tactical decision-making (Griffin & Patton, 2005). In these approaches, small-sided games or competitive situations are used as a foundation for developing athletes' skills. Although widely used, GBA explicitly emphasize and deliberately work on only two of Janelle and Hillman's four aspects. Wrisberg (2007) suggested a model labelled 'total skill practice', in which three aspects were included in the form of technical, tactical and mental skills. In an extension of these models, the model of *four pieces of the jigsaw puzzle* is proposed. Although some sort of movement is central to practice (i.e., technical execution), it is possible to build in different sequences, much like a jigsaw puzzle. Thus, the four pieces of athletic performance can be combined in various combinations within the puzzle frame. This model will make it easier for coaches to focus on specific areas in need of athletes' improvement and serves as a tool to diversify the sporting experience. Instead of primarily focusing on the type of activity the

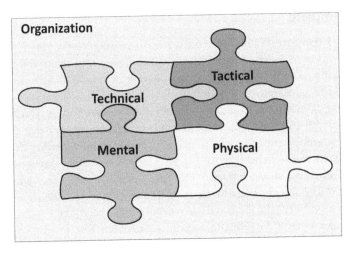

FIGURE 5.4 The four pieces of a jigsaw puzzle.

athletes undertake, it is possible to incorporate all pieces regardless of the type of activity (e.g., small-sided game or isolated practice).

Arguably, incorporating more than one piece at the same time during practice is underscored by plenty of research covering transfer of learning (cf. Abernethy, Farrow, Gorman, & Mann, 2012). At least two pieces should be integrated simultaneously to enhance transfer from the practice to the competition, but it is possible to use three or four pieces at once. Integration will make practice more competition-like. It is possible to combine pieces in every conceivable way but the 1-2-3 template described below will introduce a temporal structure for this. One caveat though, 'competition-like' is not to be perceived as winning being the most important goal when it comes to youth sports. Contrastingly, this serves to make practice as fun, meaningful, challenging and useful as possible at the same time, instead of going through the motions 'just because coach said so'. The four pieces exist within an organizational context (i.e., frame of the puzzle), as Figure 5.4 shows. This context is open for manipulation from coaches as well, but the primary means of improving athletic development lie in the four pieces.

> Which one of the four pieces do you consider your strongest suit as a coach?
> Which one of the four pieces do you consider the strongest suit of the athletes you are coaching?
> Which one of the four pieces do you think you need to develop the most?
> How would you go about to improve your competence in this piece?
> Which one of the four pieces do you think the athletes you are coaching would need to improve the most?

1-2-3 Template

The 1-2-3 template (Table 5.2) consists of three stages of a practice activity: *organization*, *new learning* and *better learning*. Its purpose is to temporally incorporate and integrate the four pieces into a coherent structure, challenging athletes for all round development Extending on the practical applications using the STTEP model (Grout & Long, 2009) and GBA (Serra-Olivares, García-López, & Calderón, 2016), this framework grounds its adjustments in what dimension of sporting competence the athlete needs to improve upon, rather than taking off in adjustments of the activity *per se*. Any activity during practice can be divided into three distinct stages. The first stage is *organization*, which is the structure of the activity the athletes are going to engage in. The second stage is *new learning* and here the focus will be working on a specific technique or learning to make tactical decisions in a specific situation. The third stage involves *better learning* where the focus is set on improving a technique or decision making by alternating the demands mentally and/or physically. Thus, in better learning, no new technique or a new decision is introduced. By manipulating mental and physical demands the athlete is challenged. This is also useful if an athlete says that he/she 'is able to do this drill now', meaning that it is getting boring or repetitive. By dividing practice into organization, new learning and better learning, coaches are provided a rationale for practice activities. Actually, it is advantageous to use an organization the athletes are familiar with, as this leads to minimal time spent in organization. The task for the coach then becomes to manipulate the demands within this organization. Below, a brief description of each stage is provided.

Organization

Organization is the structures of the activity that the athletes need to know in order to execute the practice activity, such as number of athletes involved, purpose, amount of time allowed, where to move, distances, rules etc. However important organization is, it is not the determining factor of athletic expertise. What really matters is how well developed an athlete four pieces are and not how many drills, exercises, play forms (i.e., types of organizations) an athlete knows. First, the athletes get an explanation of the organization of the activity they are about to engage in. Then, they should be allowed some time to learn this organization while trying it out. During this time, it will be inefficient for a coach to

TABLE 5.2 Stages of practice according to 1-2-3 template.

Stage	Focus
1. Organization	Learning the structure and rules of the activity
2. New learning	Technical/Tactical
3. Better learning	Mental/Physical

tax their working memory too much by emphasizing or feedbacking technical or tactical components (Ong & Hodges, 2012). Finally, when most athletes seem to have gotten a grip of the basic organization of the activity, it should be given a name. Involvement from the athletes in the naming procedure likely increase their perception of meaningfulness as they suggest names that means something to them. The next time this organization is used, the athletes probably recall much, if not all, of the information of the organization through hearing the name, as this is an efficient way of storing information (Buschke, 1976). This creates more time to emphasize the next two stages, which are more important for athletic development.

New Learning (Technical/Tactical)

Technical refers to *how* a movement is executed. *Tactical* contains decisions made by the athlete regarding *when* the movement is executed or *what* movement to select from possible alternatives. Depending on the type of sport, technique is used to accomplish an outcome (e.g., open skill sports such as invasion games), or as a purpose on its own (e.g., artistic gymnastics, where points are given for execution). In many sports, there are some decisions to be made by the athlete during competition. If so, technical execution is a sort of way to solve a tactical problem (e.g., technical execution of driving home a backhand volley to the corner that the opposing tennis player is not running to, solves the tactical problem of placing the ball out of reach for opponent). Practicing for these types of sports, it is advocated to include decision-making to a large extent during practice when working on technique. Initially, it might be as simple as choosing between two options with unlimited time at disposal. Degree of difficulty may then be increased by the coach by, just to mention a few examples: including more than two options, decreasing the available time to make a decision and making the information for decisions more ambiguous.

Better Learning (Mental/Physical)

By using a familiar organization to practice some known technical and/or tactical skill, it is possible to increase degree of difficulty through manipulation of mental or physical demands. Below are some of the possible means to adjust the challenge by incorporating aspects from the mental and physical pieces listed.

Mental

Stress Management

Add auditive or visual distractions, raise the stakes for participation (e.g., 'you have to do this, otherwise…'), randomly add incorrect decisions from the referee, create uneven situations or increase uncertainty in what happens.

Focus/precision

Decrease the area of accuracy, add visual distractions, or increase the mental load by adding something that occurs simultaneously (e.g., having to remember something such as what happened in the previous play sequence – who did something, etc., demanding that two subsequent repetitions cannot use the same choice of technique/tactic, or making the athlete count backwards in threes from 100).

Goal-setting/confidence

Use different types of goals – which are presented in somewhat progressively increasing difficulty – such as *absolute numbers* (e.g., make a total of five good executions), *time* (e.g., keep going for a set number of minutes), *absolute numbers in a specific time frame* (e.g., make a total of five good executions in two minutes), *relative frequency* (e.g., make five good executions out of ten attempts), *consecutively* (e.g., make five consecutive good executions in a row). Of course, all types are open for increase of difficulty in themselves (e.g., absolute numbers – five executions are easier than seven executions).

Physical

Speed

Decrease the distance that is used, shorten the work intervals, throw balls at a higher velocity, add reaction activities such as having to respond to a cue and make a change of direction before the primary skill is executed, add a short sprint before the primary skill is executed, or add defenders that reduce the available time for the athlete.

Strength

Add body contact, add outside resistance, or use heavier equipment.

Endurance

Increase distances/spaces, use longer work interval, use more repetitions, or move the activity to later on in the practice or after some activity that has taxed athletes physically.

Different Organizations of Practice Activities

Pedagogical methods and 1-2-3 template can be used in conjunction with each other in many combinations, as does the different organizations of practice activities described here. During practice, primarily three organization of activities is used. They are *formal exercises*, *playful games* and *game situations*. The most important distinction is between the first category of organizations and the last two. While the first one uses movement as a means to an end, the latter two uses a context for the training. In formal exercises practice is undertaken because the coach says so, the training program prescribes a specific amount of time, or an athlete feels the need to get a number of repetitions in. Work load, form, time, etc. are usually easily monitored during formal exercises, thus making them handy when a specific and somewhat narrow part needs improvement. Cushion, Harvey, Muir, and Nelson, (2012) called this 'training state'. However, I think 'formal exercises' is a better label as it conveys a message of formality. 'You work out to a specific number of repetitions', or 'for a specified time-frame', whereas 'training' sounds like undefined practice.

Nevertheless, sometimes formal exercises are subjected to dullness, non-self-determined motivation and lack of understanding. This is where it is important for a coach to have extra resources in the coaching toolbox in the form of playful games and game situations. In contrast to formal exercise, when using playful games or game situations, training is undertaken for the sake of accomplishing something that provides immediate stimulation and enjoyment (e.g., competing in a game). Athletes will benefit from experiencing a purpose with the practice activities (McCaughtry & Rovegno, 2003). Playful games are described as an activity where there are rules and a short-term goal, although not necessarily resembling the full-scale sporting competition. An example of a playful game is 'knee tag' where athletes are going one on one trying to tag each other on the knees. The first athlete to three tags wins. While the coach's purpose might be to improve the athletes' change of direction quickness, athletes do not necessarily need to know this purpose as they often are content with enjoying the game itself. Playful games would typically be dissimilar to the specific sport that is practiced, but nonetheless useful to improve specific skills, be it mental, physical, technical or tactical. Recently, plenty of studies in the coaching and sport literature have examined game-based approaches to practice. This is often carried out as small-sided games resembling the full-scale activity and mostly used in team invasion sports (Kinnerk, Harvey, MacDonncha, & Lyons, 2018), but spans other types of sports as well. Game situations are defined as a part of the full-scale competition that has been broken down. A typical example of this is the small-sided game three vs. three in ice hockey. Both playful games and game situations provide a context and heightened meaningfulness, something that has been proposed to be vital (Antonovsky, 1987).

Playful Games

Play is sometimes looked upon as a waste of valuable time and lacking positive developmental consequences within sport. In contrast, nothing could be further from the truth as play has been found to be beneficiary for development

(Nijhof et al., 2018), especially for, but not exclusively to, younger people. What is considered play lies very much in the eyes of the beholder. Arguably, play as a construct is somewhat hard to define. In this text, *playful games* are used as a label that integrates focused learning being guided by the coach (Miller & Almon, 2009) with intrinsic motivation, flexibility and positive affect (Krasnor & Pepler, 1980). The idea is to have high coach input *and* high athlete initiative. In playful games, coaches are guiding learning by providing rich experiential opportunities for development, while experiencing immediate stimulation. Below are two categories of playful games highlighted. In both types, it is advocated to take advantage of athletes' own ideas. Remember, a key concept is to experience meaningfulness, and what is meaningful to the coach might not always be the same as for the athlete.

Rule-based Play

In this kind of games, rules are agreed upon. Common examples are tag and catch the flag. These kind of games are probably the ones that come to mind first when thinking of play.

> Use this form to come up with ideas for rule-based play. Start with a rule-based play that the athletes you are coaching are familiar with and like. Then try to integrate at least one of the four pieces that you want to practice within this specific organization, such as *physical* in the form of core stability that is used in plank position to rescue a peer in the rule-based play of tag.
>
> | Organization (+ name) | What piece is practiced and how? |
> |---|---|
> | | |
> | | |

Role-based Play

In this kind of games, the athlete enters a role when performing a skill. Roles can consist of other humans, animals or even non-living objects. Its purpose is to make use of something familiar for the athlete to execute a less familiar movement. The long-term developmental purpose of using role-based play is that entering a role can, aside from creating a great engagement in a young athlete, carry the same benefits as metaphors in that they convey lots of information without taxing working memory as much. By having a relevant and purposeful role for how posture or execution is desired to be (e.g., quick, long, or fluid), the athlete will be using a higher degree of automaticity leading to better movement (Wulf, McNevin, & Shea, 2001). Neurological studies have found that a personally relevant verbal statement depicting movements elicit greater brain activity in motor regions compared to statements that lack personal relevance to an individual (Beilock, Lyons, Mattarella-Micke, Nusbaum, & Small, 2008). The role has to be culturally relevant and make sense for the athlete in order to be effective and engaging. Telling urban kids who have never seen a crab, to move like a crab when trying to make them start with the outside leg in a basketball slide is of little use. Additionally, it has to be generationally appropriate. 'Finish strong like Carl Lewis' has been replaced by Usain Bolt's finish (until he too retired). Accordingly, coaches need to constantly update their role-based tool kit. Athletes, especially young ones, will be a great source of information, keeping the references up to date. Interested coaches are referred to Winkelman's (2020) excellent work on creating effective analogies.

> Use this form to come up with ideas for role-based play. Start with a specific piece that you want to improve. Then try to come up with a 'role' that convey the message of how this skill is supposedly executed. Remember to give the role an appropriate name (from the athletes' point of view). An example is to improve the piece of physical, and specifically landing on balance after a two-legged jump. This is executed by coming down with as little sound as possible landing close with low centre of gravity. The role-based play could be to 'land like a cat'.
>
> | What piece is practiced? | How it is executed ('role') | Metaphor/Name |
> | --- | --- | --- |
> | | | |
> | | | |

Game Situations

Usage of small-sided games or other break down games has garnered much interest over the past two decades. In this text, the umbrella term *game situations* is used. Game situations consist of a part of the real-life, full-scale competition that is taken out and used as a context for a practice activity. Nevertheless, empirical studies comparing such approaches to the traditional 'technique first' approach have been somewhat equivocal in their effects as some have found larger improvements in tactical decision making for groups practicing with game situations (Chatzopoulos, Drakou, Kotzamanidou, & Tsorbatzoudis, 2006), while others have found the traditional approach to be as effective (Harrison et al., 2004). In total, game situations are likely at least as effective activities as formal exercises, and perhaps better. The purpose of using game situations is to implicitly introduce a tactical problem to the athletes. To accomplish this, the coach has to start with the decision-making that should be practiced and from there create an appropriate game situation that will elicit opportunities to work on this particular decision (Turner & Martinek, 1999). There are primarily three means for a coach to create these situations, namely *adapting, focusing* and *enhancing*. Adapting involves modifying rules, number of athletes, space, point system and using specific sequences within the full-scale competition. Focusing involves asking questions, freezing play and using replays of specific sequences. Enhancing involves presenting the athletes with specific challenges (e.g., 'try to score only on one-timers during the 3 v 3 game') or handicapping a specific athlete or team in order to make the game more even (Martens, 2012; Turner, 2005). The observing coach intervenes through any of these manipulations. It is important to remember that they should not only be used initially, but as fluid tools to continuously shape the situation to match the athletes' responses and challenge their skills optimally.

Adapting

The rules determine what can and cannot be done by the athletes. Changing of rules modifies the athletes' behaviour, such as banning a specific technique. Number of athletes involved can be altered in either team, such as loading offence-defence ratio. Area of the activity can be altered. It is possible to slant the point scoring system in a way to promote certain behaviours. A specific game sequence that the athlete recognize from competition is a great starting point for adapting the game.

Focusing

Ideally, in a game situation, the game itself works as the teacher, thus it is better to perform a desired behaviour because it leads to positive consequences within the game (e.g., scoring points or keeping opponents at bay), rather than 'obeying the coach, who says so'. Yet, some explicit measures will be beneficial. Providing the athlete with a purpose of the activity is one such means. The purpose can draw upon potential usage in the future competitions. Questioning is another valuable tool to use during game situations. Also, the coach can freeze the play at crucial moments where something either went well or not so well. In the former case, the coach will highlight what led to the positive outcome, small details that might not be obvious to the athletes. In the latter case, the coach can let the athletes run a replay from a certain point of the play to give them another chance at improving the execution. A freeze replay is an excellent way to explore alternative solutions, even in the event of a desired outcome. In all, being vigilant as a coach during game situations will provide plenty of teachable moments.

Enhancing

The third way to impact game situations is with manipulations for the individual athlete within the game. This would probably best be used for athletes who are a little more advanced, perhaps in comparison to the other athletes in the same game situation. The coach can challenge individual athletes to perform a specific action a set number of times or a percentage of the time. It can also include handicapping specific athletes by restricting movement or techniques. The handicap can be known by the other athletes, thus further increasing the level of difficulty as they can take advantage of this knowledge, or it could be private for the individual. One word of caution though, when using individualization like this, it is important to convey this message in a manner that will not be perceived as unfair treatment by neither the concerned individual nor the rest of the team.

> Use this form to come up with ideas for game situations. Start with the kind of skill you want to practice and then create an appropriate organization for a game situation. After that, consider a few adjustments that are useful to get the athletes to further develop the specific skills of choice.
>
> | Organization | What piece is practiced? | Adjustments (adapting/focusing/enhancing) |
> | --- | --- | --- |
> | | | |

Questions

In many pedagogical methods, questions are central. Similarly, it is also a means to enhance athletes' autonomy. Naturally, questions serve as a valuable pedagogical tool in any coaches' toolkit. Studies investigating the coaches' usage of questions during competitions and practices have found strikingly low frequencies ranging from 2% (Smith & Cushion, 2006) to 8% (Partington & Cushion, 2013) of all coaching behaviours. Questioning has been proposed to elicit more cognitive elaboration, athlete ownership of his/her development, encourage creativity and deeper learning (Whitmore, 2002). However, those assumptions depend on how the questions are used and answered. Research has also found some ambiguous results when investigating the outcomes of usage of questioning in school settings (Jiang & Elen, 2011). In sports, the research is sparser in this area. Yang (2006) cautions against the belief that universally effective questions exist irrespective of context and athletes' competence. Instead, questions must be viewed, and evaluated, on their subjective effect for the athlete (e.g., did the question create engagement, participation and lead to development).

Nevertheless, this section can prove to be a fruitful ground for ideas for coaches, and as always, it is important to take a reflective approach in evaluating its effects during practice. The first step to incorporating questions in practice is often to create a few questions in preparation of the practice. As proficiency increases, the coach needs to be able to let questions emerge during interactions with athletes. Emerging questions require more from the coach and are rather difficult to prepare for as he/she does not know in advance how the athletes will respond and act during practice (Ornstein, 1988).

Types of Questions

Many different conceptualizations of questions exist, such as convergent-divergent, open-closed and low-high order. Although there are similarities, some differences exist between these categories. A more comprehensible label is *simple-complex*. Simple questions aim for a specific answer, rote memory or factual responses. This type of question often starts with 'what', 'who', 'when' or 'where'. Although they have a place, coaches should not overstate them, as they are substantially more used than complex questions (McNeil, Fry, Wright, Tan, & Rossi, 2008). Meanwhile, complex questions are more stimulating and challenging as they often lack a single true correct answer. Sometimes, the correct answer is not even the most important, rather weighing or valuing of different alternatives as their primary purpose is to engage the athlete cognitively (cf. reflection Chapter 2). This kind of question often starts with 'why' or 'how'. If a 'what-question' is posed, advantageously it is followed up with 'why' (Ornstein, 1987). Ornstein (1988) presented some guidelines for how questions are used skilfully. Questions should be *concise* (e.g., definitely avoid stating two questions at once), *challenging* (e.g., do they engage athletes cognitively and lead to problem formulation on their behalf), *group orientated* (e.g., first ask the question and then decide who gets to respond; using the word 'we' may induce group spirit and unity), *adapted to age and ability* and *varied* (e.g., objective vs value laden, what and who vs how and why). Traditionally, questions have been used to evaluate knowledge, but perhaps a more prosperous scope is to stimulate thinking (van Zee & Minstrell, 1997). Finally, Martin (1979) found that students not used to complex questions could experience negative attitudes towards them. To preempt disgruntled athletes, the wise coach should inform the athletes in advance of this procedure, purpose and effects.

Sequence for Questions

Kidman and Hanrahan (2011) suggest a five-step sequence for questions. First, prepare the question by considering purpose, content, athletes' level and appropriate language. Second, ask the question and show how the athletes are supposed to respond (e.g., verbally or physical demonstration), provide time for response, and decide who is going to respond. Third, encourage responses by giving them time to process the question, and help them with additional cues – if necessary. Fourth, process the responses by giving the athletes feedback, probe for additional information or encourage reactions. Fifth, reflect upon the process, such as analysing the questions used, athletes' answers, assess response patterns and evaluate reactions. Commonly, exchanges involving questions from coaches follow a more narrow-minded sequence where the response is evaluated against a true/false criterion and few probes or follow-up questions are used (Forrest, 2014). Thus, the fourth step is critical in order to initiate qualitative dialogue.

Potential Questioning Traps

In an investigation of coaches' questioning practices, Cope and colleagues (2016) identified three different traps the coaches risk falling into, which are elaborated below.

Expecting Immediate Answer

The time immediately after asking a question is called wait time 1, while the time starting after the response is provided from an athlete is called wait time 2. Often, the wait time is one second or less. Rowe (1986) showed strong support for increasing wait time to three seconds has positive consequences for learning. Rowe reported that it is normal for teachers who have started to use longer wait time to relapse into old habits by the third or fourth week. To prevent this deterioration, it is advocated to talk to someone about the experience and receive social support. Wait time 2 seems to be even more important than wait time 1 as it gives the opportunity for the athletes to elaborate on their answers, thus thinking more deeply about the subject at hand. Moreover, longer wait time 2 increases the likelihood of athletes themselves posing questions, which is another sign of cognitive processing. Finally, contradicting intuition, longer pauses decrease the risk for behavioural problems within a classroom setting (Rowe, 1986).

Leading Questions

For a coach looking for a specific answer, it is easy to resort to asking leading questions, perhaps as a testimonial to own coaching competency (e.g., 'if the athletes think as I want them to, then I'm a skilled coach'). Conceivably, leading questions result in the coach's nonverbal response being strongly influenced by the 'correctness' of the answer from the athlete. Consequently, athletes will be hesitant to answer truthfully as they likely will see through this and try to please the coach, rather than provide their honest opinion. Certainly, the risk is heightened with younger and less experienced athletes.

For them, the present coach might very well be the first and only source of sport-specific knowledge they have encountered in their careers. Therefore, answers from the athletes' risk being of an 'adjusted variety' even if the coach does not intend so. To counter this, a coach can encourage athletes' creativity by having them come up with ideas they have not heard from the coach. Additionally, Dodd and Bradshaw (1980) drew attention to potential distortions on memory from presumptions through leading questions. Accordingly, athletes might implicitly be influenced to a position that they not really agree on, which will lead to confusion in coach–athlete communication. To avoid asking a leading question, it is advocated to start with the 'question-word' (e.g., what, how) and to receive the response from the athlete in a quite neutral manner.

Monologue Form

Cope, Partington, Cushion, and Harvey (2016) provided an example of a coach getting caught up in a back-and-forth questioning with a single athlete, and within this interaction dominating the talking space considerably. This can happen when the coach includes more information than actually concern the question. Perhaps, this is a result of the coach likening his/her own voice a little too much. Tost, Gino, and Larrick (2013) showed that formal leaders' domination of verbal interactions led to followers deferring and consequently impacted performance negativaley. This effect was more pronounced the more powerful the leader felt. Thus, a flat hierarchical structure within the group is advisable to decrease this risk.

Examples on How to Use Questions

In contrast to the traps, there are some serviceable manners to questioning practice. Harvey and colleagues (Harvey & Light, 2015; Harvey, Cope, & Jones, 2016) propose a series of sound hands-on advice on how to implement questioning during live practice activities. Either the coach stops the entire activity and asks the whole group or the coach asks a single athlete/small group that is either working on their own or currently non-involved in the whole group activity.

'Question Starters'

Below is a sample of question stems that can be used for complex questions (Kracl, 2012). Relating the stems to the four pieces of a jigsaw puzzle, questions probing into technical skill investigate how the movement was executed, while questions probing tactical skill examining what type of technique is desirable under the current circumstances. Correspondingly, questions can probe perceptions and interpretations of context (tactical skill), which could be formulated as 'what did you perceive in this situation?' Of course, coaches are more than welcome to construct their own prepared questions.

> (Assessing) How could you improve...
> (Comparing) What are the similarities/differences between...
> (Evaluating) What is the most important (and why)...
> (Analyzing) What kind of options do you have...
> (Substituting) What is another way to...
> (Generalizing) What general rule can...
> (Summarizing) How would you describe...

'Debate of Ideas'/'Tactical Timeout'

In a break during a competitive activity, the coach may interact with an athlete using a four-step model with prepared questions. This could also be used within a group of athletes on the same team during practice as a sort of 'tactical time-out' (Gréhaigne, Richard & Griffin, 2005). First, what are the strengths of the opponents? Second, what did you do well to cope with these strengths in the previous sequences? Third, what do you need to do to counteract the strengths of the opponents? Fourth, how will you carry that out during the upcoming sequences?

'The Reflective Toss'

As a more advanced way of engaging athletes in a conversation, with a tilt towards emerging rather than prepared questions, van Zee and Minstrell (1997) suggest the reflective toss. The coach tries to toss back the questions and statements that are uttered to either the same athlete or preferably another athlete. The responsibility returns to the athlete and the coach acts more like a facilitator instead of a source of knowledge. This discourse is far removed from the traditional way of viewing questions as a means to primarily evaluate athletes' knowledge.

Instructor Ingram uses the reflective toss with his basketball team during a break in a 4 v 4 half-court scrimmage.

INGRAM: *What caused you to gain a time advantage compared to the defence on the left side?*
ATHLETE A: *We managed to move the ball from the opposite side.*
INGRAM: *How did you manage to do that?*
ATHLETE B: *We had good timing in our movements when A was ready to pass the ball.*
INGRAM: *How come the passes arrived so precise then?*
ATHLETE A: *We had firm speed in our passes.*
ATHLETE C: *...and nice spacing in between us.*
INGRAM: *I see. When did you decide to move into the open area then?*
ATHLETE C: *When B caught the ball, I saw that the area was open.*

INGRAM: *Could you have accomplished the same thing in any other way?*
ATHLETE D: *Yes, we could have moved more spaced out and then it would have been an opportunity for me instead.*
INGRAM: *Can someone please elaborate on this?*
ATHLETE B: *If I would have moved over here, and D up there, D would have had more space to attack the defender.*

As the conversation infers, Ingram's purpose is not to interrogate individual athletes' knowledge, but rather to get them to collectively explore the sequence and come up with new ideas, thus generating new knowledge.

> How do you use questions today during practice (e.g., simple-complex, frequency)?
> What kind of questioning traps do you see as an issue to prevent in your coaching?
> How can you improve your usage of questions?

Practical Implementation of Pedagogy
Reflection Card

1-2-3 template			Date: _____
Organization & New learning	Better learning	Effects	Coach's thoughts/ emotions

Formulate a goal that consists of what kind of new learning the athlete (-s) should practice. In order to be able to use better learning, it is desirable to use an activity that practice skills that the athlete (-s) have a reasonable chance to perform at a level that will necessitate an increased challenge. The action plan then consists of choosing from the mental and physical pieces how to step up the degree of difficulty.

In the first column (*Organization & New learning*), describe a specific practice activity. Additionally, describe what technical and/or tactical skills practiced in that activity. This is prepared before practice. In the second column (*Better learning*), describe an adjustment of mental and/or physical demands in the activity.

Either, this adjustment is prepared ahead of practice or (at least eventually) the coach comes up with this variation during the practice. In the third column (*Effects*), describe effects on the athlete (-s) that are perceived. In the fourth column (*Coach's thoughts/emotions*), note some reactions emanating either from the adjustment itself or the observed effect on the athlete (-s).

Secondary Reflection

> Use the questions below and/or the formula for shared reflection in Chapter 2.
>
> How did the practice activity and athletes' performance influence your thoughts?
>
> With the used reflection card in hand, what do you think when you look back at that specific situation and the athlete during the practice?
>
> How would you interpret your thoughts and emotions from this particular moment?
>
> What do you now think will be the effects for the athlete after your intervention?
>
> In what way is the chosen intervention related to your coaching philosophy/idea of what you wanted to accomplish during the practice?
>
> Would you do anything differently as you look back at this specific event? If so, elaborate on this.
>
> What is the main lesson learnt that you take away from the experience?

Reflection Sheet

First to third columns are completed before practice. Fourth and fifth columns are completed after practice.

Pedagogical Methods			Date:	
Organization and Purpose of practice activity.	Circle the pedagogical method of choice.	Description of how the chosen behaviour is going to be implemented (e.g., presentation of information, prepared questions, etc).	Briefly answer the following questions: How did it feel to use the chosen method? How did the athletes respond to the chosen method? How could this method have been more effective?	What were your own thoughts and emotions during this part of the practice?

170 Pedagogy

```
DI
TM
PT
GD
PS

DI
TM
PT
GD
PS

DI
TM
PT
GD
PS
```

Reflective Summary

 When trying to implement the 1-2-3 template during practice, what has been the most important learning for you?
How are you going to capitalize on this lesson learnt in the future?
When working with a new pedagogical method, what has been the most important learning for you?
How are you going to capitalize on this lesson learnt in the future?
From your readings of pedagogy, your answers to the application exercises, and your reflective activities, how would you best use pedagogy in your coaching?

Challenging Pedagogical Assumptions

A month later, the three gathered again.

"I'm so curious to hear about your progress. What has happened since last time?" Ellen opened the meeting.

Both Leah and Collin started simultaneously. Ellen had to calm them down.

"One at a time, she said."
"I actually had great success with having the guys working more in pairs", Collin began.
"Please, explain what was so great about this", Ellen begged.
"When the guys give each other feedback, it gets more diverse of course but I also think they learn from helping each other out more. They have started

- communicating much more during competitions. I also, get a little more time to spend with the newcomers who don't have as good fundamentals, while the others partner up", Collin detailed.
- "It sounds like you have realized the benefits of observational learning from other than expert models", Ellen smiled at him. "Now, what about you Leah? You were quite distraught last time. How are you now?"
- "Much better actually. I've tried to use a smaller number of setups when it comes to activities, and in these structures, I've shortened running distances and made them go with a defender chasing from behind, put in some outside resistance by having them press against each other, and sometimes I've started the drills from laying down so they've to use more core strength just to get up", Leah said rapidly.
- "Anything else?" Ellen asked, seeing that Leah had something else on her mind.
- "Yes, as a matter of fact, I used some distractions to pressure their minds a little bit. In one drill, I had them screaming at the person running trying to get them to lose the technique", Leah elaborated confidently.
- "So, by using time more efficiently, the athletes can go into better learning rather than organization?" Ellen asked.
- "Definitely. We even tried some games they loved when they were younger. I just told them to go over a smaller area. They really worked on reaction speed without me telling them. And best of all, they loved every second of it!" Leah couldn't hide her excitement.
- "How have the athletes' performance been during competitions then, aside from talking more?" Ellen wondered, turning back to Collin.
- "Maybe a little better, but I don't know if I can tell already. I have tried to emphasize the effect of the movement and finding everyone's own optimal technique", Collin answered with an afterthought.
- "'Cause that's what counts, when it comes down to it, don't you think, Collin? The more problem-solving approach might pay off in the long-run. Do you think you can be that patient?" Ellen wrapped up.

Collin nodded back.

Quiz

1. What statement is most correct regarding different theories of learning?
    a. Behaviourism argues that individuals determine their own behaviours.
    b. Social cognitive theory argues that an important way of learning is observation.
    c. Constructivism argues that without feedback individuals will not learn.
2. What statement is most correct about the five pedagogical methods?
    a. Direct instruction means more practice time for the athletes.
    b. Peer teaching is not exactly the same as working in pairs.
    c. Problem-solving method means that the coach lets the athlete work on their own.

3. What statement is most correct about presentation of information for the athletes?
    a. Demonstrations have to be provided by an expert model.
    b. Instructions should be exhaustive for best effect on athletes.
    c. Instructions focusing on external objects are more effective than when focusing on body parts.
4. What statement about different types of practice activities is most correct?
    a. Formal exercise is very structured.
    b. Playful games will seldom lead to athletic development.
    c. Game situations primarily teach athletes the importance of competing and winning.
5. What statement is most correct about the three stages of practice activities?
    a. Organization will determine the athlete's development.
    b. New learning is the stage that is most relevant for the athlete's progress.
    c. Better learning means that the challenge of known activities is increased.
6. What statement about questioning is most correct?
    a. Rapid questions are generally more effective.
    b. Question should primarily be used to check the athletes' understanding.
    c. Coaches generally tend to ask simple questions.

References

Abernethy, B., Farrow, D., Gorman, A. D., & Mann, D. L. (2012). Anticipatory behaviour and expert performance. In N. J. Hodges, & A. M. Williams (Eds.), *Skill acquisition in sport: Research, theory and practice* (2nd ed., pp. 287–305). London: Routledge.

Antonovsky, A. (1987). *Unravelling the mystery of health*. San Francisco, CA: Jossey-Bass.

Bandura, A. (1977). Self-efficacy: Toward a unifying theory of behavioral change. *Psychological Review, 71*, 191–215.

Bandura, A. (1989). Social cognitive theory. In R. Vasta (Ed.), *Annals of child development. Vol. 6. Six theories of child development* (pp. 1–60). Greenwich, CT: JAI Press.

Beilock, S., Lyons, I. M., Mattarella-Micke, A., Nusbaum, H. C., & Small, S. L. (2008). Sports experience changes the neural processing of action language. *Proceedings of National Academy of Sciences, 105*, 13269–13273.

Berliner, D. C. (1991). Educational psychology and pedagogical expertise: New findings and new opportunities for thinking about training. *Educational Psychologist, 26*, 145–155.

Buchanan, J. J., & Dean, N. J. (2010). Specificity in practice benefits learning in novice models and variability in demonstration benefits observational practice. *Psychological Research, 74*, 313–326.

Buschke, H. (1976). Learning is organized by chunking. *Journal of Verbal Learning and Verbal Behavior, 15*, 313–324.

Cadopi, M., Chatillon, J. F., & Baldy, R. (1995). Representation and performance: Reproduction of form and quality of movement in dance by eight and eleven-year-old novices. *British Journal of Psychology, 86*, 217–225.

Cassidy, T., Jones, R., & Potrac, P. (2009). *Understanding sports coaching: The social, cultural and pedagogical foundations of coaching practice* (2nd ed.). Abingdon, UK: Routledge.

Cervone, D., Mor, N., Orom, H., Shadel, W. G., & Scott, W. D. (2011). Self-efficacy beliefs and the architecture of personality: On knowledge appraisal, and self-regulation. In K. D. Vohs, & R. F. Baumeister (Eds.), *Handbook of self-regulation: Research, theory, and applications* (2nd ed., pp. 461–484). New York: Guilford Press.

Chatzopoulos, D., Drakou, A., Kotzamanidou, M., & Tsorbatzoudis, H. (2006). Girls' soccer performance and motivation: Games vs technique approach. *Perceptual and Motor Skills, 103*, 463–470.

Cope, E., Partington, M., Cushion, C. J., & Harvey, S. (2016). An investigation of professional top-level youth football coaches' questioning practice. *Qualitative Research in Sport, Exercise and Health, 8*, 380–393.

Cushion, C., Harvey, S., Muir, B., & Nelson, L. (2012). Developing the coach analysis and intervention system (CAIS): Establishing validity and reliability of a computerised systematic observation instrument. *Journal of Sports Sciences, 30*, 203–218.

Dodd, D. H., & Bradshaw, J. M. (1980). Leading questions and memory: Pragmatic constraints. *Journal of Verbal Learning and Verbal Behavior, 19*, 695–704.

Domjan, M. (1998). *The principles of learning and behavior* (4th ed.). Pacific Grove, CA: Thomson Brooks/Cole Publishing.

Feltz, D., Short, S., & Sullivan, P. (2008). *Self-efficacy in sport*. Champaign, IL: Human Kinetics.

Forrest, G. (2014). Questions and answers: Understanding the connection between questioning and knowledge in game-centred approaches. In R. Light, J. Quay, S. Harvey, & A. Mooney (Eds.), *Contemporary developments in games teaching* (pp. 167–177). London: Routledge.

Goodson, I. F., Biesta, G. J. J., Tedder, M., & Adair, N. (2010). *Narrative learning*. Abingdon, UK: Routledge.

Gréhaigne, J.-F., Richard, J.-F., & Griffin, L. L. (2005). *Teaching and learning team sports and games*. New York: RoutledgeFalmer.

Griffin, L. L., & Patton, K. (2005). Two decades of teaching games for understanding: Looking at the past, present, and future. In L. L. Griffin, & J. I. Butler (Eds.), *Teaching games for understanding: Theory, research, and practice* (pp. 1–17). Champaign, IL: Human Kinetics.

Grout, H., & Long, G. (2009). *Improving teaching & learning in physical education*. New York: McGraw-Hill.

Harrison, J. M. et al, (2004). The effects of two instructional models - tactical and skill teaching - on skill development and game play, knowledge, self-efficacy, and student perceptions in volleyball. *Physical Educator, 61*, 186–199.

Harvey, S., Cope, E., & Jones, R. (2016). Developing questioning in game-centered approaches. *Journal of Physical Education, Recreation and Dance, 87*, 28–35.

Harvey, S., & Light, R. L. (2015). Questioning for learning in game-based approaches to teaching and coaching. *Asia-Pacific Journal of Health, Sport and Physical Education, 6*, 175–190.

Hattie, J. (2009). *Visible learning: A synthesis of over 800 meta-analyses relating to achievement*. Abingdon, UK: Routledge.

Janelle, C. M. & Hillman, C. H. (2003). Expert performance in sport: Current perspectives and critical issues. In J. Starkes, & K. A. Ericsson (Eds.), *Expert performance in sport: Advances in research on sport expertise* (pp. 19–48). Champaign, IL: Human Kinetics.

Jiang, L., & Elen, J. (2011). Instructional effectiveness of higher-order questions: The devil is in the detail of students' use of questions. *Learning Environments Research, 14*, 279–298.

Jones, R. L. (2007). Coaching redefined: An everyday pedagogical endeavour. *Sport, Education and Society, 12*, 159–173.

Kember, D., & Wong, A. (2000). Implications for evaluation from a study of students' perceptions of good and poor teaching. *Higher Education, 40*, 69–97.

Kidman, L., & Hanrahan, S. J. (2011). *The coaching process: A practical guide to becoming an effective sports coach*. Abingdon, UK: Routledge.

Kinnerk, P., Harvey, S., MacDonncha, C., & Lyons, M. (2018). A review of the game-based approaches to coaching literature in competitive team sport settings. *Quest, 70*, 401–418.

Kracl, C. L. (2012). Review or true? Using higher-level thinking questions in social studies instruction. *The Social Studies, 103*, 57–60.

Krasnor, L. R., & Pepler, D. J. (1980). The study of children's play: Some suggested future directions. *New Directions for Child and Adolescent Development, 1980*, 85–95.

Landin, D. (1994). The role of verbal cues in skill learning. *Quest, 46*, 299–313.

Liao, C-M. & Masters, R.S.W. (2001). Analogy learning: A means to implicit motor learning, *Journal of Sports Sciences, 19*, 307–319.

Magill, R. A. (2011). *Motor learning and control: Concepts and applications*. (9th ed.). Singapore: McGraw-Hill.

Martens, R. (2012). *Successful coaching* (4th ed.). Champaign, IL: Human Kinetics.

Martin, J. (1979). Effects of teacher higher-order questions on student process and product variable in a single-classroom study. *The Journal of Educational Research, 72*, 183–187.

McCaughtry, N., & Rovegno, I. (2003). Development of pedagogical content knowledge: Moving from blaming students to predicting skillfulness, recognizing motor development, and understanding emotion. *Journal of Teaching in Physical Education, 22*, 355–368.

McCullagh, P., & Weiss, M. R. (2001). Modelling: Considerations for motor skill performance and psychological responses. In R. N. Singer, H. A. Hausenblas, & C. M. Janelle (Eds.), *Handbook of sport psychology* (2nd ed., pp. 205–238). New York: Wiley.

McNeil, M. C., Fry, J. M., Wright, S. C., Tan, C. W. K., & Rossi, T. (2008). Structuring time and questioning to achieve tactical awareness in games lessons. *Physical Education and Sport Pedagogy, 13*, 231–249.

Metzler, M. W. (2005). *Instructional models for physical education* (2nd ed.). Scottsdale, AZ: Holcomb Hathaway.

Miller, E., & Almon, J. (2009). *Crisis in the kindergarten: Why children need to play in school*. College Park, MD: Alliance for Childhood.

Mosston, M., & Ashworth, S. (2002). *Teaching physical education* (5th ed.). San Francisco, CA: Benjamin Cummings.

Nijhof, S. L. et al. (2018). Healthy play, better coping: The importance of play for the development of children in health and disease. *Neuroscience and Biobehavioral Reviews, 95*, 421–429.

Ong, N. T., & Hodges, N. J. (2012). Mixing it up a little: How to schedule observational practice. In N. J. Hodges, & A. M. Williams (Eds.), *Skill acquisition in sport: Research, theory and practice* (2nd ed., pp. 22–39). London: Routledge.

Ornstein, A. C. (1987). Questioning: The essence of good teaching. *NASSP Bulletin, 71*, 71–79.

Ornstein, A. C. (1988). Questioning: The essence of good teaching – Part II. *NASSP Bulletin, 72*, 72–80.

Partington, M., & Cushion, C. (2013). An investigation of the practice activities and coaching behaviors of professional-level youth soccer coaches. *Scandinavian Journal of Medicine & Science in Sports, 23*, 372–382.

Rowe, M. B. (1986). Wait time: Slowing down may be a way of speeding up! *Journal of Teacher Education, 37*, 43–50.

Serra-Olivares, J., García-López, L. M., & Calderón, A. (2016). Game-based approaches, pedagogical principles and tactical constraints: Examining games modification. *Journal of Teaching in Physical Education, 35*, 208–218.

Shea, C. H., Wulf, G., Whitacre, C., & Wright, D. L. (2000). Physical and observational practice afford unique learning opportunities. *Journal of Motor Behavior, 32*, 27–36.

Simon, D. A., & Bjork, R. A. (2001). Metacognition in motor learning. *Journal of Experimental Psychology: Learning, Memory, and Cognition, 27*, 907–912.

Slavin, R. E. (2009). *Educational psychology: Theory and practice* (9th ed.). Upper Saddle River, NJ: Pearson.

Smith, M., & Cushion, C. J. (2006). An investigation of the in-game behaviours of professional, top-level youth soccer coaches. *Journal of Sports Sciences, 24*, 355–366.

Snowman, J., & McCown, R. (2015). *Psychology applied to teaching* (14th ed.). Stanford, CA: Cengage Learning.

Tost, L. P., Gino, F., & Larrick, R. P. (2013). When power makes others speechless: The negative impact of leader power on team performance. *Academy of Management Journal, 56*, 1465–1486.

Turner, A. P. (2005). Teaching and learning games at the secondary level. L. L. Griffin, & J. I. Butler (Eds.), *Teaching games for understanding: Theory, research, and practice* (pp. 71–89). Champaign, IL: Human Kinetics.

Turner, A. P., & Martinek, T. J. (1999). An investigation into teaching games for understanding: Effects on skill, knowledge, and game play. *Research Quarterly for Exercise and Sport, 70*, 286–296.

van Zee, E., & Minstrell, J. (1997). Using questioning to guide student thinking. *The Journal of the Learning Sciences, 6*, 227–269.

Whitmore, J. (2002). *Coaching for performance: GROWing people, performance and purpose* (3rd ed.). Naperville, IL: Nicholas Brealey.

Winkelman, N. (2020). *The language of coaching: The art & science of teaching movement.* Champaign, IL: Human Kinetics

Woollard, J. (2010). *Psychology for the classroom: Behaviourism.* Abingdon, UK: Routledge.

Wrisberg, C. A. (2007). *Sport skill instruction for coaches.* Champaign, IL: Human Kinetics.

Wulf, G. (2007). *Attention and motor skill learning.* Champaign, IL: Human Kinetics.

Wulf, G., McNevin, N., & Shea, C. H. (2001). The automaticity of complex motor skill learning as a function of attentional focus. *The Quarterly Journal of Experimental Psychology, 54*, 1143–1154.

Wulf, G., & Weigelt, C. (1997) Instructions about physical principles in learning a complex motor skill: To tell or not to tell… *Research Quarterly for Exercise and Sport, 68*, 362–367.

Yang, M. (2006). A critical review of research on questioning in education: Limitations of its positivistic basis. *Asia Pacific Education Review, 7*, 195–204.

Zimmerman, B. J., & Kitsantas, A. (2005). The hidden dimension of personal competence: Self-regulated learning and practice. In A. J. Elliot & C. S. Dweck (Eds.), *Handbook of competence and motivation* (p. 509–526). New York: Guilford.

6
FEEDBACK

Aim of the chapter: Develop an understanding of how feedback can be used to enhance athletes' performance and development.
Theoretical learning goals of the chapter:
Grow an understanding of…

1. the four functions of feedback.
2. how feedback can be used effectively to inform athletes.
3. how feedback can be used effectively to motivate athletes.
4. how implicit theories influences the impact of feedback.
5. how feedback can hamper athletes by creating feedback dependence.
6. methods for decreasing the likelihood of feedback dependence.
7. how feedback can be used effectively to reinforce athletes.
8. characteristics and consequences of different feedback modalities.

Practical learning goals of the chapter:

1. Become aware of how you provide feedback depending on its function during practice by using reflection card.
2. Become aware of your feedback provision tendencies during practice by using reflection sheet.

Vignette

For once, Ellen was running a little late to their meeting.

> "What's going on?" She said, still catching her breath.
> "Well, I'll give you some feedback", Collin uttered triumphantly. "You're exactly twice as late as Leah to this meeting. Four minutes and 22 seconds. Leah, clocked in at two minutes and eleven seconds."

"Are you so sure about that?" Leah asked.

"Of course, that's because I'm a meticulous person, while you seem a little sloppier", he kept on.

"It can happen to everyone", Ellen excused herself. "Let's focus on your coaching. Tell me a little about your general provision of feedback to the athletes."

"I don't really know how to describe it, but I try to be as positive as possible", Leah started.

"Mmhm, what kind of performances are we talking about here Leah?" Ellen probed.

"Pretty much every time they execute a technique or decision-making, I try to give them some feedback so they know where they stand", Leah answered.

"I'd like to tell you about my latest practice", Collin interjected.

"Please do", Ellen said curiously.

"We had a pretty darn good practice. At the gathering at the end of the practice I told the guys that they are naturals at this. They were so good", Collin said proudly.

"Can you see any downside to that kind of statement?" Ellen questioned him.

"Not that I can think of. They really liked the boost of hearing they are talented", he replied.

"In what way can you impact their view of themselves with these 'motivational boosts'?" Ellen kept going.

"Maybe, the athletes will be motivated as long as they feel better than the opponent", Leah took the opportunity to add her point of view as Collin was introspecting.

"Doesn't anyone want that?" Collin asked rhetorically.

"How would they react if you focused on their behaviours and strategies more than on them as persons?" Ellen asked.

"That way you could reinforce behaviours even if they wouldn't come out on top", Leah added.

"Now, what about the amount of feedback you provide during a typical practice, Leah. Can there be any drawbacks?" Ellen turned to Leah.

"I do get quite tired and sore in my throat after practice, I have to confess", she replied.

"So, if you try to reduce the frequency of feedback, your own burden would ease a little?" Ellen elaborated.

"Quite possibly, perhaps the athletes will rest their ears as well", Leah finished.

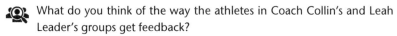 What do you think of the way the athletes in Coach Collin's and Leah Leader's groups get feedback?
How do Collin and Leah, respectively, view feedback?

Functions of Feedback

Feedback has been one of the most investigated areas in sport psychology with a comparably long history dating back to early 20th century. It has a rich association with motor learning, although over the last couple of decades researchers have broadened the field by extending it to include affective and cognitive outcomes such as motivation and implicit theories. Schmidt and Wrisberg (2000) highlighted four different functions of coaches' feedback: *inform*, *motivate*, *create dependence* and *reinforce* (see Figure 6.1).

The functions are not mutually exclusive, but rather interact and overlap, though for clarity they will be reviewed separately. As a sports performance typically consists of many simultaneously existing aspects, the coach has the option to provide feedback for different purposes in response to a single action from an athlete. Additionally, an important distinction between learning and performance has to be made as many studies investigating feedback effects used one or both, sometimes in a confusing manner. Learning is defined as relatively permanent consequences acquired from practice, while performance is considered a more transitory effect. Sometimes, these two constructs are in accord (i.e., temporary performance mirrors long-term learning), although at other times, and under some conditions, they appear to contradict one another (e.g., performance might be due to a concurrent artefact which effects disappear upon withdrawal, rather than a stable improvement within the athlete; Salmoni, Schmidt, & Walter, 1984). Performance is seen momentarily during a single task-execution, while learning must be inferred over time as it is only the trajectory of multiple performances that does tell the story of learning (Soderstrom & Bjork, 2015). Typically, in research, learning has been assessed through either retention or transfer tests. A retention test is where the person, after a time of non-practice, undertakes another repetition of the exact identical task (although often without guiding aides such as feedback that could have been provided during the practice phase). That supposedly simulate conditions common in sports, where the athlete often is left to a large extent to perform on his/her own during competition. On the other hand, transfer is usually tested through some variation of the previously practiced task, such as changing temporal relationship of sub-components (e.g., switching from a 2-beat kick to a 4-beat kick in freestyle swimming), distances or angles. In some way, this resembles conditions during competition in open skills sports where parameters for skill execution are constantly changing. However, much of the research conducted has used simple laboratory tasks. Findings from simple skills do not necessarily generalize to complex skills. Simple skills in this

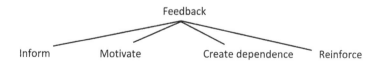

FIGURE 6.1 Four functions of feedback.

respect can be defined as having few degrees of freedom. They are often of relatively low difficulty, which demands a lower amount of practice trials for the participant to develop a rough movement representation. Also, they can be seen as somewhat artificial. Conversely, real-life sport skills are characterized with many degrees of freedom and require lots of practice before the developmental trajectory levels off significantly, approximating a plateau (Wulf & Shea, 2002). Additionally, in many studies, retention tests have used tasks without feedback on the outcome of the movement. It is doubtful whether real-life sport skills are executed without any outcome information. Usually, athletes' own perception provides information about the outcome of the movement. Moreover, many experiments have used withdrawal of essential information (e.g., vision or hearing) for the purpose of testing the development of the generalized motor programme (Russell & Newell, 2007). This practice, while not being entirely unfounded, clearly has its drawbacks and emanates from a belief that motor skills are stored in a programme within the brain, readily available for retrieval regardless of contextual information. Whether motor skills are learnt and executed in this manner has come into much question over the past decades (Summers & Anson, 2009; Thelen & Smith, 2006). Sigrist, Rauter, Riener, and Wolf (2013b) highlight the fact that many laboratory tasks have been designed to test a specific tenet of a feedback theory. Hence, feedback research tasks are frequently artificial and in dire lack of ecological validity. For a practitioner, it could be more useful to have experimental feedback design built around a real sporting task and examine its effectiveness in this situation. Nevertheless, plenty of research exist on feedback, its functions and consequences within the sporting domain. Because of the aforementioned troubles and conflicting ideas, there are more contradictive results than one would like. Finally, it could probably be stated that the general usefulness of feedback increases with task novelty and decreases with the athlete's experience (Guadagnoli & Lee, 2004).

Inform

Perhaps, the most commonly known purpose of feedback is to inform the athlete about his/her performance. This function pertains to how the feedback will guide the athlete towards skill improvement. Four different aspects influence how feedback informs an athlete of his/her performance – *origin*, *content*, *timing* and *focus*.

Origin (Intrinsic or Augmented)

Feedback can have two different origins, *task-intrinsic* or *augmented*. Task-intrinsic feedback is a natural consequence of the task and is provided to the athlete either from within the own body or from external sources (e.g., seeing where a javelin throw lands, or hearing sound of impact in a dive into the water). Augmented feedback is added from an additional outside source, such as a coach. As this book is about coaching development, most attention will be on augmented feedback. Magill (1994; 2011) contend that augmented feedback can have various impacts. Augmented feedback can be essential, unnecessary, may enhance learning or may hinder learning. Which impact augmented feedback has depends on the athlete's characteristics and the task or skill at hand.

Essential for Learning

When augmented feedback is deemed to be essential for learning, at least three situations exist. First, some performances inhibit the possibility for task-intrinsic feedback, such as when a golf shot is occluded by trees. Second, because of injury or similar circumstances, some athletes might not have the sensory pathways for detection of task-intrinsic information that is necessary for learning. Third, in some situations, the athlete's sensory system might be capable of detecting necessary information, but the athlete is unable to use this information, such as when inexperience inhibits the possibility to determine how large the knee-bend angle in a squat is.

Unnecessary for Learning

Contrastingly, there are situations when augmented feedback proves to be unnecessary for learning. Such situations occur when the athlete is performing a task that provides sufficient task-intrinsic feedback through salient external referents within the environment that the athlete uses to evaluate the appropriateness of the execution. One example of this is when a golf putt is performed on an easily read green by an athlete watching the ball until the putter strikes it. This type of situation provides the athlete with sufficient information to evaluate the execution. Furthermore, opportunities for observational learning through viewing similar athletes have been found to improve movement outcomes at least as much as athletes provided with augmented feedback, such as the tennis players in Hebert and Landin's (1994) study. Improvements on movement outcomes may more often deem augmented feedback unnecessary than improvements in movement form, as the former is generally easier to perceive through task-intrinsic feedback.

May Enhance Learning

Some tasks lend themselves to be learnt without augmented feedback, but can be improved more rapidly or to a higher skill level when augmented feedback is provided. Most sport skills fall into this category. Take, for example, the task of running as fast as possible over a short distance. In initial stages of development, it can be somewhat easy to tell if one sprint was faster than the last one, but as the athlete progresses, improvement will become more incremental. Augmented feedback will enhance continued development as it can provide more detailed information difficult for the athlete alone to discover. In complex skills that require multi-limb movements, feedback on movement qualities will facilitate learning. For augmented feedback to enhance learning, the feedback has to give the athlete some information which the athlete can use to change some movement characteristic.

May Hinder Learning

Finally, and contrary to intuition, there are some situations where feedback will hinder learning as it can inappropriately change movement patterns or make the athlete inattentive to task-intrinsic feedback. This will be discussed under the headline of *feedback dependence* later in this chapter.

In sum, the difference between situations that determine the impact of augmented feedback is not crystal clear. As a coach, though, the main thing is to be aware of the not necessarily linear relationship between amount of augmented feedback and athletes' improvement. With this awareness, it is then beneficial to analyze the task at hand, and the athletes' responses to determine whether the feedback has a positive effect or not. The weight given to augmented in comparison to task-intrinsic feedback differs with age. Younger athletes (e.g., 6–8 years old) put more emphasize on augmented feedback compared to older athletes (12–14 years old), as the latter may have greater task-knowledge to draw upon when judging their performances (Amorose & Weiss, 1998).

Content (Result or Performance)

Feedback can contain information about the effect of the movement or information about the kinematic execution. The former is called *Knowledge of Results* (KR) and conveys information about the outcome. The latter is called *Knowledge of Performance* (KP) and contains information about joint movements during the task. A majority of research investigating feedback within the sporting domain has studied KR. For most skills and situations in real-life practice though, KR should be almost obvious to the athlete (Russell & Newell, 2007). For this reason, it might be more valuable for the athlete with provision of KP feedback from the coach (or other sources). Two potential pitfalls have to be addressed with KP feedback. First, the purpose of the movement has to be established as it could be either the movement itself or the effect of the movement that is the goal within the specific sport (Gentile, 1972). In the case of the former, KP should be prescribed towards the 'correct' movement execution. In the case of the latter, KP should be used to get the athlete to understand the connection between movements and outcomes or explore other potential movements, rather than trying to get the athlete to execute a predetermined movement template (Brisson & Alain, 1996). Second, while providing KP feedback, it is important not to induce an internal focus of attention in the athlete (see section below on focus). This might seem like a paradox as KP should inform the athlete about the movement itself.

However, this can be mitigated through using analogies or by connecting the movement to the outcome (i.e., KR). Considering the accuracy of the feedback, McNevin, Magill, and Buekers (1994) examined incorrect feedback. They found that erroneous feedback was detrimental not only to performance of the specific task where feedback was provided but also to development of more general error-detection strategies that hampered execution of similar yet not completely identical tasks as well. Presumably, the earlier the erroneous feedback is given in a developmental phase, the more harmful it could be to long-term development. Early in the development, it could be wise to make sure that the feedback is less precise, but correct, instead of trying to be overly detailed and risk being erroneous. Precision of feedback can be qualitative (i.e., displaying the direction of the error, such as to the right or too wide) or quantitative (i.e., displaying both direction and magnitude of error). According to Wright, Smith-Munyon, and Sidaway (1997), athletes benefit from having large errors described quantitatively in order for them to be able to correct upon next repetition. Meanwhile, it is unclear whether smaller errors are best described quantitatively or qualitatively. The research could be interpreted as it does not matter for smaller errors. Consequently, coaches do not need to be overly nit-picking when it comes to highlighting the magnitude of small errors, which could be difficult to quantify exactly even for an experienced coach's eye.

Timing (Concurrent or Terminal)

Feedback can be provided either during the performance, *concurrent feedback*, or after the performance, *terminal feedback*. In turn, terminal feedback can be delivered immediately following a performance or with a delay. Concurrent feedback is thought to have very strong guiding effects on task execution, but also risks preventing the athlete to pay attention to task-intrinsic information during the performance. However, the detrimental effects of concurrent feedback are most prevalent on simple tasks. Contrastingly, Sigrist, Rauter, Riener, and Wolf (2013a) argued that the more complex a skill is, the more benefit from concurrent feedback is derived. Concurrent feedback can actually prevent cognitive overload in the early phases of skill development as it may be easier to attend to a simple cue from the coach, rather than the entire complex movement.

It has also been shown that withdrawal of concurrent feedback is more detrimental to the athlete the later in the learning process this is done, at least when it comes to visual information (Blandin, Toussaint, & Shea, 2008). Ranganathan and Newell (2009) showed that concurrent feedback changes the coordinative pattern compared to terminal feedback, and also in comparison to situations where the concurrent feedback is withdrawn. Generally though, one outcome can be achieved by more than one coordinative solution (Todorov & Jordan, 2002). Athletes who receive concurrent feedback react to the feedback and use more different strategies, as was found by Ranganathan and Newell. This somewhat scattered approach was less sustainable when the participants were asked to perform without the same feedback. However, the researchers also found that presenting information about the test conditions (i.e., that the concurrent feedback would be unavailable) mitigated the detrimental effect of concurrent feedback. For coaches, it seems important to consider restrictions inherent in the specific sport's competition, and especially if this situation makes concurrent feedback impossible or not. If so, coaches need to make a decision if concurrent feedback should be provided during practice.

Another way of preventing the detrimental effects of withdrawing concurrent feedback for an athlete is to provide terminal feedback after the same task-repetition, which has been found to be better than alternating concurrent and terminal feedback on different task-repetitions (Park, Shea, & Wright, 2000). Likely, this is because the athlete has the opportunity to attend to intrinsic feedback and develop error- and search strategies by proprioception rather than augmented feedback on the repetitions without augmented feedback. For a coach providing lots of concurrent feedback, it could be wise to intersperse some repetitions without feedback to allow the athlete to develop these strategies.

Concerning terminal feedback, there are two time frames that have been investigated after an athlete's performance. (Schmidt & Lee, 2005). The first one is called *feedback delay* and the second one is called *post-feedback delay* (Figure 6.2).

The feedback delay period seems to neither enhance nor degrade learning unless it is almost non-existing (i.e., zero seconds delay after task completion). In this instance, immediate feedback provision degrade long-term learning for the participants (Swinnen, Schmidt, Nicholson, & Shapiro, 1990). The argument for this is similar to what was presented as an argument against concurrent feedback. It overtakes the athlete's own responsibility of error detection and awareness of task-intrinsic feedback. On complex tasks, immediate KR feedback could give the athlete a hard time figuring out what degree of freedom to intervene during the upcoming repetition. Conversely, it could be more effective to let the athlete use task-intrinsic feedback first. Liu and Wrisberg (1997) found that the decisive factor for long-term motor learning was not necessarily the delay period *per se*, but rather that the participants consciously attended to task-intrinsic feedback. The feedback delay period has also been investigated by having participants execute some other irrelevant bogus task before receiving

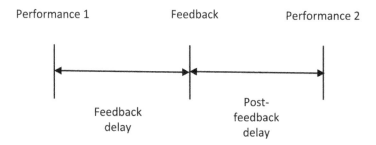

FIGURE 6.2 Time periods between first and second performance in relation to feedback.

the feedback. Generally, irrespective of the inserted activities being motor or verbal, that hampers learning. Probably, this is because information-processing or memory is blocked by these irrelevant activities. Terminal feedback is beneficial if no other competing activity is performed in-between task-execution and feedback. If feedback is provided with delay, the athlete would be best served being focused on the task in the delay period. Naturally, the feedback delay period is not intended to be interpreted such as that a coach should wait until next practice before providing feedback. The post-feedback delay period has been examined to comparably smaller extent, usually through manipulations of the time-interval duration (Salmoni et al., 1984). The findings seem to indicate no detrimental effects of having that time period extended rather than shortened. Additionally, looking at the evidence for random practice (i.e., when different tasks are mixed) compared to block practice (i.e., the same tasks are repeated in a block before moving on to the next task), it is reasonable to believe that the post-feedback delay period is not susceptible to interference of other tasks before executing the original task again (Brady, 2004). In applied settings, such as a regular practice, it is conceivably more norm than exception that there will be some other activities (e.g., talking to another athlete, thinking about what time it is, performing another skill in a small-sided game) before the athlete can execute the particular task again. Terminal feedback should offer the possibility to improve upon the performance. Therefore, it is imperative that the athlete gets another chance to perform the task. If the terminal feedback is provided at the end of the practice, a brief reminder could be useful right before next practice, priming the athlete's memory, like a little warm-up for his/her attention.

Focus (Internal or External)

Feedback can highlight either the athlete's own body parts (i.e., *internal focus*) or on some effect of the movement (i.e., *external focus*), such as the difference of focusing on the feet versus the shoes. Consistently, athletes using an external focus of attention have been shown to produce superior performances and learning development compared to athletes using an internal focus. Reasons for this have been provided from various studies. It could be that individuals' thinking about their own movement and/or body are more prone to become self-conscious and, consequently, emotions like nervousness might hamper execution (Baumeister, 1984). Wulf, Shea, and Park (2001) add that an external focus allows more natural self-organization that is not interfered by conscious controlling, which an internal focus is much more susceptible to. Through feedback, it is possible to influence athlete's focus. To test this assumption, Wulf, Chiviacowsky, Schiller, and Avila (2010) went back to a previous published study to investigate if a simple rewording of feedback statements (from internally to externally focused) produced different results for the participating football players practicing throw-ins. While the original study found that learning was better when feedback was less frequent, the replication demonstrated the opposite, when an external focus was induced by the feedback. Thus, small changes in wordings can have pronounced effects. It remains a little unclear though, if this effect should be attributed primarily to informational properties of the feedback or if it was due to athletes being frequently reminded to use an external feedback. Regardless, externally focused feedback seems beneficial. This effect has been shown in plenty of applied studies resembling real-life sports practice in as different contexts as volleyball (Wulf, McConnel, Gärtner, & Schwarz, 2002), dart throwing (Becker & Fairbrother, 2019) and injury prevention (Gokeler et al., 2015). Interestingly, the advantage of an external focus seems to be independent of personal preferences, as individuals who prefer, and use, an internal focus during balancing tasks perform worse than those who prefer, and use, an external focus (Wulf et al., 2001). Not to be forgotten, the quality of feedback is important, focus notwithstanding. That is, the feedback should contain information about the most task-relevant features. Polsgrove, Parry, and Brown (2016) demonstrated that the difference between wordings of 'pushing off from the ground' and 'running as short path as possible' made a significant difference during an agility sprint even as both statements are externally focused. Thus, not just any external-referenced feedback is useful for the athlete.

In general, what kind of content does your feedback mostly contain (Knowledge of Result or Knowledge of Performance)?
How could you improve the content of your feedback provision?
In general, do you mostly provide concurrent or terminal feedback?
How could you improve the timing of your feedback provision (e.g., delaying terminal feedback)?
How could you formulate feedback that emphasize external focus for some key skills within your sport?

Motivate

Feedback can motivate (or demotivate) an athlete to keep trying. In the early stages of practice, feedback can provide an important tool to enhance motivation as the athlete may struggle with performances. When the feedback accentuates autonomy (i.e., informational feedback), and ego involvement (i.e., controlling feedback) is avoided, motivation will be improved as stated by Self-Determination Theory (see Chapter 3). Recently, a meta-analysis by Wisniewski, Zierer, and Hattie (2020) found that feedback has a lower impact on motivation compared to cognitive and motor skill outcomes. However, as predicted by SDT, this relationship seems to be due to the fact that the feedback used in many interventions is uninformative or controlling, such as simple rewards and punishments. Contrary, Badami, VaezMousavi, Wulf, and Namazizadeh (2011) showed that feedback after good performances resulted in higher perceptions of competence, and consequently, increased intrinsic motivation, compared to when participants received feedback after poorer performances. Interestingly, negative feedback does not have any worse effect on intrinsic motivation than no feedback at all. Especially, if some instruction is added to the negative feedback, athletes could actually experience enhanced motivation. Also, a coach who, by the athlete, is considered knowledgeable and respected, acts as a buffer for detrimental effects on motivation of negative feedback. Thus, in order to create necessary 'room' for negative feedback, coaches need to create a close relationship with the athlete. If the negative feedback simultaneously conveys a message of high expectations, this will further soften the motivational blow (Fong, Patall, Vasquez, & Stautberg, 2019). Feedback that communicates lower competence in the athlete should try to neutralize this potentially inhibiting effect on motivation by having a positive autonomy-supportive message. This can be accomplished by providing options for working on improving the specific skill, or by supplying a rationale for the critique, such as referring to a criterion (Mouratidis, Lens, & Vansteenkiste, 2010). Amorose and Weiss (1998) compared *evaluative* and *informational* feedback after successful and unsuccessful performances. Evaluative feedback contains emotional statements that goes beyond simple acknowledgement of the performance or outcome revealing an evaluation from the feedback provider. Informational feedback contains either descriptive or prescriptive statements that the athlete should be able to use on subsequent performances. Following successful performances, athletes perceived evaluative feedback as the most desired, while unsuccessful performances were preferred to be followed by informational feedback. Informational feedback after a successful performance, especially after a relatively easy task, could be interpreted as signalling low competence in the athlete, which would lower self-determined motivation. Contrastingly, after an unsuccessful performance, athletes preferred informational feedback, while evaluative feedback (i.e., criticism) led to lower perceptions of competence and future expectations. Of course, this should not be viewed as an all or nothing proposition for coaches to react to successful or unsuccessful performances. Sometimes, it is good to be informational after successes as well, especially in the light of many expert coaches' inclination to provide constructive instructions during training. Given that though, it could be easy to forget to celebrate athletes' successes and just let them enjoy them moment rather than focus on improvement for the future.

Kluger and DeNisi (1996) argued that three different potential situations arise when comparing the athlete's performance to a set standard. First, no discrepancy between performance and standard is found. If so, feedback will motivate the athlete to maintain effort. Second, performance exceeds the standard. In this case, positive feedback is provided. If the athlete then believes in the possibility to reach another goal, the standard is raised and effort increased. If the athlete does not believe in higher goal attainment, then effort is reduced as the current goal did not need as much exertion. Third, if the performance does not reach the standard, negative feedback is provided. In this case, the athlete has two options, either to increase or reduce effort, perhaps even quit. Quitting might be a product of an athlete having an entity implicit theory, which will be revisited below. An increase in effort leads to a new situation, and in turn new feedback, either positive (if the discrepancy is narrowed) or negative (if the discrepancy is unchanged). If the athlete perceives the discrepancy to be smaller due to increased effort, this effort should be maintained or even increased further. If the athlete still does not experience progress towards the goal-standard, his/her belief in future success determines the continuing strivings. If the athlete believes in success, attention will be turned toward learning, which promotes continued motivation. If the athlete does not believe in success, attention will be turned to the self. Thus, self-consciousness can inhibit motivation as the feedback serves as a threat to oneself similar to what is experienced in a performance motivational climate. For a coach, it is important that the athlete does not perceive whatever feedback is provided as a threat to self-esteem, otherwise motivation will be hampered.

Implicit Theories

Individuals possess implicit beliefs regarding constructs such as intelligence, athleticism and competence. Athletes either believe that these concepts are stable or malleable. The former is called *entity theory*, while the latter is called *incremental theory*. These implicit theories affect intrinsic motivation and the choices an athlete makes when it comes to task difficulty. Feedback should focus on controllable aspects of the performance (e.g., effort, strategies, concentration and preparation), which is labelled incremental feedback. Orbach, Singer and Murphey (1997) found that a relatively small manipulation of the wording in the communication to athletes lead them to perceive greater personal control. Interestingly, participants who received functional attributions (e.g., possible to improve and everyone is able to progress) improved their performance over time compared to participants who were told that performance of this task was to a large extent dependent on innate ability. Effort-attributions seem to be most effective for intermediate-difficulty task (Schunk, 1982). For more challenging tasks, it is advantageous to attribute not only to effort, but also to strategies or other malleable factors pertaining to the quality of development, because effort alone is not a guarantee for success as the tasks increase in difficulty. Feedback highlighting innate abilities such as talent affects motivation negatively compared to feedback highlighting effort. The same impact has been found for performance, persistence, and enjoyment, that all benefit from incremental feedback (Mueller & Dweck, 1998). One problem with feedback that draws attention to stable characteristics rather than changeable features in the athlete, is that the former's focus on an end-product also leads to a focus on the self. Thus, for the individual with that mindset, protection of self-esteem is more important than taking potential risks as failures will not be viewed as temporary, but as an indication of permanently low value. Apparently, this is the case even if the feedback is positive (e.g., 'you ran the obstacle course quickly thanks to your speed talent', or 'you are the best I have ever seen on executing this technical skill').

Within the educational domain, formative assessment has been promoted over the last decades. This approach connects nicely with an incremental implicit theory, as it focuses on the process of development. One aspect that is important in this endeavour is that feedback is given at multiple times during the developmental process and not only at the end. This approach will provide multiple opportunities for practice and development. For a coach, this means that feedback for a specific skill ought to be provided during practices, and not only at competition. Additionally, the focus on process over product will be further immersed if the coach views feedback of athlete performance as an opportunity for the coach's own development and improvement of the coaching practice. This can be accomplished by having the athlete provide feedback to the coach about what is working best and consequently trying to adapt practices for continued athlete improvement (Nicol & Macfarlane-Dick, 2006). There is also the potential for coaches own implicit theory to shape coaching behaviours and communication. Some tentative findings correlate coaches' incremental theory with being empathetic during losses, respectful and predictable in their interactions with other people, willing to seek out help and advice, and placing greater emphasize on the athlete and sports compared to competition and winning (Hennessy, 2016).

 How do you currently use feedback to motivate the athletes (e.g., evaluative/informational feedback)?

How could you improve your feedback provision in order to enhance the athletes' motivation?

How could you formulate feedback to highlight controllable aspects of the performance?

Feedback Dependence

Research has demonstrated a perhaps counterintuitive relationship between amount of feedback and learning. Due to its strong guiding properties, feedback helps the athlete to perform better. However, the same feedback might lead to overuse of short-term corrections, which make stable movement patterns more difficult to reach. Frequent feedback may even become a part of the task itself for the athlete and overshadow task-intrinsic feedback, thus creating feedback dependence. Potentially, long-term learning is inhibited with high frequencies of feedback. This phenomenon is more likely for tasks that in relation to the athlete's skill level are relatively easy. More complex and difficult tasks still benefit from relatively high frequencies of feedback. Accordingly, a coach needs to carefully consider a specific skill's degree of difficulty (and compare it to the athlete's skill level) before deciding how to implement the information on feedback dependence. A thorough examination of the literature by Marschall, Bund, and Wiemeyer (2007) showed some factors that determine the occurrence of feedback dependence. One such factor seems to be a larger number of practices (e.g., > 90) leading to an increased risk for dependency. This is possibly of high interest for coaches, as sport skills are usually practiced with large amounts of practice. As the athlete becomes more proficient in task-execution, a greater reliance on proprioceptive information is assumed (Blandin et al., 2008; Tremblay & Proteau, 1998). When the task at hand is challenging in comparison to the athlete's own skill level, more feedback can be given without dependence being developed as the feedback eases task-execution to a more reasonable level while the athlete at the same time needs to pay attention to task-intrinsic feedback to handle the task (Guadagnoli & Lee, 2004). The primary objective of feedback's informational property is to facilitate the athlete's development of error detection and correction mechanisms that will enable him/her to eventually improve and perform through task-intrinsic feedback. For this reason, it is useful to know some methods to prevent feedback dependence and increase the athlete's engagement in task-intrinsic feedback, especially for relatively easy tasks.

Ways to Prevent Feedback Dependence

Fading

Research has been consistent in showing that early on in practice of a novel task, feedback (e.g., KR) is helpful for the athlete (Goodwin, 2019). Thus, frequent feedback is beneficial at the start. Contrastingly, later on in the skill development, the athlete's attention benefits from error detection through task-intrinsic feedback (if available), and this search process could be hampered by simultaneously having to process augmented feedback (Lai & Shea, 1999). To solve this issue, a fading schedule can be used. By this procedure, the coach initially uses higher frequencies of feedback and with time reduces this frequency deliberately. As the practice phase goes on and progress is made, it is natural for athletes to prefer a lower frequency of feedback (Janelle, Barba, Frehlich, Tennant, & Cauraugh, 1997), and this preference is met through a fading schedule.

Bandwidth

When providing bandwidth feedback, feedback is only provided when it exceeds a set limit deviation from the intended goal of the movement. Importantly, the athlete should be informed of the procedure of providing feedback only on large errors. Athletes' knowledge of this makes it possible for them to infer absence of feedback as positive. A broader bandwidth (e.g., 10%) deviation from the movement goal has been found to be more effective than a narrower (e.g., 5%) deviation. A broader bandwidth more naturally reduces feedback frequency over time as more and more repetitions should land within the bandwidth limits as the athlete progresses. The advantage of this is not entirely explained by reductions of feedback frequencies, though, as Lee and Carnahan (1990) found that individuals who received feedback on the exact same trials without knowledge of why did not improve as much. Athletes need to be informed of the bandwidth procedure in order to maximize its positive effects.

Summary

Summary feedback is provided when a number of repetitions or performances are given feedback simultaneously. For example, an athlete gets feedback after every tenth repetition for each one of the ten preceding repetitions. This delay of augmented feedback increases athletes' cognitive effort and increases attention to task-intrinsic feedback such as limb positions and kinaesthetic information (Anderson, Magill, Sekiya, & Ryan, 2005).

Average

Average feedback is used when the mean error from a number of repetitions is presented as the average error during that span. This method has a lot of similarities to summary feedback, and it is proposed to work through the same mechanisms, enhancing cognitive processing in the athlete. Similarly to the summary method, a smaller number of repetitions is more effective for more complex task and larger numbers for simple tasks (Yao, Fischman, & Wang, 1994). Longer length of summary/average is better when the athlete is more task-experienced and vice versa (Guadagnoli, Dornier, & Tandy, 1996).

Estimation

When using estimation, the athlete is first asked to estimate his/her own performance before getting augmented feedback from the coach. For example, in an aiming task, participants were requested to estimate force, release angle and trajectory before being provided with KR. This process enhanced their error-detection capabilities (Liu & Wrisberg, 1997). A similar approach pertains to using questions. This procedure has been found to elicit cognitive effort, creativity and problem-solving alongside awareness of one's performance (Chambers & Vickers, 2006). Using questions as a form of feedback may also induce a greater sense of ownership in the athlete of the performance. Before being able to draw maximum benefits of estimations, the athlete needs some basic understanding of, and skill in, executing the task. Hence, estimation could be most appropriate when the athlete has at least some experience with the task, compared to being a novice (Sigrist et al., 2013a).

Self-control

Some studies have examined how often the participants prefer to receive feedback and have found a wide range of preferences (from 11% to 97% of the total trials; Wulf et al., 2010). From this it is hard to distinguish generalizable optimal preferences of feedback frequencies. Jimenez-Diaz, Chaves-Castro, and Morera-Castro (2020) examined the results from 18 studies on the effectiveness of letting the participants regulate when they wanted feedback compared to conditions where feedback was provided without participants' control. Both short-term performance as well as long-term learning seem to be enhanced with self-control. Arguably, when an athlete is in charge of the frequency of feedback provision, he/she determines when most receptive for or interested in feedback information. Thus, the effect of feedback should be higher during self-controlled condition. For a coach, this can be arranged by telling the athlete that feedback is available upon request (even if feedback is provided from the coach at another schedule as well). By encouraging athletes to request feedback their task involvement and cognitive effort should increase. Self-control also enhances perceived autonomy, increasing self-determined motivation (Lewthwaite & Wulf, 2017).

> In general, how often do you provide augmented feedback to the athletes during practice today?
> To what extent do you think the athletes you are coaching risk becoming feedback dependent?
> What kind of ways of preventing feedback dependence could you use?

Reinforce

Feedback serves to reinforce a specific behaviour, by creating associations between stimuli and movement (Schmidt & Lee, 2005). Positive and negative reinforcements strengthen the connection between stimulus and behaviour (see Figures 5.1 and 5.2), while punishment and extinction weaken the same relationship. Potentially, self-efficacy is an important moderator for athletes connecting stimuli and behaviour. Usually, positive feedback is primarily thought of when considering increases in self-efficacy, but the relationship might be slightly more complicated. Athletes can be strengthened in their strivings for achievement, even if they receive feedback about what they did not perform well. Tzetzis, Votsis, and Kourtessis (2008) showed this when negative information was provided along with positive feedback on other aspects and included information on how to improve. Therefore, positive and negative feedback will be reviewed below.

Positive vs Negative Feedback

Ferdinand and Kray (2013) demonstrated that positive feedback contains more task-relevant information in comparison to negative feedback. Perhaps this comes from the fact that information about what worked well offers more direction on how to behave, while information about what did not work just eliminates one of an infinite number of possible movements. Other sport-related studies have been somewhat ambiguous when it comes to effects of positive and negative feedback. Some studies have demonstrated greater learning when receiving feedback after good trials compared to when receiving feedback after poor trials (Chiviacowsky & Wulf, 2007). Arguably, children learn more from positive feedback, while adults can actually derive more benefit from negative feedback. Whether the feedback is positive or negative has a stronger effect on adolescents then younger or older people. The adolescent brain is more sensitive to rewards compared to children and adults, which can make adolescents prioritize greater risk in order to achieve some kind of success. Further, positive or negative feedback have not equally strong effects depending on the risk level in the behaviour preceding the feedback which was investigated by Zhuang, Feng, and Liao (2017). Regardless if the feedback was positive or negative after conservative choices, the participants performed equally well the next time. Meanwhile, a risky choice led participants to perform much better when provided with positive compared to negative feedback. Thus, negative feedback after a high-risk event seem to impede learning. For a coach, it is important to be careful when deciding upon feedback provision after an athlete takes a risk. A typical decision is to decide if positive feedback should be provided to encourage a brave action or if negative feedback should be provided to inform about failed skill execution.

After providing negative feedback to an athlete in a typical group practice venue, it would be wise for a coach to make a concerted effort to focus on the same athlete until the coach is able to provide positive feedback, preferably concerning similar behaviours. Otherwise, it is easy to lose track of the balance between positive and negative feedback. This procedure allows the coach to catch the athlete executing something successfully, and consequently is able to provide positive feedback genuinely. Likely, this will increase the athlete's trust in the coach that he/she will provide sincere feedback regardless of positive or negative feedback. In extension, the athlete could be more responsive for negative feedback in the future, through understanding that the coach's feedback is aimed at improving skills, and not judging or bashing the athlete. Positive feedback has been shown to facilitate individuals' consolidation of motor skills (Sugawara, Tanaka, Okazaki, Watanabe, & Sadato, 2018), as it both enhances the motivation, but also elicits positive emotions that further its positive impact. Moreover, a coach needs to decide upon the purpose of the feedback, or rather what function of feedback is currently most effective for the athlete. Magill (2011) argued that information about positive aspects is better for motivation, while information about negative aspects is better for skill development.

Some coaches use public positive feedback as a means to provide stimulation for the other athletes as they get a positive model of behaviour. Another purpose might be to increase power of the reinforcement as others witnessing the praise is thought to make the praised individual feel even better. Although intentions are good, this procedure has clear drawbacks. Public feedback tends to be connected to a performance motivational climate (see Chapter 3). Furthermore, Horn (1985) found that athletes who received more positive feedback in public reported lower perceptions of their own competence, arguably since the athletes compared the amount of positive feedback to the other athletes' and drew the conclusions that the coach had lower expectancies for them. If a coach gives two different kinds of feedback for the same level of performance (e.g., positive vs neutral, or neutral vs negative), it conveys important expectancy information to the athletes, even if unintended by the coach. Additionally, athletes have to be provided with quality and contingent positive feedback if it is to have any value. Praise for the sake of praise will be easy to see through by the athletes and will erode athletes' confidence in the coach's competence and intentions.

Clearly though, receiving feedback after good performances, even if learning is not necessarily that much greater, increases the athlete's confidence in future capacity (Carter, Smith, & Ste-Marie, 2016). In addition, for more complex tasks, feedback should also include aspects that were not as well-executed. Tzetzis and colleagues (2008) showed in a badminton study that participants who received information about good and bad aspects of their performance of complex backhand shots improved both skill level, as well as confidence in this skill, compared to participants who only got information about what they did well. Thus, despite negative feedback, it is possible for an athlete to improve self-confidence as long as it induces a sense of control for the athlete. Schunk (1982) found that for increases in task involvement, skill development and self-efficacy, it is more effective to reinforce past efforts rather than to encouraging future work.

A commonly suggested template for provision of negative feedback is to use the sandwich method. This is done with first a positive statement, then the negative statement, and finally another positive statement (Martens, 2012). The intention of this approach is to get the recipient of the feedback to be more receptive by first providing something positive and to end of a good note with the second positive remark. However, as always, following any recipe uncritically runs the risk of being both mechanical and inefficient. For example, an athlete getting used to the coach always providing some negative feedback after an initial positive remark could end up not paying any attention to the first statement. Perhaps, an overuse of the sandwich method could also lead to the athlete feeling a little conned by the coach if the latter is not perceived as sincere and uses the positive statements just to hide the negative. In general, it is an appropriate approach to provide more positive feedback than negative, although some additional methods would be useful to have at a coach's disposal. Therefore, it is advocated to mix the feedback sandwich up with simply providing a positive statement, period. Likewise, a provision of a negative feedback statement followed by some encouragement referring earlier successes might be suitable. Research on expert coaches has found their ratios of positive to negative feedback to be very varying, ranging from roughly twice as many positive statements (Bloom, Crumpton,

TABLE 6.1 Sensitive words, possible implications and alternatives.

Word	Potential implication for the listener (i.e., receiver of communication)	Possible alternative formulations
But	Ignoring the first half of the statement that comes before *but*.	Use a full stop and start a new sentence or use conjunctions such as *and, at the same time, also*.
Why	*Why* can seem intruding and accusing.	Use wordings such as *how come...* or *what is the reason for...?*
Must, Should	*Must* and *should* can be perceived as controlling and lead to non-self-determined motivation.	Use 'softer' and less direct words such as *could*.
Never, Always, No one, All etc.	These words are generalizations that are seldom true.	Be more specific by using wordings such as *this time, in your last repetition* or *right now*.

& Anderson, 1999) to more than 25 times as many (Horton, Baker, & Deakin, 2005). Reasons for this are unclear and could be methodological artefacts or dependent on the group of athletes. However, it needs to be mentioned that most studies investigating expert coaches have found a heavy reliance on an instructional approach, and high-quality information could potentially off-set negative feedback as previously mentioned.

Sensitive Words

When providing verbal feedback to an athlete, it is useful to be cautious about phrases and wordings that are easily perceived as either emotionally loaded or bring a subtle negative connotation. Some words also make the feedback statement ambiguous and confusing to the athlete. Examples of such words are described in Table 6.1.

 How do you reinforce desirable actions from the athletes today? How could you avoid using sensitive words in your feedback?

Modality

With the advent of technological progress, research has debated the merits of different modalities of feedback provision. There are three distinct modalities that feedback can be conveyed through: *visual, auditive* and *haptic* (i.e., tactile and kinaesthetic). Few sport studies have compared the effectiveness of these modalities. Even less is known about the effectiveness of combinations of two or more of the modalities. Nonetheless, Sigrist and colleagues (2013a) speculated that combinations would be more effective for complex tasks rather than simple tasks. According to dual coding theory (Paivio, 1991), working memory is not overloaded if different channels are used. This theory is derived from cognitive psychology and primarily focuses on visual and verbal channels. Thus, providing feedback through visual and auditive modality simultaneously should be possible for the athlete to handle, as long as the information's complexity in relation to athlete's competence and experience is not too high. Rhoades, Da Matta, Larson, and Pulos (2014) investigated studies comparing visual and verbal feedback and found a positive effect for the addition of visual feedback. Even if the effect was quite small, it is possible that this addition is a deciding factor in the competitive sports world. It seems that visual feedback alone is no better and perhaps less efficient than verbal feedback, but the combination of the two could prove beneficial (Akinci & Kirazci, 2020). The source of information that is deemed the most appropriate to facilitate performance is established fairly early in skill development. After that point, it could be detrimental to withdraw this source (Tremblay & Proteau, 1998). Accordingly, if the competition conditions state that one modality of feedback is ineligible, it could be wise not to include it in early practice.

Visual

Visual modality of feedback contains both physical demonstrations from the coach of an athlete's execution, video, execution in front of a mirror or more abstract information such as force production curves displayed on a monitor. To date, the studies examining concurrent feedback have mostly used visual feedback. Tasks that are well suited for this are not aiming tasks, since it would occupy visual resources from the athlete. More appropriate tasks are rather some type of force production activities or balancing acts, such as slalom simulator or standing on a balance board. For complex tasks, concurrent visual feedback is believed to induce a more external focus as the athlete attends to the feedback instead of the body parts, which helps to facilitate execution (Wulf, Shea, & Matschiner, 1998). If so, the focus tends to be used even when feedback is withdrawn. For simple tasks with fewer degrees of freedom, visual concurrent feedback seems to interfere with long-term learning (Schmidt & Wulf, 1997). Conceivably, this occurs because it is easier to make small repetition to repetition changes in simpler tasks, trying to 'please' the feedback source every time. Meanwhile, when performing more complex tasks, it is possible that the athlete is satisfied with a broader solution and therefore those moment-to-moment changes are bypassed for an overall fairly accurate movement solution, rather than a 'perfect' movement.

Coaches tend to use more positive modelling when it comes to providing demonstrations compared to showing the athlete what they did wrong (Cushion & Jones, 2001; Smith & Cushion, 2006). Mirrors are another popular tool for providing concurrent KP feedback in sports such as dance, weight lifting and swimming. Their presence provides the opportunity for the athlete to use the feedback in a self-controlled manner. Today, plenty of apps and computer programs exist for coaches who want to explore the possibilities of visual feedback, not to mention the convenience of modern cell phone recordings. Some applications lend themselves to both sharing the video with the athlete's device as well as drawing lines and arrows to highlight specific areas. Feedback through video serves well to a self-controlled schedule as the athlete easily can determine when and what performances to watch. One possible way of laying a foundation for this is to have a camera rolling during practice connected to a screen that the athlete can watch whenever interested in a specific task execution. Depending on task complexity, terminal (simpler tasks) or concurrent (more complex tasks) visual feedback could prove most effective (Sigrist et al., 2013b).

Auditive

Auditive modality of feedback contains both verbalized words and other signals. Reasonably, the most convenient and applicable means of providing auditive feedback for a sports coach is through spoken words. Surprisingly, this is, when it comes to investigations of the auditive modality, the least studied. Contrastingly, studies have used a variety of alarms and sonified signals to highlight when and where the athlete is moving compared to a predetermined pattern (Sigrist et al., 2013a). For coincidence-anticipation tasks (e.g., hitting a baseball pitch or catching a pass in American football), verbal information is redundant to visual as this is the primary modality for such tasks (Magill, Chamberlin, & Hall, 1991). Possibly, verbal KR adds little beyond the error information the athlete derives from visual information during task execution. Compared to other modalities of feedback, Altavilla, Cejula, and Caballero-Pérez (2018) found that verbal feedback was seen as more personal, which can explain the motivational boost received from this type of feedback. Perhaps, verbal feedback is best used for KP information, reinforcing desirable behaviours or enhancing motivation.

For a coach working in a group practice environment, it could be wise to start the feedback provision to an individual athlete with the athlete's name. A well-known phenomenon is the 'cocktail party effect' where a personally highly relevant stimulus, such as one's own name, can capture the person's attention in spite of a cacophony of noise. Briefly after this attention-grabbing signal, the athlete is more perceptive for the content of the feedback (Wood & Cowan, 1995). Additionally, by using such a distinct and pointed cue as the name of the athlete in question, the risk for the apathy phenomenon 'bystander effect' is reduced. Research in social psychology has shown that in ambiguous situations people tend to look to others for cues on how to act (Garcia, Weaver, Moskowitz, & Darley, 2002). In line with this phenomenon, it is easy for an athlete the coach wants the attention of, to keep going just like the other athletes, unless something very specific calls for his/her attention. This inattention to the coach feedback is precluded with the use of the athlete's name. Moreover, using the names of the athlete when providing feedback has been argued to be a sign of an athlete-centred approach (Vinson, Brady, Moreland, & Judge, 2016). Finally, a word of caution. Provision of auditive feedback can be difficult to keep private as others in close proximity can overhear, to the potential dismay of the intended athlete (Funk, Heusler, Akcay, Weiland, & Schmidt, 2016).

Haptic

Haptic modality of feedback contains both *tactile*, 'outside' sensations that can be felt by contact with skin, and *kinaesthetic*, 'inside' sensations that can be experienced through muscles, joints and tendons. Many studies investigating this feedback modality have used high-technology equipment, which might not be readily available to most coaches (cf. Funk, Heusler, Akcay, Weiland, & Schmidt, 2016). More reasonable uses of haptic feedback are from physical touch either from a person (e.g., peer's arms on the lower legs when trying a handstand in between the peer's arms) or a relatively convenient equipment (e.g., touching a string that hangs from the roof right behind the athlete during a squat indicates that the movement is a little too far back). Haptic feedback might be less convincing than verbal feedback, when they are conflicting, perhaps partly because the latter could be expressed in an authoritative manner (Sarlegna, Gauthier, & Blouin, 2007). Still, it could be useful and help the athlete become more aware of task-intrinsic proprioceptive feedback. Sigrist and colleagues (2013b) claimed that haptic feedback is most beneficial for error augmentation (i.e., increasing error and variability through physical contact in order to have the athlete develop a feel for when errors occur) of simple skills, rather than trying to reduce errors.

Physical contact can be a sensitive and complicated issue for coaches (Piper, Garratt, & Taylor, 2013; Sports Coach UK, 2009), as recently there has been a greater emphasis on the potential risks of abusive contacts within sports (Johansson, 2013). However, Thompson (2016) wondered when guidelines for practice will catch up with the theoretical and empirical evidence for the positive effects of touch, as a no-touch rule could bring more drawbacks than first realized by policy-makers (Öhman & Quennerstedt, 2017). Touch can communicate emotions and serve as a powerful social reward (Løseth, Leknes, & Ellingsen, 2016), which for a coach can be utilized in a way such as an energetic high-five. An investigation of the opinions of high school students in physical education revealed that physical contact was appreciated when it facilitates learning new technique, prevent injury, or convey closeness or emotions. It was deemed inappropriate by the students when teachers interfere with students' feelings of being capable on their own, and when touching was not required to perform the activity (Caldeborg, Maivorsdotter, & Öhman, 2019). An agreement between coach and athletes seems pivotal when it comes to the use of haptic feedback.

 What modality do you currently prefer to use for feedback?
What modality do you think the athletes prefer?

Practical Implementation of Feedback

Reflection Card

	Feedback		Date: _____
Situation	Purpose of feedback	Description of feedback	Coach's thoughts/ emotions
	☐ Inform ☐ Motivate ☐ Reinforce		

The goal of this reflective activity is to deliberately implement some of the previously presented information on feedback. A broad action plan should be developed for feedback provision. Since feedback often is highly dependent on the practice activity and athlete's performance, it may be better with a more general plan than one that is too specific. In the first column (*Situation*), describe a specific athlete's performance during a practice activity. In the second column (*Purpose of feedback*), mark the primary intention of feedback provision, whether it is to inform, motivate or reinforce the athlete. In the third column (*Description of feedback*), describe briefly the feedback that was provided to the athlete. The first three columns could be prepared before practice, but by now, with the practice from the previous reflection cards, it is advocated to try to think on the feet during practice. A hallmark of skilled feedback provision is to be able to react to an athlete's performance that cannot be prepared meticulously. Certainly, when reading the preceding parts in this chapter and doing the application exercises, some broad guidelines for personal feedback provision might start to evolve. Still, the final craftmanship should be executed during practice, in real-time. In the fourth column (*Coach's thoughts/emotions*), note some reactions from either the feedback provision itself or the observed effect on the athlete.

Secondary Reflection

 Use the questions below and/or the formula for shared reflection in Chapter 2.

What made you decide upon the primary purpose of the feedback provided in the reflection card?

How could you have provided this feedback in another modality, and what would have been the consequences then?

> Did you experience that you missed any opportunities to provide feedback to an athlete during the practice? If so, what was the cause that you did not seize the opportunity/made an intervention? What was the main reason for the intervention being made at the time it actually was?
>
> With the used reflection card in hand, what do you think when you look back at that specific situation and the athlete during the practice?
>
> How would you interpret your thoughts and emotions from this particular moment?
>
> What do you now think will be the effects for the athlete after your feedback?
>
> What other purpose could you have focused on when providing feedback in this situation? How would that have been carried out? What would the consequences have been?
>
> What is the main lesson learnt that you take away from the experience?

Reflection Sheet

In this chapter, two reflection sheets are provided. Reflection sheet 2 is more advanced, and it is recommended to use Reflection sheet 1 first, and if looking to take feedback awareness to yet another level, move on to Reflection sheet 2. In either Reflection sheet, the first column is completed before practice. Second to fifth columns are completed after practice. In Reflection sheet 2, the purpose is not to get the percentages exactly correct, but to think about the relative frequency of various aspects of feedback. Some might be harder to estimate than others and after some practices a few of the questions may not be applicable. By doing this after practice, the coach has a foundation for becoming more self-aware when providing feedback during future practices.

Reflection sheet 1: *Feedback* Date: _____

Organization and Purpose of practice activity.	Circle function of feedback of emphasis.	Describe how the chosen feedback function was implemented (e.g., how did you inform the athletes about their performance trying to induce an external focus, or how did you formulate feedback avoiding sensitive words).	Briefly answer the following questions: How did it feel to use the chosen feedback function? How did the athletes respond to the chosen feedback function? How could this feedback function have been more effective?	What were your own thoughts and emotions during this part of the practice?
	Inform Motivate Dependence Reinforce			
	Inform Motivate Dependence Reinforce			
	Inform Motivate Dependence Reinforce			

Reflection sheet 2: *Feedback*

Date: _____

Description of and Purpose of practice in general	Function of feedback			
	Inform	Motivate	Feedback dependence	Reinforce
	Approximately, how often was my feedback KR? ____ % Approximately, how often was my feedback KP? ____ %	Approximately, how often was my feedback controlling? ____ %	Approximately, how often did I provide feedback after the athlete had time to process task-intrinsic feedback? ____ %	Approximately, how often was my feedback positive? ____ % Approximately, how often was my feedback negative? ____ %
	Approximately, how often was my feedback concurrent? ____ % Approximately, how often was my feedback terminal? ____ %	Approximately, how often after a successful performance did I provide evaluative feedback? ____ % Approximately, how often after an unsuccessful performance did I provide informational feedback? ____ %	Approximately, how often did I use one of the methods for preventing feedback dependence? ____ %	Approximately, how often did I avoid using sensitive words in my feedback? ____ %
	Approximately, how often was my feedback internally focused? ____ % Approximately, how often was my feedback externally focused? ____ %	Approximately, how often was my feedback promoting an incremental implicit theory? ____ %	Approximately, how often did I provide feedback when a relatively easy skill was executed? ____ %	Approximately, how often did I purposefully withhold feedback to extinguish an undesirable behaviour? ____ %

Reflective Summary

> When working with feedback during practice, what has been the most important learning for you?
> How are you going to capitalize on this learning in the future?
> Which one of the four feedback functions do you currently consider your strongest suit?
> Is any feedback function more difficult to manage in your view?
> What could you do to improve your skills managing this feedback function?
> From your readings of feedback, your answers to the application exercises, your reflective activities, how would you best use feedback in your coaching?

Challenging Feedback Assumptions

For the next meeting Ellen made sure she was on time by some margin. This time the one missing was Collin.

> "Speaking of the devil, you're late", Leah smiled at Collin, as he entered the door.
> "I had to talk to a disgruntled parent", Collin replied shamefully.
> "Does that make you a sloppy person?" Ellen asked politely.
> "I guess… or perhaps that can happen to anyone", he replied silently.
> "Behaviours don't necessarily reveal who we are on the inside", Ellen said with a soothing voice.
> "No, I tried to apply that mindset when I've been giving the guys feedback lately as well", Collin quipped.
> "What kind of statements have you used then?" Ellen queried.
> "I've tried to focus more on things they can control rather than what they are", he replied.
> "And what have you found with that procedure?" Ellen asked.
> "More athletes are trying harder, especially among the lesser talented", Collin continued.
> "I guess you have a hard time abandoning the mindset completely that people are or are not", but I am impressed by your effort", Leah laughed a little.

Ellen looked somewhat surprised by Leah's abruption.

> "The coach's own implicit theory may impact behaviours and communication in a subliminal way. How have you managed to reduce the amount of feedback, Leah?" Ellen spun in her chair towards Leah.

"I got an idea when I used the reflection sheet you gave me. After a few practices, I saw a pattern where I used very high frequencies of feedback", she answered.

"Was it for mostly difficult tasks?" Ellen probed.

"Actually, it was for pretty much everything", Leah replied.

"How would you go about it now then?" Ellen kept asking.

"I really like the estimation and self-control procedures for more routine drills. The athletes have been told that they can request feedback at any time, which isn't that often compared to when I was deciding myself on when to give feedback. And when I now do decide to give feedback, I let them guesstimate their own performance before I tell my opinion", Leah said.

"What have you noticed with this approach, then?" Ellen asked.

"As far as I can tell, the athletes are paying more attention when they do ask for feedback. I also think they are into the activity when I'm not giving constant concurrent feedback", Leah said as she looked at Collin who seemed like he was thinking about something.

"Yeah, I've given more visual KP feedback instead of relying almost exclusively on KR. That also helps not being overly focused on them as persons or the end-product, I think. Certainly, for the newcomers this has helped them getting a grasp of the techniques we're using", Collin spoke out.

"Sounds good that you are both so aware of your feedback practice by now", Ellen wrapped up.

Quiz

1. Which are the four functions of feedback?
    a. Motivate, inform, dependence, reinforce.
    b. Augmented, intrinsic, summary, bandwidth.
    c. Immediate, delayed, external, internal.

2. When it comes to informing the athlete about performance, which statement is most correct?
    a. Augmented feedback is always useful for the athlete.
    b. Concurrent feedback is more effective in the long-term for athlete development.
    c. Externally focused feedback is better than internally focused.

3. When it comes to using feedback to enhance athlete motivation, which statement is most correct?
    a. More feedback is more motivating.
    b. Feedback is most motivating when it is not a threat to self-esteem.
    c. Negative feedback is worse than no feedback at all for motivation.

4. How can feedback convey a message of incremental implicit theory?
   a. Feedback should be given quietly.
   b. Feedback should highlight controllable aspects.
   c. Feedback should exclusively be positive.

5. Which statement is false about how feedback can create dependence in the athlete?
   a. Task-intrinsic feedback may be overshadowed by augmented feedback.
   b. Frequent feedback might cause too many short-term changes from the athlete which inhibits long-term learning.
   c. Athletes who have received mostly negative feedback become more dependent on the coach.

6. What is the main purpose of methods for preventing feedback dependence?
   a. Ease the work load for coaches.
   b. Prohibit athlete's guessing and uncertainty of own performance.
   c. Engage the athlete cognitively in processing of information.

7. When it comes to reinforcing athletes with positive or negative feedback, which statement is most correct?
   a. Positive feedback should be provided in public for optimal effect.
   b. Athletes learn most from negative feedback.
   c. After providing negative feedback, it would be wise for a coach to try to find something positive before too long.

8. Which statement is most correct concerning different modalities of feedback?
   a. Visual feedback can only be provided as terminal feedback.
   b. Auditive feedback is usually less motivating.
   c. Haptic feedback can be worrisome for coaches to provide.

References

Akinci, Y., & Kirazci, S. (2020). Effects of visual, verbal, visual + verbal feedback on learning of dribbling and lay-up skill. *Sport Mont, 18*, 63–68.

Altavilla, C., Cejuela, R., & Caballero-Pérez, P. (2018). Effect of different feedback modalities on swimming pace: Which feedback modality is most effective? *Journal of Human Kinetics, 65*, 187–195.

Amorose, A.J., & Weiss, M.R. (1998). Coaching feedback as a source of information about perceptions of ability: A developmental examination. *Journal of Sport & Exercise Psychology, 20*, 395–420.

Anderson, D. I., Magill, R. A., Sekiya, H., & Ryan, G. (2005). Support for an explanation of the guidance effect in motor skill learning. *Journal of Motor Behavior, 37*, 231–238.

Badami, R., VaezMousavi, M., Wulf, G., & Namazizadeh, M. (2011). Feedback after good versus poor trials affects intrinsic motivation. *Research Quarterly for Exercise and Sport, 82*, 360–364.

Baumeister, R. F. (1984). Choking under pressure: Self-consciousness and paradoxical effects of incentives on skilful performance. *Journal of Personality and Social Psychology, 46*, 610–620.

Becker, K. A., & Fairbrother, J. T. (2019). The use of multiple externally directed attentional focus cues facilitates motor learning. *International Journal of Sports Science & Coaching, 14*, 651–657.

Blandin, Y., Toussaint, L., & Shea, C. H. (2008). Specificity of practice: Interaction between concurrent sensory information and terminal feedback. *Journal of Experimental Psychology: Learning, Memory, and Cognition, 34*, 994–1000.

Bloom, G. A., Crumpton, R., & Anderson, J. E. (1999). A systematic observation study of the teaching behaviors of an expert basketball coach. *The Sport Psychologist, 13*, 157–170.

Brady, F. (2004). Contextual interference: A meta-analytic study. *Perceptual and Motor Skills, 99*, 116–126.

Brisson, T. A., & Alain, C. (1996). Should common optimal movement patterns be identified as the criterion to be achieved. *Journal of Motor Behavior, 28*, 211–223.

Caldeborg, A., Maivorsdotter, N., & Öhman, M. (2019). Touching the didactic contract – A student perspective on intergenerational touch in PE. *Sport, Education and Society, 24*, 256–268.

Carter, M. J., Smith, V., & Ste-Marie, D. M. (2016). Judgments of learning are significantly higher following feedback on relatively good versus relatively poor trials despite no actual learning differences. *Human Movement Science, 45*, 63–70.

Chambers, K. L., & Vickers, J. N. (2006). Effects of bandwidth feedback and questioning on the performance of competitive swimmers. *The Sport Psychologist, 20*, 184–197.

Chiviacowsky, S., & Wulf, G. (2007). Feedback after good trials enhances learning. *Research Quarterly for Exercise and Sport, 78*, 40–47.

Cushion, C. J., & Jones, R. L. (2001). A systematic observation of professional top-level youth soccer coaches. *Journal of Sport Behavior, 24*, 354–376.

Ferdinand, N. K., & Kray, J. (2013). Age-related changes in processing positive and negative feedback: Is there a positivity effect for older adults? *Biological Psychology, 94*, 235–241.

Fong, C. J., Patall, E. A., Vasquez, A. C., & Stautberg, S. (2019). A meta-analysis of negative feedback on intrinsic motivation. *Educational Psychology Review, 31*, 121–162.

Funk, M., Heusler, J., Akcay, E., Weiland, K., & Schmidt, A. (2016). Haptic, auditory or visual? Towards optimal error feedback at manual assembly workplaces. In *PETRA '16: Proceedings of the 9th ACM International Conference on PErvasive technologies related to assistive environments*. New York: Association for Computing Machinery.

Garcia, S. M., Weaver, K., Moskowitz, G. B., & Darley, J. M. (2002). Crowded minds: The implicit bystander effect. *Journal of Personality and Social Psychology, 83*, 843–853.

Gentile, A. M. (1972). A working model of skill acquisition with application to teaching. *Quest, 17*, 3–23.

Goodwin, J. E. (2019). Scheduling concurrent visual feedback in learning a continuous balance task. *Journal of Motor Learning and Development, 7*, 261–272.

Gokeler, A., Benjaminse, A., Welling, W., Alferink, M., Eppinga, P., & Otten, B. (2015). The effects of attentional focus on jump performance and knee joint kinematics in patients after ACL reconstruction. *Physical therapy in sport, 16*, 114–120.

Guadagnoli, M. A., Dornier, L. A., & Tandy, R. D. (1996). Optimal length for summary knowledge of results: The influence of task-related experience and complexity. *Research Quarterly for Exercise and Sport, 67*, 239–248.

Guadagnoli, M. A., & Lee, T. D. (2004). Challenge point: A framework for conceptualizing the effects of various practice conditions in motor learning. *Journal of Motor Behavior, 36*, 212–224.

Hebert, E. P., & Landin, D. (1994). Effects of a learning model and augmented feedback on tennis skill acquisition. *Research Quarterly for Exercise and Sport, 65*, 250–257.

Hennessy, L. (2016). 2016 Games Development Conference Keynote Presentation. Retrieved from https://www.youtube.com/watch?v=1JKCnNtPJ_A

Horn, T. S. (1985). Coaches' feedback and changes in children's perceptions of their physical competence. *Journal of Educational Psychology, 77*, 174–186.

Horton, S., Baker, J., & Deakin, J. (2005). Experts in action: A systematic observation of 5 national team coaches. *International Journal of Sport Psychology, 36*, 299–321.

Janelle, C. M., Barba, D. A., Frehlich, S. G., Tennant, L. K., & Cauraugh, J. H. (1997). Maximizing performance feedback effectiveness through videotape replay and a self-controlled learning environment. *Research Quarterly for Exercise and Sport, 68*, 269–279.

Jimenez-Diaz, J., Chaves-Castro, K., & Morera-Castro, M. (2020). Effect of self-controlled and regulated feedback on motor skill performance and learning: A meta-analytic study 2020 Jul 5:1–14. doi: 10.1080/00222895.2020.1782825. Epub ahead of print.

Johansson, S. (2013). Coach-athlete sexual relationships: If no means no does yes mean yes? *Sport, Education and Society, 18*, 678–693.

Kluger, A. N., & DeNisi, A. (1996). The effects of feedback interventions on performance: A historical review, a meta-analysis, and a preliminary feedback intervention theory. *Psychological Bulletin, 119*, 254–284.

Lai, Q., & Shea, C. H. (1999). Bandwidth knowledge of results enhances generalized motor program learning. *Research Quarterly for Exercise and Sport, 70*, 79–83.

Lee, T. D., & Carnahan, H. (1990). Bandwidth knowledge of results and motor learning: More than just a relative frequency effect. *The Quarterly Journal of Experimental Psychology A: Human Experimental Psychology, 42A*, 777–789.

Lewthwaite, R., & Wulf, G. (2017). Optimizing motivation and attention for motor performance and learning. *Current Opinion in Psychology, 16*, 38–42.

Liu, J., & Wrisberg, C. A. (1997). The effect of knowledge of results delay and the subjective estimation of movement form on the acquisition and retention of a motor skill. *Research Quarterly for Exercise and Sport, 68*, 145–151.

Løseth, G., Leknes, S., & Ellingsen, D-M. (2016). The neurochemical basis of motivation for affiliative touch. In H. Olausson, J. Wessberg, I. Morrison, & F. McGlone (Eds.), *Affective touch and the neurophysiology of CT afferents* (pp. 239–264). New York: Springer.

Magill, R. A. (1994). The influence of augmented feedback on skill learning depends on characteristics of the skill and the learner. *Quest, 46*, 314–327.

Magill, R. A. (2011). *Motor learning and control: Concepts and applications.* (9th ed.). Singapore: McGraw-Hill.

Magill, R. A., Chamberlin, C. J., Hall, K. G. (1991). Verbal knowledge of results as redundant information for learning an anticipation timing skill. *Human Movement Science, 10*, 485–507.

Marschall, F., Bund, A., & Wiemeyer, J. (2007). Does frequent augmented really degrade learning? A meta-analysis. *E-Journal Bewugung und Training, 1*, 75–86.

Martens, R. (2012). *Successful coaching* (4th ed.). Champaign, IL: Human Kinetics.

McNevin, N., Magill, R. A., & Buekers, M. J. (1994). The effects of erroneous knowledge of results on transfer of anticipation timing. *Research Quarterly for Exercise and Sport, 65*, 324–329.

Mouratidis, A., Lens, W., & Vansteenkiste, M. (2010). How you provide corrective feedback makes a difference: The motivating role of communicating in an autonomy-supporting way. *Journal of Sport & Exercise Psychology, 32*, 619–637.

Mueller, C. M., & Dweck, C. S. (1998). Praise for intelligence can undermine children's motivation and performance. *Journal of Personality and Social Psychology, 75*, 33–52.

Nicol, D. J., & Macfarlane-Dick, D. (2006). Formative assessment and self-regulated learning: A model and seven principles of good feedback practice. *Studies in Higher Education, 31*, 199–218.

Öhman, M., & Quennerstedt, A. (2017). Questioning the no-touch discourse in physical education from a children's right perspective. *Sport, Education and Society, 22*, 305–320.

Orbach, I., Singer, R., & Murphey, M. (1997). Changing attributions with an attribution training technique related to basketball dribbling. *The Sport Psychologist, 11*, 294–304.

Paivio, A. (1991). Dual coding theory: Retrospect and current status. *Canadian Journal of Psychology, 45*, 255–287.

Park, J-H., Shea, C. H., & Wright, D. L. (2000). Reduced-frequency concurrent and terminal feedback: A test of the guidance hypothesis. *Journal of Motor Behavior, 32*, 287–296.

Piper, H., Garratt, D., & Taylor, B. (2013). Child abuse, child protection, and defensive 'touch' in PE teaching and sports coaching. *Sport, Education and Society, 18*, 583–598.

Polsgrove, M. J., Parry, T. E., & Brown, N. T. (2016). Poor quality of instruction leads to poor motor performance regardless of internal or external focus of attention. *International Journal of Exercise Science, 9*, 214–222.

Ranganathan, R., & Newell, K. M. (2009). Influence of augmented feedback on coordination strategies. *Journal of Motor Behavior, 41*, 317–330.

Rhoades, M. C., Da Matta, G. B., Larson, N., & Pulos, S. (2014). A meta-analysis of visual feedback for motor learning. *Athletic Insight, 6*, 17–33.

Russell, D. M., & Newell, K. M. (2007). No-KR tests in motor learning, retention and transfer. *Human Movement Science, 26*, 155–173.

Salmoni, A. W., Schmidt, R. A., & Walter, C. B. (1984). Knowledge of results and motor learning: A review and critical reappraisal. *Psychological Bulletin, 95*, 355–386.

Schmidt, R. A., & Lee, T. D. (2005). *Motor control and learning: A behavioral emphasis* (4th ed.). Champaign, IL: Human Kinetics.

Schmidt, R. A., & Wrisberg, C. A. (2000). *Motor learning and performance: A problem-based learning approach* (2nd ed.). Champaign, IL: Human Kinetics.

Schmidt, R. A., & Wulf, G. (1997). Continuous concurrent feedback degrades skill learning: Implications for training and simulation. *Human Factors, 39*, 509–525.

Schunk, D. H. (1982). Effects of effort attributional feedback on children's perceived self-efficacy and achievement. *Journal of Educational Psychology, 74*, 548–556.

Sarlegna, F. R., Gauthier, G. M., & Blouin, J. (2007). Influence of feedback modality on sensorimotor adaptation: Contribution of visual, kinesthetic, and verbal cues. *Journal of Motor Behavior, 39*, 247–258.

Sigrist, R., Rauter, G., Riener, R., & Wolf, P. (2013a). Augmented visual, auditory, haptic, and multimodal feedback in motor learning: A review. *Psychonomic Bulletin Review, 20*, 21–53.

Sigrist, R., Rauter, G., Riener, R., & Wolf, P. (2013b). Terminal feedback outperforms concurrent visual, auditory, and haptic feedback in learning a complex rowing-type task. *Journal of Motor Behavior, 45*, 455–472.

Smith, M., & Cushion, C. J. (2006). An investigation of the in-game behaviours of professional, top-level youth soccer coaches. *Journal of Sports Sciences, 24*, 355–366.

Soderstrom, N. C., & Bjork, R. A. (2015). Learning versus performance: An integrative review. *Perspectives on Psychological Science, 10*, 176–199.

Sports Coach UK. (2009). *Code of practice for sports coaches: Rights/relationships/responsibilities*. Leeds: Sports Coach UK.

Sugawara, S. L., Tanaka, S., Okazaki, S., Watanabe, K., & Sadato, N. (2018). Social rewards enhance offline improvements in motor skill. *PLoS One, 7*, e48174.

Summers, J. J., & Anson, G. J. (2009). Current status of the motor program: Revisited. *Human Movement Science, 28*, 566–577.

Swinnen, S. P., Schmidt, R. A., Nicholson, D. E., & Shapiro, D. C. (1990). Information feedback for skill acquisition: Instantaneous knowledge of results degrades learning. *Journal of Experimental Psychology: Learning, Memory, and Cognition, 16*, 706–716.

Thelen, E., & Smith, L. B. (2006). Dynamic systems theories. In R. M. Lerner & W. Damon (Eds.), *Handbook of child psychology: Theoretical models of human development* (pp. 258–312). John Wiley & Sons Inc.

Thompson, E. H. (2016). The effects of touch. In H. Olausson, J. Wessberg, I. Morrison, & F. McGlone (Eds.), *Affective touch and the neurophysiology of CT afferents* (pp. 341–353). New York, NY: Springer.

Thompson, J. (2003). *The double-goal coach*. New York, NY: HarperCollins.

Todorov, E., & Jordan, M. I. (2002). Optimal feedback control as a theory of motor coordination. *Nature Neuroscience, 5*, 1226–1235.

Tremblay, L. & Proteau, L. (1998). Specificity of practice: The case of weightlifting. *Research Quarterly for Exercise and Sport, 69*, 284–289.

Tzetzis, G., Votsis, E., & Kourtessis, T. (2008). The effect of different corrective feedback methods on the outcome and self confidence of young athletes. *Journal of Sports Science & Medicine, 7*, 371–378.

Vinson, D., Brady, A., Moreland, B., & Judge, N. (2016). Exploring coach behaviours, session contexts and key stakeholder perceptions of non-linear coaching approaches in youth sport. *International Journal of Sports Science & Coaching, 11*, 54–68.

Wisniewski, B., Zierer, K., & Hattie, J. (2020). The power of feedback revisited: A meta-analysis of educational feedback research. *Frontiers in Psychology, 10*, 3087.

Wood, N., & Cowan, N. (1995). The cocktail party phenomenon revisited: How frequent are attention shifts to one's name in an irrelevant auditory channel? *Journal of Experimental Psychology: Learning, Memory, and Cognition, 21*, 255–260.

Wright, D. L., Smith-Munyon, V. L., & Sidaway, B. (1997). How close is too close for precise knowledge of results? *Research Quarterly for Exercise and Sport, 68*, 172–176.

Wulf, G., Chiviacowsky, S., Schiller, E., & Avila, L. T. (2010). Frequent external-focus feedback enhances motor learning. *Frontiers in psychology, 1*, 190.

Wulf, G., McConnel, N., Gärtner, M., & Schwarz, A. (2002). Enhancing the learning of sport skills through external-focus feedback. *Journal of Motor Behavior, 34*, 171–182.

Wulf, G., & Shea, C. H. (2002). Principles derived from the study of simple skills do not generalize to complex skill learning. *Psychonomic Bulletin & Review, 9*, 185–211.

Wulf, G., Shea, C. H., & Matschiner, S. (1998). Frequent feedback enhances complex motor skill learning. *Journal of Motor Behavior, 30*, 180–192.

Wulf, G., Shea, C., & Park, J-H. (2001). Attention and motor performance: Preferences for and advantages of an external focus. *Research Quarterly for Exercise and Sport, 72*, 335–344.

Yao, W-Y., Fischman, M. G., & Wang, Y. T. (1994). Motor skill acquisition and retention as a function of average feedback, summary feedback, and performance variability. *Journal of Motor Behavior, 26*, 273–282.

Zhuang, Y., Feng, W., & Liao, Y. (2017). Want more? Learn less: Motivation affects adolescents learning from negative feedback. *Frontiers in Psychology, 8*, 76.

7
COACH–ATHLETE RELATIONSHIP

Aim of the chapter: Develop knowledge of the coach-athlete relationship and its importance.

Theoretical learning goals of the chapter:
Grow an understanding of…

1. components of the coach-athlete relationship.
2. coaches' ability to read the athlete.
3. what can be done to maintain or improve the coach-athlete relationship.
4. how athletes perceive the coach.
5. conversational techniques.
6. active listening.

Practical learning goals of the chapter:

1. Improve empathic accuracy during practice by using reflection card.
2. Improve conversation techniques by using reflection sheet.

Vignette

Another post-practice meeting started as Leah and Collin rushed in.

"Collin, you seem bothered by something", Ellen begun.
"Well, some athletes are just so sensitive", Collin almost screamed back.

The other two looked at each other in surprise.

"When they don't keep at it during our conditioning and I tell them to not to quit, they get upset. Like it's my fault they fold under pressure", he continued.
"How do you sound when you tell them not to quit, Collin?" Ellen asked tentatively.

"What do you think?" Collin snapped back, still upset. "Sure, I'm mad at them. There are no worse things than kids who don't leave it all out there."

"You don't sound like you are really nice to them at those moments", Leah queried, as if to save Ellen from getting a tirade.

"Can you give us an example of your wordings?" Ellen asked gently.

"Maybe something along the lines of 'If you don't have any ambition, I'm not wasting time watching you feeling sorry for yourselves'", Collin said as he started to calm down a little bit.

"How do you think, that will impact your relationship, say in terms of closeness?" Ellen questioned.

"Probably not so well", he replied.

"Leah, do you have any issues with your athletes' relationships?" Ellen turned towards Leah.

"Some of them are hard to get a hold of. I don't know what they really feel when we see each other", Leah told.

"It can be difficult being a mind reader", Ellen filled in. "What do you do to get that hold of them then?"

"Not much, I guess. I try to read their body language. If it's positive or…", Leah couldn't finish her sentence before Collin added:

"Maybe you need to show them who's in charge."

Leah looked puzzled at him.

"Anyway, nonverbal behaviours are not necessarily universal in what emotions they convey", Ellen said. "Perhaps you could benefit from asking the athletes what they feel as well."

"I'm a little uncertain if that will be perceived as too intrusive, but I'll give it a try", Leah concluded.

"Collin, how do you think you could encourage the athletes' work ethic while not harming their egos?" Ellen asked him.

"I don't really know. I need to think about it first", he replied slowly.

> What do you think of Collin's and Leader's relationships with their respective athletes?
> How do Collin and Leah, respectively, view their coach-athlete relationships?

Components of the Coach-Athlete Relationship

Compared to the other areas presented in the previous chapters, the coach-athlete relationship has a much younger research history as it basically began at the turn of the millennium. Prior to this, the coach and the athlete were more viewed as individual entities rather than a dyad in an interdependent relationship. Old-fashioned leadership gave the coach non-negotiable mandate for decision-making and power. Thus, the relationship was of a one-way variety as the athlete was totally dependent on the coach, while the coach was seen as independent of the athletes. Contemporary views of leadership are aware of the interdependence of leader and follower. Without followers there are no leaders, and today's athletes are not hesitant to change group, organization or even sport altogether. Also, coaches are influenced by athletes just as much as athletes are influenced by coaches, both when it comes to well-being and sporting goal-attainment. Profound support for cooperation compared to working individually, or even in opposition, was shown by Johnson and Johnson (2005), affecting various outcomes that are of high interest for both coach and athlete. Apparently, a coach has much to gain from nurturing a positive relationship with the athletes, instead of getting caught in a power struggle or a 'my-way or high-way' stance. The relationship is influenced by individual characteristics (e.g., age, gender, experience, personality), socio-cultural aspects (e.g., norms, roles, sporting context) and some relational factors, such as if the relationship is typical or atypical of coach-athlete, duration and whether participants have the same gender. Relationships work through interpersonal communication that in turn influence feelings, thoughts and behaviours of both participants. From their interaction, outcomes on both intrapersonal (e.g., inner satisfaction, affects, motivation, individual performance), interpersonal (e.g., relationship satisfaction, conflict, relationship maintenance) and group level (e.g., team cohesion, role acceptance or ambiguity, team performance) are affected (Jowett & Poczwardowski, 2007).

Relationships are described by Jowett (2005) as characterized along two separate dimensions. The dimensions are successful (versus unsuccessful) and effective (versus ineffective). Successful relationships are those that have reached a certain objective level of performance achievement (e.g., medal at international competition), while unsuccessful relationship have failed to reach a predetermined performance standard. In contrast, an effective relationship is one that is characterized by the coach helping the athlete to growth, development and psychological well-functioning beyond sporting performance measures. Athletes' relationships are potentially valuable whether they focus more on sporting performance or relational aspects. This can be affected by the duration of the relationship as it is common for longer coach-athlete relationships to extend into more existential parts, while shorter relationships usually stay focused on sport performance aspects (Storm, Henriksen, Larsen, & Christensen, 2014). Additionally, some coaches might be idiosyncratically inclined towards creating a relationship leaning towards one or the other dimension. A coach who has a clear preference for either one would be wise to try to involve other people who provide athletes with complementary relationships aspects. Athletes are also open to keeping relationships with previous coaches, and a current coach must not view this as a threat to his/her authority, but rather see the relational benefits for the athlete.

Athletes go through developmental phases in their career, as do coaches and relationships. Reasonably, these developments will intertwine and influence each other (Sandström, Linnér, & Stambulova, 2016). It is complex to examine the relative impact from coach, athlete and relationship as all three are dynamic. Relationships tend to follow an arc of development which can be divided into different phases. The developmental phases of honeymoon, conflict, and stability are typically salient, even though other categorizations exist. Relationship development models more often than not capture the same development trajectory irrespective of how many phases they contain (Solomon & Roloff, 2018). Presumably, in the first phase, participants view each other in a positively biased way, sort of warranting having made a good choice to enter the relationship (even if an athlete might have the coach elected by others). In the second phase, conflicts arise more frequently than in the others. Into the third phase, only the relationships that manage to ride out conflicts in the second phase and reconcile opinions survive (Sened et al., 2017). Depending on the duration of the coach-athlete relationship, it can be anything from a newly initiated linkage or long-standing solid partnership. If it has survived for a longer time, it is reasonable, but not guaranteed, that the relationship is functional. Exceptions, for example, will be in a team sport situation where the coach has the board's confidence rather than the athletes' or if the team as a whole has a working relationship with the coach, but a few athletes do not.

Within sports coaching, the relationship between coach and athlete will naturally be influenced by the maturity of the athlete, frequency and duration of contacts and whether the sport is individual or team orientated. The relationship between coach and athlete is made up of three fundamental components: *closeness*, *commitment* and *complementarity*. Alongside these dimensions, *co-orientation* describes the degree of similarity within the three aforementioned components between coach and athlete (Jowett, 2007).

Closeness

This dimension covers the affectional dimension of the relationship. Feelings of trust, liking and respect make up the core of closeness. While some argue that feeling close within a relationship is an outcome of thoughts and behaviours, it is likely a circular relationship where feelings also lead to behaviours and thoughts (LaVoi, 2007). Factors influencing closeness in a relationship are, according to Berscheid, Snyder, and Omoto (1989); number and variety of mutual activities, frequency of time spent alone together, and how strongly the participants are influenced by each other. For a coach-athlete relationship to grow closer, it may be positive to carry out activities away from the sporting venue, such as playing bowling for fun, having a movie night with the team, cooking a dinner together or taking a cultural excursion on an off-day during a tournament. Of course, these activities have to be fitted to age, commitment and interests of both parties. Furthermore, a coach setting aside one-on-one time for a chat in connection with practice time could prove valuable in developing a closer bond. While many athletes recognize that the development of closeness is a two-way street, it is not uncommon for athletes to place more responsibility on the coach for this purpose (LaVoi, 2007).

Commitment

Commitment characterizes the cognitive dimension of the relationship. This dimension pertains to how much the individual is committed to keep the relationship for the longer term. When evaluating the current relationship, *satisfaction* and *dependence* affect the individual's commitment. Satisfaction is determined through implicit (or explicit) comparisons between the current relationship and previous relations, peer's relations and through comparing outcomes for both parties. How much an individual is perceived to put into the relationship (e.g., number of hours spent preparing and conducting practices) are judged against the other's investment. If the ratio is perceived similarly, it will feel satisfying. Importantly, the over-benefitting individual may very well feel stressed out and guilty, just as the under-benefitting person likely feels frustrated and hurt from 'receiving less than their share'. In addition, the extent that a person links his/her own identity to the specific relationship works towards commitment. Dependence hinges on availability of alternative relationships; if attractive alternatives exist, dependence will be lower and vice versa. The interaction within the relationship also affects degree of dependence. For example, commitment is enhanced if a person can experience freedom within the relationship to be one's best self, and also if a person feels that he/she would not be the same without the other. However, dependence is a double-edged sword as some relationships are experienced as involuntary, but due to lack of alternatives the individual is forced to stay. Poor alternatives and high investment can cause a strong commitment even in the presence of high dissatisfaction (Rusbult & Buunk, 1993).

Complementarity

Complementarity represents cooperation and reciprocal acts from one of the individuals within the relationship. This dimension pertains to the behavioural aspect of the relationship and can be divided into *corresponding* and *reciprocal* behaviours (Sadler, Ethier, & Woody, 2011). Corresponding behaviours are similar in degree of affiliation to one another (e.g., a coach who talks about feelings with the athlete who similarly is open with his/her feelings). Reciprocal behaviours happen when a dominant behaviour by one individual is followed by a submissive one by the other or vice versa. An example of this occurs when an athlete follows the coach's instructions. In this example both are affiliated with one another, while the coach is dominant and athlete submissive. These expressions are not meant to be interpreted in a way that the relationship as a whole is incompatible with equality between coach and athlete. An interesting approach is to have the coach lead during practice, while the athlete takes more of a lead role during competition, where the coach might have less opportunities for input, switching between dominant and submissive roles (Jowett & Carpenter, 2015). For this to work, it is essential that practices allow athletes to develop necessary skills in order to make decisions during competition. Complementarity is easier to observe since it consists of observable behaviours, compared to the dimensions of closeness and commitment, which reside within the individual. Accordingly, some argue that behaviours are easier to change compared to thoughts and emotions as they are under stronger conscious control. Therefore, when wanting to improve the relationship it will be wise for a coach to deliberately use complementary behaviours. An example of complementarity is when the coach pays attention to what the athlete has to say and acts on this. Poczwardowski, Barott, and Henschen (2002) uncovered a circular relationship between interaction/activity and feelings of concern. The more coach and athlete interacted, the more they cared for each other. Increases in care led to similar increases in shared activity.

> What are your feelings of your relationships with the athletes?
> What are your thoughts of your relationships with the athletes?
> What kind of behaviours are corresponding and reciprocal between yourself and the athletes?

Plenty of ideas have been presented on how to improve upon each component of the coach–athlete relationship and some of these are presented in Table 7.1 (Jowett & Shanmugam, 2016).

Co-orientation

This dimension captures the coach's and the athlete's consensus on their mutual relationship. Each participant in the relationship views the relationship in two ways. This is captured in a *direct perspective* and a *metaperspective*. The direct perspective is the view the first person has of the other (e.g., 'I trust my athlete), while the metaperspective is the view that the first person thinks the other has on the first person (e.g., 'I think my athlete trusts me'). A combination of these views uncovers three aspects of co-orientation, namely *actual similarity*, *assumed similarity* and *empathic accuracy* (see Figure 7.1). Actual similarity describes how similar both persons' views of the other are (e.g., comparison of 'I trust my coach' and 'I trust my athlete'). Assumed similarity describes the agreement between one person's view of the other and the same person's view of how the other sees him-/herself (e.g., 'I trust my athlete' and 'I think my athlete trusts me'). Empathic accuracy is the correlation between how a person believes the other views him-/herself and how that other person actually views him-/herself (e.g., 'I think my athlete has good confidence' and 'I [athlete] am confident in

TABLE 7.1 Suggestions on how to improve the 3 C's of a coach-athlete relationship.

	Component to improve	
Closeness	Commitment	Complementarity
Be objective in conflicts and do not choose sides until you have 'all' the facts.	Create developmental plans that will have the athletes feel your commitment.	Lead by example.
Express your feelings (and not just facts).	Listen to and learn from the athletes.	Create an environment that is positive, engaging, innovative.
Be honest.	Show that you take action.	Be responsive to athletes' actions.
Pay attention to athletes' individual accomplishments and contributions, no matter how small.	Make sure that responsibilities such as roles, rules, or expectations are defined in a clear manner.	Provide structure, challenge and organization through instilling a quality work ethic.
Honour your promises.	Ensure that every athlete knows that you value them.	Explain consequences of not following rules.
Be reliable/consistent/predictable.	Spell out benefits for the athletes who stays with you as a coach.	Be flexible to athletes' actions, needs and desires.

my athletic skills'). The three views are valid for both coach and athlete (Jowett, 2007), but as the topic of this text is coaching, the coach perspective is the one in focus. Shared knowledge and common understanding increase co-orientation between coach and athlete (Jowett & Cockerill, 2003).

Assumed similarity is often biased in a close relationship, as it is appealing to consider the partner as more similar to oneself then what really is the case (Kenny & Actielli, 2001). Partly, this is explained by the self-serving bias, according to which individuals are prone to perceptions that are favourable to the self. In a voluntary relationship, a well-behaving partner reflects back on the individual for making a sound judgement in choosing this partner. In the case of coaching, it may be interpreted as the coach working effectively and influencing the athlete in a positive direction. Accordingly, a favourable self-perception increases the likelihood that the other will be perceived positively. Assumed similarity was found by Jowett and Clark-Carter (2006) to be strongly correlated with both

		Coach's	
		Direct perspective	Metaperspective
Coach's	Direct perspective	-	Assumed similarity
Athlete's	Direct perspective	Actual similarity	Empathic accuracy

FIGURE 7.1 Relationships between direct and metaperspective.

relationship quality and satisfaction with training and performance from both participants in the coach-athlete relationship.

Few studies have investigated the impact of the coach-athlete relationship on coaches' outcomes. Yet, it is highly likely that coaches are affected in similar ways as the athletes. For a coach this means that having a positive metaperspective of closeness, commitment and complementarity will be a source of confidence, motivation, and satisfaction (Jowett, 2008). Specifically, Lorimer (2009) argued that the association between coach's satisfaction and relationship is impacted by coach's satisfaction on how the athlete behaves towards them. Proactively, a coach will profit from explicitly explaining this to the athlete, both increasing the probability of the athlete conforming and acting in a positive manner, as well as showing some vulnerability which improves the odds of ameliorating the relationship itself.

> Think of one of your athletes. How do you view your relationship?
> How do you think the athlete views the relationship with you? (Similarly or differently?)
> Is there any athlete that you have more trouble getting a quality relationship with? If so, why?

Measuring the Coach-Athlete Relationship

 In the appendix, the Coach-Athlete Relationship Questionnaire (CART-Q: Jowett, 2009; Jowett & Ntoumanis, 2004) is provided. There are two versions, one for athletes' direct perspective and one for coaches metaperspective. The athletes' rating of their direct perspective provides an insight into their experience of the coach-athlete relationship. By comparing the athletes' direct perspective and the coach's metaperspective, an assessment of the coach's empathic accuracy is received.

> When you view the athletes' direct perspective of how they view their coach-athlete relationship, what do you think?
> When you compare the athletes' direct perspective with your metaperspective, what do you think about your empathic accuracy?

Reading the Athlete

In close relationships, there is a strong motivation for having an accurate perception of the other as accuracy is helpful to both the relationship and the self. Motivation to be accurate has been shown repeatedly to be more important than stable factors such as gender (Ickes, Gesn, & Graham, 2000). Through the development of a relationship, motivation for empathic accuracy will be greatest early on. Initially in a relationship, each participant usually is eager to please the other before asserting own needs. This stage will often decide whether the relationship will last or terminate. If the coach is unaware of the athletes' desires such as level of closeness, the athlete will withdraw or seek out others for this purpose, and the relationship will likely deteriorate before it has been firmly established. Any friction occurring is necessary to settle in a manner that is positive for each member. For this to happen, having a sound grasp of each other's true emotions and thoughts is vital. If not, it will be difficult to find out if the relationship is suitable for one's own motives. Later on, it is easier for relationship members to resort to shared knowledge and routine instead of making a concerted effort to be empathically accurate in each specific moment. Relationships that ride out the potentially stormy second phase have a solid foundation for long-term companionship. However, there can be circumstances that demotivate an accurate perception, such as if the perceiver is not able to handle potentially disturbing information from the other (e.g., if the other is severely depressed and the perceiver has no resources to handle this), or if the other is annoyed with some minor issue within the relationship in contrast to the perceiver (who has no better option than to stay in the relationship). In those cases, it could be wise for the coach to avoid having an accurate perception of the athlete's thoughts and feelings, as this paradoxically can help stabilize the relationship. At least, tuning out of the other's relationship-threatening thoughts and feelings can be beneficial when these are deemed to present only short-term, temporary threats. For a coach, it could be beneficial not to investigate too deeply into a single instance of an athlete ignoring the coach's eye-contact after having an argument during a competition, if this is an abbreviation of the athlete's normal behavioural pattern. Generally though, being able to have a grasp of the athlete's inner states is of great advantage for coaches, and if the same relationship threat resurface, neglecting them will probably be ineffective in solving the underlying issue (Rollings, Cuperman, & Ickes, 2011). Verbal communication is paramount between coach and athlete. Additionally, it is helpful for coaches to be skilled in eliciting thorough verbal information, understand that information and also attend to nonverbal cues. Sometimes, an athlete will consciously or unconsciously withhold information from the verbal channel. Some idiosyncrasies can be difficult to verbalize as they are potentially unknown to the athlete or just not desirable to make explicit. In instances like these, coaches still need to elicit valuable information. Coaches can draw inferences about both more stable traits such as personality and more transient states such as mental skills or subjective well-being. Inferences can of course concern both affective and cognitive content.

Empathy

For a coach, being skilled at understanding the individual athlete is very beneficial in building a positive relationship. If a coach recommends an athlete to seek professional counselling because of depressive symptoms, or has a stern talking to the athlete because of lack of focus during practice, these judgements better be accurate. Otherwise, the athlete's perceptions of closeness, through lowered trust of the coach, and commitment, through doubts about coach's competence, likely suffers. Athletes' perceived empathy from the coach is strongly connected to both quality of coach–athlete relationship and athletes' satisfaction with training and instruction (Jowett, Yang, & Lorimer, 2012). Logically, a coach's level of empathy is crucial, of which various definitions exist. While it is not always necessary to have an absolute definition, it is advantageous to have a somewhat clear view of the concept. Many times, there are confusion between some adjacent concepts, primarily between *sympathy* and *empathy*. Whereas sympathy revolves around feeling *for* another person (e.g., perception of sadness in athlete entails coach's feelings of concern), empathy cause feeling *as* another person (e.g., perception of sadness in athlete entails coach's feeling of sadness).

Components

Recently, empathy has been suggested as a multidimensional construct consisting of three interactive components, outlined in Figure 7.2. They are *motor*, *emotional* and *cognitive* components. *Motor empathy* is defined as synchronization of body language during observation of the other. One example of this kind of mimicry happens when a yawn from one person elicits yawn in another. Primarily, this type of empathy occurs on an automatic and subconscious level. *Emotional empathy*

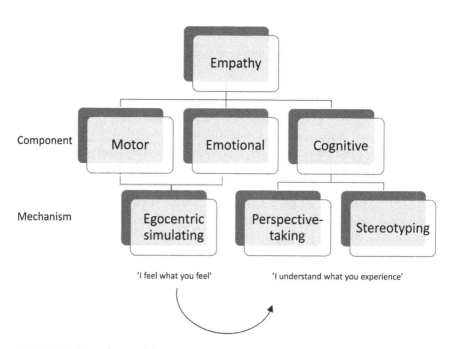

FIGURE 7.2 Empathy model.

is defined as the ability to detect and resonate with the emotional state of another person. This is done through more conscious observation compared to motor empathy. By recognizing athlete's emotions, physiological changes will occur in the observer. This helps perceiving the athlete's experience. *Cognitive empathy* is defined as the ability to comprehend other's inner states. Motor and emotional empathy may facilitate correct inferences of the athlete's inner state (i.e., 'I feel what you feel'), but in order to truly understand his or her experience cognitive empathy (i.e., 'I understand what you feel') is also needed (Bekkali et al., 2020).

Mechanisms

Motor and emotional empathy act in a bottom-up manner, using external stimuli to trigger the coach's own reactions. Meanwhile cognitive empathy works in top-down fashion, using coach's knowledge and cognitions to interpret the athlete's state. To get a more elaborate comprehension of how a coach's emotional inference of an athlete's inner state work, three distinctive mechanisms contribute. They are *egocentric simulating*, *perspective-taking* and *stereotyping*.

Motor and emotional empathy use egocentric simulating and through this mechanism, the coach tries to infer the athlete's state by using own reaction patterns. Emotions, tendency to infect others is a striking example of this mechanism, such as where one person's laughter leads to another one's smile, making the second person feeling joyful and drawing the conclusion that the first person is happy. Another way of egocentric simulating is deliberately adopting the athlete's body language, such as stance, posture or movement, making it easier to experience the same emotions (Epley & Waytz, 2010). In total, egocentric simulating is data driven (i.e., the coach uses the athlete's expressions to form an impression).

Since egocentric simulating uses the coach's own experience of the perceived feelings, it risks biasing the inference towards how the coach feels, rather than how the athlete experiences or even project the coach's state (Kammann, Smith, Martin, & McQueen, 1984). Thus, the cognitive component with its two theory-driven mechanisms is vital. By theory-driven, it means that the coach uses knowledge or previous experience to understand the athlete's inner state. What at first glance seems like one expression of an inner state, might not be so when further dissecting it. The arrow in Figure 7.2 illustrates the interaction where motor and emotional empathy help perception formation and facilitate cognitive empathy, which is somewhat superordinate in conceptualizing this perception.

When using perspective-taking, the coach tries to deliberately perceive the athlete's view of a specific situation. This can be accomplished either from imagining how the coach would experience the same event or from imagining how the athlete experiences the situation. However slight that difference might sound, it essentially implies different outcomes. Imagining how another perceives the situation elicits empathy, whereas when imagining how you would experience the situation provokes personal distress. In the event of a negative situation, the former approach evokes altruism and understanding Meanwhile, in the same situation, the latter approach creates feelings of discomfort when witnessing another's state and seems to lead to a more self-orientated emotional response (Batson, Early, & Salvarani, 1997). Consequently, it is advocated to try to imagine how the athlete experiences the situation and not how you yourself would experience the situation. Moreover, stereotyping is also useful. Especially with unfamiliar athletes, stereotypes provide a good source for inferencing the athlete's states. Certainly, not all stereotypes have valid information and they often have a bad reputation pertaining to prejudice, but to the extent that stereotypes mirror real group characteristics their usage lead to increased accuracy. If the target is unacquainted, such as a relatively new athlete in the group, the coach can increase accuracy by drawing from stereotypes on how to judge the athlete's inner state. This is done by assuming how a similar athlete would likely react in a similar situation. Still, risks arise when an athlete's emotional and cognitive reactions diverge from the stereotypical (e.g., feeling relieved when being cut from a competition squad due to high levels of competitive stress). In short, a coach needs to be vigilant when stereotyping (Lewis, Hodges, Laurent, Srivastava, & Biancarosa, 2012).

> In general, do you consider athletes' emotions or thoughts to be most difficult to recognize?
> In what way do you rely on egocentric simulating, perspective-taking and stereotyping when trying to read the athletes?

Factors Affecting Empathy

Factors affecting the judgements of others are both related to athlete, coach and their relation (see Figure 7.3). Athletes can be high or low in expressivity of inner states, making their inner states more or less visible to observers.

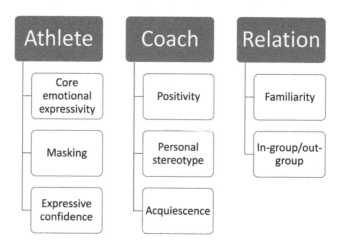

FIGURE 7.3 Factors influencing coach's judgement of athletes.

Although coaches have a much better chance at predicting highly expressive athletes' cognitions and emotions, this does not mean that it is impossible to infer states in low expressivity athletes. Neither does it imply that highly expressive athletes feel stronger emotions themselves, as there is no relationship between self-reported affective experiences and how easy one is to read (Zaki, Bolger, & Ochsner, 2008). An individual's expressivity consists of *core emotional expressivity, expressive confidence* and *masking* (Gross & John, 1998). Although situational factors potential for influencing an individual's expressivity are unexplored by research, intuitively an environment allowing non-judgemental displays of emotions will at least not hamper the individual's tendency to show emotions clearly. Likely, expressive confidence will increase in a permitting environment with reliable others and the need for masking will decrease if the individual feels secure in expressing both positive and negative states. Still, an athlete's emotional outbursts can present a threat to the rules of the specific sport and/or others in the team. This is somewhat of a balancing act the coach needs to pay close attention to.

Characteristics within the coach that influence the perception are primarily *positivity* (i.e., coach's tendency to view others in general positively or negatively), *personal stereotype* (i.e., coach's idiosyncratic view of athletes across many different traits or states) and *acquiescence* (i.e., coach's inclination to infer superlatives or modesty in judgements). An example of personal stereotype is one coach who believes that athletes in general feel nervous at competition, while another coach thinks that athletes in general are excited by competition. All of these characteristics will impact the coach's judgements of athletes' states.

Relational factors work through *familiarity* with the athlete and whether or not the target belongs to *in-group/out-group* compared to the coach. Familiarity with the athlete will gradually lead to increased possibilities to make detailed judgements of the athlete's states. If the coach identifies the athlete as belonging to another group (i.e., out-group) as oneself, such as ethnicity, sex or even favourite team (just to mention a few group belongings that have been investigated), it will lead to less differentiated judgements, and more 'they all look the same' (Kenny, 2020). Critically examining how these factors influence a coach's ability to read an athlete will lay a foundation for more accurate perceptions. One bias to be aware of is peoples' propensity to attribute others actions to traits and stable causes when judging negative events, while believing that positive events for others are largely due to situational factors (Malle, 2006). Another bias to be watchful of is the halo-effect, where a perception of one aspect shapes a different observation, which might make a coach mistake an athlete's personality trait (e.g., extraversion) for a sign of an emotional state.

People in greater power generally show less empathy, show less interest for others' mental states, take others' perspective to less extent and are less accurate drawing inferences about others' inner world (Epley & Waytz, 2010). For this reason, a coach needs to make a concerted effort to empathize with the athlete.

Accordingly, a coach will be well-served creating a democratic and open atmosphere in the group in order to minimize the power distance between coach and athlete. In line with coaches being somewhat blind to their own behaviours, Haselwood and colleagues (2005) found that athletes rated coaches' competence of reading athletes significantly lower than coaches themselves, which mirror people's tendency to overrate their capability of reading others' states (Ames & Kammrath, 2004). A coach needs to be vigilant on bias and overrating one's ability in this area.

Recent studies have uncovered that verbal information conveys more information compared to nonverbal (Gesn & Ickes, 1999; Hall & Schmid Mast, 2007; Zaki, Bolger, & Ochsner, 2009). To prevent a coach from spending limited attentional resources observing ineffective cues, it is vital to know which sources are most effective. Unfortunately, a widely spread belief is that verbal information contributes minimally to understanding a message from a person. Often, Mehrabian and Ferris (1967) study is referred to, when this argument comes up. In this study, the researchers examined how vocal and facial components contributed to how positively the communicators attitude were interpreted. Results showed the well-known 7/38/55 percentages (speech/tonality/body language) that have been widely interpreted as nonverbal information is vastly more important than verbal information for understanding communication. Hopefully, the more recent evidence will find its way to coaches helping them read the athletes correctly and build flourishing relationships.

 What athletes in your current group are easier or harder for you to read?

What athletes in your group do you think have a high core emotional expressivity?

Are there any athletes in your group that you think have high degrees of masking or low levels of expressive confidence?

How would you rate your characteristics of positivity, personal stereotype and acquiescence respectively?

Think of an athlete identified as in-group with you and a specific event this athlete was involved in, would you have reacted any different in this situation if the athlete was from an out-group.

Improving Coaches' Empathic Accuracy

Contrary to many peoples' belief, empathy is heightened under conditions of deliberate processing and not gut feeling alone (Ma-Kellams & Lerner, 2016). This is promising for coaches looking to improve their understanding of athletes' states, as it hints a dynamic – and not static – skill. Fortunately, this goes hand in hand with the reflective approach adopted within the present book as the cognitive forcing strategies used with reflection cards demands deliberate processing. Before delving into ways to improve the coach's ability of empathic accuracy, it is necessary to highlight that empathic accuracy is highly dependent of the sender's expressiveness, even more so than a product of a skilled perceiver (Ickes & Buysse, 2000). Thus, it is important for a coach to encourage athletes to express their true feelings by avoiding judging and creating an open climate of acceptance. Intervention studies investigating how to improve empathic accuracy have had success with two complementary approaches. First, it is advantageous to learn more about communication skills (Cunico, Sartori, Marognolli, & Meneghini, 2012), such as perspective-taking and active listening. Second, explicitly trying to infer another person's inner state and receiving feedback on these inferences has been used successfully in both nursing and sports coaching (Lobchuk et al., 2018; Lorimer & Jowett, 2010). Recurring practice of inferring other's inner states will increase empathic accuracy as theoretical knowledge alone will not suffice (Barone & Hutchings, 2005). For this reason, the reflection card in the present chapter allows practice of this.

Number of athletes within the group has been shown to correlate with empathic accuracy. Lower number of athletes is connected to better empathic accuracy (Hanson & Gould, 1988). Intuitively, this makes sense as a coach who has fewer individuals to manage has more opportunities of interaction per athlete compared to a coach who has a larger number of athletes to take care of. Furthermore, Lorimer and Jowett (2009) found that coaches for individual sports were more accurate compared to team sport coaches, and this effect was explained by a greater amount of shared cognitive focus in individual sports. Shared cognitive focus is defined as the actual similarity of the content of thoughts and feelings at a given time. If both parties in a relationship think of the same thing, it is easier to draw inferences about others' states. Let's say that the athlete is focusing on the instruction the coach is giving, they have a shared cognitive focus. Shared cognitive focus can be accomplished by increased familiarity. Two persons who know one another are more likely to share cognitions. Another factor is the length of the practice sessions, which is positively correlated with empathic accuracy (Lorimer & Jowett, 2009). Arguably, a longer practice makes it possible to take time to really listen and pick up on nonverbal clues, whereas a shorter practice might put more pressure on executing the practice plan rather than being flexible and open for unexpected reactions from the athletes. Longer practices will also make room for interactions somewhat unrelated to the sport-specific content, benefitting familiarity and shared cognitive focus. Practice time is often a scarce commodity for many amateur or youth organizations. However, a crafty coach finds ways to extend the allotted time. For example, warm-ups can often be performed before the practice facility is available (e.g., using the locker rooms, adjacent venue outdoors). Another example of extending the time spent together is through joint travel with an athlete (e.g., car-pooling, public transportation). Some fitness work can be carried out after regular practice time is over (e.g., calisthenics on the side-lines, aerobic work in the stairs, stretching on poolside deck). Finally, by arriving slightly ahead of the official start time for practice, a coach can create additional time for meetings, either structured or spontaneous.

Aside from making observations trying to infer inner states, coaches should elicit verbal information from the athletes regarding their thoughts and feelings. Through this verbal interaction, coaches get feedback on their assumptions about athletes' states, which has been shown essential in improving empathic accuracy (Lorimer & Jowett, 2009). Later in this chapter a section covers conversational technique that aid coaches in their strivings to get info from athletes.

 To what extent do you create an environment conducive to athletes' expressing their true feelings?
How can you improve your empathic accuracy?

Maintaining the Relationship

When it comes to maintaining the coach-athlete relationship, threats have to be countered and they can emanate from within as well as from outside the relationship. Lydon and Quinn (2013) highlight three hazards that need to be avoided. First, attractive alternatives have to be matched or ignored. People that are satisfied with their current relationship tend to spend less time watching potential alternatives. Ignoring, may not be possible, though. In sports (particularly elite sports), there is always the prospect of getting recruited to another organization, by an agent or by another coach. Another option is to devalue the alternatives, as this makes them less of a threat to the current relationship. Countering attractive alternatives for an athlete should not be viewed by the coach as a call for back-stabbing by talking down another organization. Rather, the coach should try to nurse the current relationship so that the athlete consider the alternatives less attractive through free will. Second, transgressions by the partner are a threat to the relationship, such as when disobeying rules or using foul language. This can be handled in a number of ways. One alternative is to ignore the transgression itself, something that could be advisable if it is minor in nature. Being forgiving is another appropriate way of handling breaches of agreements from the other. Attributions of the partner's underlying reasons when he/she misbehaves can be crucial in this case. A coach who attributes a misdemeanour by an athlete to internal, permanent and controllable factors is more likely to get upset with the athlete as a person compared to a coach who attributes the same action to external, temporary or uncontrollable factors. The former attribution pattern is detrimental to the relationship. Naturally, there are situations and actions that have a clear-cut and objectively correct attribution, but more often than not the reasons for people's actions are muddy water. In those cases, a benevolent attribution is more helpful for relationship maintenance. For an excellent source and easy read on attribution retraining, Seligman and colleagues (1995) is recommended. If an athlete consistently attributes transgressions in a dysfunctional manner, it is possible to train the athlete into making more functional attributions. The athlete will no doubt benefit from this in other aspects as well, such as handling setbacks during competitions. Third, conflicting personal and relationship goals pose another threat. If these types of goals are incongruent, a sacrifice has to be made on behalf of relationship maintenance by prioritizing the goals that are to the benefit of the relationship. However, the motive for the concession seems to have an important impact, as people who sacrifice to obtain positive relational outcomes report more happiness compared to individuals who sacrifice in order to avoid negative development of the relationship.

> What do you currently think of how you and your athlete handle the following relationship threats?
> Alternative attractiveness.
> Partner transgressions.
> Goal conflicts.

Maintenance behaviours must be ongoing, and interestingly, females both perceive and conduct these behaviours to a larger extent than males (Stafford, 2020). Gender differences in relationship maintenance has been sparsely investigated within the sporting domain. Research in other domains has revealed some differing approaches between men and women, though. For example, women tend to care more about dyadic relationships and are therefore inclined to work harder to promote such relationships. Men, on the other hand define themselves in terms of relationships at group level rather than dyads. Furthermore, women show more forgivingness and idealization within the relationship (Lydon & Quinn, 2013). Among the maintenance behaviours, women use more positivity, openness, assurances, social networks, sharing tasks, and forgiveness. Additionally, the underlying reasons for using these behaviours show gender differences. While men tend to use these behaviours as a reaction to perceived relationship threats, women use them more routinely, regardless of their perception of the status of the relationship. Similarly, women prefer to discuss relationship issues more directly than men generally do (Fiori & Rauer, 2020). A marital or dating relationship is probably different in some aspects than the typical coach-athlete relationship in sports, such as participants' age and life experience. Still, coaches benefit from paying attention to aforementioned aspects in their relationships with athletes. Even if dyadic relationships are more important to women than to men, male coaches should not interpret this as responsibility for maintaining the coach-athlete relationship should be left to others (e.g., female athletes or coaching colleagues). Male coaches might rather have to consider their effort if they want to maintain (or enhance) their coach–athlete relationships. Recently, coach–athlete relationship maintenance in sports has been explored. Several strategies for maintenance have been deducted that were all related to the quality of coach–athlete relationship which were illustrated by the acronym COMPASS. All of them are useable by coaches and athletes alike. Below, each category is covered briefly based upon the work of Rhind & Jowett, 2012; Rhind and Jowett (2010), unless otherwise noticed.

Conflict Management

Conflicts revolve around cognitive, affective and behavioural responses to perceived disagreements between the parties. Conflicts are at times functional, such as when playing time, practice content or competition tasks are in focus. This can get the athletes to focus on improving and be reminded that skills development and performance improvements are central to the sporting endeavour. Contrastingly, when conflicts are social, concentrating on relational or personal issues, they are harder to solve and likely have more severe consequences for the relationship. Men engage in more conflicts with their peers than women. Strategies that aim directly at the person instead of the actual problem are less effective, cause more harmful feelings and often lead to an escalating conflict (Wachsmuth, Jowett, & Harwood, 2017).

When trying to solve a conflict it is worthwhile to put some preparation time in, to be certain on what to say, what the reasons are, and form a preconception of the other's potential arguments. Doing this will not only convey a clearer message, but also create a better foundation for handling potential negative emotions before they go overboard. On the other hand, lack of awareness of a conflict being present, its seriousness and content, will hamper conflict management. Another barrier is willingness to try reconcile the conflict, sometimes due to other priorities. Disagreement on what initially has been agreed upon and how it is monitored can further prove inhibiting (Wachsmuth, Jowett, & Harwood, 2018). Additionally, being understanding and showing patience during conflicts, trying not to lose temper, and handling disagreements by listening and co-operating, facilitate conflict management. Again, empathic accuracy plays a crucial role in reading the other's intentions and emotions even during times of conflict. I-statements, elaborated later, are another effective tool. Finally, when a quick decision has to be made or when multiple athletes are involved, a coach has greater leeway for more forceful, authoritative strategies to manage a conflict.

Openness

Being open towards one another makes for a relationship maintenance behaviour in itself, but also increases the knowledge of each other leading to enhanced opportunities for empathic accuracy. Athletes who are low on the personality trait agreeableness are more likely to be somewhat egocentric and have a harder time reciprocating sharing and giving from others, as was shown by Jowett and colleagues (2012). For this reason, a coach needs to persist in being open with this kind of athlete, and rather act as a role model for sharing thoughts and emotions that also builds the athlete's trust in the coach and eventually leads to reciprocity. Openness includes stating one's own opinions regarding goal-setting, being open about one's own feelings, and providing feedback to each other, including praise (when appropriate).

Motivational

This dimension covers behaviours demonstrating motivation to keep the relationship going and motivating the other to do the same. For this to happen, coaches need to prove that their competence fits the needs of the athlete (e.g., recreational athlete might want more social skills). Motivational strategies have been found to have a strong influence on the relationship commitment experienced by athletes (Rhind & Jowett, 2011). This includes working hard to achieve goals, showing passion for sport, and displaying abilities as a coach (or athlete).

Preventative

Preventative behaviours aim to forestall conflicts between coach and athlete. This includes talking about the relationship regularly, talk about expectations of each other, and providing feedback to each other when expectations are not met. Facilitating a positive environment in general is also conducive of pre-empting conflict. Further strategies that serve to prevent conflicts are role clarification, sharing information in a transparent manner and goal-setting (Wachsmuth et al., 2017).

Assurance/Support

Assurance/Support relates to being responsive to the others issue both in- and outside of sport. From adolescence up until family formation, a coach is many times an athlete's closest ally, serving as a friend, counsellor or mentor. Coaches should cherish and nurture an athlete's trust to be seen as such a valuable resource. This includes showing the athlete that the coach is reliable even in times of trouble, being considerate of events in the other's personal life, and showing the other that he/she can talk to the coach about anything. Assuring to the athlete that the coach will be interested in a long-term relationship is valuable. All considered, highly anxious athletes do not perceive support as clearly as the others do (Hülya Aşçi, Kelecek, & Altintaş, 2015), which make them need this support even more.

Social Networks

This includes socializing with the other (sometimes outside of training), and talking about, as well as spending time with, mutual friends and contacts. Travels to competition and practice camp locations provide an opportunity for socializing with each other. Athletes tend to view the coach more of a friend, whereas coaches view their relationship more in terms of teacher-student or family (Jowett & Carpenter, 2015). In general women have both larger, more supportive, and more diverse social networks around them from which they will draw support (Fiori & Rauer, 2020). Overall, shared networks (e.g., mutual friends) are more useful than non-shared. Sometimes, the latter actually introduces problems into the relationship. An athlete keeping a relationship with a previous coach was mentioned earlier in this chapter as potential resource, but can apparently have downsides as well, such as when contradicting advice is given to the athlete. It is proposed that social networks as a strategy is less prevalent at elite level sports compared to lower levels (i.e., recreational and youth) as Rhind and Jowett (2011) indicated that coaches used social networks more when lacking high levels of complementarity and commitment within their relationship.

 Which ones of the relationship maintenance strategies (COMPASS) do you currently use?
Which strategy could you use more or better?
Do you think any of the athletes are more difficult to maintain your relationship with?
If so, what could be done to improve your coach-athlete relationship?

Athletes' Perception of Coaches

Knowledge of how athletes perceive coaches will help both in conveying desired messages and understanding athletes, as it is possible to use non-verbal information to one's advantage. Athletes' initial impression of a coach is formed on three sources: *static cues* (e.g., age, gender), *dynamic cues* (e.g., eye contact, tone of voice, facial expressions) and *third-party reports* (e.g., coaching experience, qualifications, reputation). The last two sources were deemed by athletes as most important, which is promising for coaches as these sources are more malleable than static cues (Manley et al., 2008). Clothing has also been found to influence athletes' perception of coaches. Sporting attire is seen as most appropriate during training and enhances the athletes' perception of a coach's ability to work on technical skills and build character. A lean physique, compared to a larger build, has been linked to higher perceptions of competence (Manley, Greenlees, & Thelwell, 2017).

An abundance of research investigating what is known as thin-slices of expressivity, has found that people make very quick judgements during short observations of another person's behaviours and traits. Five seconds of observation has been shown to be as accurate as five minutes (Ambady & Rosenthal, 1992). Therefore, paying attention to the first meeting with a new group of athletes is critical. Knowing the first couple of sentences by rote on what to say and how to say it, is a proven concept for insecure lecturers, that also works to install added confidence in the speaker. Interestingly, Kammrath, Ames, and Scholer (2007) reported that there is varying durability for the early impressions of different traits. Impressions of agreeableness, conscientiousness (e.g., being organized, reliable, adhering to rules) and emotional stability are easier overcome by later information compared to extraversion and openness. Thus, a coach wanting to form a certain impression of extraversion and openness should make a concerted effort conveying these at the initial meeting.

Although people in general have quite an accurate perception of how others view them, this view is predominantly undifferentiated across individuals. Because of this generalization, it is easy to be inaccurate on specific individual's unique perceptions. That is, even if a coach has a fairly precise impression on how he/she is viewed by athletes in general, chances are he/she is not very accurate in predicting each and every athlete's unique impression of him/her. Kenny and DePaulo (1993) suggested several reasons for this insensitivity. First, self-protecting bias leads us to protect our self-concept, which we have invested a lot in and want to keep. This concern can easily become more important than being accurate of others' perception of us. Second, people are principally unwilling to give each other feedback (see Chapter 1 for a discussion of distinguishing between coach and coaching). Thus, the available data upon which to infer another individual's unique perception is parsimonious. Third, confirmation bias is another form of bias that leads us to interpret other's opinions as a validation of our previous perception of ourselves rather than actually picking up the true content of the message that is being conveyed. Our metaperception (i.e., how we think others view us) can be formed through three different ways (Kenny, 2020). *The naïve theory* postulates that a person monitors others' reactions through their verbal and nonverbal feedback to get information on how one is perceived. There are some problems with this approach, though. Again, people are generally not providing very honest feedback on how much they like another. This is especially the case when there is a power discrepancy, as exists between coach and athlete. It would be incautious for an athlete to be too blunt in expressing his/her opinion about a coach who later dictates who gets to perform in a competition or start in a match. The second approach for metaperception is that of *self-observations*. By alleging to this, an individual monitors his/her own behaviour, and from there draws inferences of how the other perceives oneself. Notoriously, people are weak at monitoring their own behaviours (cf. Chapter 4), particularly so when interacting with others, something that requires a lot of attentional capacity. Finally, the *self-theory* route suggests passivity in individuals' formation of metaperception, as they use their own self-image to a large extent. Consistent with this, we generally overestimate how well others know our internal states. The way that determines most of people's metaperception is self-theory. Hence there is a correlation between our self-perception and how we think others view us, although, as mentioned earlier, this is on average and not specific for unique individuals' perception of us.

> What kind of perception do you think the athletes have of you as a coach today?
> Would you like to change this perception?
> If so, how would you go about doing that?

Conversational Technique

Conversation is a two-way endeavour as it consists of both sending and receiving messages, which are intertwined to a large extent and should not been viewed as entirely separate. Yet, for pedagogical purposes they are here presented compartmentalized. The first section (*sending effective messages*) briefly covers some findings from the literature on how to convey information. Gradually, in the subsequent sections the content will move towards receiving messages. In this area (just as in many others covered within this book), there is no panacea, but rather different aspects to take into consideration depending on various situational and interpersonal factors as well as depending on purpose. Thus, the presented information needs to be digested by the individual coach and applied into real-life situations.

Sending Effective Messages

Communication and relationships have a reciprocal connection. A good relationship leads to better communication, just as good communication leads to a better relationship (Davis, Jowett, & Tafvelin, 2019). Much has been said and written about the importance of coaches inspiring pre-game speeches, but less has been scrutinized scientifically. So far, there are definitive doubts whether highly emotional speeches have tremendous positive impact on athletes as a whole (Rubio, Hernandez, Sánchez-Iglesias, Cano, & Bureo, 2018). Contrastingly, competitions in themselves are often anxiety-inducing, which indicates risk that a coach's added input raises arousal over optimal level. Accordingly, coaches should provide more individual treatment when it comes to pre-competition talks. Some athletes need to be fired up, while others' need to be relaxed. A recurring theme in this text has been the differences between coaches' own experience and perception of others. Communication is no different, as coaches believe their messages are clearer, easier to understand and contain better language than the athletes do. Furthermore, self-disclosure is an important skill for communicators and it has been found to generally be higher among female coaches, than for male coaches (Haselwood et al., 2005). A word of caution is mandated, though. Some coaches seem to like being in the spotlight so much that they ramble on with personal anecdotes. The purpose of self-disclosure needs to be connected to the athletes' needs, such as talking about coach's own mistakes (e.g., missing a game-winning shot in high school) as a way to console or illustrate that mistakes are part of a learning process. Keeping messages short, concise and specific will reduce the cognitive effort needed to attend to them. Another aspect to consider is tempo of speech, as slower talk generally is easier to understand, and it is common for anxious presenters to speed up their tempo. Additionally, coaches should avoid sarcasm and put-downs, instead focusing on positive aspects. When checking for understanding of a message, a common method is asking a closed question (e.g., 'Do you copy?'), although it is much more effective to ask someone to summarize the content as this gives both a much better view of the actual grasp from the athletes as well as opens up for questions from the athletes (Hargie, 2010; Martens, 2012). Some of our nonverbal behaviours are under conscious control, while others are not. For example, it is possible to change posture when standing up, while pupil dilution is not. Eye-contact while speaking is generally seen as credible, although it is more difficult to search for words and thoughts while looking someone in the eye. Thus, being prepared, knowledgeable about the content and simultaneously being able to handle potential emotions that arise in the moment, is something the coach has to pay attention to (Hargie, 2010).

I-statement

When it comes to handling tough issues, an effective means to convey a message is called *I-statement*. Instead of accrediting or accusing the recipient, the sender starts with how the issue is viewed by him-/herself. When addressing the other's part in the issue, it is paramount to describe behaviours that are possible to observe, and not thoughts, traits or intentions, which are likely impossible to be sure of. As discussed previously in this text, behaviours are possible to change, which conveys an optimistic approach on the other's opportunities. Furthermore, I-statements use descriptive instead of evaluative language, and they are more tentative rather than certain in their expressions of 'facts'. Actually, they share commonalities with informational limit-setting (cf. Chapter 3). I-statements are located in between talking *for* another (e.g., 'You always think that I am mad') and talking *to* another (e.g., overly begging). Messages sent in this manner protect the other's self-esteem. It also refrains the conflict from escalating into personal issues, instead it focuses on neutral and observable aspects. A sound I-statement often starts with the word 'I', although not every rant using 'I' as first word necessarily qualifies (e.g., 'I hate your apathetic attitude!'). To construct an effective, I-statement, Table 7.2 provides an easy-to-use framework. Below are two examples applied to a sports coaching context.

Instructor Ingram (Using I-statement)

232 Coach–athlete relationship

TABLE 7.2 Framework for constructing an I-statement.

	Critical situation	Person involved and his/her behaviour	Your feelings	Consequences for your relation in the long-term	Behaviours that you prefer the other to do instead
Ingram	Finishing gym training	Lisa have not put the weights back onto the racks	Irritation	Poorer practice planning	Hang up the weights

'*I feel irritated when you do not put the equipment back in the gym, which makes me want to shy away and pout. It makes me clean up all night after practice, and that time I would rather spend planning tomorrow's practice. I would like you Lisa to obey the rules for the gym keeping it neat, so I can focus on practice planning.*'

Tina Trainer (Not Using I-statement)

'*You're not able to hang up the weights back on the rack. I get so annoyed when you don't care about the rules of the gym.*'

> In what types of situation do you think it is important to send an effective message to the athletes?
> How would you describe your body language?
> How can you make use of I-statements as a coach?

Listening

There is a dearth of research exploring sport coaches' listening, although this is commonly investigated within the therapeutic domain. Still, it is very advantageous for a coach to have knowledge of and develop listening skills, for example when trying to interpret the athlete's emotions as has been discussed earlier. Figure 7.4 illustrates the communication process. Listening is more complex than many believe, and Yukelson (2006) described three different levels of increasing quality. First, *arrogant listening* implies that listeners are mostly interested in what they themselves are going to say when given the opportunity, basically waiting for pauses in the speech to voice their own opinion. Second, *superficial listening* alludes to listeners tuning out immediately when they have what they deem the most essential information. Although this approach may allow for a basic understanding of what is being said, it is by no means the most effective way of eliciting information. Third, *active listening* is best described as listeners trying to pick up both content, and underlying emotions and cognitions from the speaker in an attempt to capture the true and intended meaning of the message. Listening is carried out by both verbal and nonverbal behaviours. When listening, displaying immediacy with the speaker

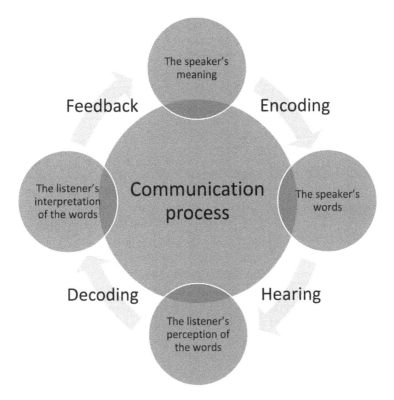

FIGURE 7.4 The communication process.

through eye-contact, head nods, and forward body lean show attentiveness and involvement. Verbal behaviours include acknowledging and elaborating the speaker's message, helping to articulate and explore the speaker's feelings, as well as putting experiences into a wider context. In order to be perceived as a good listener, verbal behaviours are more important than nonverbal (Bodie & Jones, 2012). A meticulous way to detail active listening is the HURIER model. *Hear, understand, remember, interpret, evaluate* and *respond* are the parts that make up the active listening process and will be described below using Brownell (2020) unless otherwise noticed.

Hear

Easily overlooked in listening is the essential ingredient of first actually hearing what is being said. Too many small things can divert our attention away from the speaker, such as cell phones, other noise and inner contemplations. Instead, deliberately direct the attention towards the speaker. Reducing internal distractions are often more difficult than external ones. Because we think faster than the speaker speaks, a vacuum is created where our mind easily drifts away. To counter this, silently repeat the spoken word or silently pose questions about what is said. Staying silent for a while after the speaker appears to have stopped talking might elicit further verbalizations from the speaker, while hurrying to cut the silence short with your own words risks impeding the speaker. It will also give more time for the next phase, understanding of what has just been told.

Understand

After the coach has made sure the message is heard, it is time to understand it. A vital tool for improving understanding is questions. Although questions have been forwarded in Chapter 5 (primarily through the use of complex questions), probes or follow-up questions are more important here. A probing question aims to dig deeper into something the speaker is talking about. By framing the question towards personal agency more than external influences, the speaker will attend to constructive aspects of the experience (Healing & Bavelas, 2011). Avoid focusing solely on content, as it is important to dig into the underlying emotional tone the speaker is conveying. Resist the urge to interrupt only to advance your own agenda, such as telling an anecdote that you were reminded of from something that was said, which might have little to no value for the speaker. Learning more about the speaker is an appropriate goal to zero in on this dimension.

Remember

Obviously, it is imperative to remember what is said, both for being able to process that information and also to honour the speaker with attention. There are numerous memory skills to learn to improve memory. One common technique is to place bits of information into a created story. When listening to someone, who actually tells a story, visualization of the things that are told will often suffice. Another useful tool is the written word. Beginning therapists often feel insecure when being advised to take notes during therapy, frequently worrying that the client will feel neglected when he/she does not keep eye contact, etc. for the sake of notetaking. Contrarily, though, many clients feel there is an added seriousness when the therapist keeps notes. Just make sure to inform beforehand of this procedure. All that needs to be said is something along the line of 'Is it alright if I take some notes during our conversation, as I want to make sure that I get what you are saying correctly? If you'd like, you can see what I have written down.'

Interpret

Interpreting messages depends largely on empathy. This has been covered previously in this chapter.

Evaluate

When evaluating a message, it is recommended to consider what credibility the speaker has on the topic. Does the speaker know what he/she is talking about? Is the speaker trying to 'sell' a point with the message (e.g., an athlete arguing for a change of practice content)? Another area to take into account is ethics. Does the message include any dubious subliminal attitudes or is it fair (e.g., an athlete blaming 'lazy' teammates for one's own performance during competition)? Additionally, external evidence needs to be considered in relation to the message. Is there any other information supporting or contradicting the message (e.g., other athletes' opinion on a conflict)? Identification of emotional appeals from the speaker needs to be done. Many times, emotional appeals are harmless, but they can also be used (intentionally or unintentionally). Finally, keep an open mind when evaluating a message.

Respond

After evaluating the message (or a part of it) there is a call for a response on the listener's behalf. Depending on the content of the message received, different responses are appropriate. If the speaker made some kind of request, it might be appropriate to be assertive. This is done by standing up for your beliefs and using an I-statement. Other ways of responding include *paraphrasing*, *reflecting* and *summarizing*. Paraphrasing involves providing alternative expressions to the words used by the speaker. Through this, it is possible to uncover more accurate or more positive meanings, such as when 'impatient' is paraphrased into 'active'. Reflecting when it comes to conversation has a different meaning in comparison to the reflective approach used for enhancing coaches' learning and development. Here, reflecting means that the listener makes an educated guess of the underlying meanings of the spoken words. Emotional and hands-on content are useful to explore through reflecting. Summarizing happens when statements from the speaker are repackaged in a concise manner with the words of the listener focusing on the main points. This serves well for the listener to check for understanding of a long passage or many shorter statements. Additionally, the speaker gets clarification on long-winded messages that were not so clear in his/her own mind. When a speaker gets feedback through an elaborate response from the listener, it is possible for the speaker to explore further into his/her inner world. In extension, the speaker may reach insights that were previously not visible, which leads to a deeper conversation (Miller & Rollnick, 2013).

> How do you currently listen to the athletes?
> Are there any of the HURIER-aspects that you are currently more skilled at? Less skilled at?
> What can be done to improve your listening?

Measuring Conversational Technique

 In the appendix, the HURIER Listening Profile (Zohoori, 2013) is provided measuring listening in the six dimensions.

 When you view the result on the HURIER Listening Profile, what do you think?

Practical Implementation of Coach–Athlete Relationship
Reflection Card

Empathic accuracy   Date: _____

Situation	Internal states	Coach's thoughts/emotions
	Distressed Proud	
	Excited Irritable	
	Upset Happy	
	Guilty Ashamed	
	Scared Inspired	
	Focused Nervous	
	Hostile Determined	
	Jittery Active	

This reflection card is slightly different from the ones encountered in the previous chapters. The objective of this reflective exercise is to improve empathic accuracy and this has been shown to be accomplished when coaches receive feedback on their assessments of others' states. Therefore, the reflection card creates an opportunity to make a read of a specific athlete during a practice (or competition if so chosen). In the first column (*Situation*), describe a specific situation where the coach tries to make a read of an athlete's internal state. The situation does not have to be particularly extraordinary, but may consist of simple events such as making a successful pass, getting a very friendly smile from a teammate, or performing just slightly worse than usual. Importantly, both mainly positive and mainly negative events can be used. Many coaches prefer to focus on highly salient reactions, and while those may be easier to interpret, they are not necessarily the most important nor provide the best material for practicing empathic accuracy. The same reasoning applies when choosing the type of athlete to read (e.g., outspoken or reserved). An athlete that is soft-spoken or laid-back needs to be understood just as well, so coaches are reminded not to forget these kinds of athletes when using this reflective exercise. Perhaps the name of the athlete has to be included if the group is large or multiple reflection cards are used within the same practice session.

In the second column (*Internal states*) rate the different states that are listed on a scale from 1 to 5 describing to what extent the athlete experiences them in the chosen situation. 1 corresponds to 'very slightly or not at all' while 5 corresponds to 'extremely', with 3 'moderately' in the middle. The approach of using a list of states has successfully been used in interventions resulting in perceiver's improved empathic accuracy (Ma-Kellams & Lerner, 2016). This kind of rating of one's states has proved both reliable and valid for different timeframes and flexible enough to be used with different wordings eliciting various aspects of emotional experience from the rater (Watson, Clark, & Tellegen, 1988). In the reflection card presented, 16 adjectives describing internal states are included. It is not necessary to rate all states. A selection could be used depending on understanding, age of athletes, or purpose chosen by the coach. Nonetheless, it will be a more thorough examination if not only attending to already known or 'easy' words, as this potentially unlocks new aspects for the coach to be cognizant of in athletes' reactions. After the practice (or competition) is over, the athlete is asked to complete a similar evaluation on their own in an empty reflection card. Some coaches prefer (sometimes depending on the type of practice session) to give the athlete the reflection card immediately after the situation instead of waiting for the end of the practice. This enhances the possibility of getting an accurate rating of the emotions as they actually appeared. For younger athletes with shorter attention span, this could prove particularly effective. To get the athlete's immediate attention to the situation and his/her states the coach needs to notify the specific athlete immediately to remember states of the particular situation and then rate coach's perception of the athlete's experience in the second column. The athletes should be informed before practice that some situation will be chosen and the involved athlete will be notified during the session. Remember to have a pen along with a copy of the reflection card ready for the athlete. To decrease risks for athletes feeling singled out, it helps if the coach is positioned close to the athletes, instead of shouting across the venue. Afterwards, the coach compares the two appraisals, which gives the coach the feedback necessary to improve his/her empathic accuracy. A high correlation indicates a greater accuracy on the coach's behalf.

In a typical sport's practice setting, a coach is more likely to be able to observe the athlete's body language than to hear a verbal statement from the athlete. Thus, inferring athletes' emotional states is a useful skill for coaches. Finally, the reflection card has been used by some coaches as basis of discussion with the athlete. Such a discussion serves as a valuable tool both to increase the athlete's understanding of own reactions and to improve the relationship between coach and athlete. In the third column (*Coach's thoughts/emotions*), note immediate thoughts or reactions upon trying to read the athlete's inner state (e.g., feeling proud as a coach for the way the athlete handled her-/himself, feeling puzzled

Secondary Reflection

> Use the questions below and/or the formula for shared reflection in Chapter 2.
> To what extent did you make a correct judgement of the athlete's feeling?
> What was difficult with this exercise?
> What would you do next time to keep improving your empathic accuracy (e.g., choose another athlete or type of situation)?
> With the used reflection card in hand, what do you think when you look back at that specific situation and the athlete during the practice?
> How did the athlete's expressivity influence your thoughts?
> How did the athlete's expressivity influence your emotions?
> What is the main lesson learned that you take away from the experience?

Reflection Sheet

First column is either completed before practice or after a conversation. The second to fourth columns are completed after practice or after a conversation with an athlete.

Conversational techniques			Date: _____
Description of a practice in general or description of a conversation with an athlete.	To what extent did you manage to use any of the conversational techniques? Provide examples of situations and verbal formulations where appropriate, in order to dig deeper into your actual use of them. I-statement Listening	Briefly answer the following questions: How did it feel to use the chosen method? How did the athletes respond to the chosen method? How could this method have been more effective?	What were your own thoughts and emotions during this part of the practice?

by the athlete's reactions or disappointed because it is a coach's job to prepare the athlete better for this type of situation).

Reflective Summary

> When trying to read athletes' inner states, what has been the most important lesson learnt for you?
> How are you going to capitalize on this lesson learnt in the future?
> When working with conversational techniques, what has been the most important lesson learnt for you?
> How are you going to capitalize on this lesson learnt in the future?
> From your readings of coach-athlete relationship, your answers to the application exercises, and your reflective activities, how would you best use your knowledge of coach-athlete relationship in the future?

Challenging Relational Assumptions

"I have something to show you", Collin said proudly.

He took out his cell phone and displayed a text message. Ellen smiled as she read the message from one of Collin's athletes, who thanked him for the last couple of weeks' coaching.

> "That was very neat. It looks like you really made improvements. Tell us a little bit how you now handle misdemeanours from athletes", Ellen wished.
> "I thought about what you showed me about the impact of not ascribing thoughts, feelings and intentions to the athletes. You can't really know what's inside them", he said confidently.
> "It seems like you have come to very valuable insights", Ellen praised him.
> "You're right, but I do believe that you *can* read their feelings, at least to some extent", Leah interjected. "I did some nice progress as well in this area", she added.
> "Good to hear. Let's hear about how you used the reflection cards, Leah", Ellen said.
> "Mm, the most important thing hasn't actually been when I've written in the cards, although the emotions mentioned there is an aha-experience as it makes you aware of more feelings than the ones you normally think of. The best part has been getting the feedback afterwards from the athletes, both when they've filled out their own card, but also when we've talked about their experiences. I have actually focused more on the cards as a convenient way into a very personal talk." Leah could have kept going, but was interrupted by Collin:
> "I think I've become better at listening to my athletes as well. We've more dynamic back-and-forth interactions now. They accommodate to my behaviours, and I try to be responsive to them too."

"When I talk with the athletes about other stuff, they both seem more open than before, but I also pick-up nonverbal clues that I recognized from their actions in other situations", Leah made her voice heard again.

Suddenly, Leah and Collin were so fired up they talked without listening to one another.

"Okay, I'm very pleased you're so excited about your development", Ellen tried to calm the moment down. "How would you capitalize on all of your lessons learnt during the season?"

"Sometimes it's tedious to write so much, but it gives me great satisfaction when I look back at my first reflection cards. It's a confidence boost to see hands-on how much I've improved. My reflections are way more elaborate today. I've also found new areas I've never thought of that are interesting", Leah replied.

"I'll definitely keep measuring my progress in other areas than the ones we've been working on during the year. Statistics may be dull, but they don't lie and they give you direction and feedback on how you're doing. It's just a matter of figuring out how to measure what you want to do", Collin contributed.

"Like actual coaching behaviours?" Ellen asked.

"Yeah...", Collin replied.

"My interactions with the athletes are at a deeper level now. They seem to think highly of me as a coach when I show that I want to improve too. Previously, my focus was mostly the sport itself, but now I've realized that the people is the main thing", Leah managed to get the last word with a curious smile.

Quiz

1. What are important components of the coach-athlete relationship?
   a. Initiation, growth, termination.
   b. Warm-up, activity, cool-down.
   c. Closeness, commitment, complementarity.

2. What can be done to enhance coaches' empathic accuracy?
   a. Increase practices' length.
   b. Observe more during practice.
   c. Conduct organized practices.

3. What acronym serves as a reminder for maintaining the coach-athlete relationship?
   a. COMPASS.
   b. HURIER.
   c. 3C's.

4. What is most correct about how athletes perceive coaches?
   a. Athletes do not use external sources.
   b. Coaches view of themselves form how they believe athletes see them.
   c. Longer observations provide a much more accurate impression than very brief.
5. What does it mean to use an I-statement?
   a. You have your goals at the forefront.
   b. You use more descriptive and less evaluative language.
   c. You try to boost the other person's self-esteem.
6. What contributes the most to being a skilled listener?
   a. Nonverbal behaviours.
   b. Verbal behaviours.
   c. Equally nonverbal and verbal behaviours.

References

Ambady, N., & Rosentahl, R. (1992). Thin slices of expressive behavior as predictors of interpersonal consequences: A meta-analysis. *Psychological Bulletin, 111*, 256–274.

Ames, D. R., & Kammrath, L. K. (2004). Mind-reading and metacognition: Narcissism, not actual competence, predicts self-estimated ability. *Journal of Nonverbial Behavior, 28*, 187–209.

Barone, D. F., & Hutchings, P. S. (2005). Increasing empathic accuracy through practice and feedback in a clinical interviewing course. *Journal of Social and Clinical Psychology, 24*, 156–171.

Batson, C. D., Early, S., & Salvarani, G. (1997). Perspective taking: Imagining how another feels versus imagining how you would feel. *Personality and Social Psychology Bulletin, 23*, 751–758.

Bekkali, S. et al. (2020). Is the putative mirror neuron system associated with empathy? A systematic review and meta-analysis. *Neuropsychological Review*. https://doi.org/10.1007/s11065-020-09452-6

Berscheid, E., Snyder, M., & Omoto, A. M. (1989). The relationship closeness inventory: Assessing the closeness of interpersonal relationships. *Journal of Personality and Social Psychology, 57*, 792–807.

Bodie, G. D., & Jones, S. M. (2012). The nature of supportive listening II: The role of verbal person centeredness and nonverbal immediacy. *Western Journal of Communication, 76*, 250–269.

Brownell, J. (2020). *The listening advantage: Outcomes and applications*. New York: Routledge.

Cunico, L., Sartori, R., Marognolli, O., & Meneghini, A. M. (2012). Developing empathy in nursing students: A cohort longitudinal study. *Journal of Clinical Nursing, 21*, 2016–2025.

Davis, L., Jowett, S., & Tafvelin, S. (2019). Communication strategies: The fuel for quality coach-athlete relationships and athlete satisfaction. *Frontiers in Psychology, 10*, 2156.

Epley, N., & Waytz, A. (2010). Mind perception. In S. T. Fiske, D. T. Gilbert, & G. Lindzey (Eds.), *Handbook of social psychology* (5th ed., pp. 498–541). New York: Wiley.

Fiori, K., & Rauer, A. (2020). Gender and race perspectives on relationship maintenance. In B. G. Ogolsky & J. K. Monk (Eds.), *Relationship maintenance: Theory, process, and context* (pp. 265–283). New York: Cambridge University Press.

Gesn, P. R., & Ickes, W. (1999). The development of meaning contexts for empathic accuracy: Channel and sequence effects. *Journal of Personality and Social Psychology, 77*, 746–761.

Gross, J. J., & John, O. P. (1998). Mapping the domain of expressivity: Multimethod evidence for a hierarchical model. *Journal of Personality and Social Psychology, 74*, 170–191.

Hall, J. A., & Schmid Mast, M. (2007). Sources of accuracy in the empathic accuracy paradigm. *Emotion, 2*, 438–446.

Hanson, T. W., & Gould, D. (1988). Factors affecting the ability of coaches to estimate their athletes' trait and state anxiety levels. *The Sport Psychologist, 2*, 298–313.

Hargie, O. (2010). *Skilled interpersonal communication: Research, theory and practice* (5th ed.). London: Routledge.

Haselwood, D. M., et al (2005). Female athletes' perceptions of head coaches' communication competence. *Journal of Sport Behavior, 28*, 216–230.

Healing, S., & Bavelas, J. B. (2011). Can questions lead to change? An analogue experiment. *Journal of Systemic Therapies, 30*, 30–47.

Hülya Aşçi, F., Kelecek, S., & Altintaş, A. (2015). The role of personality characteristics of athletes in coach-athlete relationships. *Perceptual & Motor Skills: Exercise & Sport, 121*, 399–411.

Ickes, W., & Buysse, A., et al. (2000). On the difficulty of distinguishing good and poor perceivers: A social relations analysis of empathic accuracy. *Personal Relationships, 7*, 219–234.

Ickes, W., Gesn, P. R., & Graham, T. (2000). Gender differences in empathic accuracy: Differential ability or differential motivation? *Personal Relationships, 7*, 95–109.

Johnson, D. W., & Johnson, R. T. (2005). New developments in social interdependence theory. *Genetic, Social, and General Psychology Monographs, 131*, 285–358.

Jowett, S. (2005). On enhancing and repairing the coach-athlete relationship. In S. Jowett, & M. V. Jones (Eds.), *Psychology of sport coaching* (pp. 14–26). Leicester, UK: British Psychology Society.

Jowett, S. (2007). Interdependence analysis and the 3+1Cs in the coach-athlete relationship. In S. Jowett, & D. Lavallee (Eds.), *Social psychology in sport* (pp. 15–27). Champaign, IL: Human Kinetics.

Jowett, S. (2008). What makes coaches tick? The impact of coaches' intrinsic and extrinsic motives on their own satisfaction and that of their athletes. *Scandinavian Journal of Medicine and Science in Sport, 18*, 664–673.

Jowett, S. (2009). Factor structure and criterion-related validity of the metaperspective version of the coach-athlete relationship questionnaire (CART-Q). *Group Dynamics: Theory, Research, and Practice, 13*, 163–177.

Jowett, S., & Carpenter, P. (2015). The concept of rules in the coach-athlete relationship. *Sports Coaching Review, 4*, 1–23.

Jowett, S., & Clark-Carter, D. (2006). Perceptions of empathic accuracy and assumed similarity in the coach-athlete relationship. *British Journal of Social Psychology, 45*, 617–637.

Jowett, S., & Cockerill, I. M. (2003). Olympic medallists' perspective of the athlete-coach relationship. *Psychology of Sport and Exercise, 4*, 313–331.

Jowett, S., & Ntoumanis, N. (2004). The coach - athlete relationship questionnaire (CART – Q): Development and initial validation. *Scandinavian Journal of Medicine and Science in Sports, 14*, 245–257.

Jowett, S., & Poczwardowski, A. (2007). Understanding the coach-athlete relationship. In S. Jowett, & D. Lavallee (Eds.), *Social psychology in sport* (pp. 3–14). Champaign, IL: Human Kinetics.

Jowett, S., & Shanmugam, V. (2016). Relational coaching in sport: Its psychological underpinnings and practical effectiveness. In R. J. Schinke, K. R. McGannon, & B. Smith (Eds.), *Routledge international handbook of sport psychology* (pp. 471–484). Abingdon, UK: Routledge.

Jowett, S., Yang, X., & Lorimer, R. (2012). The role of personality, empathy, and satisfaction with instruction within the context of the coach-athlete relationship. *International Journal of Coaching Science, 6*, 3–20.

Kammann, R., Smith, R., Martin, C., & McQueen, M. (1984). Low accuracy in judgements of others' psychological well-being as seen from a phenomenological perspective. *Journal of Personality, 52*, 107–123.

Kammrath, L. K., Ames, D. R., & Scholer, A. A. (2007). Keeping up impressions: Inferential rules for impression change across the Big Five. *Journal of Experimental Social Psychology, 43*, 450–457.

Kenny, D. A. (2020). *Interpersonal perception: The foundation of social relationships.* (2nd ed.). New York: Guilford Press.

Kenny, D. A., & Actielli, L. K. (2001). Accuracy and bias in the perception of the partner in a close. *Journal of Personality and Social Psychology, 80*, 439–448.

Kenny, D. A., & DePaulo, B. M. (1993). Do people know how others view them? An empirical and theoretical account. *Psychological Bulletin, 114*, 145–161.

LaVoi, N. M. (2007). Expanding the interpersonal dimension: Closeness in the coach-athlete relationship. *International Journal of Sports Science & Coaching, 2*, 497–512.

Lewis, K., Hodges, S. D., Laurent, S. M., Srivastava, S., & Biancarosa, G. (2012). Reading between the minds: The use of stereotypes in empathic accuracy. *Psychological Science, 23*, 1040–1046.

Lobchuk, M., et al (2018). Heart health whispering: A randomized, controlled pilot study to promote nursing student perspective-taking on carers' health risk behaviors. *BMC Nursing, 17*, 21.

Lorimer, R. (2009). Coaches' satisfaction with their athletic partnerships. *International Journal of Coaching Science, 3*, 57–66.

Lorimer, R., & Jowett, S. (2009). Empathic accuracy in coach–athlete dyads who participate in team and individual sports. *Psychology of Sport and Exercise, 10*, 152–158.

Lorimer, R., & Jowett, S. (2010). Feedback of information in the empathic accuracy of sport coaches. *Psychology of Sport and Exercise, 11*, 12–17.

Lydon, J. E., & Quinn, S. K. (2013). *Relationship maintenance processes.* In J. A. Simpson, & L. Campbell (Eds.), *The Oxford handbook of close relationships* (pp. 573–588). Oxford: Oxford University Press.

Ma-Kellams, C., & Lerner, J. (2016). Trust your gut or think carefully: Examining whether an intuitive, versus a systematic, mode of thought produces greater empathic accuracy? *Journal of Personality and Social Psychology, 111*, 674–685.

Malle, B. F. (2006). The actor-observer asymmetry in attribution: A (surprising) meta-analysis. *Psychological Bulletin, 132*, 895–919.

Manley, A. J., et al. (2008). Athletes' perceived use of information sources when forming initial impressions and expectancies of a coach: An explorative study. *The Sport Psychologist, 22*, 73–89.

Manley, A., Greenlees, I., & Thelwell, R. (2017). Athlete expectancies of coaches and their consequences. In R. Thelwell, C. Harwood, & I. Greenlees (Eds.), *The psychology of sports coaching: Research and practice* (pp. 142–155). New York: Routledge.

Martens, R. (2012). *Successful coaching* (4th ed.). Champaign, IL: Human Kinetics.

Mehrabian, A., & Ferris, S. R. (1967). Inference of attitudes from nonverbal communication in two channels. *Journal of Consulting Psychology, 31*, 248–252.

Miller, W. R., & Rollnick, S. (2013). *Applications of motivational interviewing. Motivational interviewing: Helping people change* (3rd edition). New York: Guilford Press.

Poczwardowski, A., Barott, J. E., & Henschen, K. P. (2002). The athlete and the coach: Their relationship and its meaning. Results of an interpretive study. *International Journal of Sport Psychology, 33*, 116–140.

Rhind, D. J. A., & Jowett, S. (2010). Relationship maintenance strategies in the coach–athlete relationship: The development of the COMPASS model. *Journal of Applied Sport Psychology, 22*, 106–121.

Rhind, D. J. A., & Jowett, S. (2011). Linking maintenance strategies to the quality of coach-athlete relationships. *International Journal of Sport Psychology, 42*, 1–14.

Rhind, D. J. A., & Jowett, S. (2012). Development of the coach-athlete relationship maintenance questionnaire (CARM-Q). *International Journal of Sports Science & Coaching, 7*, 121–137.

Rollings, K. H., Cuperman, R., & Ickes, W. (2011). Empathic accuracy and inaccuracy. In L. M. Horowitz, & S. Starck (Eds.), *Handbook of interpersonal psychology: Theory, research, assessment, and therapeutic interventions* (pp. 143–156). Hoboken, NJ: John Wiley & Sons.

Rubio, V. J., Hernandez, J. M., Sánchez-Iglesias, I., Cano, A., & Bureo, R. (2018). The effects of coaches' pre-game speeches on young players' self-efficacy. *Journal of Sport Psychology, 27*, 59–66.

Rusbult, C. E., & Buunk, B. P. (1993). Commitment processes in close relationships: An interdependence analysis. *Journal of Social and Personal Relationships, 10*, 175–204.

Sadler, P., Ethier, N., & Woody, E. (2011). Interpersonal complementarity. In L. M. Horowitz, & S. Starck (Eds.), *Handbook of interpersonal psychology: Theory, research, assessment, and therapeutic interventions* (pp. 123–142). Hoboken, NJ: John Wiley & Sons.

Sandström, E., Linnér, L., & Stambulova, N. (2016). Career profiles of athlete-coach relationships: Descriptions and interpretations. *International Journal Sports Science & Coaching, 11*, 395–409.

Seligman, M. E. P., Reivich, K., Jaycox, L., & Gillham, J. (1995). *The optimistic child*. Boston, MA: Houghton, Mifflin.

Sened, H., et al. (2017). Empathic accuracy and relationship satisfaction: A meta-analytic review. *Journal of Family Psychology, 31*, 742–752.

Solomon, D. H., & Roloff, M. E. (2018). Relationship initiation and growth. In A. L. Vangelisti & D. Perlman (Eds.), *The Cambridge handbook of personal relationships* (pp. 79–89). New York: Cambridge University Press.

Stafford, L. (2020). Communication and relationship maintenance. In B. G. Ogolsky & J. K. Monk (Eds.), *Relationship maintenance: Theory, process, and context* (pp. 109–133). New York: Cambridge University Press.

Storm., L. K., Henriksen, K., Larsen, C. H., & Christensen, M. K. (2014). Influential relationships as context learning and becoming elite; Athletes' retrospective interpretations. *International Journal of Sports Science & Coaching, 9*, 1341–1356.

Wachsmuth, S., Jowett, S., & Harwood, C. (2017). Conflict among athletes and their coaches: What is the theory and research so far? *International Review of Sport and Exercise Psychology, 10*, 84–107.

Wachsmuth, S., Jowett, S., & Harwood, C. G. (2018). Managing conflict in coach-athlete relationship. *Sport, Exercise, and Performance Psychology, 7*, 317–391.

Watson, D., Clark, L. A., & Tellegen, A. (1988). Development and validation of brief measures of positive and negative affect: The PANAS scales. *Journal of Personality and Social Psychology, 54*, 1063–1070.

Yukelson, D. P. (2006). Communicating effectively. In J. M. Williams (Ed.), *Applied sport psychology: Personal growth to peak performance* (5th ed., pp. 174–191). New York: McGraw-Hill.

Zaki, J., Bolger, N., & Ochsner, K. (2008). It takes two: The interpersonal nature of empathic accuracy. *Psychological Science, 19*, 399–404.

Zaki, J., Bolger, N., & Ochsner, K. (2009). Unpacking the informational bases of empathic accuracy. *Emotion, 9*, 478–487.

Zohoori, A. (2013). A cross-cultural comparison of the HURIER listening profile among Iranian and US students. *The International Journal of Listening, 27*, 50–60.

8
LONG-TERM DEVELOPMENT

Theoretical learning goals of the chapter:
　Grow an understanding of...

1. behavioural modification principles.
2. expertise.

Practical learning goals of the chapter:

1. Become able to use reflection card/reflection sheet to new learning materials and areas.

Introduction

There are several options to work with the content of this book long-term. Although coaching is a multifaceted endeavour containing all topics in one form or the other during a single practice session, it is beneficial to focus on one subject. This is not in contrast to the aforementioned holistic approach advocated within the book. Instead, focusing on 'one subject' will elicit critical reflection, which in all likelihood will incorporate aspects of other areas as the coach sees fit. For example, let's say a coach chooses to work on improving the motivational climate within the group. When reflecting upon the motivational tasks used during practice, likely the coach has to consider effects of and on areas such as pedagogical methods and coach-athlete relationship. While focusing on one subject, some things that have come to the coach's attention worthy of intervention (perhaps through a questionnaire or application exercise) may be worked on for two months before moving on to another area. At the end of that period, getting some feedback from the athletes or from an observer would be a good evaluation of the coach's work and provide direction for future efforts. An evaluation of this kind may give insight into the specific coaching behaviours used (*What*) or the quality of the approach undertaken in order to develop these behaviours (*How*). By choosing one specific area to focus on, it is easier to really improve coaching within this area, motivation may be enhanced, noticing and evaluating success is more straightforward, which in turn leads to better confidence when it comes to making future improvements.

For example, a coach could work with the book by setting aside some time every week, such as 30–60 minutes, for going through the theory of a specific chapter and from there create a plan for how to implement the theory during the upcoming week's practices. The implementation can be done by using reflection cards or reflection sheets. The biggest advantage of using reflective activities during practices is that it both allows the coach to adapt the theory to situational, coach's and athletes' constraints, needs and peculiarities, but it simultaneously provides a workout for the coach's cognitive skills and self-awareness. One of the more prominent findings of learning is that spacing practice over time with other activities in interspersed in between enhances learning (Donovan & Radosevich, 1999). Two reasons for this are a facilitation of memory consolidation and deeper learning. Memory consolidation occurs through protein synthesis in the brain after practice and requires sleep. Basically, this process transfers cognitions from short-term memory into long-term memory making it more robust against forgetting. Deep learning happens because the learning material is not only stored in short-term memory but also has to be retrieved each time. Furthermore, by adding other events, learning materials and cognitive focuses in between (e.g., having a competition day, a day with non-sport activities), deep learning is enhanced as the particular learning material is contrasted with other information.

Another possibility of using the book is to involve a group of coaches working collaboratively on improvement. A group working on the same areas of improvement provide many benefits. Coaching colleagues may inspire each other and facilitate motivation, assist in understanding of theory and provide more real-life experiences after testing during practices that will give a more nuanced problematization of the theory. A diverse group working on the same topic helping each other, perhaps also in some form of mentor relationships, provides a fruitful ground for informal learning many coaches appreciate (Culver & Trudel, 2006).

> What would be an appropriate amount of time for you to regularly set aside for working on coaching improvement? What would be an appropriate time of week for this work?
>
> Are there any groups of coaches that you could involve or join in coaching improvement?

Behavioural Modification

This book is about improvement and change in coaching practice. Rather than just going with the gut-feeling of what appears desirable at a specific moment, long-lasting improvement and behavioural modification require a structured approach. Behaviours entail observable ones, but also cognitive, such as a coach's thoughts during practice. Possible behaviours to modify range from using more reciprocal pedagogical method during strength training, to thinking about athletes' playing position before providing feedback, or to use less conditional regard in interactions with athletes, to just mention some examples. Specific behaviours may be increased or decreased, and it is beneficial to operationalize them so they become measurable. By decreasing the required effort for the desired behaviour, increasing the effort for unwanted behaviours or adjusting situational factors, behavioural modification is facilitated.

Let's say a coach wants to keep messages shorter during time-outs. First, operationalization has to be done of what shorter messages means, in measurable terms, 'mentioning only one offensive and one defensive point', for example. Second, investigation of competing behaviours has to be undertaken. In this example it might be that the coach feels more competent when plenty of areas are covered during one timeout and believes that it makes a good impression on the athletes. Third, the efforts needed and reinforcers for each behaviour has to be adjusted to a more desired balance, which in the current example might be done through having an assistant coach make a comment whenever the coach mentions more than one point for either offence or defence (i.e., adjust reinforcers). Another way is to step away from the group for the first 20 seconds of the timeout (i.e., adjust situational factors), which makes it more difficult to cover more points in the remaining time (Miltenberger, 2008).

Michie, van Stralen, and West (2011) propose that three conditions are needed for a person to undertake a specific and desired behaviour, namely *capability*, *opportunity* and *motivation*. Capability means that the person has to have the psychological capacity including the needed knowledge to engage in desired behaviour. For a coach looking to improve upon coaching, reading and trying out the application and reflective exercise in this book provides ample possibilities to develop necessary declarative knowledge and skills. Opportunity entails factors outside of the individual that either makes the behaviour possible or even prompt it. Opportunities can be restricted or facilitated by social factors. For a coach looking to improve, it is wise to influence the social environment so that it will be conducive of change. For example, the coach might talk to athletes about his/her own developmental journey and goal for coaching development in a way that they will be more understanding of some trial-and-error on the coach's behalf. Another way to influence social factors is surrounding oneself with supportive people in coaching staff or even choose an organization that values a developmental mindset among coaches even if that comes with some mistakes or inefficiency in the short-term. Motivation in general has been detailed in Chapter 3 including coaches' own motivation. In that section a coach looking to improve his/her own motivation finds many helpful suggestions. Coaches who have high level of capability, opportunity and motivation have a solid foundation for improving their coaching.

> ✏ For you to improve as a coach, do you need to enhance any of your capability, opportunity or motivation? If so, how would you go about that?

In all change-related work, there are potential for setbacks and traps. Long-term improvement sometimes takes tedious work. Duckworth, Grant, Loew, Oettingen, and Gollwitzer (2011) differ between three paths to goal commitment: *indulging, dwelling* and *mental contrasting*. Indulging means fantasizing of a positive future without taking into consideration obstacles present in reality standing in the way of realization of the desired future. Dwelling, on the other hand, entails thinking about negative aspects of the present, without any elaboration of wanted future. Both of these approaches are one-sided ways of thinking. Instead, mental contrasting is recommended. This involves elaborating the present reality and its obstacles, as well as the desired future state. Through this, the two temporal aspects are simultaneously accessible for the individual, which creates a strong connection between them. The positive future is elaborated first and then potentially inhibiting obstacles are penetrated. Seemingly, this order (i.e., positive first, negative second) elicits more functional response compared to the opposite (Duckworth et al., 2011).

Table 8.1 describes important phases of the behaviour change process which have been derived from Prochaska, Redding, and Evers (2008), and Rothman, Baldwin, Hertel, and Fuglestad (2011). Before reaching the first phase though, there is the risk of getting stuck in procrastination, weighing pros and cons to no end, instead of moving forwards. It is tempting to postpone action today for thinking about or 'pseudo-planning' action tomorrow, and then repeat the same cycle tomorrow. This may provide a false sense of achievement. In comparison, at the preparation phase, the hands-on change process is intended to start within a month. Necessary advice, courses or books are sought out and researched and evolve into a plan. After creating an action plan, there is commonly a sense of optimism and hope, which often carries over into the initiation phase. Those positive feelings may be accompanied by nervousness and uncertainty.

Self-efficacy has most relevance in the initiation phase, where a person has to 'prove' to oneself that he/she has the capacity to overcome initial obstacles. Higher expectations elicit higher rates of behavioural initiation. Initially focusing on advancement, growth and accomplishments is facilitative in getting the change process going.

In the continuation phase, there can be tension between one's ability to perform the new behaviour and motivation on one hand and unpleasant experiences

TABLE 8.1 Phases of behavioural change.

Phase	Preparation	Initiation	Continuation	Maintenance	Habit
Defining feature	Action plan is constructed.	Hands-on effort to change behaviour.	Continued effort to establish new behaviour.	Sustained effort that is perceived as easier then previously.	New self-perpetuating pattern of behaviour.
Critical issues	Important steps taken towards action, such as entering into a developmental program, buying a self-help book etc.	Beliefs in and expectations of success.	Initial rewards from new behaviour and demands of the change process.	Satisfaction with new behaviour.	Prior behaviour.
Marker of end of phase/ transition to next phase	The person enters into the context in which the new behaviour will be carried out.	First reliable performance of new behaviour.	Consistent performance of behaviour and confidence in one's ability to perform it repeatedly.	Consistent performance of behaviour without consideration of its value.	Evaluation whether the habit is worthwhile or should be modified.

through challenges on the other hand. The length of this phase is highly variable between persons and contexts.

During the maintenance phase, less temptation is experienced in returning to old habits or behaviours. One thing to be vigilant of at that point, is the potential for less reinforcements and compliments from others people. Perhaps fewer positive feelings will appear as excitement of novelty wears off and performance of the specific behaviour starts to be taken for granted. People may remain indefinitely in this stage and continuously evaluate the behaviour's cost-benefit balance.

Finally, when the behaviour has been incorporated into regular everyday endeavours without any particular conscious effort, it is a habit. At that phase, the behaviour's consequences are not evaluated, and instead the behaviour is reinforced and sustained by itself. Going from this habit to the preparation phase requires deliberate contemplation whether the habitual behaviour is worthwhile. If so, the individual may start a new change process. In sum, habits are hard to form, easy to maintain, and possibly difficult to improve upon.

When a behaviour is turned into habit, it seems functional to shift to a prevention focus emphasizing security, duty and meeting obligations. Individuals who have this focus have a better prospect at maintaining the changes undertaken (Rothman, Baldwin, Hertel, & Fuglestad, 2011). Behavioural changes through deliberate, structured and continuous work have a good chance to be relatively permanent for coaches, thus reaching habit phase (Cheon & Reeves, 2013).

> ✏️ Think of a skill or behaviour you want to change. In what phase would you place yourself when it comes to making an important change/improvement today?
> What is the main point to get you to next phase?

While most people probably have heard of the effectiveness of goal-setting (see Chapter 4), less is known to the general public about *implementation intentions* (II). In addition, Gollwitzer (1999) describes another intention, namely goal intention. The two intentions make up the components of an if-then statement. II corresponds to the 'if-part', while goal intentions match the 'then-part'. Whereas, the latter details what is to be done (e.g., 'I intend to achieve x!'), the former specifies a cue linked to a behaviour instrumental for reaching the goal. Thus, II delivers *when, where* and *how* the person will instigate the behaviour (e.g., 'If situation y happens, then I will initiate goal-directed behaviour z'). An II links an environmental situational cue to a behavioural response. Eventually, when this cue is encountered, the behaviour is executed automatically and with less effort. II has been shown to increase individuals' awareness of these critical cues compared to people who only have set a goal. A critical cue can be anything such as time during practice, a feeling, a certain place, a practice activity or even a specific person. By having specified a cue and specified an accompanying behaviour, the goal is protected from unwanted influences, and disengagement from failings, while efforts are increased leading to a smaller discrepancy between what is intended and what is actually achieved. Various traps to consider when creating the II are highlighted in Table 8.2. Forming an II consists of first identifying a response (e.g., behavioural or cognitive) that will facilitate goal achievement, and second assume a suitable moment when this response is to be initiated. Finally, rehearsal of the created II's cue-response link increases likelihood to use it in real-life situation (Gollwitzer & Sheeran, 2006).

Tina Trainer's goal is to increase the feedback delay period to at least two seconds on at least 90% of her feedback provisions during a specific practice activity. She created the following II: '*When an athlete jumps, I will listen to the sound of her landing, then I will count silently to five before saying anything.*'

Instructor Ingram's goal is to use individualized consideration before practices start. He created the following II: '*When I reach the rallying point prior to the practice, I will ask the present athletes about their day at school.*'

Often, the time it takes to complete a task or reach an achievement is underestimated, which is called *planning fallacy*. This happens because people create mental scenarios on how a project will develop. Since it is unimaginable to take every possible factor into account, mental scenarios lack several alternative events that can occur along the way. This makes plans often more straight-forward and extending over shorter times than reality. To counter this bias, II help in decreasing number of interruptions to a plan, thus decreasing the number of misjudgements in the path to reaching one's goal (Koole & Spijker, 2000).

Long-term development 251

TABLE 8.2 Potential barriers for goal completion and remedies.

Barrier	Processes	Remedies
Failing to get started	Difficulties to remember to act.	Shorten the time between preparing II and opportunity to act. Include II on practice plan that is reviewed during practice.
	Difficulties to seize the opportunity despite remembering to act.	Clearly specify situational cue in II and be very clear about how the behaviour is carried out.
	Difficulties to resist short-term rewards ahead of long-term achievements.	Consider the most attractive alternatives and specify them in the II and what behaviour to carry out when they appear.
Getting derailed	Difficulties to keep attention on the goal, instead attending to distracting and vivid stimuli.	Corral situations that provide attentional disruptions, and either work to avoid those situations or work out an appropriate II in response to these situations.
	Difficulties to act appropriately during mood swings.	Identify antecedents of mood swings and work out II for these antecedents. View good mood as a feature of unproblematic situations, which might neither be optimally challenging or conducive of expertise development (see section below).
	Difficulties to progress in the light of negative feedback.	Include negative feedback in II as a natural stepping stone.

 What of the following areas do you deem most important for you to improve in your coaching over the next couple of months?

Motivational skills

Your own motivation

Sport-specific coaching behaviours

Social competence coaching behaviours

Pedagogy

Feedback provision

Coach-athlete relationship

Choose a specific goal for your coaching development in the specified area:

How are you going to measure goal progress?

Create an II with the following steps.

How will you get started? Identify appropriate behaviour facilitative of goal achievement.

Identify situational cues (when, where) that will elicit the specified behaviour:

Identify potential barriers or challenges to your progress:

How will you stay on track towards your goal when any of these barriers or challenges arise?

What is a reasonable date for you to reach your goal?

Expertise

Coaching expertise should not be confused with coaching experience. Although, development of expertise takes time, it is not necessarily equivalent with hours spent coaching. Some features that experts do in comparison to novices forwarded in the literature are listed below (Berliner, 2001; Nash, Martindale, Collins, & Martindale, 2012; Zimmerman, 2002):

- Produce innovative and novel solutions to problems
- Possess and utilize a large declarative knowledge base
- Structure their knowledge in a more efficient way, easing the cognitive load
- Recognize patterns quicker
- Take longer time to start solving problem, due to more deliberation and gathering of information
- Solve problem with better quality, and often also faster as a whole
- Give greater and more diverse meaning to single events
- Are flexible and adaptable to the current situation
- Regulate their learning proactively, instead of reactively, by setting goals and self-monitoring systematically

The question then remains, how does a coach develop expertise? According to Côté, Erickson, and Duffy (2013) coaches use the learning situations elaborated in Chapter 2 and experiences during athletic career and coaching to develop their expertise. Early on, coaches focus on hands-on drills and gradually shift focus to more abstract concepts of coaching trying to create a coherent style of coaching and not just bits of pieces scrambled together. Eventually, coaches may reach a stage where they use the athlete as a starting point for decision-making, trying to figure out what is best for each specific athlete rather than apply general principles. Then coaches are more flexible in their methods turning coaching into skilled craftmanship. An expert coach uses science and art interchangeably.

The cognitive learning coaches go through on their way to expertise mirror the phases of behavioural modification to some extent. First, declarative knowledge and slow processing characterize the learning as the person is rehearsing verbally through silent thoughts or audible words while performing the task. This resembles many peoples' experience of learning how to drive a manual car. The initial memorization of coordinating hand and foot movement when shifting gears is anything but smooth, albeit necessary for getting rolling. Later, it progresses into associative stage where connections between different factors are made by the learner leading to a smoother task execution. Error detection is more efficient. Still, the person remembers the explicit rules used in the earlier stages and can go back to them if so needed. After working through the associative stage, the skills evolve into automatic. Tasks require less conscious processing and attentional resources making it possible to focus on other areas. A skilled driver rarely remembers how and when the gear was shifted during a drive as attention was turned towards the other vehicles on the road. Though, the occasional slip happens even for the best experts. Like an athlete needs to keep in shape and sporadically go back to work on fundamentals, a coach should hone some coaching skills every now and then by making a concentrated effort to deliver a great performance at whatever so small an issue (e.g., provide a extra clear demonstration for a common drill or try to hear every single syllable an athlete utters in a conversation). The higher the skill level, the smaller the progress (Anderson, 2005). For expertise to develop, deliberate practice is emphasized. Deliberate practice is characterized by sharp focus, lots of feedback and not always inherently enjoyable (Ericsson, Krampe, & Tesch-Romer, 1993). Among other factors, *effort* is essential for the individual to be able to engage in deliberate practice. The effort expended has to be at maximum level, but it is also mandated that recovery such as sleep and mentally relaxing activities are not forgotten. When deliberate practice is conducted it is better to go at it with high focus and intensity for a shorter time, then to go through the motions just to get hours under your belt. In analogy, Kuhlmann and Ardichvili (2015) found that workplace development in an applied context is driven by accepting optimal challenges in comparison to one's current skill level. Simple tasks rarely lead to expertise attainment. Thus, the maxim of challenging one's comfort zone has merit. For a coach, this could play out in the form of accepting one more athlete into the group that already is 'full' or choosing a slightly more detailed form for practice planning. An applied context such as coaching provide more on-the-job learning opportunities and time and less in formal education. Everyday coaching consists of performing rather than practicing. Therefore, a coach wanting to develop expertise has to find ways to practice on the job.

In contrast to a perhaps overly simplified linear model of novices developing to the end-product of expertise, Grenier and Kehrhahn (2008) propose that expertise exists at different states. Even if the coach previously has developed expertise, it is not necessarily a permanent state as it needs to be redeveloped to some extent if *content, environment* or *constituency* are changed or expanded. The content is revised in sports as sport-specific rules, training methods and techniques constantly evolve. An expert coach needs to update knowledge and skills in accordance. The environment is changed for example when a coach changes coaching role, age-groups or country. The constituency may also be altered. It is not enough for a coach to have knowledge and skills to be considered an expert since expertise undoubtedly is tied to its social utility as there needs to be an audience which recognizes and legitimizes the coach as expert. A coach's 'audience' consists among others of board, parents and athletes. In total, an expert coach may be forced into another state of expertise, that ranges from dependence to independence to finally transcendence (see Table 8.3).

Clearly, an expert coach needs to have plenty of declarative knowledge underpinning decision-making and drawn upon when in discussions with colleagues, athletes or other stakeholders. It is difficult to provide a rationale for in-practice or in-competition decisions if the coach does not have a vast knowledge of the related issues. In some way this makes it perhaps more difficult to coach than

TABLE 8.3 States of expertise.

State of expertise	View of and handling of information	Critical actions
Dependence	Relying on others for information	Relearning some aspects to succeed
Independence	New information supplements the existing knowledge	Experimentation during practice, seeking out resources for new information
Transcendence	Ownership of knowledge that is somewhat unconscious eliciting a feeling of confidence	Freedom to improvise and challenge practices with continued experimentation that adds to existing knowledge

to be an athlete, as the former needs to possess both declarative knowledge and procedural skill simultaneously. Before coaches are scared away of all that needs to be known and done, a quote many attribute to Mark Twain is appropriate: 'It ain't what you don't know that gets you into trouble, it's what you know for sure that just ain't so'. Thus, the most important thing for a coach is not to know everything or do everything perfectly, but to be constantly inquiring, searching for information and feedback, evaluating the current practice including his/her own cognitions, emotions and values. In short, the greatest virtue of a coach is being permanently curious.

What characteristics of expert coaches do you identify in your own coaching?
What characteristic would you most need to improve?
Do you need to improve your effort to achieve this improvement?

Modifying Reflective Activities

In the prior chapters, the reflective activities use a recurring theme, which are now described to provide templates for coaches who want to expand the areas (*What*) of the structured coaching improvement not limiting oneself to this book's content. The reflection cards are basically built using four phases. First, an interesting situation is found and described in practice. Second, a decision is made regarding some kind of intervention. Third, the intervention is carried out. Fourth, the influence on the coach's inner states is noted. This last step is important in developing coaches' reflection engagement. Thoughts and emotions are significant to aid self-awareness, reach deep learning, and make for a greater understanding of how the implementation is best carried out in the long run. Through these phases, it is possible to construct a new reflection.

Reflection Card

[Chosen subject]			Date:_____
[Prepared situation]	[Decision to intervene]	[Intervention]	Coach's thoughts/ emotions

Use the above reflection card on a novel subject either not covered within this book or not used in conjunction with a reflection card (e.g., goal-setting, sport-specific area or use of questions). Work out a preferred goal and action plan from the chosen area. Relabel the first column as is deemed appropriate and fill it out before practice. Relabel the second and third columns appropriately for the chosen subject and fill them out during a specific situation in practice. Finally, complete the fourth column afterwards.

Berliner (2001) mentions that experts are more flexible in their thinking and teaching. Thus, eventually a coach should be able to pick up any kind of situation in a reflection card and construct an intervention on the spot. However difficult that might sound, it is possible to improve a coach's vigilance and decision-making by frequent usage of a structured and reflective mindset.

Expert			Date:_____
Event	Intervention rationale	Intervention execution	Coach's thoughts/ emotions

In this reflection card, 'anything is possible'. No boxes are prepared beforehand. In the first column (*Event*), a noteworthy situation that occurs during a practice is described. By highlighting a particular situation, a coach's cognitive processes are already underway as this takes deliberate monitoring. In the second column (*Intervention rationale*), the underlying thought processes for a suitable coaching intervention is described. This is where the coach frames the problem and as previously mentioned, more expert coaches take longer time to get the problem-solving process going. A coach should not be afraid to spend some additional time in this phase before coming up with an intervention. To accomplish this, the coach has to search through a range of various subjects in order to find the appropriate intervention. The inquiries can for example be pondering whether an athlete has poor technique, whether an athlete is uncomfortable within a specific group or whether an athlete has an unfulfilled need of autonomy. Thus, a goal for this practice cannot be prepared like the previous reflection cards have made possible. In this manner, the goal, and definitely the plan has to be made up on the spot in the heat of the moment. As hard as it seems, this is the pinnacle of skilled coaching and reflection-in-action. It is also the most authentic coaching, as a coach needs to be able to react to events and situations during practice that cannot always be foreseen. Handling such issues is a hallmark of expert coaching and allows for great flexibility in the coaching. In the third column (*Intervention execution*), the way the intervention was carried out is described. It is important to distinguish between the decision and the execution as one may be good but not the other, and this makes it easier to evaluate how a similar event is best handled in the future. In the fourth column (*Coach's thoughts/emotions*), the coach's reactions to either the event, the intervention or its effect on the athlete (-s) is noted.

Secondary Reflection

The secondary reflection can be built with an underlying structure as seen below. Through the secondary reflection, the intervention is evaluated in relation to its effect of the coach's inner states and conversely, how the coach's thoughts and emotions influenced the event.

 How did the situation and [chosen intervention] influence your thoughts?

How did the situation and [chosen intervention] influence your emotions?

How did your thoughts influence the effect of the [implementation of intervention]?

How did your emotions influence the effect of the [implementation of intervention]?

In what way is the [chosen intervention] related to your coaching philosophy/idea of what you wanted to accomplish at the practice?

With the used reflection card in hand, what do you think when you look back at that specific situation and the athlete during the practice? For example, do you view the situation any differently now compared to during the practice?

Would you do anything different as you look back at this specific event? If so, elaborate on this.

What is the main lesson learnt that you take away from the experience?

Reflection Sheet

The reflection sheet may also be generic with five columns and used with a novel subject like the reflection card. The first column describes the practice content at various times (practice activity 1 on row 1, etc). The second column details *What* is to be included in the practice at appropriate time points (thus the different rows in the reflection sheet as one *What* may be appropriate during practice activity 1, while something else is used during practice activity 2). The third column evaluates the implementation in comparison to the intention in second column. The fourth column tries to reflect upon possible pros and cons of the implementation and preferably with a depth of dialogic or critical reflection. The fifth column lets the coach reflect upon own emotional and cognitive reactions during the implementation.

[Chosen subject]				Date: _____
Description of and Purpose of practice activity	Description of how [chose subject] is intended to be implemented.	Evaluation of the actual implementation of the [chosen subject].	What pros and cons do you see with the implementation of the [chosen subject]? (Try to think of effects for the athletes as athletes/as individual persons/as a group/for the society.)	What were your own thoughts and emotions during this part of the practice?

Reflective Summary

The reflective summary presented in Chapter 2 is also generic and advantageous to complete after working with a specific subject for a specific time (e.g., trying to use another pedagogical method for two months). Below, additional questions (worthwhile to consider after a period of structured work on improving the coaching) are presented.

> Now it is valuable to revisit the evaluation of your reflections provided in Chapter 2. What reflection depth do you generally see in your reflection sheets?
>
> Also, compare some of your earliest reflective activities with some of your later ones. What kind of differences do you see?
>
> What does these comparisons say about your development as a coach?
>
> How would you use this lesson learnt in the future on your continuing development?
>
> Choose a particularly significant event over the last months where you have been working with coaching development. Go back to the final 12 questions in Chapter 2's reflective summary and answer them in relation to the chosen significant event.
>
> Using the same particular significant event, try to categorize your learning from this event by using the framework for levels of learning in Chapter 2.

Quiz

1. Why are Implementation Intentions effective for reaching a goal?
   a. They outline specific and critical cues along with behaviour that is used in the situation.
   b. They raise the importance of the goal.
   c. They focus the goal in particular.

2. What is a characteristic of expertise in relation to novice?
   a. Quicker to get a problem-solving underway.
   b. More traditional solutions are used.
   c. More flexibility in adapting to the situation.

References

Anderson, J. R. (2005). *Cognitive psychology and its implications* (6th ed.). New York: Worth Publishers.

Berliner, D. C. (2001). Learning about and learning from expert teachers. *International Journal of Educational Research, 35*, 463–482.

Cheon, S. H., & Reeve, J. (2013). Do the benefits from autonomy-supportive PE teacher training programs endure?: A one-year follow-up investigation. *Psychology of Sport and Exercise, 14*, 508–518.

Côté, J., Erickson, K., & Duffy, P. (2013). Developing the expert performance coach. In D. Farrow, J. Baker, & C. MacMahon (Eds.), *Developing sport expertise: Researchers and coaches put theory into practice* (2nd ed., pp. 17–28). New York: Routledge.

Culver, D., & Trudel, P. (2006). Cultivating coaches' communities of practice: Developing the potential for learning through interactions. In R. L. Jones (Ed.), *The sports coach as educator: Re-conceptualising sports coaching* (pp. 97–112). London: Routledge.

Donovan, J. D., & Radosevich, D. J. (1999). Meta-analytic review of the distribution of practice effect: Now you see it, now you don't. *Journal of Applied Psychology, 84*, 795–805.

Duckworth, A. L., Grant, H., Loew, B., Oettingen, G., & Gollwitzer, P. M. (2011). Self-regulation strategies improve self-discipline in adolescents: Benefits of mental contrasting and implementation intentions. *Educational Psychology, 31*, 17–26.

Ericsson, K. A., Krampe, R. T., & Tesch-Romer, C. (1993). The role of deliberate practice in the acquisition of expert performance. *Psychological Review, 100*, 363–406.

Gollwitzer, P. M. (1999). Implementation intentions: Strong effects of simple plans. *American Psychologist, 54*, 493–503.

Gollwitzer, P. M., & Sheeran, P. (2006). Implementation intentions and goal achievement: A meta-analysis of effects and processes. *Advances in Experimental Social Psychology, 38*, 69–119.

Grenier, R. S., & Kehrhahn, M. (2008). Toward an integrated model of expertise redevelopment and its implications for HRD. *Human Resource Development Review, 7*, 198–217.

Koole, S., & Spijker, M. (2000). Overcoming the planning fallacy through willpower: Effects of implementation intentions on actual and predicted task-completion times. *European Journal of Social Psychology, 30*, 873–888.

Kuhlmann, D. O., & Ardichvili, A. A. (2015). Becoming an expert: Developing expertise in an applied discipline. *European Journal of Training and Development, 39*, 262–276.

Michie, S., van Stralen, M. M., & West, R. (2011). The behaviour change wheel: A new method for characterizing and designing behaviour change interventions. *Implementation Science, 6*, 42.

Miltenberger, R. G. (2008). *Behavior modification: Principles and procedures* (4th ed.). Belmont, CA: Thomson Wadsworth.

Nash, C., Martindale, R., Collins, D., & Martindale, A. (2012). Parameterising expertise in coaching: Past, present and future. *Journal of Sports Sciences, 30*, 985–994.

Prochaska, J. O., Redding, C. A., & Evers, K. E. (2008). The transtheoretical model and stages of change. In K. Glanz, B. K. Rimer, & K. Viswanath (Eds.), *health behavior and health education: Theory, research, and practice* (4th ed., pp. 97–121). San Francisco, CA: Jossey-Bass.

Rothman, A. J., Baldwin, A. S., Hertel, A. W., & Fuglestad, P. T. (2011). Self-regulation and behavior change: Disentangling behavioral initiation and behavioral maintenance. In K. D. Vohs, & R. F. Baumeister (Eds.), *Handbook of self-regulation: Research, theory, and applications* (2nd ed., pp. 106–122). New York: Guilford Press.

Zimmerman, B. (2002). Becoming a self-regulated learner: An overview. *Theory into Practice, 41*, 64–70.

Appendix A
QUESTIONNAIRES

Self-Reflection and Insight Scale (Coach Rating Coaching)

> Here are some statements about how you usually do in your coaching role. Read each statement and then choose the most appropriate rating. There are no right or wrong answers.

		Strongly disagree					Strongly agree
1	I don't often think about my thoughts.	1	2	3	4	5	6
2	I rarely spend time in self-reflection.	1	2	3	4	5	6
3	I frequently examine my feelings.	1	2	3	4	5	6
4	I don't really think about why I behave in the way that I do.	1	2	3	4	5	6
5	I frequently take time to reflect on my thoughts.	1	2	3	4	5	6
6	I often think about the way I feel about things.	1	2	3	4	5	6
7	I am not really interested in analyzing my behaviour.	1	2	3	4	5	6
8	It is important for me to evaluate the things that I do.	1	2	3	4	5	6
9	I am very interested in examining what I think about.	1	2	3	4	5	6
10	It is important to me to try to understand what my feelings mean.	1	2	3	4	5	6
11	I have a definite need to understand the way that my mind works.	1	2	3	4	5	6
12	It is important to me to be able understand how my thoughts arise.	1	2	3	4	5	6
13	I am usually aware of my thoughts.	1	2	3	4	5	6

		Strongly disagree				Strongly agree	
14	I'm often confused about the way that I really feel about things.	❏1	❏2	❏3	❏4	❏5	❏6
15	I usually have a very clear idea about why I've behaved in a certain way,	❏1	❏2	❏3	❏4	❏5	❏6
16	I'm often aware that I'm having a feeling, but I often don't quite know what it is.	❏1	❏2	❏3	❏4	❏5	❏6
17	My behaviour often puzzles me.	❏1	❏2	❏3	❏4	❏5	❏6
18	Thinking about my thoughts makes me more confused.	❏1	❏2	❏3	❏4	❏5	❏6
19	Often, I find it difficult to make sense of the way I feel about things.	❏1	❏2	❏3	❏4	❏5	❏6
20	I usually know why I feel the way I do.	❏1	❏2	❏3	❏4	❏5	❏6

Scoring Key	Reflective skill	Your rating
Reflection engagement	(add 3, 5, 6, 8 to 12, reverse 1, 2, 4, 7) divide by 12	
Reflection insight	(add 13, 15, 20, reverse 14, 16 to 19) divide by 8	

Reversed items means that a box marked '1' equals a rating of six, while a box marked '6' equals a rating of one. Estimated time for completion of questionnaire: 10 min.

Problems in Sport Questionnaire (Coach Rating Coaching)

On the following pages you will find a series of vignettes. Each one describes an incident and then lists three possible ways of responding to the situation. Think about each response option in terms of how appropriate you consider it to be as a mean of dealing with the problem described in the vignette. There are no right or wrong ratings on these items.

There are 8 vignettes with 3 possible options for each. Please be sure to evaluate each of the proposed options for every vignette.

Situation A

Jeremy is an athlete that generally performs as well as his teammates. However, for the past couple of weeks he has appeared preoccupied and listless. During trainings, he does what he is asked to do but his coach feels that he does not give 100%. The most appropriate thing for Jeremy's coach to do is:

		Very inappropriate		Moderately appropriate			Very appropriate
A1	Impress upon Jeremy that it is really important to work as hard as possible at each training session for his own good.	❏ 1	❏ 2	❏ 3	❏ 4	❏ 5	❏ 6 ❏ 7
A2	Talk to Jeremy and try to help him work out the cause of his listlessness.	❏ 1	❏ 2	❏ 3	❏ 4	❏ 5	❏ 6 ❏ 7
A3	Warn him that if he does not put more effort into training, you will have to impose negative consequences (extra training sessions, suspension).	❏ 1	❏ 2	❏ 3	❏ 4	❏ 5	❏ 6 ❏ 7

Situation B

The team Northern Dragons has been performing poorly since the beginning of the season. What would be the best way for the coach to help them?

		Very inappropriate		Moderately appropriate			Very appropriate
B1	Schedule additional practices and offer tangible rewards to athletes when they are performing well.	❏ 1	❏ 2	❏ 3	❏ 4	❏ 5	❏ 6 ❏ 7
B2	Make a chart showing each athlete's individual performance and emphasize the importance of this chart.	❏ 1	❏ 2	❏ 3	❏ 4	❏ 5	❏ 6 ❏ 7
B3	Have some discussions with the team as a whole and facilitate their devising some solutions for improving their performance.	❏ 1	❏ 2	❏ 3	❏ 4	❏ 5	❏ 6 ❏ 7

Situation C

At the beginning of the season, when you selected the players that would be part of your team, you were not sure about selecting Ben. You had then discussed the situation with him. At the end, you had selected him and he has been working hard since, improving quickly and getting closer and closer to the level of other players on the team. You should now...

		Very inappropriate		Moderately appropriate			Very appropriate
C1	Point out to Ben that if he continues to improve at this rate, he will keep his place in the team and then watch his performance closely.	❏ 1	❏ 2	❏ 3	❏ 4	❏ 5	❏ 6 ❏ 7
C2	Mention to Ben that you noticed his efforts and his progress.	❏ 1	❏ 2	❏ 3	❏ 4	❏ 5	❏ 6 ❏ 7
C3	Continue to emphasize that he has to work hard and further improve his performance.	❏ 1	❏ 2	❏ 3	❏ 4	❏ 5	❏ 6 ❏ 7

Situation D

Jennifer is one of your athletes and she does not always pay attention to your instructions. She often distracts her training partners and is not very receptive to your feedback. You are concerned that she might not improve as much as the others and that she might even end up affecting the performance of your other athletes. The best thing for you to do in such a situation is...

		Very inappropriate		Moderately appropriate			Very appropriate
D1	Emphasize how important it is for Jennifer to pay attention to your instructions if she wishes to perform well.	❏ 1	❏ 2	❏ 3	❏ 4	❏ 5	❏ 6 ❏ 7
D2	Insist that the instructions must be followed and give Jennifer a sanction when she does the opposite.	❏ 1	❏ 2	❏ 3	❏ 4	❏ 5	❏ 6 ❏ 7
D3	Address the problem with Jennifer and try to determine the best solution with her.	❏ 1	❏ 2	❏ 3	❏ 4	❏ 5	❏ 6 ❏ 7

Situation E

Nancy, one of your athletes, has just started a part-time job, in addition to going to school and her training. She loves her new job and is proud of now being able to earn her own pocket money.

However, you are worried because she seems tired and stressed during training. You decide that the best thing to do is:

		Very inappropriate	Moderately appropriate	Very appropriate
E1	Ask her how she plans to balance work, her studies and her training.	❏1 ❏2 ❏3	❏4 ❏5	❏6 ❏7
E2	Tell her that she ought to be careful to keep a balance between work, school and training and suggest that she focuses more on her athletic performance than on her part-time job.	❏1 ❏2 ❏3	❏4 ❏5	❏6 ❏7
E3	Insist that she cut down on her part-time job hours; you can't allow it to interfere with her training.	❏1 ❏2 ❏3	❏4 ❏5	❏6 ❏7

Situation F

Among the group of young athletes you are coaching, there is an athlete named Margy who has a hard time fitting in with the group. She is quiet, a little clumsy and has been the butt of many jokes from other athletes. In spite of the efforts of many previous coaches, other athletes have not yet accepted Margy. Your intuition would guide you to:

		Very inappropriate	Moderately appropriate	Very appropriate
F1	Prod her into interactions and provide her with much praise for any social initiative.	❏1 ❏2 ❏3	❏4 ❏5	❏6 ❏7
F2	Talk to her and emphasize that she should make friends so she'll be happier during training.	❏1 ❏2 ❏3	❏4 ❏5	❏6 ❏7
F3	Invite her to talk about her relations with the other athletes, and encourage her to take small steps to gradually get closer to them when she's ready.	❏1 ❏2 ❏3	❏4 ❏5	❏6 ❏7

Situation G

For the past few weeks, things have been disappearing from the locker room during training sessions. Today, you surprised Daniel rummaging in the locker of another athlete. The best thing to do is:

		Very inappropriate			Moderately appropriate			Very appropriate
G1	Talk to him about it, express that you are confident that he will not do it again and attempt to understand why he did it.	1	2	3	4	5	6	7
G2	Give him a good scolding; stealing is something that cannot be tolerated and he has to learn that.	1	2	3	4	5	6	7
G3	Emphasize that it was wrong and have him apologize to his training partners and promise not to do it again.	1	2	3	4	5	6	7

Situation H

Jacob is a talented athlete. In competitions or tournaments, he performs adequately, but you are convinced that he could do even better. A useful approach might be to:

		Very inappropriate			Moderately appropriate			Very appropriate
H1	Encourage Jacob to talk about what his performance means to him and whether he has any ideas that could help him improve.	1	2	3	4	5	6	7
H2	Stress to Jacob that he should do better, and that he won't achieve higher levels if he continues at his current level of performance.	1	2	3	4	5	6	7
H3	Watch his performance more closely; praise him for every improvement, and point out whenever he could do better.	1	2	3	4	5	6	7

Scoring key	Motivational style	Your rating
Highly autonomy supportive	(add A2, B3, C2, D3, E1, F3, G1, H1) multiply by 3	
Moderately controlling	subtract A1, B2, C3, D1, E2, F2, G3, H2	
Highly controlling	(add A3, B1, C1, D2, E3, F1, G2, H3) multiply by (−3)	
Total motivational style (add the three rows):		_____

Estimated time for completion of questionnaire: 15 min.

The Perceived Motivational Climate in Sport Questionnaire-2 (Athletes Rating Coaching)

Mark one box for each statement that is most appropriate in your mind. Answer how often the following statement occur according to you. There are no right or wrong answers, just be as honest as possible. Please indicate how much you agree or disagree with each statement.

		Strongly disagree				Strongly agree
1	On this team, the coach wants us to try new skills.	1	2	3	4	5
2	On this team, the coach gets mad when an athlete makes a mistake.	1	2	3	4	5
3	On this team, the coach gives most of his or her attention to the stars.	1	2	3	4	5
4	On this team, each athlete contributes in some important way.	1	2	3	4	5
5	On this team, the coach believes that all of us are crucial to the success of the team.	1	2	3	4	5
6	On this team, the coach praises athletes only when they outperform teammates.	1	2	3	4	5
7	On this team, the coach thinks only the starters contribute to the success of the team.	1	2	3	4	5
8	On this team, athletes feel good when they try their best.	1	2	3	4	5
9	On this team, athletes are taken out of a competition for mistakes.	1	2	3	4	5
10	On this team, athletes at all skill levels have an important role on the team.	1	2	3	4	5
11	On this team, athletes help each other learn.	1	2	3	4	5
12	On this team, athletes are encouraged to outperform the other athletes.	1	2	3	4	5
13	On this team, the coach has his or her own favourites.	1	2	3	4	5
14	On this team, the coach makes sure athletes improve on skills they're not good at.	1	2	3	4	5
15	On this team, the coach yells at athletes for messing up.	1	2	3	4	5
16	On this team, athletes feel successful when they improve.	1	2	3	4	5
17	On this team, only the athletes with the best 'stats' get praise.	1	2	3	4	5
18	On this team, athletes are punished when they make a mistake.	1	2	3	4	5
19	On this team, each athlete has an important role.	1	2	3	4	5

		Strongly disagree				Strongly agree
20	On this team, trying hard is rewarded.	1	2	3	4	5
21	On this team, the coach encourages athletes to help each other.	1	2	3	4	5
22	On this team, the coach makes it clear who he or she thinks are the best athletes.	1	2	3	4	5
23	On this team, athletes are 'psyched' when they do better than their teammates in a game.	1	2	3	4	5
24	On this team, if you want to play in a game, you must be one of the best athletes.	1	2	3	4	5
25	On this team, the coach emphasizes always trying your best.	1	2	3	4	5
26	On this team, only the top athletes 'get noticed' by the coach.	1	2	3	4	5
27	On this team, athletes are afraid to make mistakes.	1	2	3	4	5
28	On this team, athletes are encouraged to work on their weaknesses.	1	2	3	4	5
29	On this team, the coach favours some athletes more than others.	1	2	3	4	5
30	On this team, the focus is to improve each competition/practice.	1	2	3	4	5
31	On this team, the athletes really 'work together' as a team.	1	2	3	4	5
32	On this team, each athlete feels as if they are an important team member.	1	2	3	4	5
33	On this team, the athletes help each other to get better and excel.	1	2	3	4	5

Scoring key	Motivational climate	Your rating
Mastery climate		
Cooperative learning	(add 11, 21, 31, 33) divide by 4	
Important role	(add 4, 5, 10, 19, 32) divide by 5	
Effort/Improvement	(add 1, 8, 14, 16, 20, 25, 28, 30) divide by 8	
Performance climate		
Intra-team member rivalry	(add 6, 12, 23) divide by 3	
Punishments for mistakes	(add 2, 7, 9, 15, 18, 27) divide by 6	
Unequal recognition	(add 3, 13, 17, 22, 24, 26, 29) divide by 7	
Total rating of motivational climate from an athlete (add the first three rows, subtract the last three):		
Calculate the average rating of all athletes' ratings:		

Estimated time for completion of questionnaire: 15 min.

Coach Motivation Questionnaire (Coach Rating Coaching)

Below are some reasons why coaches coach. Answer how true the following statements are for you. There are no right or wrong answers, just be as honest as possible.

Please indicate how much you agree or disagree with each statement answering the question:

Why do you coach your sport?

		Not true at all			Somewhat true			Very true
1	Because I find it stimulating.	❏1	❏2	❏3	❏4	❏5	❏6	❏7
2	Because coaching is fundamental to who I am.	❏1	❏2	❏3	❏4	❏5	❏6	❏7
3	Because it contributes to my development as a person.	❏1	❏2	❏3	❏4	❏5	❏6	❏7
4	Because I don't want to let my athletes down.	❏1	❏2	❏3	❏4	❏5	❏6	❏7
5	To be respected by others.	❏1	❏2	❏3	❏4	❏5	❏6	❏7
6	I often think my coaching efforts are a waste of time.	❏1	❏2	❏3	❏4	❏5	❏6	❏7
7	Because I get a good feeling out of it.	❏1	❏2	❏3	❏4	❏5	❏6	❏7
8	Because coaching is integral to my life.	❏1	❏2	❏3	❏4	❏5	❏6	❏7
9	Because it is moving me towards my personal goals.	❏1	❏2	❏3	❏4	❏5	❏6	❏7
10	Because if I quit it would mean I'd failed.	❏1	❏2	❏3	❏4	❏5	❏6	❏7
11	To get recognition from others.	❏1	❏2	❏3	❏4	❏5	❏6	❏7
12	Sometimes I don't know why I coach anymore.	❏1	❏2	❏3	❏4	❏5	❏6	❏7
13	Because I enjoy the effort I invest.	❏1	❏2	❏3	❏4	❏5	❏6	❏7
14	Because it personifies my values and beliefs.	❏1	❏2	❏3	❏4	❏5	❏6	❏7
15	Because it allows me to achieve my personal goals.	❏1	❏2	❏3	❏4	❏5	❏6	❏7
16	Because I feel responsible for the athletes' performance.	❏1	❏2	❏3	❏4	❏5	❏6	❏7
17	Because I want to be appreciated by others.	❏1	❏2	❏3	❏4	❏5	❏6	❏7
18	Sometimes I feel the costs outweigh the benefits.	❏1	❏2	❏3	❏4	❏5	❏6	❏7

	Not true at all			Somewhat true			Very true
19 Because I enjoy the interaction I have with athletes.	❏ 1	❏ 2	❏ 3	❏ 4	❏ 5	❏ 6	❏ 7
20 Because I feel pressure from myself to win.	❏ 1	❏ 2	❏ 3	❏ 4	❏ 5	❏ 6	❏ 7
21 Because I like the extrinsic rewards (i.e., money) associated with winning.	❏ 1	❏ 2	❏ 3	❏ 4	❏ 5	❏ 6	❏ 7
22 Sometimes I question my desire to continue coaching.	❏ 1	❏ 2	❏ 3	❏ 4	❏ 5	❏ 6	❏ 7

Scoring Key	*Coach's motivation*	*Your rating*	*(Total rating)*
Intrinsic	(add 1, 7, 13, 19) divide by 4	_____	multiply by 3
Integrated	(add 2, 8, 14) divide by 3	_____	multiply by 2
Identified	(add 3, 9, 15) divide by 3	_____	multiply by 1
Introjected	(add 4, 10, 16, 20) divide by 4	_____	multiply by (-1)
External	(add 5, 11, 17, 21) divide by 4	_____	multiply by (-2)
Amotivation	(add 6, 12, 18, 22) divide by 4	_____	multiply by (-3)

Total rating of your motivation (add the scores in the right column, i.e., 13 + -3 = 10):

Estimated time for completion of questionnaire: 10 min.

Coaching Behaviour Scale for Sport (Athletes Rating Coaching)

Some athletes have a single coach and others work with a coaching team. If you have more than one coach, think of the coach, or the coaches most responsible for that area. Mark one box for each statement that is most appropriate in your mind when answering the following question. Answer how true the following statements are for you. There are no right or wrong answers, just be as honest as possible.

How frequently do you experience the following coaching behaviours?

The coach(es) most responsible for my physical training and conditioning...

		Never			Fairly often			Always
1	Provides me with a physical conditioning programme in which I am confident.	1	2	3	4	5	6	7
2	Provides me with a physically challenging conditioning programme.	1	2	3	4	5	6	7
3	Provides me with a detailed physical conditioning programme.	1	2	3	4	5	6	7
4	Provides me with a plan for my physical preparation.	1	2	3	4	5	6	7
5	Ensures that training facilities and equipment are organized.	1	2	3	4	5	6	7
6	Provides me with structured training sessions.	1	2	3	4	5	6	7
7	Provides me with an annual training programme.	1	2	3	4	5	6	7

The coach(es) most responsible for my technical skills...

		Never			Fairly often			Always
8	Provides me with advice while I'm performing a skill.	1	2	3	4	5	6	7
9	Gives me specific feedback for correcting technical errors.	1	2	3	4	5	6	7
10	Gives me reinforcement about correct technique.	1	2	3	4	5	6	7
11	Provides me with feedback that helps me improve my technique.	1	2	3	4	5	6	7
12	Provides visual examples to show how a skill should be done.	1	2	3	4	5	6	7
13	Uses verbal examples that describe how a skill should be done.	1	2	3	4	5	6	7
14	Makes sure I understand the techniques and strategies I'm being taught.	1	2	3	4	5	6	7
15	Provides me with immediate feedback.	1	2	3	4	5	6	7

The coach(es) most responsible for my mental preparation...

		Never			Fairly often			Always
16	Provides advice on how to perform under pressure.	1	2	3	4	5	6	7
17	Provides advice on how to be mentally tough.	1	2	3	4	5	6	7

		Never			Fairly often			Always
18	Provides advice on how to stay confident about my abilities.	1	2	3	4	5	6	7
19	Provides advice on how to stay positive about myself.	1	2	3	4	5	6	7
20	Provides advice on how to stay focused.	1	2	3	4	5	6	7

The coach(es) most responsible for my goal-setting...

		Never			Fairly often			Always
21	Helps me identify strategies to achieve my goals.	1	2	3	4	5	6	7
22	Monitors my progress toward my goals.	1	2	3	4	5	6	7
23	Helps me set short-term goals.	1	2	3	4	5	6	7
24	Helps me identify target dates for attaining my goals.	1	2	3	4	5	6	7
25	Helps me set long-term goals.	1	2	3	4	5	6	7
26	Provides me support to attain my goals.	1	2	3	4	5	6	7

The coach(es) most responsible for my competition strategies...

		Never			Fairly often			Always
27	Helps me focus on the process of performing well.	1	2	3	4	5	6	7
28	Prepares me to face a variety of situations in competition.	1	2	3	4	5	6	7
29	Keeps me focused in competitions.	1	2	3	4	5	6	7
30	Has a consistent routine at competition.	1	2	3	4	5	6	7
31	Deals with problems I may experience at competition.	1	2	3	4	5	6	7
32	Shows confidence in my ability during competitions.	1	2	3	4	5	6	7
33	Ensures that facilities and equipment are organized for competition.	1	2	3	4	5	6	7

Scoring key	Sport-specific coaching behaviours	Your rating
Physical training and conditioning	(add 1 to 7) divide by 7	
Technical skills	(add 8 to 15) divide by 8	
Mental preparation	(add 16 to 20) divide by 5	
Goal-setting	(add 21 to 26) divide by 6	
Competition strategies	(add 27 to 33) divide by 7	
Calculate the average rating of all athletes' ratings:		

Estimated time for completion of questionnaire: 10-15 min.

Transformational Teaching Questionnaire (Athlete Rating Coaching)

Mark one box for each statement that is most appropriate in your mind when answering the following question. Answer how often the following statements occur according to you. There are no right or wrong answers, just be as honest as possible. Please indicate how much you agree or disagree with each statement that starts with:

My coach...

		Not at all	Once in awhile	Sometimes	Fairly often	Frequently
1	Shows that s/he cares about me.	❏ 1	❏ 2	❏ 3	❏ 4	❏ 5
2	Acts as a person that I look up to.	❏ 1	❏ 2	❏ 3	❏ 4	❏ 5
3	Creates practices that really encourage me to think.	❏ 1	❏ 2	❏ 3	❏ 4	❏ 5
4	Demonstrates that s/he believes in me.	❏ 1	❏ 2	❏ 3	❏ 4	❏ 5
5	Treats me in ways that build my respect.	❏ 1	❏ 2	❏ 3	❏ 4	❏ 5
6	Is enthusiastic about what I am capable of achieving.	❏ 1	❏ 2	❏ 3	❏ 4	❏ 5
7	Provides me with tasks and challenges that get me to think in different ways.	❏ 1	❏ 2	❏ 3	❏ 4	❏ 5
8	Motivates me to try my hardest.	❏ 1	❏ 2	❏ 3	❏ 4	❏ 5
9	Tries to know every athlete in the group.	❏ 1	❏ 2	❏ 3	❏ 4	❏ 5
10	Gets me to question my own and others' ideas.	❏ 1	❏ 2	❏ 3	❏ 4	❏ 5
11	Tries to help athletes who might be struggling.	❏ 1	❏ 2	❏ 3	❏ 4	❏ 5
12	Talks about his/her personal values.	❏ 1	❏ 2	❏ 3	❏ 4	❏ 5
13	Encourages me to look at issues from different sides.	❏ 1	❏ 2	❏ 3	❏ 4	❏ 5

		Not at all	Once in awhile	Some- times	Fairly often	Fre- quently
14	Recognizes the needs and abilities of each athlete in the group.	❑ 1	❑ 2	❑ 3	❑ 4	❑ 5
15	Is optimistic about what I can accomplish.	❑ 1	❑ 2	❑ 3	❑ 4	❑ 5
16	Behaves as someone I can trust.	❑ 1	❑ 2	❑ 3	❑ 4	❑ 5

Scoring key	Social competence coaching behaviours	Your rating
Idealized Influence	add (2, 5, 12, 16)	
Inspirational Motivation	add (4, 6, 8, 15)	
Intellectual Stimulation	add (3, 7, 10, 13)	
Individualized Consideration	add (1, 9, 11, 14)	
Calculate the average rating of all athletes' ratings:		

Estimated time for completion of questionnaire: 10 min.

Coach Athlete Relationship Questionnaire (Athlete Rating Coaching)

Mark one box for each statement that is most appropriate in your mind. Answer how true the following statement are for you. There are no right or wrong answers, just be as honest as possible. Please indicate how much you agree or disagree with each statement to how you feel with your coach:

		Strongly disagree			Moderately			Strongly agree
1	I am close to my coach.	❑ 1	❑ 2	❑ 3	❑ 4	❑ 5	❑ 6	❑ 7
2	I am committed to my coach.	❑ 1	❑ 2	❑ 3	❑ 4	❑ 5	❑ 6	❑ 7
3	I like my coach.	❑ 1	❑ 2	❑ 3	❑ 4	❑ 5	❑ 6	❑ 7
4	When I am coached by my coach, I am at ease.	❑ 1	❑ 2	❑ 3	❑ 4	❑ 5	❑ 6	❑ 7
5	I trust my coach.	❑ 1	❑ 2	❑ 3	❑ 4	❑ 5	❑ 6	❑ 7
6	I feel that my sport career is promising with my coach.	❑ 1	❑ 2	❑ 3	❑ 4	❑ 5	❑ 6	❑ 7
7	When I am coached by my coach, I am responsive to his/her efforts.	❑ 1	❑ 2	❑ 3	❑ 4	❑ 5	❑ 6	❑ 7
8	I respect my coach.	❑ 1	❑ 2	❑ 3	❑ 4	❑ 5	❑ 6	❑ 7
9	I appreciate my coach's sacrifices in order to improve performance.	❑ 1	❑ 2	❑ 3	❑ 4	❑ 5	❑ 6	❑ 7
10	When I am coached by my coach, I am ready to do my best.	❑ 1	❑ 2	❑ 3	❑ 4	❑ 5	❑ 6	❑ 7
11	When I am coached by my coach, I adopt a friendly stance.	❑ 1	❑ 2	❑ 3	❑ 4	❑ 5	❑ 6	❑ 7

Scoring Key	Athletes' perception of coach–athlete relationship	Your rating
Closeness	(add 3, 5, 8, 9) divide by 4	
Commitment	(add 1, 2, 6) divide by 3	
Complementarity	(add 4, 7, 10, 11) divide by 4	
Total perception of coach–athlete relationship (add the ratings above):		

Estimated time for completion of questionnaire: 5 min.

Coach Athlete Relationship Questionnaire
(Coach Rating Metaperspective of Athlete)

Decide first whether you want to compare your rating with a single athlete or the average of all athletes' perceptions. Mark one box for each statement that is most appropriate in your mind. Answer how true the following statement are for you. There are no right or wrong answers, just be as honest as possible. Please indicate how much you agree or disagree with each statement to how you personally think a specific athlete/all athletes in general on your squad feels about you.

		Strongly disagree			Moderately			Strongly agree
1	My athlete is close to me.	❏1	❏2	❏3	❏4	❏5	❏6	❏7
2	My athlete is committed to me.	❏1	❏2	❏3	❏4	❏5	❏6	❏7
3	My athlete likes me.	❏1	❏2	❏3	❏4	❏5	❏6	❏7
4	My athlete is at ease when I coach him/her.	❏1	❏2	❏3	❏4	❏5	❏6	❏7
5	My athlete trusts me.	❏1	❏2	❏3	❏4	❏5	❏6	❏7
6	My athlete feels that his/her sporting career is promising with me.	❏1	❏2	❏3	❏4	❏5	❏6	❏7
7	My athlete is responsive to my efforts when I train him/her.	❏1	❏2	❏3	❏4	❏5	❏6	❏7
8	My athlete respects me.	❏1	❏2	❏3	❏4	❏5	❏6	❏7
9	My athlete appreciates the sacrifices I make in order to improve performance.	❏1	❏2	❏3	❏4	❏5	❏6	❏7
10	My athlete is ready to do his/her best when I train him/her.	❏1	❏2	❏3	❏4	❏5	❏6	❏7
11	My athlete adopts a friendly stance when I train him/her.	❏1	❏2	❏3	❏4	❏5	❏6	❏7

Scoring Key	Coach's metaperception of athletes' experience of coach–athlete relationship	Your rating
Closeness	(add 3, 5, 8, 9) divide by 4	
Commitment	(add 1, 2, 6) divide by 3	
Complementarity	(add 4, 7, 10, 11) divide by 4	
Total metaperception of coach–athlete relationship (add the ratings above):		

Estimated time for completion of questionnaire: 5 min.

Summarizing Coach Athlete Relationship Questionnaire scores

Athletes' perception of the coach–athlete relationship (add their total scores and divide by number of athletes): _____

To evaluate your empathic accuracy, either compare a single athlete with your metaperspective of the same athlete, in which case you have to ask the athlete to provide his/her rating non-anonymously, or compare the average of all athletes' ratings on the 3C's with your own rating.

HURIER Listening Profile (Coach Rating Coaching)

Zohoori, A. (2013). A cross-cultural comparison of the HURIER Listening Profile among Iranian and US students. *The International Journal of Listening*, 27, 50–60. Reprinted by permission of The International Listening Association, www.Listen.org.

> Respond to each of the following questions concerning your perception of your listening behavior.
> Mark one box for each statement that is most appropriate in your mind. Choose one specific listening context (e. g., during a practice, in a meeting) and answer all questions with that situation in mind. This will help you be more consistent in your responses.

		Almost never		*Some- times*		*Almost always*
1	I am constantly aware that people and circumstances change over time.	❏ 1	❏ 2	❏ 3	❏ 4	❏ 5
2	I take into account the speaker's personal and cultural perspective when listening to him/her.	❏ 1	❏ 2	❏ 3	❏ 4	❏ 5
3	I pay attention to the important things going on around me.	❏ 1	❏ 2	❏ 3	❏ 4	❏ 5
4	I accurately hear what is said to me.	❏ 1	❏ 2	❏ 3	❏ 4	❏ 5
5	I understand my partner's vocabulary and recognize that my understanding of a word is likely to be somewhat different from the speaker's.	❏ 1	❏ 2	❏ 3	❏ 4	❏ 5

(Continued)

		Almost never		Some- times		Almost always
6	I adapt my response according to the needs of the particular situation.	❏ 1	❏ 2	❏ 3	❏ 4	❏ 5
7	I easily follow conversations and can accurately recall which member contributed which ideas in small group discussions.	❏ 1	❏ 2	❏ 3	❏ 4	❏ 5
8	I consider my partner's personal expertise on the subject when he/she tries to convince me to do something.	❏ 1	❏ 2	❏ 3	❏ 4	❏ 5
9	I do not let my emotions interfere with my listening or decision-making.	❏ 1	❏ 2	❏ 3	❏ 4	❏ 5
10	I can remember what the instructor has said in class even when it's not in the book.	❏ 1	❏ 2	❏ 3	❏ 4	❏ 5
11	I recognize my 'hot buttons', and don't let them influence my listening.	❏ 1	❏ 2	❏ 3	❏ 4	❏ 5
12	I take into account the person's motives, expectations and needs when determining the meaning of the message.	❏ 1	❏ 2	❏ 3	❏ 4	❏ 5
13	I provide clear and direct feedback to others.	❏ 1	❏ 2	❏ 3	❏ 4	❏ 5
14	I let the speaker know immediately that he/she has been understood.	❏ 1	❏ 2	❏ 3	❏ 4	❏ 5
15	I overcome distractions such as the conversation of others, background noises and telephones, when someone is speaking.	❏ 1	❏ 2	❏ 3	❏ 4	❏ 5
16	I enter communication situations with a positive attitude.	❏ 1	❏ 2	❏ 3	❏ 4	❏ 5
17	I am sensitive to the speaker's tone of voice in communication situations.	❏ 1	❏ 2	❏ 3	❏ 4	❏ 5
18	I listen to and accurately remember what my partner says, even when I strongly disagree with his/her viewpoint.	❏ 1	❏ 2	❏ 3	❏ 4	❏ 5
19	I encourage information sharing by creating a climate of trust and support.	❏ 1	❏ 2	❏ 3	❏ 4	❏ 5
20	I concentrate on what the speaker is saying, even when the information is complicated.	❏ 1	❏ 2	❏ 3	❏ 4	❏ 5
21	I consider how the speaker's facial expressions, body posture and other nonverbal behaviours relate to the verbal message.	❏ 1	❏ 2	❏ 3	❏ 4	❏ 5
22	I weigh all evidence before making a decision.	❏ 1	❏ 2	❏ 3	❏ 4	❏ 5
23	I take time to analyze the validity of my partner's reasoning before arriving at my own conclusions.	❏ 1	❏ 2	❏ 3	❏ 4	❏ 5
24	I am relaxed and focused in important communication situations.	❏ 1	❏ 2	❏ 3	❏ 4	❏ 5
25	I listen to the entire message without interrupting.	❏ 1	❏ 2	❏ 3	❏ 4	❏ 5
26	I make sure that the physical environment encourages effective listening.	❏ 1	❏ 2	❏ 3	❏ 4	❏ 5
27	I recognize and take into account personal and cultural differences in the use of time and space that may influence listening effectiveness.	❏ 1	❏ 2	❏ 3	❏ 4	❏ 5
28	I ask relevant questions and restate my perceptions to make sure I have understood the speaker correctly.	❏ 1	❏ 2	❏ 3	❏ 4	❏ 5

		Almost never		Some- times		Almost always
29	I listen carefully to determine whether the speaker has solid facts and evidence or whether he/she is relying on emotional appeals.	❏ 1	❏ 2	❏ 3	❏ 4	❏ 5
30	I am sensitive to my partner's feelings in communication situations.	❏ 1	❏ 2	❏ 3	❏ 4	❏ 5
31	I have a wide variety of interests which helps me approach tasks creatively.	❏ 1	❏ 2	❏ 3	❏ 4	❏ 5
32	I distinguish between main ideas and supporting evidence when I listen.	❏ 1	❏ 2	❏ 3	❏ 4	❏ 5
33	I am ready to focus my attention when a presenter begins his/her talk.	❏ 1	❏ 2	❏ 3	❏ 4	❏ 5
34	I readily consider new evidence and circumstances that might prompt me to reevaluate my previous position.	❏ 1	❏ 2	❏ 3	❏ 4	❏ 5
35	I can recall what I have heard, even when I am in stressful situations.	❏ 1	❏ 2	❏ 3	❏ 4	❏ 5
36	I take notes effectively when I believe it will enhance my listening.	❏ 1	❏ 2	❏ 3	❏ 4	❏ 5

Scoring Key		Your rating
Hearing	add (4, 15, 16, 20, 24, 33)	
Understanding	add (5, 11, 25, 28, 32, 36)	
Remembering	add (3, 7, 10, 18, 31, 35)	
Interpreting	add (2, 12, 14, 17, 21, 30)	
Evaluating	add (1, 8, 22, 23, 29, 34)	
Responding	add (6, 9, 13, 19, 26, 27)	

Estimated time for completion of questionnaire: 15-20 min.

Appendix B
KEYS

Quiz Chapter 1
    1a
    2c
    3c

Quiz Chapter 2
    1b
    2b
    3a
    4a
    5a
    6b
    7c

KEY TO REFLECTION DEPTH

Leah Leader

Telling

She does not reflect on her own thoughts, emotions, or role in the situation, nor does she investigate any potential effects of her actions. Instead, she focuses solely on describing the event as it played out.

Coach Collin

Descriptive Reflection

He does consider information provided at the coaching education in an unproblematized manner. The one perspective he explores is sports, and the same goes for effects which are thought about only in terms of sport. He shows little awareness of previous or future events when reflecting.

Tina Trainer

Dialogic Reflection

She does consider different perspectives in the form of how her decision will influence their relationship as well as others in the group. Problematizing is displayed when she weighs acting quickly and maintaining relationships. She also highlights her own role in how she normally does, her engagement and how her tone of voice plays a part.

Instructor Ingram

Critical Reflection

He takes into account historical aspects when considering the groups previous experiences with another coach. An inner discussion is seen when he argues with himself about time and activity levels. His own preparedness is weighed into the situation, and he deliberately contemplates how his decision will make it easier for him later on. Multiple perspectives are used as the situation is also viewed from outside of the sporting context.

Quiz Chapter 3
1b
2b
3a
4c
5a
6c
7a
8c

Quiz Chapter 4
1c
2b
3a
4b
5c
6b
7c
8a

Quiz Chapter 5
1b
2b
3c
4a
5c
6c

Quiz Chapter 6

1a
2c
3b
4b
5c
6c
7c
8c

Quiz Chapter 7
1c
2a
3a
4b
5b
6b

Quiz Chapter 8
1a
2c

INDEX

Note: Page numbers in *italics* refer to figures. Page numbers in **bold** refer to tables.

1-2-3 template 155, 156, **156**, 158

Acceptance and Commitment Therapy 102
Achievement Goal Theory 65, 77, 81

Behavioural modification 247, 252
Behavioural problems 109, 110
Behaviourism 135, 137, 139, **151**

Closeness 120, 197, 212–13, **215**, 216–18
Coach education 5
Coaching behaviours: controlling behaviours 72; reactive behaviours 97, **98**; supportive behaviours 70, **71–2**, 84; 'social competence' 103, 107; spontaneous 97, **98**; 'sport-specific' 97, **98**, 99, 107
Coaching efficacy 116
Cognitions 28–33, 35, 39, 41, 43, 70, 100, 120, 219, 221, 223, 232, 246, 254
Cognitive Behavioural Therapy 102
Coping strategies 80, 102, 114
Commitment 27, 99, 101–2, 104, 120, 212, 213, **215**, 216, 218, 227, 228, 248
Competition 4, 6, 29, 70, 74–5, 78, 81, **83–4**, 85, 100–3, 105–6, 112–14, 117–18, 137, 139, 141, 154–5, 157, 159, 161–3, 178, 183, 188, 195, 211, 214, 217, 220–21, 225–6, 228–30, 253
Complementarity 213–14, **215**, 216, 228
Constructivism 143–6, **151**

Controlling 68, 70, 72, **73**, 74–6, 86, 115, 185, **194**
Co-orientation 212, 214–15

Deliberate practice 37, 253
Demonstration 147, 150, 152–3, 164, 195, 253
Direct instruction 146–8, **151**
Dynamical systems theory 100

Ego-involvement **73**, 75, 80, 185
Ego-orientation *78*, 80, **82–3**, 112–13
Emotions 24, 26, 30, 34–5, 43, 66, 69, 70, 100, 102, 104, 107–9, 117–18, 136, 139, 184, 192, 197, 214, 217, 219, 221, 226–7, 231–2, 254
Empathic accuracy 214, *215*, 216, 222–3, 226, 236–7
Empathy 112, 114, 119, 137, 147, 217, *218*, 219–22, 234
Expectations 5, 45, 101, 105–6, 108, 115–6, 150, 186, **215**, 227, 248, **249**
Expertise 8, 13, 31, 135, 145, 156, **251**, 252–3, **254**
Expressivity 220–21, 228
External focus 101, 117, 184–5, 195, 200
Extinction 136–8, 191

Feedback: concurrent 182–3, 195–6; delay 182, *183*, 184; dependence 178, 188–91; modality 194–7; terminal 182–4, 196

Game situations 159, 161–3
Goal orientation 77, 78, 81, **82–3**
Goal-setting **71**, 101, 141, 158, 227, 250
Guided discovery 147, 149–50, **151**

Informational 68, 74–6, 86, 111, 185–6, 189, 231
Information processing theories 99–100
Implementation Intentions 250, **251**
Implicit theories 3, 178, 187–9
Idealized influence 104–5
Individualized consideration 104, 107
Inspirational motivation 104, 106
Instruction **98**, 104, 107–8, 113–14, 116, 147–8, 150, **151**, 153–4, 186, 194, 213, 218, 223
Intellectual stimulation 104, 106–7
I-statement 226, 231–2, 235, 238

Knowledge of performance 181, 195–6
Knowledge of result 181–3, 190, 196

Laissez Faire 104, 150
Learning: better learning **156**, 157, 168; deep learning 26, **27**, 28, 32, 34, 40, 246, 254; new learning **156**, 157, 168; surface learning 26, **27**

Mastery climate **79**, 80–1, **82–3**, 84, 86
Metaperception 229–30

Observation 12–13, 97, 101, 109, 121, 139, 142, 145, 149, 153, 180, 218–19, 221, 224, 229
Organization **98**, 116, **156**, 156–7, **215**

Peer teaching 147, 148–9, **151**, 153
Performance climate **79**, 81, **82–3**, 112–13
Playful games 45, 110, 159, 160
Problem-solving 33, 40, 145, 147, 150, **151**, 153, 190, 255
Punishment 16, 66, 86, **98**, 105, 108–10, 113, 139, 185, 191

Questioning 25, 29, 34, 41, 142, 163–7, 231

Reflection: primary reflection 43–4, 46; reflection card 13, 41, 43–6, 87, 121, 168, 198, 222–3, 236–7, 246, 255–6; reflection depth 13, 51, 54; reflection engagement 34–5, 43–4, 254; reflection-in-action 36–8, 44–5, 49, 256; reflection insight 34–5, 43–6, 48; reflection-on-action 38, 48; reflection sheet 13, 43–4, 48, 54, 88, 122, 169, 199–201, 238, 246, 256–7; reflective summary 49, 89, 125, 170, 202, 239, 257–8; retrospective reflection 38, 49; secondary reflection 43, 45–6, 88, 122, 169, 198–9, 238, 256; shared reflection 46, *47*, 48
Regression fallacy 108
Reinforcement **98**, 108–9, 113, 116, 121, 136–9, 191–2, 249; negative 109, 136, 191; positive 108, 109, 113, 116, 121, 136, 139, 191; reinforcement schedule 137
Response cost 109, *110*, 138
Rewards 66, **71**, **73**, 74–5, **79**, 81, **83**, 86, 105, 110, 139, 185, 192, 197, **249**, **251**
Role-based play 160–61
Rule-based play 160

Sanctions by reciprocity 110
Self-awareness 24, 32–5, 39, 40, 49, 55, 77, 121, 246, 254
Self-Determination Theory 65, *66*, 70, 81, 85, 185
Self-efficacy 118, 139–41, 191, 193, 248
Self-esteem 112, 118, 187, 231
Self-monitoring 32, 34–5, 83, 86, 229, 252
Self-regulation 119, 140, *141*, 144
Shaping 108, 137
Skill: closed 100, 142; mental 101, 117, 154, **156**, 157–8, 168, 217; open 100, 157, 178; physical 99, 117, 154, **156**, 157–9, 168; reflective 29–30, 32, 34, 42, 45, 48, 53, **54**, 55; tactical 117–8, 154, **156**, 157, 159, 166; technical 99–100, 117, 154, **156**, 157, 159, 166, 168, 228
Social Cognitive Theory 139–41, 144, **151**
Stereotype 220–21
Stress 27, 42, 85, 102, 113–14, 157, 213, 219, 220

Task involvement 78, 81, 193
Task method 145, 147, **151**, 153
Task-orientation 78, 81, **82–3**
Time-out 102–3, 138–9, 247
Token economy 110, 138
Transactional leadership 104–5
Transformational leadership 103–5